PRAISE FOR
A MIRROR IN THE ROADW

"Blending cultural history and literary biography with the barest traces of memoir, Dickstein has produced in his newest essay collection that rarest of species of literary criticism: one as genial to the general reader as to the academic." —*Library Journal*

"[An] admirable new collection of critical essays. . . . [E]very page in the volume displays curiosity, incision and surprise." —Ilan Stavans, *Forward*

"The great achievement of the book lies . . . [in] Dickstein's love of reading, the vast amount he has done, and his critical acumen. They have enabled him to organize his essays into a coherent and wide-embracing vision. His own style, marked by free and abundant use of adjectives and adverbs, ignores modernist proscriptions but enables him to express the intensity of his reading experience." —Norman Kelvin, *Sewanee Review*

"If Mr. Dickstein were a less intelligent critic, his book might be more aggressively polemical. As it is, what he offers is . . . a series of thoughtful studies. The book makes one envy Mr. Dickstein's students who get to be introduced to these writers . . . by a critic of such warm and varied sympathies. And even an experienced reader will make some new acquaintance in these pages." —Adam Kirsch, *New York Sun*

"A particular strength of this volume is its deft combination of historical and formal reading practices; Dickstein brings together literature's social and aesthetic registers to produce insightful discussion of canonical authors. . . . A strong contribution to American literary criticism." —*Choice*

"Dickstein is a deeply read and securely grounded critic, willing to greet a book first as a reader, but then able to register and evaluate its thematic ambition and its responsiveness to historical pressures. He is as succinct as he is insightful, especially when he turns his focus to mid-20th-century literary culture. . . . Dickstein is a supple writer, free of ideological tether." —Sven Birkerts, *Boston Globe*

"*A Mirror in the Roadway* presents an unusually coherent gathering of essays, introductions and reviews. . . . [Dickstein] is particularly strong on American literature in the early decades of the last century, on the books that Modernism 'put out of fashion,' by writers such as Theodore Dreiser and Sinclair Lewis and Upton Sinclair. . . . [H]e quotes so skillfully as to make one want to read the books he writes about." —Michael Gorra, *Times Literary Supplement*

"A firm traditionalist, Dickstein takes issue with deconstructive theorists, who see literature as a separate, self-referential world of language, and with new historicists who deny fiction its integrity by grounding it too stubbornly in a social context that may not be relevant to the writer's purposes. . . . The best pieces engage in a quirky and personal way with their subjects."
—Madeleine Minson, *Times Higher Education Supplement*

"Morris Dickstein's *A Mirror in the Roadway* is refreshing criticism, particularly in its contrast to our current chorus of Resentment. Like Edmund Wilson, his precursor, Dickstein favors realism and reality over theories of theories. Dickstein is admirable on Jewish writers (Kafka, Agnon, Bellow, Malamud, Philip Roth, Ozick) who in a sense are his true subject."
—Harold Bloom, literary critic

"In arguing for an exuberant and dynamic notion of realism, Morris Dickstein reanimates a great and nearly vanished tradition of literary and cultural criticism that speaks to the common reader."   —Ross Posnock, Columbia University

"Morris Dickstein has neither theories nor hobbyhorses. His critical tools are the old fashioned ones: a vast range of reading, fellow feeling for the author he is discussing, and the urge to put the work in the context of the life. He is as illuminating about Cather as about Celine, as perceptive about Philip Roth as about Upton Sinclair."   —Richard Rorty, Stanford University

"Morris Dickstein gives the phrase 'the art of criticism' real meaning. He makes literature in writing about literature. His essays are rare birds. They only soar."   —Roger Rosenblatt, commentator and journalist

"Morris Dickstein is one of the few critics who still can bridge, vigorously and engagingly, the gap between the academic world and the common reader. These essays are especially fine on American writing of the 1920's and 30's, exhibiting balanced judgment, insight, and a rich fund of knowledge about American literary and cultural history. One can apply to Dickstein a phrase he uses for Edmund Wilson—that he is able to apply a wide range of resources 'to hold fast to the elusive human dimension of literature.'"
—Robert Alter, University of California, Berkeley

"Dickstein's essays are original, genially reflective and, at apt moments, invitingly autobiographical. He consistently shows himself to be a fair-minded but exacting critic who is not afraid to tell us what books are worth reading and why. His critical commentaries are saturated with the knowledge accumulated over years of attentive and sympathetic encounters with some of the most distinctive writers of modern American and European letters."
—Maria DiBattista, Princeton University

A MIRROR IN THE ROADWAY

A MIRROR IN THE ROADWAY

LITERATURE AND THE REAL WORLD

Morris Dickstein

PRINCETON UNIVERSITY PRESS

PRINCETON AND OXFORD

Requests for permission to reproduce material from this work should be sent
to Permissions, Princeton University Press

Published by Princeton University Press, 41 William Street,
Princeton, New Jersey 08540

In the United Kingdom: Princeton University Press, 3 Market Place,
Woodstock, Oxfordshire OX20 1SY

Second printing, and first paperback printing, 2007
Paperback ISBN-13: 978-0-691-13033-0
Paperback ISBN-10: 0-691-13033-7

The Library of Congress has cataloged the cloth edition of this book as follows
Dickstein, Morris.
A mirror in the roadway : literature and the real world / Dickstein, Morris.
p.   cm.
Includes bibliographical references and index.
ISBN 0-691-11996-1 (cl : alk. paper)
1. Literature, Modern—20th century—History and criticism.   I. Title.

PN771.D55 2004
809'.04—dc22   2004053514

British Library Cataloging-in-Publication Data is available

This book has been composed in Goudy

Printed on acid-free paper. ∞

press.princeton.edu

Printed in the United States of America

3   5   7   9   10   8   6   4   2

For
Eugene Goodheart
and
in memory of
Alfred Kazin

CONTENTS

READING AND HISTORY

PREFACE

WHY WRITE ABOUT literature? Certainly not to be rewarded with money, fame, and love, as Freud suggested about artists, and not from any assurance of being widely read. General readers may dip into reviews of new books but seldom feel compelled to read literary criticism, especially now that books and writers are less central to American culture than they were fifty years ago. Even professors of literature rarely assign critical works to their students, much as they may borrow from them, since literature itself rightly fills out the syllabus. Critics confronting the other arts have the bracing challenge of translating paintings or string quartets or jazz performances into another medium; literary critics too often play a losing game of paraphrase as their language competes with the works they are describing. Criticism can do much to illuminate all kinds of art, but few works, even famously difficult ones, actually cry out for criticism.

Critics write about literature for the same reasons writers write about anything: for the pleasure of forming graceful sentences that sort out their own reactions to books, or simply to be part of a conversation about the human dilemma that goes back to the beginnings of culture. But why, you might ask, have I written about these writers rather than others, about Günter Grass rather than Alain Robbe-Grillet, about Willa Cather rather than Frank Norris, about Philip Roth rather than William Gaddis? Simply put, these are writers whose way with language or outlook on life mattered deeply to me. They provoked the shock of recognition that, like some magic mirror, offers revealing glimpses of one's half-hidden selves. In reading Roth, for example, I'm always arguing with him, admiring him, feeling outraged by him, and implicitly defining myself through him. Such hotly divided feelings may be the ones most congenial to criticism. There is no writer in this book who is of merely conceptual interest to me.

Many of the essays published here were written for occasions not strictly of my own choosing—commissioned reviews, conferences, public lectures, essay collections, introductions to reprints of classic works. But I wrote them out of a strong intuition that they might enlighten readers while enabling me to remain a student, to keep on learning. Critical writing, like teaching or any exchange of ideas, can complete one's own reading experience. I wrote an introduction to Upton Sinclair's *The Jungle* because I had just been teaching it at the University of Paris in a course on "The City in American Culture," and found it more revealing book than I had expected. I agreed to review difficult works like Grass's *The Flounder* and Gabriel García Márquez's *The Autumn of the Patriarch* because I had been bowled over by *The Tin Drum* and *One Hundred Years of Solitude* and guessed that they could never write anything that wouldn't engage me. I was game to keynote a conference on Céline's impact on American writers because twenty years earlier, recuperating from a strep infection in a small village in Provence, I had read *Death on the Installment Plan* in a fever of excitement and was struck by some uncanny similarities to a newly published book by Philip Roth, *Portnoy's Complaint*.

These points of appeal gave me a personal stake in the books I was writing about, which is as much a sine qua non of lively criticism as of any worthwhile writing. But there was also something intrinsic to the books themselves that drew me to them. These were ambitious works that packed a huge emotional charge. They brought a significant chunk of world with them, and drove it home to readers with the unusual intensity that literature can summon. Even when the emotions seemed to have been subtracted, as in the influential short fiction of Raymond Carver, they were no less potent for remaining unspoken. The anesthetized surface of Carver's stories could be as freighted with feeling as the histrionic arias of Céline's or Roth's loquacious protagonists. Moreover, Carver's stories, with their dead-end settings in the blue-collar world of the Pacific Northwest, are rooted in a social location as specific as Sinclair's industrial Chicago, Grass's prewar Danzig, García Márquez's Caribbean lowlands, Céline's shopkeeper Paris, Richard Ford's Montana and Wyoming, or Roth's suburban New Jersey.

This keen sense of the writer's relation to a larger world is one theme that led me to bring these essays together, for, despite the Marx-inflected criticism of Georg Lukács and the Frankfurt school, the relation of literature to the world around it—the world recreated inside it—played little role in twentieth-century criticism. The technical innovations of modernism demanded a close attention to the text, while its points of reference to the real world, including the actual lives of writer and reader alike, would fall victim to the epistemological scruples of postmodern theorists. Deconstructionists like Paul de Man and Jacques Derrida insisted that the language of literature was performative and self-referential rather than representational, and neopragmatists like Richard Rorty argued that statements about the world could never correspond to the way things actually are. The referentiality of art, its varied reflections of a world outside itself, became as unfashionable as any sense of objective truth. The essays in this book, on the other hand, belong with what George Orwell described as his own "semi-sociological literary criticism"—*semi* because they are attuned to aesthetic concerns along with social ones, and are addressed to general readers rather than specialists. Orwell undoubtedly used this qualifier because, like Virginia Woolf, Edmund Wilson, Cyril Connolly, Mary McCarthy, and Alfred Kazin, he saw himself as a literary journalist, a freelance intellectual whose essays and reviews were intuitive, occasional, and unsystematic.

Such critics, whose work I studied in *Double Agent*, constituted something of a backwater amid the technical advances, the new professionalism, of twentieth-century criticism. They wrote as *littérateurs*, essayists, not technicians of interpretation. They were influenced by the historical approach of an earlier era, including Marxism, at a time when it had largely gone out of fashion. They saw literature in broadly social terms, but their approach was invariably more personal, less programmatic, than the Marxist one. They connected literature to a wider world but, thanks to the advances of modernism, they were no longer wedded to any simple notions of realism. They realized that modern writers, philosophers, psychoanalysts, and scientists alike had complicated the whole question of representation. The world itself had grown more complex, more elusive, less amenable to direct documentation. Nevertheless, they would have understood what Edward Said meant in the introduction to *The World, the Text, and the Critic* (1983) when he said that "each essay in this book affirms the connection between texts and the existential actualities of human life, politics, societies, events."

I hope this is true of my own collection as well. Said's title might have suited this book had he not already claimed it, but I would have substituted "reader" for "critic," since critics essentially are more alert, more articulate readers, readers raised to a higher power, fully attentive to the seismic shock of the written word. As Said makes clear, the academic scene around him was dominated by an omnivorous notion of "textuality" that saw language itself as the substance of literature and reduced the world to the language in which it is described, the "texts" which interpret it. As Derrida put it in his oft-quoted formulation: "there is no outside-the-text." De Man put this even more clearly in his best-known essay, "The Resistance to Theory," when he questioned whether "literature is a reliable source of information about anything but its own language." Critics of this persuasion debunked the human basis of literature, as they deconstructed the human subject itself, the illusion of selfhood. They focused instead on the intricacies of language, with its vertiginous metaphors and undermining subtexts, and on what they saw as the ideological character of all representation. They substituted linguistics for aesthetics, isolating the binaries of language from its capacity to generate meaning. New Critics and the Russian formalists had already treated history and biography as little more than the raw material for art; they severed criticism from the real-world concerns that engaged ordinary readers. But where those earlier critics idealized art as a privileged language set apart from the idols of the tribe, later theorists excavated literary works for the discursive and cultural assumptions that linked them with many other kinds of texts. Deconstruction and post-structuralism, especially in the United States, completed the separation of art from life that fin-de-siècle aestheticism and critical formalism had initiated. As Said wrote, "literary theory for the most part isolated textuality from the circumstances, the events, the physical senses that made it possible and render it intelligible as the result of human work." Even the return to a more historical approach in the 1980s was heavily influenced by rhetorical theories of textuality, discourse, and ideology it first came to counteract. It searched out the traces of social power in literature, and often mobilized history in a way that devalued art.

The work in this book belongs to a different tradition, intuitive, experiential, historicist and "semi-sociological" in the older way. It negotiates a middle ground between art and the human world that art sets out to reconstruct. It is based on the notion, now no longer fashionable, that the most fully realized art also yields the richest insight into its subject, as well as its time and place, that aesthetic commentary can also be a form of historical understanding. A reviewer once noted, with some astonishment, that in *Leopards in the Temple* I wrote about characters in fiction not as words on the page but as if they were real people facing actual problems. This surprised me, but I was happy to agree. It is an effect that art cunningly achieves, not an approach I somehow decided to take. This "reality effect," as Roland Barthes called it, was the bête noire of deconstructive critics, as it had been for the formalist critics who preceded them. But artistic representations of the real world are never merely literal and factual, and certainly never strictly accurate or objective. They are transformative, for they are always filtered through the mind of the subject and the medium of language.

The first section of this book, "American Realism," takes us back to a time, early in the twentieth century, when writers could still rely on masses of painstakingly acquired social information, thick description, and atmospheric detail to construct a whole social milieu. They created characters who were at once individual and representative: an immigrant family in the Chicago stockyards, an unfulfilled woman in a small town in Minnesota, a lone survivor of the pioneer days in Nebraska. Writers like Upton Sinclair and Sinclair Lewis were demon researchers whose methods were rooted in journalism. The inner lives of their characters interested them less than their social meaning.

The two world wars of the twentieth century changed all this. The conventions of realism no longer seemed adequate to a darkly altered sense of reality. The age demanded new forms that would combine metaphysical anguish and psychological complexity with new social truth. For the writers discussed in the second section, "A Different World," the old stable sense of self and society is under siege. These essays show how writers, under the extreme, often fragmented conditions of modern life, can rely neither on the techniques of reportage nor on representative figures. Instead they filter the world though the prism of interior monologue, satire, allegory, or fantasy, not to escape from the real but to convey it more sharply. In this sense, modernism can be seen as a more acute, more desperately inventive phase of realism.

But for the subsequent writers I discuss, in "Postwar Fiction in Context," modernism itself has lost its privileged position. Its techniques have been assimilated but they give no comfort. In the Second World War and the nuclear standoff that followed, the world peered once more into a frightful abyss of its own making. These writers turn to recent forebears like Céline and Heming-way not for experimental forms but for a different voice, an extreme, distinc-tive rhythm for conveying experience. They channel the world through the perceptions of a keen if unbalanced observer. If they seem self-absorbed, it is because there is little else they can now trust. In Mailer, Bellow, and Roth, the central figure is not a social type but usually some version of the authorial self. Life is refracted in rich sensory detail through their own minds. In this post-Freudian era, writers document the world by probing their own baroque demands upon it. But they rarely lose touch with their historical moment, despite this heightened subjectivity.

Harold Bloom was right to say that the imagination resists being confined by the literal. Part of my problem with the New Historicism is that it literal-izes the impact of class and power on literary texts, though more subtly, less mechanically, than most Marxist critics had done. It brings together text and context in ways that can be insightful but also puzzlingly selective; it chooses its examples and anecdotes more arbitrarily than art itself. The last section of this book, "Reading and History," offers some examples of this historical ap-proach, which can go badly awry, as in Marjorie Levinson's tendentious read-ing of Wordsworth's "Tintern Abbey," which, despite the disclaimers, reads more like an indictment than an interpretation. A character in Tony Kush-ner's play *Angels in America* puts the relation between life and art this way: "Imagination can't create anything new, can it? It only recycles bits and pieces of the world and reassembles them into visions." I've tried to show, as Kush-ner's play ultimately does, that the imagination can indeed create something new, but always stitched together from pieces of the real world, a process fa-miliar to most readers and playgoers but seriously troubling to advanced theo-rists. On this point, like Dr. Johnson, I rejoice to concur with the common reader.

I've largely confined this book to essays on fiction, though many poets like Wordsworth, Crabbe, Blake, Keats, Whitman, and Hopkins can be densely concrete in their depiction of the real world. Often this served a larger pur-pose. For Hopkins it pointed to the splendor of creation: "Glory be to God for dappled things." Wordsworth saw poetry as an instrument for the education of the feelings, a means of nurturing our decency and humanity, rescuing our fel-low feeling from the numbing effects of modern life. Walter Benjamin echoed Wordsworth (and in a sense anticipated the Internet) when he described the impact of daily journalism, with its overload of information, in dulling the sensibilities of readers. But where Wordsworth appealed to poetry for resis-tance, Benjamin looked to storytelling, with its links to an oral tradition. By the middle of the nineteenth century, the novel had effectively begun to re-place poetry as a means of repairing tattered human bonds.

The ascendancy of the novel came about not only because it was attuned to the social changes that everyone experienced but thanks to its increasingly complex storytelling and subtle characterization. As literacy spread but classi-cal learning waned, readers lived in these novels as they no longer lived easily in the language of poetry. Though some novelists—think of Evelyn Waugh and other satirists—kept their readers disengaged from the characters, in most classic novels the narrative promotes identification. The empathy Wordsworth sought to awaken through poetry was transferred to prose fiction, and novels succeeded or failed to the degree that they conveyed a credible world. For writers as different as Howells and Hemingway, the work of Tolstoy became the gold standard; his novels, especially *War and Peace*, were seen as a trans-parent window on the real, a window that seemed to be closing down all through the twentieth century.

As I noted earlier, this transparency was no more than a wonderfully achieved illusion, a technical feat as well as a feat of the imagination. Stend-hal called the novel a "mirror carried along a roadway," but this did not mean for him that novels reproduced the larger world by a mechanical process of re-flection. The moving mirror, like a hand-held movie camera, offers us con-stantly shifting images, each fleetingly accurate yet framed into meaning by choice, happenstance, and sequence. This framing and montage constitute form in fiction, as they do in film. The process is interpretive, not simply reflective. When the historian Peter Gay castigates fiction as a "distorting mir-ror," or when J. M. Coetzee's surrogate Elizabeth Costello, lecturing on realism, says that "the word-mirror is broken, irreparably it seems," they confirm that relations between life and art have grown more problematic, but they scarcely confirm Costello's grim suspicion that "the bottom has dropped out," that lit-erature itself may be obsolete.

Through much of the twentieth century, art veered away from realism with-out in any sense abandoning the real. Literature has no viable equivalent to abstraction in painting or music, since there is always a referential element in language. The words we use, however qualified by overtone and suggestion, are always "about" something. But the individual vision of any writer and the selective, subjective qualities of a literary work complicate any trite notion of realism. Each apparition seen in the mirror of art varies in shape, surface, and texture and has its own way of picturing what it reveals. Every great writer has a different feel, a signature style or voice. When the suppressed second half of Richard Wright's autobiography was finally published in the late 1970s, I was captivated by a familiar voice I'd never expected to hear again. I've had a sim-ilar experience each time I returned, after long absence, to the work of a fa-vorite writer. The effective realism of individual writers can be traced as much to their distortions, their subjective "visions," as to the bits and pieces of the world that feed into them. Novels project possible worlds, accented worlds, not one world on which they can all agree.

In a forum on pulp fiction, Maria DiBattista complained that the aim of pulp writers "was not to understand reality but to experience it in a heightened form." Yet to some degree this is the method of all art, the intensification of what is actual in the world by what is actual in the mind. This is certainly true of all the writers discussed in this book, even the most committed realists. A novel is an organized set of experiences, unfolding in a certain rhythm, no matter how lifelike it may seem. By giving his immigrant family a worst-case scenario in *The Jungle*, where everything possible goes wrong, Upton Sinclair makes them stand for every hapless worker caught in the industrial maw, but he never at any point departs from the social facts. Uproarious satirists like Sinclair Lewis and Mary McCarthy, with their highly developed sense of the ridiculous, may exaggerate and caricature, but they remain recognizably true to their subjects. Dostoevsky intensifies, like his master, Dickens, without becoming less of a realist, and this gives his work an almost hallucinatory power, while modernists like Kafka and Beckett craft extreme fables that probe the limits of human endurance and disorientation, surreal situations made all the more credible by their dark comedy and precise circumstantial detail. They are doing what all artists do, not betraying reality but heightening its effects in ways that yield meaning. What empirically minded scholars like Peter Gay call distortion is little more than what an earlier theorist called significant form. As the Israeli novelist Aharon Appelfeld once wrote, reality can allow itself to appear random, disorganized, even incoherent and incredible. In a novel, the world is held to a higher standard. We experience literature as a world that makes sense, even where it looks most senseless. The essays in this book explore how writers take hold of the raw material of experience, the dross of the real world, and make it less arbitrary and opaque, more believable, a vision that is also a kind of revelation.

New York, NY
May 2004

ACKNOWLEDGMENTS

MOST OF THE chapters of this book originated as lectures, essays, reviews, or conference papers. Many have been substantially revised for this volume, with the help of some excellent suggestions from my first editor at Princeton University Press, Mary Murrell, and from two outside readers, Maria DiBattista and Ross Posnock. My new editor, Hanne Winarsky, brought all her energy and enthusiasm to the project. I'm grateful to all the original editors and conveners, who in a number of cases contributed valuable ideas, including John Atherton, Peter Biskind, Claire Bruyère, Jackson R. Bryer, Emily Miller Budick, Ezra Cappell, Marc Chénetier, George Core, Thomas Cushman, Lewis Dabney, Lindsay Duguid, Anne Fadiman, Blanche Gelfant, Larry and Suzanne Graver, Peter C. Herman, Alice Kaplan, Roger Kimball, Hilton Kramer, Wendy Lesser, Suzanne Mantell, Mario Materassi, Jefferson Morley, Ruth Prigozy, John Rodden, John Seelye, Alan Shapiro, Harvey Shapiro, Sarah Spence, Milton R. Stern, Jean Tamarin, and Art Winslow. I owe a special debt to my friend Richard Locke, who first invited me to write for the *New York Times Book Review*; to Caroline Rand Herron, my most recent editor there, who never failed to come up with challenging subjects; and to the late William Phillips, who, over several decades, despite occasional differences, provided a congenial home for my work at *Partisan Review*, a magazine whose impact on American intellectual life in its heyday will probably never be equaled. I am deeply grateful to my wife, Lore, who read each of these essays with a keen literary eye and impeccable taste and sense of style before they were published, and to my staunch agents and friends Georges Borchardt and his Paris colleague Michelle Lapautre, as well as DeAnna Heindel. Timothy Krause and Denell Downum provided great help in bringing these essays together. Among friends I'm happy to single out Mark Bauerlein, Marshall Berman, Larry Graver, and Anne Roiphe for their advice and conversation. Through bad times and good, Eugene Goodheart has been one of my soul mates in thinking about literature and criticism. The late Alfred Kazin, an inspired writer and talker, lent me some of his overflowing love of literature and his sense of purpose as a critic. He permitted me to dedicate the essay on New York writers to him when it first appeared. I hope he wouldn't mind my transferring that dedication to the book as a whole.

A MIRROR IN THE ROADWAY

.

INTRODUCTION: A MIRROR IN THE ROADWAY

ONCE THERE WAS a common assumption that along with everything else that gave meaning to literature—the mastery of language and form, the personality of the author, the moral authority, the degree of originality, the reactions of the reader—hardly anything could be more central to it than the text's interplay with the "real world." Literature, especially fiction, was unapologetically about the life we live outside of literature, the social life, the emotional life, the physical life, the specific sense of time and place. This was especially true after the growth of literary realism in England in the eighteenth century with Defoe and Richardson; in France in the early nineteenth century with Stendhal and Balzac; in Russia at midcentury with Tolstoy; in England again with George Eliot, Dickens, and Trollope; and finally in America with Mark Twain, Henry James, and William Dean Howells, who became the tireless promoter of a whole school of younger realists.

Much as we may still enjoy their work as effective storytelling, readily adaptable to other media, the main assumptions of these writers about the novel and the world around it are now completely out of fashion. That is, everywhere except among ordinary readers. Since the modernist period and especially in the last thirty years, a tremendous gap has opened up between how most readers read, if they still read at all, and how critics read, or how they theorize about reading. As common readers, we sometimes read books (or go to the movies) simply to escape, to get away from our own mundane lives, but part of the time we read for meaning as well. Books can tell us volumes about ourselves, but also about people and places remote from us, in different corners of society or in the distant past. Perhaps the writer could not actually have been there, yet we are transported: we come to trust the imaginative reality the work creates. Coleridge called this the "willing suspension of disbelief," a state of mind that indulges not only the staged dilemmas of fictional characters but the "factual" circumstances of their lives. Even fully imagined works contain a large quotient of information—about other people's sex lives, for example, or their politics; about how they look and dress, or how they behave in social situations. Some of these descriptive functions of literature have been taken over by journalism or pop sociology—by literary nonfiction, as we call it today—or by visual media like photography, film, and television. Yet despite the revolutions of modernist writing, which sometimes threatened to replace realism with fantasy, dream logic, internal monologue, disjunctive montage, and other verbal experiments, it takes a great deal of realistic detail to make these styles credible, as serious readers know and ordinary readers instinctively appreciate.

Without this tissue of correspondence to the real world, literature would be little more than a language game, a self-enclosed world operating entirely by its own rules. Whatever passion or energy goes into a game, the moves have no reference to anything outside the frame; and when it's over, it's over—until the next game begins. Literature, on the other hand, especially fiction, has an open grid. We live on intimate terms with the characters in any effective novel. They sometimes seem more real to us than the people we know, in part because they're purged of accident or contradiction, purified into whatever they essentially are. We may feel shocked and impoverished when a novel ends, and even speculate about what might happen after the curtain goes down. Literary form lays down strict rules (such as rhyme and meter in certain kinds of poetry), but in any actual work these rules are constantly being stretched and modified, even flouted. The creative process involves a curious alchemy between our perceptions and the words we find to express them, between the signifiers of language and the object world to which it beckons.

During the early part of the twentieth century, novelists tried to reduce their dependence on linear plot, background, and setting, just as poets made bold departures from regular rhyme and meter. Fiction writers found their Victorian predecessors bulbous and wordy, their works organized by a narrative logic that no longer seemed convincing. But this new generation also resisted the documentary impulse, the abundance of journalistic detail, that was crucial for the first modern writers, who had emerged in the 1890s under the tutelage of Howells and the influence of Zola. As Ezra Pound and William Carlos Williams turned to the minimalism of the image, publishing poems that were as condensed as haiku, Hemingway and Fitzgerald stripped storytelling down to essentials, using descriptive language and dialogue that seemed bare yet were rich with implication. Responding to *The Great Gatsby*, Edith Wharton was struck by the erasure or omission of Gatsby's background. As a true social novelist, she wrote to Fitzgerald that "to make Gatsby really Great, you ought to have given us his early career . . . instead of a short resumé of it. . . . But you'll tell me that's the old way, & consequently not *your* way." We don't generally think of Willa Cather as a modernist, in part because her narrative manner is crisp and straightforward and she harbored a growing disdain for the modern world. But in the 1920s, she wrote some remarkable books, as spare as *The Great Gatsby* and *The Sun Also Rises*, by purging circumstantial detail and searching out the social and emotional center of her characters' lives. Yet the world of these tightly written later books like *A Lost Lady* and *The Professor's House* is no less realistically described than the immigrant worlds portrayed in *O Pioneers!* and *My Ántonia* which she remembered from her childhood in Nebraska.

To make a case for her new style, Cather boldly redefined realism in her critical writings, later collected in a 1936 book called *Not Under Forty*, whose very title was meant to challenge the younger generation. In "The Novel

Démeublé"—written in 1922, the year of *The Waste Land* and *Ulysses*—she called for a less upholstered kind of fiction, free of "journalism" and "mere verisimilitude." She saw hopeful signs in the new modern writers, whose work confirms her feeling that "the higher processes of art are all processes of simplification." Like Virginia Woolf throwing down the gauntlet to Arnold Bennett, she thinks "how wonderful it would be if we could throw all the furniture out of the window . . . and leave the room as bare as the stage of a Greek theatre." But in renouncing the inert detail of documentary realism, Cather grasps at the essence of realism: the link between descriptive writing and the minds and lives of the novel's characters. She notes that in Tolstoy's work the details of the physical setting—the dress, the furniture, the houses—"seem to exist, not so much in the author's mind, as in the emotional penumbra of the characters themselves." Cather was exasperated by Balzac's overflowing documentation, but Erich Auerbach (in *Mimesis*) saw exactly this fusion of character and milieu as the key to his realism. In Balzac's visual inventory of Madame Vauquer's *pension* in *Le père Goriot*, Auerbach emphasizes "the harmony between Madame Vauquer's person on the one hand and the room in which she is present, the pension which she directs, and the life which she leads." In short, "*sa personne explique la pension, comme la pension implique sa personne.*"

For all their swerve away from the accumulative methods of the Victorian novelists, the French naturalists, and the American realists, the writers of the 1920s shared their faith that works of literature powerfully reflected a world outside themselves. They differed only on the most effective ways of doing so. In *The Professor's House* Cather used several contrasting "houses," including ancient Pueblo cliff-dwellings, as emblems of her characters' state of mind, yes, but also their different way of being: pre-Columbian, small-town traditional, and sleekly modern. As Fitzgerald did with the parties in Gatsby's rented mansion and Hemingway did with bullfighting, Cather made the economy of a grand metaphor do the work of detailed description. These writers objected not to the realism of their predecessors but to their literalism. When scene and character are fused in Tolstoy, Cather says, "literalness ceases to be literalness—it is merely part of the experience," as readers have always understood. But what ordinary readers readily knew can be something many scholars, literary theorists, and postmodern philosophers do *not* know, or at least find highly problematic.

Objectivity may indeed be an elusive goal but, as the philosopher Bernard Williams points out in *Truth and Truthfulness*, accuracy and sincerity are not only highly valued by most people but are considered, at least in a relative sense, obtainable. George Orwell had the same view. His case against modern politics, and especially against the new forms of absolute dictatorship, was not simply directed against the machinery of surveillance and the distortions of language; worst of all, these systems conspired against one's sense of reality, which they treated as if it were a potter's clay. When Winston Smith gives way to his tormentor, O'Brien, near the end of *Nineteen Eighty-Four*, he becomes a kind of postmodernist, renouncing his sense of fact, his adherence to truth, the very evidence of his senses. "The fallacy was obvious," he says of his earlier empirical faith. "It presupposed that somewhere or other, outside oneself, there was a 'real' world where 'real' things happened. But how could there be such a world? What knowledge have we of anything, save through our own minds?" Under the pressure of mental and physical torture, he surrenders his individuality along with his sense of fact and takes refuge in solipsism. For Orwell this represents his complete breakdown, his loss of faith in his own perception of the world.

But even today the word "real" remains honorific, not chimerical, as in quirky colloquial phrases like "get real." The proliferation of reality-based TV shows, which began in 1992 with MTV's *The Real World*, may be attractive to networks because they're so cheap to put on. Like the first English novels, which claimed to be merely factual accounts, they appeal to viewers because they show actual events happening to "real" people—events that are competitive, often titillating, occasionally unpredictable. They cater to a blatant voyeurism, yet what the audience sees is in effect simulated: the participants are carefully chosen—they must be young, attractive, easily typed, outgoing— and the programs are edited along crudely "dramatic" lines from thousands of hours of "candid" footage. This editing process, which imposes a largely fake narrative on supposedly spontaneous material, is grist for the mill of theorists who argue that we have no direct access to what is real and true, only to patterns of representation that shape our perception of what we see and read.

We associate this viewpoint today with poststructuralism, especially the work influenced by French theorists like Michel Foucault and Jacques Derrida, but it became a virtual consensus in literary studies over the past thirty years. Foucault argued that the way we see and describe things is never merely empirical, let alone objective. Nor is it merely *subjective*. It is defined by what he called "discursive practices," the social ideologies that enforce relationships of power in any given society. So where Matthew Arnold, in his quaint humanistic way, described literature as a "criticism of life," for Foucault and the critics who followed him, writers could never truly subvert the values of their age, since they were invariably conditioned by its assumptions. They could not be critical of power since they were complicit with it, unable to break with their society's habits of mind. Derrida and Paul de Man added the idea that language itself, far from being a transparent medium of communication helping us make sense of the world, was full of rhetorical snares and contradictions, especially metaphors and other figures of speech that burdened us with inescapable traces of other people's metaphysics. Like Blake's sunflower, always turned longingly toward the sun, we pine for the real, we aspire to objective knowledge but always remain rooted in the mental soil from which we sprang.

The poststructuralist outlook was not completely new; the "hermeneutics of suspicion," which greets all rhetorical formations with skepticism, goes back at least 150 years. But once it was established as an academic orthodoxy, it changed the face of literary criticism. Instead of describing how writers made sense of the world, American Studies scholars, for example, labored to show how they distorted the world, portrayed it along preconceived lines, and collaborated with social forces and institutions they imagined they were criticizing. This does not mean that if these writers were more honest, more talented or independent-minded, they could have portrayed their world in a more accurate light. According to these skeptics, none of us has access to any objective reality—the thing as it is—to any fundamental truth or foundation; all we have is our particular angle of vision, which is invariably partial and contingent. Nietzsche, one of the godfathers of poststructuralism, called this "perspectivism." In criticizing positivism, the scientific, empirical view that the inquirer must somehow determine "the facts," Nietzsche wrote: "*No*, facts are precisely what there is not, only interpretations. We cannot establish any fact 'in itself': perhaps it is folly to want to do such a thing." But he added, "In so far as the word 'knowledge' has any meaning, the world is knowable; but it is *interpretable* otherwise, it has no meaning behind it, but countless meanings."

Elsewhere, in words that would be echoed by pragmatist thinkers from William James to Richard Rorty, Nietzsche wrote: "Will to truth is a making firm, a making true and durable, an abolition of the false character of things, a reinterpretation of it into beings. 'Truth' is therefore not something there, that might be found or discovered—but something that must be created and that gives a name to a process, or rather to a will to overcome that has in itself no end." This notion of truth as a process, as something changing and dynamic rather than fixed and found, was later developed by William James in his lectures on pragmatism: "The truth of an idea is not a stagnant property inherent in it. Truth *happens* to an idea. It *becomes* true, is *made* true by events. Its verity *is* in fact an event, a process: the process namely of its verifying itself, its veri-*fication*. Its validity is the process of its valid-*ation*."

Nietzsche and James seem to be arguing that, at least in the sphere of understanding, there is no objective reality, nothing out there to be found and discovered, only a shifting series of interpretations (though James insists that once an idea *is* verified and validated, its truth has been established). By this view, the relation of literature to what we anomalously call "the real world" is either settled or meaningless, since objective truth is an illusion. In one blow the rationale for the modern realist aesthetic crumbles. The emerging realism developed with the novel in eighteenth-century England, was traced to Dutch genre painting in Hegel's lectures on aesthetics, became a rallying cry for art critics, literary critics, painters, and novelists in mid-nineteenth-century France, became a force in American painting with the work of Homer and Eakins, and changed the whole direction of American literature under the influence of Howells. Many facets of realism have been familiar for so long that it's hard to grasp why they encountered such resistance. They include: the more faithful depiction of everyday life, a new emphasis on individual psychology and personal destiny that reflected the rise of the middle class, and a more prosaic style that accorded dignity to low-born figures like Defoe's Moll Flanders, Wordsworth's leech-gatherer, and Balzac's or Stendhal's Young Men from the Provinces, trying to storm the gates of wealth and power. Of course we must distinguish between realism, a varied set of conventions and period styles, and reality itself, which can be approached or simulated by many different styles, some of them far from "realistic." As James Wood has written in *The Broken Estate*, "everything flows from the real, including the beautiful deformations of the real; it is realism that *allows* surrealism, magic realism, dream, and so on." But Wood goes perhaps too far when he adds: "Moments of truth in fiction may be only in small part related to the lifelike; rather they flow toward and withdraw from the lifelike." Surely the lifelike has always been an essential element in fiction. The elements of realism I just described all entail an objective world in which the young may rise, living subjects expending energy and passion to make their way, and real centers of power and divisions of class, with ambitions in play, conditions exposed. In the nineteenth century, as the text itself grows more "objective" and lifelike, the author withdraws and becomes increasingly invisible as compared to the playful puppet master of earlier fiction, who freely intervened in the action.

This sense of an objective world is an essential feature of "realism" in philosophy as well as in fiction. In *Philosophy and the Mirror of Nature* and other books and essays, Rorty describes this as the "correspondence" theory of truth, the notion that our minds can discover the facts that will enable our ideas to correspond with what is actually there. For this Rorty substitutes a "coherence" theory of truth, suggesting that the best we can achieve is an effective consistency rather than objective certainty. Elsewhere he distinguishes between "the claim that the world is out there," which he accepts as common sense, and "the claim that truth is out there," which he sees as dependent on the language we use to make sense of the world. While this separates Rorty from philosophical realism, and especially from positivism, it distinguishes him far less from literary realism, since any novel is less an objective inquiry than a subjective heterocosm, a second world, or one of many possible worlds. A novel comments on the world we know by verbally reconstituting it, and it aims to be consistent and credible rather than strictly faithful to that larger world. Not surprisingly, of all philosophers Rorty is perhaps the most attuned to fiction, especially in *Contingency, Irony, and Solidarity* (1989). Nevertheless, one of the best-known definitions of the novel flows from a classic image of the "mirror of nature" that Rorty's work directly challenges.

In the epigraph to chapter 13 of *The Red and the Black*, among the greatest of all realist novels, Stendhal famously wrote: "The novel is a mirror being carried along a road." This saying, undoubtedly by Stendhal himself, is attributed to a seventeenth-century French historian named Saint-Réal, who actually existed, though no such remark has been found in his work. With his fanciful ebullience and playful interventions in the narrative, Stendhal was anything but the Hidden God of his own fiction; an artist of the put-on, he often amused himself with bits of pseudoscholarship. He took pleasure in leading pedantic readers astray, notably his own later editors. He tended to make up these epigraphs, often inventing the author as well, but here he chooses a writer who happens to be "real," a sort of saint of the real, as if to underline the realism he aims to define. Stendhal's mirror image has been derided by critics and philosophers as evidence of the epistemological naiveté of realist theory: the notion that a work of fiction simply reflects the external world in the same way that a book progresses down the path of its plot and settings. (Even so informed a scholar as René Wellek describes it in *Concepts of Criticism* as "a recommendation of literal and total imitation.") But Stendhal's metaphor is more complex than his critics have allowed.

Stendhal returns to the image later in the book, apropos of almost nothing, in a long and ambiguous parenthesis: "A novel, gentlemen, is a mirror carried along a highway. Sometimes it reflects to your view the azure of the sky, sometimes the mire of the puddles in the road. And the man who carries the mirror on his back will be accused by you of immorality! His mirror shows you the mire, and you blame the mirror! Blame, rather, the road in which the puddle lies, and still more the road inspector who lets the water stagnate and the puddle form" (translated by Lowell Bair).

Stendhal stands accused of proposing just what Rorty attacked, a naive correspondence between the mirror of art and its surrounding landscape, the world. This kind of mechanical "reflection," though dear to the commissars of socialist realism, was a notion that even Marxist critics like Georg Lukács and Raymond Williams avoided. Lukács's theory of realism emphasizes not literal replication but the "type," Hegel's concrete universal, at once convincingly singular and emblematic of large social forces and movements. Along the same lines, Williams wrote in *The Long Revolution*, "The old, naive realism is . . . dead, for it depended on a theory of natural seeing which is now impossible." Williams is saying that reality is in part created by our perception, by our complicated interchange with the material world (what Wordsworth described as "all the mighty world / Of eye, and ear,—both what they half create, / And what perceive"). Another idiosyncratic Marxist, the young Richard Wright, concurred in a 1936 manifesto called "Blueprint for Negro Writing": "The relation between reality and the artistic image is not always direct and simple. The imaginative conception of a historical period will not be a carbon copy of reality. Image and emotion possess a logic of their own."

But Stendhal's mirror image is anything but mechanical: it points not to simple seeing but to the tricky ways of seeing through art. His digression into theory aims to fend off another charge entirely—one that would be leveled at many later realists: that the writer is hanging out society's dirty linen, giving an unflattering picture of people and conditions that shouldn't be in a novel in the first place. By the criteria of seventeenth- and eighteenth-century classicism, which Stendhal attacked in his book *Racine and Shakespeare*, art should give an elevated, idealized portrait of general nature, including human nature, not the muck and mire of individual quirks and local conditions (which are perhaps accidental, and untypical). We needn't number the streaks of the tulip, as Dr. Johnson put it, perhaps thinking of the Dutch realist painters.

For Stendhal, Shakespeare was a Romantic before his time. He saw the tumultuous buzz of life in Shakespeare's plays—the mixture of styles, the range of characters and emotions, the shattering of the unities of time and place—as an antidote to the rarefied dignity of the French classical tradition. In much the same way, the mundane stuff of the new fiction, the low particularities, would challenge the decorum of older literary forms, including epic and tragedy. Don't blame the novelists for what they show us, Stendhal is saying; blame the bad condition of the road—the world—and the public officials who should have reported and improved it. Stendhal only appears to be invoking the mirror as an impersonal mechanism, a carbon copy that displays the world as it actually is. The image itself, as he positions it, belies this simplistic claim. This is not a stationary mirror fixed upon the passing show, observing the parade as from the viewing stand, but a dynamic reflector shifting position as it moves down the road. It must be held or carried by someone, and the images it provides will be framed, constantly changing, a series of partial views contributing to a larger picture. It takes in both the azure lyricism of the romantic sky and the all-too-real muck of the neglected terrain. To the modern eye this mirror eerily resembles a movie camera doing a sophisticated tracking shot—some sixty years before movies were invented, and several years before the beginnings of still photography. Or better still, these images of the sky above, the mud below, suggest a hand-held camera, which even today produces an appearance of artlessness as a token of authenticity. Initially, photography and then film gave a big push to realism in literature, especially in late nineteenth-century America, where they developed in tandem with the work of realist painters like Homer and Eakins. We might say that Mathew Brady and the photographers who worked under him were the first American realists, just as the Civil War was the first war that could be reported realistically. But by perfecting the external, descriptive aims of realism, the new visual media, with their stunning mechanical accuracy, made this kind of reproduction less important to painting and fiction. Eventually, it would sound the death knell of portrait painting as we knew it, though it also encouraged the subjective portraiture of painters like Eakins and Sargent, to say nothing of Van Gogh, Picasso, Matisse, and Bonnard. Instead, painting and fiction evolved into impressionism and modernism, where photography, with its ties to the surface of things, could not compete.

Despite an abundance of descriptive detail, the strength of the great European realists, from Balzac and Stendhal to Tolstoy and Proust, came not from mirroring the material surface of reality but from laying bare its social structure and reenacting the ferocious ambitions and frustrations of those who played out their passionate lives within it. Realist novels are inevitably the product of a society in transition. New ways of making money and amassing power eroded social barriers, and this offered openings for new men like Stendhal's Julien Sorel and Balzac's Rastignac, who lay siege to society as if it were a fortress to be stormed. But such characters also have complex interior lives. With them the novel enters a domain of psychology and individual identity that was only rudimentary in Defoe and Fielding but foreshadowed in the work of their contemporary, Samuel Richardson. Richardson's *Clarissa* has rightly been compared to Proust's novel as a work of minute, endlessly exfoli-ating self-scrutiny. Eventually, as realism became more internalized, the world surrounding the characters would sometimes grow vague and blurry, and the psychological novel would develop as an alternative to realist fiction. Yet this was also a more subtle kind of mirroring, a new way of mapping the interaction between the inner and outer world. Molly Bloom's stream of consciousness at the end of *Ulysses* was at once a breakthrough into modernism and the ulti-mate stage of realism, an interior realism that mimed the wayward flow of mental associations.

Another challenge emerging from the heart of realism itself was the novel's aspiration toward art, its unrelenting effort to perfect and codify its own tech-niques. The novel began as a catch-all of prose narrative, the popular stepchild of the arts, sometimes ragged in its writing, with shifting points of view, undi-gested historical material, and a puritan pretense that it wasn't fiction at all, simply a trove of letters or an artlessly told personal history. For much of the nineteenth century, novels commanded a fervent readership but little cultural respect, and some of the leading critics, such as Matthew Arnold, scarcely took notice of them. With his immense popularity, Dickens was the special object of highbrow condescension, especially from critics like George Henry Lewes, who were committed to the new realism. But a few writers—first Flaubert, then Henry James—set out to change all this. James's reviews, essays, and prefaces build toward a monumental project to transform fiction into a fine art by developing rigorous formal principles, including the notion that the writer should never directly intervene in the narrative, but *should* portray the action from a consistent point of view. Prolific writers like H. G. Wells, using the old slapdash techniques, never quite forgave James for this. Wells saw James not only as the creator of the Art Novel but as someone who insisted that it must provide "real through and through and absolutely true treatment of people more living than life." For Wells, impatient with such exactitude, "it might be more or less than that and still be a novel," as he says in his *Experi-ment in Autobiography*. "It isn't a constructed tale I have to tell," says Wells's artless narrator at the outset of *Tono-Bungay*, "but unmanageable realities." But Wells's informal view did not prevail; critics like Percy Lubbock (in *The*

Craft of Fiction) turned James's approach into a manual of technique, and F. R. Leavis (in *The Great Tradition*) projected it into a strenuous reading of the history of the English novel.

James's predecessor, Flaubert, had gone even further than James by putting a tremendous emphasis on style. His letters are full of the agony of the phrase, the image, of finding the right word. Such an ambition had been foreign to fiction until then, for it had generally been a loose and open form, presided over by a wayward and garrulous narrator and stocked with an abundance of worldly information. (H. G. Wells's novels look back to this tradition.) Now Flaubert expressed annoyance that the novel actually had to be *about* something. Why couldn't it be a kind of prose poem that pivoted on the perfect precision of its own language? In an 1852 letter he wrote: "What seems beautiful to me, what I should like to write, is a book about nothing, a book dependant on nothing external, which would be held together by the strength of its style . . . a book which would have almost no subject, or at least in which the subject would be almost invisible, if such a thing is possible. The finest works are those that contain the least matter. . . . I believe that the future of Art lies in this direction."

This proved to be a remarkably accurate forecast. The ambition to write a book about nothing, a book that was all form and style, was taken up languidly by aesthetes and decadents in France and England; it became part of the legacy of the fin-de-siècle writers to the early moderns. Though no writer, Flaubert included, has ever been entirely able to supersede the referential nature of language, Flaubert's fantastic wish foreshadowed both aestheticism (which saw art as feeding largely on itself) and certain strains of modernism (which drove art toward the formal investigation of its own techniques). Oscar Wilde's *Picture of Dorian Gray* is his version of Stendhal's mirror, but the glass is turned inward toward the soul rather than outward toward the world. Early on someone says, "every portrait that is painted with feeling is a portrait of the artist, not of the sitter. The sitter is merely the accident, the occasion." This is the perspective of Romantic poetry imported into fiction, for Romantic poetry, as M. H. Abrams showed long ago, embodied the shift from the mirror to the lamp, from the neoclassical artist as reflector of the world around him to the Romantic artist as the source of his or her own creative fire. But even the Romantic lamp illuminates the space around it, shedding its light on the actual world, while modern writing and painting often make no such claims. With his attraction to humble men and women in ordinary rural settings, the Romantic Wordsworth, like the urban, demotic Whitman, was one of the progenitors of realism. Whitman's catalogues are novelistic (and often photographic) in their flow of detail, their ecstatic, voluminous concreteness, and Wordsworth too, in his poems about Michael and Matthew and the "Old Man Travelling," can be poignant in his matter-of-factness, which sometimes provoked his contemporaries to parody and invective.

But there is a strand of modern painting, especially abstract painting, that is simply about the paint, or about the geometry of the image, just as modern dance can be solely about movement, or about the body, modern music about sound, and modern poetry about the language. Can any writers have taken literature further away from mirroring the world than Gertrude Stein, who modeled her work partly on the cubism of her friend Picasso but also on the pragmatism and psychological theories of her teacher William James? Stein's use of language is nothing if not concrete, but her word-bound literalism parodies and undercuts the strategies of realism. In Stein's case, Romantic self-absorption and modernist experiment lose their titanic edge and terminate in a crisis of representation.

Let me summarize the argument and build upon it:

One of the great innovations in literature, starting from the eighteenth century, was the honing of techniques, especially in fiction, that enabled it to correspond much more closely to the world around it. If poetry should offer us real toads in imaginary gardens, as Marianne Moore suggested, then fiction gives us imaginary toads—invented characters—in real gardens, that is, against a backdrop that must seem entirely credible. Paradoxically, fictional characters are often based on real people, and the background must be richly imagined to engage us as real. Thus Orwell praised Dickens for his fertility of invention by noting that "the outstanding mark of Dickens' writings is the unnecessary detail." For modernist critics like Leavis, this sheer abundance, the luxury of the irrelevant detail, was a drawback, a failure of organization, though it permitted the novelist to create a world.

Saul Bellow once argued that realism is still the great modern breakthrough. It allowed fiction to make sense of a society in perpetual upheaval. The novel's focus on the individual, especially the psychology of the individual, reflected the emergence of the new middle class, in a period when it became possible for individuals to succeed not only through birth and pedigree but by way of talent and ambition. But realism also encouraged writers to explore the social conditions created by the growth of industry, the new working class, the expansion of cities, the flow of immigrants, the changing position of women, the decline of rural life, the impact of technology, the emergence of America as a new force in the world, the impact of war and violence, the surge of nationalism and anti-Semitism, the power of race and ethnicity, the dissolution of hierarchy, the loss of religious belief, the rise of democracy and dictatorship, the accumulation of wealth, the increase in travel and leisure, the shifts in manners and morals, the development of the mass media, and hundreds of other social changes that could be condensed into the trajectory of individual lives.

In America, where literary realism supposedly never took hold, where romance was long said to be the prevailing form of fictional expression, novelists like Upton Sinclair, Theodore Dreiser, and Sinclair Lewis tackled these social subjects almost as if they were freelance journalists or intuitive sociologists—doing research, packing in massive amounts of information, finding characters and situations that typified the changes they saw all around them. They recorded regional tics of speech and quirks of behavior but also showed how power was distributed and deep personal needs were played out and thwarted. Early in *Sister Carrie*, when Dreiser sets out to describe one of the new department stores in Chicago, he begins: "The nature of these vast retail combinations, should they ever permanently disappear, will form an interesting chapter in the commercial history of our nation." These great enterprises reveal the nexus between commerce and desire, and Dreiser sees himself as their conscientious historian.

Much of this literature melding storytelling with social history and criticism appeared in the United States between 1890 and 1930, when the realist movement was at its peak. Some of it was focused on the small-town world from which the writers sprang. Hamlin Garland vividly recalled the hardscrabble life of his parents on Midwestern farms and set out in *Main-Travelled Roads* to correct the idyllic lens through which this world was commonly seen. Sarah Orne Jewett, in the spirit of Winslow Homer, sketched some indelible portraits of women's lives in small Maine fishing villages in *The Country of the Pointed Firs*, placing herself in the picture as recorder and detached observer. Harold Frederic, a London correspondent for the *New York Times*, showed remarkable insight into the religious life of a troubled minister in a small American city in *The Damnation of Theron Ware*. Stephen Crane, with far less personal experience, painted a stunning impressionist picture of life in New York's Irish slums in *Maggie: A Girl of the Streets*. Crane was influenced by the books and slide lectures of Jacob Riis, who covered the same material journalistically in *How the Other Half Lives*, using photographs, primitively reproduced, to complement his lurid, sensational reports on the turbulent underclass. Even Howells, in *A Hazard of New Fortunes*, makes his genteel but curious protagonist our tour guide to the poor immigrant districts of New York, with its ethnic restaurants, labor unrest, and heavy-handed police repression. His New York, where good apartments are hard to find, is already the modern city we know. Finally, in *Sister Carrie*, one of our greatest city novels, Dreiser built on his own journalism to describe the rise and fall of commonplace characters who inhabit his densely realized worlds of Chicago and New York.

All these books were published in a single decade between 1890 and 1900, years of serious depression, financial panic, and unprecedented social crisis in the United States. And all of them went out of fashion once modernism turned writers away from overtly social subjects and documentary approaches, toward a more refined technique for experimenting with language and exploring their characters' rich interior lives. Few critics were more responsible for the low esteem into which these realist writers fell than Lionel Trilling, who, in "Reality in America" (the opening essay in *The Liberal Imagination*), accused Dreiser and the progressive literary historian V. L. Parrington of having a coarse, simplistic, undifferentiated sense of reality. Of Parrington, he writes: "There exists, he believes, a thing called *reality*; it is one and immutable, it is wholly external, it is irreducible. Men's minds may waver, but reality is always reliable, always the same, always easily to be known. And the artist's relation to reality he conceives as a simple one," that is, one of passive "correspondence." To Parrington's charge that Hawthorne was "forever dealing with shadows, and he knew that he was dealing with shadows," Trilling responds that "shadows are also part of reality and one would not want a world without shadows, it would not even be a 'real' world." But Trilling insists that Hawthorne also "was dealing with realities, with substantial things." Far from dismissing realism, Trilling would expand Parrington's sense of "reality" to include the romantic, the psychological, the fantastic, and the moral, all the while insisting on a more intricate and active correspondence between the mind of the artist and the external world. This more nuanced understanding of realism is taken for granted today, though Trilling's viewpoint on the realist writers has been turned on its head.

In the last twenty years, scholars have rediscovered the flawed but fascinating books of the American realist tradition. Yet thanks to the influence of poststructuralism, they remain skeptical about any writer's ability to tell us much that is truthful about the real world. They see these works as vessels of ideology, shaped and distorted by their own points of view. Like Oscar Wilde, they think these portraits tell us more about the minds of the writers than about the world—not about their souls, as Wilde suggested, but about the social assumptions that were part of their mental baggage. Like Nietzsche they argue that "facts are precisely what there is not, only interpretations." But what is a novel if not an interpretation of experience, a thoroughly imagined way of rendering it? Jacob Riis, in his reports and photographs, and Dreiser, in his novels, may have thought they were giving us the social facts as they saw them; they may even have thought objectivity was possible. But their own work shows how partial and committed they inevitably were. Recent scholarship has revived interest in the realist aesthetic yet at the same time discounted its access to reality, emphasizing instead its collusion with power and with the marketplace.

The socially textured arts, from photography to documentary filmmaking to fiction, provide excellent examples of Nietzsche's perspectivism at work. Novelists may have dreamed that they were the secretaries of society, recording objective facts and conditions. But by filtering them through fictional characters and invented stories, they provide them with a personal accent, an inward resonance, a narrative shape and resolution, that gives their accounts an advantage over the work of journalists and historians. This storytelling also makes them meaningful to a whole different range of readers.

In a recent book called *Savage Reprisals*, the historian Peter Gay tries to debunk the use of novels as a way of understanding history. As an empirical scholar he feels these novels are not accurate. Dickens, he says, is too emotional, and entirely ignorant of the utilitarianism he lampoons in *Hard Times*. As a Freudian, he feels that novels are not impartial enough; they are distorted by the prejudices and neuroses of the authors, their grudge against the society that formed them. Gay, a voluminous historian of the nineteenth-century bourgeoisie, also clearly dislikes the kind of social criticism he finds in many of these writers; to him their outlook seems hostile, warped, and stereotyped. But he sets the terms of his attack too narrowly. Though the three novels he discusses by Dickens, Flaubert, and Thomas Mann contain a great deal of description and social information, no one would go to them for objectivity or strict verisimilitude. But why would a Freudian expect writers, of all people, to be coolly objective? Instead it's their *subjectivity* that gives them much of their historical *and* literary value. The subjectivity of their characters, who experience society in a personal (yet somehow typical) way, is made possible by the writer's own angle of vision; this is no mere distortion but itself a vital piece of historical evidence, shaped by the time and place as well as the formative experiences of the author. This subjective quality gives the work an emotional coloring that still connects us to it, many years later. This was Aristotle's argument for the superiority of poetry over history, which Gay aims to overturn. If these works had the balanced, rounded, impartial truth he seeks—and that theorists at the opposite extreme deny is possible—these novels would simply be documents of their time, inertly factual traces of the period in which they were written. Instead, they go far to reconcile the quotidian world and the always surprising world of art and imagination.

Novels mediate between subject and object, the perceiver and the things perceived, the hard facts of the world and the contingencies of the language we use to describe them. Novels show us that the real world, far from being simple and always available, can also be elusive and problematic. They create identifications that channel the quicksilver flow of our inner experience and redirect our social sympathies. They can be powerful tools of indoctrination. They can excite us sexually or inflame us politically. They are not simply mirrors that reflect the world but prisms that refract it, break it down. Yet they envelop us in a milieu that can seem more credible than the world we know. Novels somehow finesse the philosophical conflict between objective truth and the plurality of perspectives; they renew the world by refreshing our perception of it.

AMERICAN REALISM

The Sense of Time and Place

THE CITY AS TEXT: NEW YORK
AND THE AMERICAN WRITER

If the City is a text, how shall we read it?
—Joyce Carol Oates

CITIES ARE CONSTRUCTIONS of steel and stone, accumulations of humanity on a grand scale. Architects plan and study cities; historians trace their economic and political influence; urbanists analyze their patterns of development and social interaction. But there is also a symbolism of cities that exerts a powerful hold on our imagination. Ancient Greek and biblical cities, so small by modern standards, crystallized into large, resonant myths: Athens and Sparta, Nineveh and Babylon, Rome and Jerusalem; so too did London and Paris.

American cities are too new to carry this weight of symbolic meaning. We have no modern urban texts powerful enough to invest them with the mythic reverberations of such older cities. Instead we have media images that provide the world with instantly recognizable stereotypes. During the 1970s and 1980s, many Americans associated New York with images of crime and urban blight, with streets of sunless concrete, subways out of Dante's hell. This changed toward the end of the century, when the economy and the stock market soared, the crime rate began to decline, and the city renewed itself as a magnet for visitors and immigrants alike. Once again the prevailing image became the famous skyline, long used as a backdrop for the credits of dozens of films. After September 11, 2001, this inevitably became the wounded skyline, symbol of a nation that felt under siege, attacked on its own shores for the first time.

There were other prevailing images of the city: the bright lights of Broadway, which somehow survived the development and gentrification of the Times Square area; the Statue of Liberty, which played its symbolic role in 1989 in Tiananmen Square. Fritz Lang claimed that he took the inspiration for the 1927 film *Metropolis* from his first sight of the skyline from the New York harbor. This is a European view: New York as the capital of the future, the image of modernity. As late as the 1960s, New York still had more skyscrapers than all the world's cities combined. By 1940, according to urban historian Kenneth T. Jackson, it "had become the world's largest and richest city."

After the war, movies like *On the Town* could make a powerful impact simply by filming on location. According to dance critic Arlene Croce, who grew up in Providence, "New York had a tremendous glamor in the postwar years;

I certainly felt it in *On the Town*, and every time the 20th Century Fox orchestra played 'Street Scene' behind a New York stock shot, which it did constantly in that period, I would be paralyzed with desire." Feeding this fascination were hundreds of song lyrics that reflected New York's genius at self-promotion during this era. From Rodgers and Hart's "Manhattan" to Dubin and Warren's "42nd Street" and "Lullaby of Broadway" to "New York, New York, / It's a Wonderful Town"—now the material for instant nostalgia—New York was synonymous with bubbly wit, urbanity, and glamor.

But this bastion of industrial capitalism and urban sophistication was not the city in which most New Yorkers lived. What they knew best, what their children eventually wrote about, was Jane Jacobs's New York, a city of separate neighborhoods and ethnic groups, a city of urban villages linked by a gigantic web of trolley lines, subways, tunnels, and bridges, but also a city with a vibrant street life that somehow defied the American love affair with the automobile.

Not many American writers were attracted to New York as an icon of modernity. In *Manhattan Transfer* and *U.S.A.*, John Dos Passos tried to imitate the staccato rhythm and headlong energy of the industrial city, which he found so alien to individuality. His work, like Döblin's novel *Berlin, Alexanderplatz*, epitomizes what the sociologist Georg Simmel in his classic essay "The Metropolis and Mental Life" describes as "the *intensification of nervous stimulation*" in city life: "the rapid crowding of changing images, the sharp discontinuity in the grasp of a single glance, and the unexpectedness of onrushing impressions." Dos Passos's montage in *U.S.A.*—a noisy overlay of newsreel headlines, the fragmentary perceptions of the camera eye, and miniature biographies of real people interwoven with the threads of fictional narrative—is a transposition of urban life into an abstract, collective pattern in which the individual is submerged. As he says at the outset, he wants to write an epic of Everyman, a Whitmanesque Poem of These States, "the slice of a continent. . . . the speech of the people." But more than modern life itself, it is his own panoramic technique that impoverishes his characters and pinches their inner lives.

The modern look and feel of New York has proved more of a challenge and an inspiration to visual artists, including precisionists like Charles Sheeler and Louis Lozowick, cubists like Max Weber, and futurists like Joseph Stella, who arrived from Italy in 1906. Weber, in a brilliant series of paintings in 1915, including *New York at Night, Rush Hour, New York, New York Department Store*, and *Grand Central Terminal*, depicted the city as a hub of modernity and technology. Stella, a few years later in *The Voice of the City of New York Interpreted*, created an explosive but abstract geometry of five vivid New York scenes, in which New York's bridges and buildings, despite their Gothic touches, became almost ready-made cubist images. "New York is what all towns will be tomorrow—geometric," wrote a French visitor, Paul Morand, in 1929. "It is the simplification of line, of ideas, of feelings, the reign of directness."

Finally there were the abstract painters of the New York School after World War II, who were also inspired by the hard-edged geometry of city life. (Mondrian's "Broadway Boogie-Woogie" is perhaps the most famous example.) Working parallel to them were the European-born architects attached to the International Style, who turned from the more decorative and lush skyscrapers of the thirties, such as the Chrysler Building, to the severe formal geometry of the Seagram Building, the Lever House, and many lesser versions of the modernist glass box, which began to give a dismally rectangular quality to the Manhattan skyline.

Only a handful of American writers, like Hart Crane in parts of *The Bridge* ("To Brooklyn Bridge," "The Tunnel") and William Carlos Williams in his prose experiments of the 1920s, tried either to celebrate the city or to imitate this modernist iconology. They tried to get the buildings, the bridges, the rush of humanity into their very technique. They were reacting against the grim, apocalyptic portrayal of urban life in other modern writers like Eliot, yet Eliot's influence overshadowed theirs. His London in *The Waste Land*, with its Dantesque image of the crowd flowing across London Bridge—"so many, / I had not thought death had undone so many"—sums up the antiurban fascination and revulsion of so many post-Romantic authors. Eliot's spectral "Unreal City" is virtually an anthology of such writers, for it includes imagery not only of Dante's hell but of Dickens's dust heap in *Our Mutual Friend*, Poe's prophetic 1840 sketch "The Man of the Crowd," and Baudelaire's "*fourmillante cité, cité pleine de rêves*," which Eliot himself cites in his notes.

Poe's version of New York is called London in "The Man of the Crowd"; in a few pages it introduces an astonishing number of motifs that would later become crucial for the literature of the city. It even introduces the theme of this essay, the city as text, since it describes the narrator's effort to *read* a man—the emblem of the urban crowd—who, in the end, cannot be read. "*Er lasst sich nicht lesen*" is the first and last line of the story. The narrator's driving curiosity, his avidity to read the faces of the crowd, propels the story forward, for this is also a fable about interpretation, an open-ended detective story.

This nameless narrator resembles Poe's other curious, brooding protagonists: his detectives and the fevered, obsessional types who haunt his horror stories. But the object of this man's fascination is the city itself, more specifically, "the dense and continuous tides of population" rushing past the door of his hotel, which he first observes darkly through the "smoky panes" of his window. Almost a century before the vogue of "mass society," before the work on masses and crowds of Le Bon, Ortega, and Canetti, before King Vidor's great silent film *The Crowd*, Poe was one of the first to see the urban crowd as a single complex entity, a creature that seemed to have a life and will of its own. But he also saw it as a mystery, full of anonymous beings and unaccountable energies, something that cried out to be deciphered yet could never truly be known.

At first the narrator is detached, shielded, peering out from a distance at the kaleidoscopically changing mass, trying to read the individual faces that reel by him "in that brief interval of a glance." Then, at the exact midpoint of the story, his attention is absorbed by the idiosyncratic look on a single face, and he leaves his secure vantage point to plunge into the crowd itself. He turns from cinematic observer, before whose "keenest appetency" the street simply unreels itself, into the *flâneur*, the walker in the city, or in this case the stalker in the city. His inscrutable prey, whose behavior is a jumble of puzzling hints and signs, stands for the mystery of the crowd itself. Pursuing him all through the night and the next day, "resolute not to abandon a scrutiny in which I now felt an interest all-absorbing," he finally grows "wearied unto death." He finds the mystery at last impenetrable.

Writers like Dickens and Dostoevsky—and Poe's disciple, Baudelaire— would soon do wonders with the turbulent anonymity of the urban crowd, but the American writer who best developed the viewpoint of the *flâneur* was Whitman.[1] It has been argued that Whitman's city is really an urban pastoral, a countrified utopia, tranquil for all its turbulence. Yet Whitman, far more than Poe, made the eddying flow of the crowd not simply the subject of his work but one of its organizing principles. Responding to the "aboriginal name" of "Mannahatta" in an 1860 elegy, Whitman described New York as a city of islands nesting in bays and rivers, a city of flowing tides but also of flowing currents of humanity—"tides swift and simple, well loved by me," as well as "immigrants arriving, fifteen or twenty thousand a week. . . . Trottoirs throng'd, vehicles, Broadway, the women, the shops and shows." These busy tides and currents are translated into the structure of his best poems.

Whitman loves to make lists. His rolling Homeric catalogues are themselves word-crowds. Think of the exotic place-names that trip so liquidly off his tongue in great inventory poems like "Salut au Monde!" where Whitman becomes the *flâneur* in orbit, reeling off an immense geography, encircling the globe as he had circled the city. Whitman ingests the country and the city, the rivers and the mountains. But the ebb and flow of what Whitman names in these poems, those words that taste so good to him, infuse themselves into the rhythm and substance of greater poems, such as "Song of Myself" and "Crossing Brooklyn Ferry."

If Whitman is not fully a city poet, it's because he takes in city activity as he takes up everything else, as part of an endless current through which he reaches out to the world and assimilates it to himself. "To me the converging objects of the universe perpetually flow," he says in "Song of Myself." Yet unlike many poets who preceded him, who felt swamped and nullified by city life, Whitman takes pleasure in this eddying current, revels in its diversity. For

---

[1] Walter Benjamin's essays on Baudelaire and nineteenth-century Paris are a classic analysis of the *flâneur* and the urban crowd. See also Marshall Berman's discussions of Baudelaire's prose poems and Dostoevsky's Petersburg in *All That Is Solid Melts into Air* (1982).

Wordsworth in the seventh book of *The Prelude*, London was summed up in the freakish carnival of St. Bartholomew's Fair, melting individual identity into a monstrous amalgam. But Whitman, for all his stress on selfhood, on personality, relishes the undifferentiated quality of the urban mass. Wordsworth in London feels depressed, spiritually starved, under threat of dissolution. For Whitman this chaos is a plenitude, a blurring of the hard boundaries of the self, the separations of space and time.

Whitman assimilates the city to the rhythm of physical activity, not just the movement of the body but the systole and diastole of its inner pulsations. He personalizes the crowd without individualizing any member of it, not even himself. The "Calamus" poems, which are both sexual and political, express his dream of "a new city of friends," a community which is both plebeian and sensual. Does he takes his pen in hand, he asks, to record

> . . . the vaunted glory and growth of the great city spread around me?—no;
> But merely of two simple men I saw to-day on the pier in the midst of the crowd,
> parting the parting of dear friends.
>
> ("What Think You I Take My Pen in Hand?")

Elsewhere he writes,

> A great city is that which has the greatest men and women,
> If it be a few ragged huts it is still the greatest city in the whole world.
>
> ("Song of the Broad-Axe")

Another "Calamus" poem, one of Whitman's most flagrantly sensual tributes to New York as a city of "comrades and lovers," begins daringly, arrogantly:

> City of orgies, walks and joys,
> City whom that I have lived and sung in your midst will one day make you
> illustrious.

The gaucheness and crude boasting of this last line is a piece of essential Whitman, as well as a piece of New York. He goes on to enumerate what in the city might repay him for making it so famous:

> Not the interminable rows of your houses, nor the ships at the wharves,
> Nor the processions in the streets, nor the bright windows with goods in them,
> Nor to converse with learn'd persons, or bear my share in the soiree or feast;
> Not those, but as I pass O Manhattan, your frequent and swift flash of eyes
> offering me love,
> Offering response to my own—these repay me;
> Lovers, continual lovers, only repay me.
>
> ("City of Orgies")

As usual in Whitman, we have no way of knowing how literally to take these lines. His New York, it would seem, is both a place to pick up men and a metaphorical community of flashing eyes and intersecting glances. ("How the floridness of the materials of cities shrivels before a man's or woman's look!") The urban crowd becomes for him what Nature was for some Romantic poets: a scene of ecstatic fusion.

> I hear the sound I love, the sound of the human voice,
> I hear all sounds running together, combined, fused or following,
> Sounds of the city and sounds out of the city, sounds of the day and night.
>
> ("Song of Myself")

Emphasizing the body yet himself strangely disembodied, Whitman becomes the tutelary spirit hovering over all human activity—over the little one sleeping in its cradle, the youngsters climbing the bushy hill, the suicide sprawled on the bloody floor of the bedroom. In Whitman's crowded catalogue almost every line is a separate story, a concrete naming. These terse, vivid details supply an exact realism that anchors Whitman's euphoria, his erosion of boundaries and differences. Whitman's precise jottings are like little poems strung together, through which he plunges breathlessly, as Poe's narrator plunges into the maelstrom on the street. But where Poe's feverish narrator remains detached—observing, weighing, speculating—Whitman's theme, his essential myth, is one of connection, of something far more deeply interfused: "And these tend inward to me, and I tend outward to them. . . . And of these one and all I weave the song of myself."

After the audacities of "Song of Myself," Whitman's most daring leap (as well as his greatest city poem) was "Crossing Brooklyn Ferry." There his myth of connection sheds its vagueness and, with an uncanny gift for prophecy, he projects himself fifty and a hundred years into the future. For Whitman, whose life was split between Brooklyn and Manhattan, the ferry became what the Brooklyn Bridge would later be for writers like Hart Crane: a symbol of passage, a poetic crossing that signals their own leaps of imagination. For Whitman it is more: the link between the city and the bay, as well as a bridge between the past, the present, and the future. (Many years later Whitman, in prose, recalled his passion for ferries, comparing the "oceanic currents, eddies, underneath" with "the great tides of humanity also, with ever-shifting movements.")

Whitman's genius in the poem is to imagine not an abstract future but people in the flesh, traversing the same tide a hundred years later, and to insist that they imagine *his* personal reality, even to the point of their imagining him imagining them.

> Just as you feel when you look on the river and sky, so I felt,
> Just as any of you is one of a living crowd, I was one of a crowd.
>
> . . . .
>
> I too lived, Brooklyn of ample hills was mine,

I too walk'd the streets of Manhattan island, and bathed in the waters around it,
I too felt the curious abrupt questionings stir within me,

.   .   .   .

I too had receiv'd identity by my body

.   .   .   .

What thought you have of me now, I had as much of you—I laid in my stores in
     advance,
I consider'd long and seriously of you before you were born.

Whitman turns our perception of the past and future into an insistent moral
demand: he wants us to acknowledge that people who once lived and will live
are as real as we are, that he himself once pulsed with flesh and blood, humor
and desire. But the self-delighting narcissist in Whitman wants more than to
be recognized: he wants to be petted, known, loved; he wants to create the future, to dominate it, to merge with it sexually across time and death. In another poem that begins, "Whoever you are holding me now in hand," he tries
to control how future readers will hold his book, where they may read it, how
it might press up against their hip and feel the physical pressure of their pulse.
In "Crossing Brooklyn Ferry," the poem itself becomes the medium that "fuses
me into you now, and pours my meaning into you." The city, like the poem,
now assures his immortality, and he concludes by laying a benediction upon it,
for it is now coeval with his own body, blood of his blood, flesh of his flesh, eddying forward like his own throbbing brain.

If Whitman is the poet of urban euphoria, who saw his work as "a call in the midst
of a crowd, / My own voice, orotund, sweeping and final," then Melville, his exact
contemporary, created the most powerful contrary vision. Melville did not often
write about cities, but in a few texts he gave us indelible images of urban isolation,
anonymity, and entrapment worthy of Kafka. Alfred Kazin has written about
Melville's "angry attachment to his birthplace," where his mother, Maria Gan-
sevoort, came from an illustrious family. There he spent not only some of his early
days but his years of neglect and anonymity as a deputy customs inspector, a job
dimly reminiscent of his years at sea. *Moby-Dick* begins in Manhattan only so
that Ishmael can describe the crowd at the water's edge, to explain the irresistible
fascination of the sea. In *Moby-Dick*, cities represent the safe confinements of
domesticity and civilization, but the urban scenes in Melville's other novels are
frequently nightmarish. Pierre Glendinning's arrival in New York (in *Pierre*) is
a biblical scene of almost hellish phantasmagoria; Pierre lands in the midst of a
chaotic urban crowd—the underclass, as we would call it today—a Babel of
sexes, races, and languages that fills him "with inexpressible horror and fury."

   In indescribable disorder, frantic and diseased-looking men and women of all colors, and in all imaginable flaunting, immodest, grotesque, and shattered dresses,
   were leaping, yelling, and cursing around him.

Their language he describes as "words and phrases unrepeatable in God's sunlight, and whose very existence was utterly unknown, and undreamed of by tens of thousands of the decent people of the city." This is not the ordinary urban crowd, certainly not Whitman's benign current of humanity. This is the edge of the city, the boundary line between civilization and chaos. With its thieves'-quarters and brothels and strange foreign tongues, it is the city of vice and crime, an urban archaeology of a buried, invisible stratum of urban life.

In *Redburn*, a few years earlier, Melville had sent his hero down to explore another invisible city. Descending from his ship in Liverpool, armed only with a fifty-year-old guidebook his father had once used, Redburn finds barely the faintest resemblance between the city on paper and the "modern" Liverpool. Here change is the law of life, and everything old has been torn down and forgotten. (Melville's point is clear: our fathers' experiences, and their guidebooks, now prove less than useless.) Later he comes upon a woman and her daughters starving to death in the street, but he can find no one, not even the police, who will take the least interest in them, except, finally, to dispose of their cadavers. They too belong to the forgotten, the invisible city.

Stopping off in Constantinople on his voyage to the Near East in 1856, Melville himself experienced the narrow streets of the city as a "maze," a "labyrinth." On a long walk, as described in his journal, "found myself back where I started. Just like getting lost in a wood. No plan to streets. Pocket compass. Perfect labyrinth. Narrow. Close, shut. . . . If you could but get up into a tree, soon out of the maze. But no, no names to the streets. . . . No numbers. No anything." Only the open sea allayed the claustrophobia he felt in the city.

Some of Melville's most arresting short fiction deals with isolation or abandonment, the loneliness at the heart of great cities. In "The Two Temples" he describes a morosely comic incident in which he is first kept from entering Grace Church in lower Manhattan, then, after sneaking in, is accidentally locked in the church, then expelled by the angry beadle. In another scarcely known sketch, "Jimmy Rose," he portrays a great figure of the town, once a wealthy, generous, and convivial host, who loses all his money yet continues living—barely, pathetically—on the grudging charity of his former friends. As the island's residential life gradually moves uptown, his very house, which the narrator of the story eventually inherits, is buried in a grim commercial district. Once the center of fashion, it is now in the backwater of "progress," a forlorn symbol of the graciousness of an earlier era. But Melville's most piercing image of isolation in New York can be found in his greatest tale, "Bartleby, The Scrivener: A Story of Wall-Street." Here Melville develops brilliantly what is only rudimentary in "Jimmy Rose," the contrast between the plight of the outcast and the conventional but wholly ineffectual sympathy of the elderly narrator.

Bartleby, with his "pallid haughtiness" and iron resistance, may be the formal subject of the story, but the lawyer who employs him and finally abandons him is unquestionably the central character. Like Poe's Man of the Crowd, Bartleby and his unaccountable "preferences" are ultimately impenetrable; his refusal to examine his own work, to continue copying, or even to vacate his employer's office is certainly outrageous—for those of us who think as this lawyer does. His rebellion, always couched in the same polite formula, "I would prefer not to," is surely the mildest, purest form of negation imaginable, yet no conventional view of the world, no rational ethic of business or society, could accommodate it.

Melville's narrative impersonation of the cozy Wall Street lawyer, who is indignant at the loss of a public sinecure and so proud of the patronage of Mr. John Jacob Astor, is a tour de force of ironic ventriloquy. Known to all as "an eminently *safe* man," he has always, as he tells us proudly, "been filled with a profound conviction that the easiest way of life is the best." His snug, comfortable existence is disrupted by his troublesome copyist. But despite his liberal tolerance and his strong undercurrent of fascination with Bartleby, he never truly confronts his mysterious shadow and double, whose anonymity and immobility are the hideous underside of his own ease and sociability. He can understand Bartleby only through sentimental platitudes about human loneliness which, in a different way, *are* actually the themes of the story. He can conclude by lamenting, with great pathos, "Ah, Bartleby! Ah, humanity!" but his own humanity is too limited to comprehend Bartleby's passive resistance. Try as he may, he can neither help him nor, Pilate-like, wash his hands of him. "In vain I persisted that Bartleby was nothing to me—no more than to anyone else." In this eminently safe man, Whitman's notions of urban fellowship and mutual sympathy are tested and found wanting.

Melville's New York, so unlike Whitman's, is a hierarchy of Dickensian clerks, demanding clients, and prudential employers concerned mainly with appearances. Instead of receiving automatic deference, along with a day's work for a day's pay, this Wall Street lawyer is asked to peer into a metaphysical abyss, an exercise for which he is poorly equipped. A lax and tolerant clubman, addressing us in a style of genuine cultivation, he represents not only the business but perhaps also the literary world of the early nineteenth century, with its close links between law, letters, commerce, and the easy social milieu of the gentleman. But his paternalism and sociability cannot encompass the key images of his own working life. Once his office might have commanded an unobstructed view, but now, as Wall Street has prospered, it faces an air shaft and a grimy brick wall. Here Bartleby sits, behind a screen, copying, within reach of his master's voice but sequestered from his eyes, cut off from any sense of nature and the outside world, himself facing literally nothing.

If the watchword of Whitman's New York is fusion—the city nesting on bays, the manly contact of hands and eyes—the great theme of Melville's New York is blockage, closure: the dead wall behind the screen which Bartleby, as if in a trance, stares at in his silent reverie. Bartleby's response to blockage is immobility: not to work, not to eat, not to move, and above all, not ever to explain himself. The lawyer, out of sheer desperation, tries to interest him in other pursuits. He even offers to take him into his own home. At being asked, with a remarkable touch of black humor, if he would like to travel to Europe to "entertain some young gentleman" with his "conversation," Bartleby mildly replies, "I like to be stationary. But I am not particular." When Bartleby stubbornly refuses to move, the lawyer moves, taking his office elsewhere—a logical step, easy to rationalize, but also, as in a Hawthorne fable, some kind of unpardonable sin.

Whitman could write optimistically in *Specimen Days* that "an appreciative and perceptive study of the current humanity of New York gives the directest proof yet of successful democracy." But the relation between Bartleby and his employer shows the irreducible social, economic, and human obstacles to this urban utopia. Bartleby has been arrested for loitering on someone else's property, but the lawyer, though under no obligation, feels unable to sever his connection to him. He tries to make Bartleby's life more comfortable, and even goes to visit him. "I know you," Bartleby finally says to the lawyer, without looking at him, "and I want nothing to say to you." Starving himself to death, recoiling into immobility, he curls up in a fetal position in the courtyard of the Tombs, then already one of New York's horrendous prisons.

Though Melville himself was forgotten after the 1850s, his deeply ambivalent vision of New York lived on in the work of other writers. His treatment of the underclass, of social conflict and urban disintegration, became a staple of the naturalism of the 1890s, while his satiric portrayal of the narrow but comfortable world of the respectable middle class, as represented by the lawyer, became material for the social novels of Henry James and Edith Wharton. Amid the crude commercial values and cataclysmic social changes of the Gilded Age, these two writers, themselves products of New York gentility, painted a picture of the social hierarchy of Old New York that was acidulously critical yet at times touchingly elegiac.

The naturalists concentrated on the immediate topical world of the slum and the strike, on living conditions and working conditions. Theirs was the modern city just coming into being, with legions of immigrant workers arriving each week, squeezed into crowded, miserable living quarters and unhealthy workplaces. It was the downtown world of the tenement, the sweatshop, the Tammany ward, the union hall, the dance hall, and the gin shop—the no-longer-so-invisible world that Poe and Melville had begun to excavate. (Melville had even written a prescient sketch, "The Tartarus of Maids," about the unfortunate lives of factory girls in a huge New England mill.)

James and Wharton, on the other hand, wrote about the uptown world of great houses and magnificent dinner parties. They too dealt with the vertiginous rate of change in the city, which so dramatically altered the world they had known. Between 1860 and 1900, New York was transformed from an important commercial port and manufacturing center into a dominant force in the national economy—America's only world city. ("There's only one city that belongs to the whole country," says a character in Howells's 1890 novel *A Hazard of New Fortunes*, a testament to New York's new ascendancy.) It was also physically transformed—at the lower end by the tremendous influx of immigrants, at the upper end by the surge of new industry and wealth, which tore down old structures and inexorably pushed the development of the city northward.

In 1898 New York swallowed its own suburbs, incorporating the four outer boroughs, including Brooklyn, which was itself America's fourth largest city. When James returned to New York after a twenty-one-year-absence in 1904, he was struck, as he later wrote in *The American Scene*, by the "note of vehemence in the local life," which reflected "the appeal of a particular type of dauntless power." The crude, brash energy of the Gilded Age was everywhere: in the crush of humanity on the electric trolley lines, in the skyscrapers that dwarfed passersby and blocked his view of the churches of his boyhood, even in the conversation which, like the architecture, he felt, lacked "quiet interspaces."

James saw New York as the triumph of the onrushing future over the gracious past, of "the economic idea" over any "aesthetic view."[2] He described the skyscraper as "a huge, continuous, fifty-floored conspiracy against the very idea of the ancient graces." His own birthplace on Washington Place, right off Washington Square, had been torn down, with no "tablet" to mark his entrance into the world. "Where, in fact, is the point of inserting a mural tablet, at any legible height, in a building certain to be destroyed to make room for a sky-scraper?" (Just a few years later, James's birthplace would be the site of the notorious Triangle Shirtwaist fire, in which so many immigrant working girls perished. Today the site of this chilling juxtaposition, marked by the plaque James missed seeing, belongs to New York University.)

The disappearance of his birthplace inspired James to write one of his last great stories, "The Jolly Corner," to imagine what his life might have been like if the house had survived, if he had not left home and had instead become one of the movers and shakers of the new economic order. This is a kind of ghost story, and James imagines his hero's alter ego as a developer, an entrepreneur, an emblem of the buccaneering new city and of America itself. This alter ego comes to him as a haunting apparition, a Mr. Hyde whose unhappiness and deformity hint at the horrors of his own unlived life. This is "The Beast in the Jungle" as social history.

In *The American Scene* James writes with the same mixture of recoil and fascination about what New York had become in his long absence. On the one

[2] In "New York" (1921) Marianne Moore would quote James and play upon his ambivalence. She chooses an offbeat urban subject, the wholesale fur trade, that stands for both commerce and beauty, the savagery of the hunt and the finery of fashion. Although she knows that "estimated in raw meat and berries, we could feed the universe," in the end, she says, quoting James, "it is not the atmosphere of ingenuity, . . . it is not the plunder, / but 'accessibility to experience.' "

hand he feels a "sense of dispossession," "a horrible, hateful sense of personal antiquity." But he is also drawn to the teeming Lower East Side ghetto, even to the Yiddish theater and the crowded cafes, where, in the "torture-rooms of the living idiom," he imagines he hears the "Accent of the Future," a language for which there is no "existing literary measure."

Twenty-five years earlier, James had already marked a changing New York in *Washington Square*, a novella commemorating the world of his grandmother. Washington Square itself is merely the backdrop of the story, but in the early pages, as we learn how "the tide of fashion began to set steadily northward," James fills in the social history of the neighborhood with a tender personal accent, which still echoes through his account of lower Fifth Avenue in *The American Scene*. Though set far in the past, around 1850, the story can be read as the early life of an old maid, the oft-told tale of a woman once disappointed in love, never to love again. But the actual subject of the story, as is so often the case in James, is money. Courted by a smooth and attractive fortune hunter, Catherine Sloper is "defended" by her cold-hearted, inflexible father, who resents her for the death of her mother and cannot imagine that a handsome, eligible man could be genuinely attracted to her. His cruel sarcasm perfectly matches the cynical opportunism of her would-be lover.

James conveys the social and professional standing of Dr. Morris Sloper with a light irony that points up the man's limitations and satirizes a society that accords him so much distinction. Like the lawyer in "Bartleby," he has done his duty, won his place in the world, but lacks the milk of charity, the gift of warmth or human understanding. His urban sharpness is his undoing: he doesn't *see* people, he sees through them. He defends his daughter and his fortune with a self-satisfaction indistinguishable from cruelty. The plain Catherine, on the other hand, is very much the simple heart, a creature starved for affection and toyed with unconscionably by father and lover alike. She withdraws, turns her back on the world, seals herself into a corner of the past which is Washington Square. The city has changed but *she* has not. Her frozen fate, itself a kind of closure and entrapment, approaches the grim death-in-life of Bartleby's. Yet she proves stronger than her father or lover. Her adamant refusal to marry or to forgive—she is as resolute toward her father and her meddlesome aunt as toward her former lover—is like Bartleby's refusal to copy, or even to move. It bespeaks an iron passivity which is a bleak, oblique form of protest.

By the late 1880s James essentially had put New York and America behind him. He left it to Edith Wharton to develop fully the tragic implications of the Washington Square theme. Old New York and changing New York are not simply the settings of Wharton's novels; they are essentially the protagonists. After James, Edith Wharton was America's most piercingly intelligent social novelist. But her world was tightly enclosed: this was her limitation as well as the basis for her unusual tragic power. Like the ethnic writers who came after

her, Wharton wrote about the small world she grew up in and knew best. Most
New York writers have been able to grasp the city only through its cacophonous subcultures, but as she grew older and learned something about anthropology, Wharton came to see even New York's upper classes as a distinct tribe
with its own peculiar mores and rituals.

Just such a ritual is the brilliant dinner party at the end of her 1920 novel
The Age of Innocence, which, "in the old New York code, was the tribal rally
around a kinswoman about to be eliminated from the tribe" As the hero, Newland Archer, fully understands, the real story behind this dinner remains unspoken, fenced in by old habits of duplicity, by an iron reserve. Newland's
cousin, Ellen Olenska, with whom he has fallen in love, is being sent back to
Europe—in style. His extramarital "affair" with her, never consummated because of their ingrained New York inhibitions, has been taken for granted by
a cynical society, which assumes they are lovers, and the whole tribe has now
"rallied about his wife on the tacit assumption that nobody knew anything, or
had ever imagined anything."

> It was the old New York way of taking life "without effusion of blood": the way
> of people who dreaded scandal more than disease, who placed decency above
> courage, and who considered that nothing was more ill-bred than "scenes," ex-
> cept the behaviour of those who gave rise to them.

Despite the silent accusations that underlie this ritual, Newland and his so-
called "lover" get off easily in this "conspiracy of rehabilitation and oblitera-
tion," except, of course, that they will never be together; she will depart forever,
and the deepest part of their lives will remain unlived. Instead of defying convention and making a life together, they submit to the Old New York code of
family, propriety, and respectability—values deeply etched in their own being.

Edith Wharton was the product of these values herself, but in her books, as
in her life, she weighed them against other values: passion, spontaneity, art,
adventure. The New York she describes in *The Age of Innocence* is narrow-
minded, provincial, and self-satisfied. When Newland's mother and sister
travel abroad, they never dream of actually becoming acquainted with a for-
eigner. When a penniless French intellectual, who lives on good conversation,
inquires about a job in New York, Newland is stymied, for he is unable "to fit
M. Rivière into any conceivable picture of New York as he knew it." And
Newland's wife May finds the whole idea simply unimaginable: "A job in New
York? What sort of job? People don't have French tutors."

The satiric side of this portrait of New York in *The Age of Innocence* is the
work of the later, expatriate Edith Wharton, the woman who had to battle her
own class and breeding to become a writer, to discover passion, to leave her
marriage, the woman who, like so many younger writers of the 1920s, fled the
limitations of America for the art, culture, and freedom of Europe. For many
of these writers, who came from small towns in the Midwest, New York itself

was such a refuge: an offshore island, a lonely outpost of European sophistication in a philistine America. But not for Edith Wharton, who had come of age
at an earlier time, surrounded by ritual sanctions and constraints.

Yet *The Age of Innocence*, like *Washington Square*, also has its elegiac side.
Now that the old New York no longer existed, now that a terrible world war
had revealed an uglier, more violent world than anyone had dreamed possible,
the staid moral values of that simpler society looked more attractive to Wharton. Even in those earlier days the larger world had looked sordid enough, and
Old New York was beginning to feel beleaguered. Newland worried that "the
country was in possession of the bosses and the emigrant, and decent people
had to fall back on sport or culture."

The ambivalence, the autumnal quality of Wharton's novel, is expressed in
her title, for it alludes to a more benign and innocent time but also to an "in-
vincible innocence" like May's, armored against experience, untainted by
imagination, blind to the vast changes in the world around her. Like Harriet
Ray in *The Custom of the Country*, she is "sealed up tight in the vacuum of inherited opinion, where not a breath of fresh sensation could get at her."

These last words give us an intimation of how much more harsh Wharton's
vision of New York could be in prewar novels like *The House of Mirth* and *The
Custom of the Country*. In these books, set in a twentieth-century New York,
the new money is already in the saddle. The old-fashioned values of Washington Square are giving way to the brutal economics of Wall Street and the
equally brutal social ethics of Fifth Avenue. Here the rituals of exclusion and
displacement no longer take place "without effusion of blood," if they ever did.
Instead Wharton almost takes pleasure in pursuing her characters to their inexorable destruction. Lily Bart in *The House of Mirth* and Ralph Marvell in
The Custom of the Country are perfect products of their social world yet also
doomed to collide with it. Neither can play the money game, which is also the
marriage game. Lily is trained to be a decorative object, an adornment in some
loveless marriage. Ralph is schooled to be cultivated and useless, a gentleman
of the old school, like his venerable grandfather. Blinded by their own sensi-
tivities, these characters are no match for the coarse, the calculating, and the
ambitious—the aggressive new rich whose wealth is grounded in industry,
mining, oil, railroads, banking, stock speculation—in short, for all the explosive energies that were transforming the city and the nation.

Faced with these predatory creatures, who have history and economics on
their side, the sensitive, indolent, all-too-trusting Ralph Marvell in the end
"seemed to be stumbling around in his inherited prejudices like a modern man
in mediaeval armour." When his wife is shown to have deceived him from the
start, when "the whole archaic structure of his rites and sanctions tumbled
down about him," he takes his own life. Meanwhile, his unfaithful, unscrupulous wife, the former Undine Spragg, surmounts one obstacle after another,
one husband after another, to end up remarried to her first husband, now a

successful Wall Street tycoon. As Lily Bart is the poor but beautiful insider who, tangled up in her own half-understood scruples, becomes the outcast, Undine is the outsider who will stop at nothing to satisfy her longing for financial security and social standing—the very archetype of the survivor.

Wharton is unique in being able to endow this drama of social closure, of exclusion and inclusion, with some of the Melvillean power of tragedy. *The House of Mirth* begins as a social comedy about the marriage market; its wicked irony irresistibly reminds us of *Pride and Prejudice*. But by the time of Lily Bart's death, we're more likely to think of ritual sacrifice than of Shakespearean comedy. If the outcast Lily Bart is a Bartleby figure, then Lawrence Selden, the ironic, worldly lawyer who truly loves her, may remind us of Melville's Pilate-like narrator. Selden too is a well-meaning but ineffectual man who, despite his considerable independence of mind, cannot step out of the circle of his own reticences and prejudices. He can't save Lily because he can't reach out to her, can't help misinterpreting her behavior. A lifetime of proprieties and indirections, an elaborate semiotics of social intercourse, prevents both of them from ever speaking their minds. When he finally overcomes his scruples and comes to get her, she has already killed herself, without quite intending to do so. Even her own flirtation with death had eluded her control.

Edith Wharton brilliantly examines the ground rules of the social game and poignantly portrays its victims, but she too, despite her biting criticism, never really looks outside it. The cruelties of exclusion and hierarchy in New York are her subject, but her novels are as closed in upon themselves as the world she dissects. When Undine Spragg falls out of favor with society, she discovers she has become invisible. She can go to the opera, yet no one there actually *sees* her. Lily Bart, in her precipitous decline, finds every social avenue simply closed to her. But as far as Wharton is able to show, there simply *was* no world outside those channels, no New York apart from what she represents under the names of Washington Square, Wall Street, and Fifth Avenue. The new middle-class flats and residential hotels along West End Avenue are worse than death; from the viewpoint of society, they scarcely exist. Lily Bart does seek out a woman who is poor and takes some comfort from her survival, but she represents nothing significant in the world of the novel, no world elsewhere in which Lily could take refuge. This was the struggle of poverty as Wharton could observe it—from a distance. Lily also spurns the help of a Jewish financier and speculator, Rosedale, whose manners are bad and whose grammar is unspeakable, but who manages to buy his way up from Wall Street to Fifth Avenue. He offers to rescue her, but she cannot imagine being saved in this way.

The naturalistic writers of the turn of the century and the New York–based ethnic writers who followed them specialized in everything Edith Wharton left out or condemned: the titanic forces of the new economic machine, the despised immigrants who were its first victims but who eventually were able to use it to gain a foothold in New York. In Edith Wharton's New York there are only a handful of streets, all of them instantly readable. Her characters are defined by where they live, when they go out, whom they see: a chance indiscretion tells all. Reputations are easily ruined. Everyone knows everyone else; their families have intermarried for generations; their very names, like Newland and Archer, are grafts from their family trees. Even Wharton's style of cadenced narrative, cutting irony, and acute social observation suggests the knowing but irreverent insider, whose values continue to reflect those of the world she criticizes.

How different is the cool journalistic manner of Stephen Crane's *Maggie: A Girl of the Streets* (subtitled "A Story of New York," as Melville had called his tale "A Story of Wall-Street"). Looking for some archetypal city tale, the young Crane gives us a fable of the prodigal daughter: a story of drunken parents, coarse men, and a girl's Hogarthian descent from slum life to prostitution, abandonment, and self-immolation—in short, the material of Victorian melodrama. What *is* new about the story, what echoes down through every tenement novel in the twentieth century, through every film from Griffith's *Musketeers of Pig Alley* through *Dead End* to *The Naked City* and *Mean Streets*, is the taste and feel of the overcrowded streets, down to the thousand cooking odors streaming out of the tenement. Like Jacob Riis in *How the Other Half Lives*, Abraham Cahan in *Yekl*, Dreiser in *Sister Carrie*, Jack London in *The People of the Abyss*, and Upton Sinclair in *The Jungle*, Crane discovers a new city, foreseen by Whitman and Melville, witnessed by a genteel but sympathetic observer in Howells's *A Hazard of New Fortunes*, yet excluded from the social fiction of James and Wharton. By reporting so sharply on what most novels left out, Crane became the missing link between Whitman's passionate *flâneur*, dreaming of a "city of friends," and Alfred Kazin's *A Walker in the City*, in which every sight and sound of the old immigrant neighborhood of Brownsville glows and echoes with an astonishing emotional intensity.

I have no room here to explore the riches of the modern ethnic New York novel, which began with works by Cahan, Anzia Yezierska, Mike Gold, and Henry Roth and culminated in 1950s novels like Ralph Ellison's *Invisible Man* and Saul Bellow's *Seize the Day*—two more stories about men who feel free, only to find themselves blocked at every turn. These migrants and children of immigrants, authors who knew the invisible New York as they knew their own families, had grown up on the French and Russian novel, on the novel of "society," on modernism, never imagining that their own experiences could be material for an authentic American literature. They were under cultural pressure to assimilate, to blend into the melting pot of a bland American identity.

The world they knew was completely out of keeping with the optimism and gentility of so much American writing. But they had the example not only of Crane but of Dreiser, whose *Sister Carrie* was one of the rare works that took up Whitman's expansive sense of the exhilarating possibilities of the American city as a terrain of ambition and conquest. (As one critic remarks, Carrie is a Maggie who doesn't *have* to be punished.) Yet the book's depiction of the terrible decline of Hurstwood also conveys the other, Melvillean sense of the anonymity of city life as a scene of entrapment, closure, and disintegration. Its portrayal of the trolley strike and the lower depths to which Hurstwood sinks—especially in the chapter called "The Curious Shifts of the Poor"—exerted a strong influence on the grim social novels of the Depression years.

We began with the symbolism of cities, the real cities that had also become cities of imagination. If the city was originally a symbol of civilization, for twentieth-century writers it became the symbol of civilization in decay. And no city came to represent crime, poverty, racial conflict, and social disintegration more than New York. The underside of the prosperity of cities was always its concentrations of inhuman misery, the vast disparities of fortune and social welfare between people living so close together. Michael Gold's 1930 novel *Jews Without Money*, was set three decades earlier, at exactly the moment Henry James was touring the Lower East Side and Edith Wharton was writing *The House of Mirth*. Written in a tone of high excitement, almost manic recollection, it was a Whitmanian prose poem that inverted Whitman's optimism: it was a catalogue of squalor and desperation. If the immigrant city *seems* a more open and fluid place than Edith Wharton's tight little world, it was also a city of gruesome enclosure in which people could live their whole lives within a few feverishly crowded blocks.

From Whitman, Gold borrowed the nervous, bustling energy of the plebeian city, the emotional intensity, the wild variety of sights, sounds, smells. The jagged rhythm of New York, which Whitman had caught in the movement of his verse, becomes the style of the city in Yezierska, Gold, and Henry Roth, whose bleak, claustral visions of the ghetto are far closer to Melville and Crane than to Whitman. And Roth's *Call It Sleep* brilliantly captures an immigrant child's pervasive *fear* of the city, so full of dark, sexual cellars and dangerous streets, as well as the Babel of strange languages that so disgusted Melville's Pierre and unsettled Henry James.

Like *Call It Sleep*, Ellison's *Invisible Man* is a modern bildungsroman, since the city, as far back as Hawthorne's great story "My Kinsman, Major Molineux," has always been seen as the site not only of a culture's but also of an individual's coming of age. The prototypical New York writer whom Ellison most resembles is not Whitman or Melville but Horatio Alger, whose moral fables about innocent country boys trying their fortune in the great city became guidebooks for real country boys making their way in large numbers into the urban maze. But Ellison's young hero's invisibility is more drastic than anything encountered by Edith Wharton's social outcasts. All through the city he finds rampant duplicity: everyone strikes poses, everyone tries to manipulate him. Instead of a success story, the novel becomes a *Candide*-like fable of innocence and experience, exposure and disenchantment. This young man goes not from rags to respectability (as in Alger) but from naiveté to cynicism, telling his story from yet another cellar, a Dostoevskian hole in the ground. But just as Roth's young protagonist, as he moves beyond his home turf, discovers the city as a scene of growth and possibility, Ellison's hero revels in the shape-shifting transformations of city life. Having told his story, he emerges from his lair on the final page, ambiguously renewed.

With postwar writers like Ellison and Bellow we move from naturalistic documentation of the darker side of city life to metaphysical rumination, in which New York comes to stand for the collapse of modern society. In Bellow's early New York novels, like *The Victim* and *Seize the Day*, the city is a scene not of freedom and possibility, not even of tenements and ghettoes, but of an obscure unease, of blockage and failure that seem to lie at the heart of the human enterprise. It's revealing that Saul Bellow (like Dreiser in *Sister Carrie*) locates the expansive possibilities of city life in Chicago, the rough-and-ready place where Bellow grew up, while ascribing the malaise and disintegration of modern life to New York, the city to which he later came as an aspiring writer. It's a long way from the buoyant adventures of Augie March to the sense of entrapment and suffocation in *Seize the Day* and the saturnine outlook of Mr. Sammler. (Both books include versions of the angry, censorious, "successful" father, perhaps a distant echo of Dr. Sloper in *Washington Square*.) By the time of *Mr. Sammler's Planet*, which depicts New York in the Swinging Sixties, individual failure and unhappiness have given way to large-scale social apocalypse—epitomized for Bellow by black criminals, disrespectful students, and sexually voracious women.

The primitivist fantasies of some modern writers, Bellow says, have become the daily fare of the New York streets: "The dreams of nineteenth-century poets polluted the psychic atmosphere of the great boroughs and suburbs of New York." "From the black side, strong currents were sweeping over everyone. Child, black, redskin—the unspoiled Seminole against the horrible Whiteman. Millions of civilized people wanted oceanic, boundless, primitive, neckfree nobility, experienced a strange release of galloping impulses, and acquired the peculiar aim of sexual niggerhood for everyone." In this grim, arguably racist fantasy, New York had become a wholly terrifying city, a locus of appetite and anarchy for the grasping middle class as well as the ferocious underclass. Yet at the very same time, the rest of the world was drawn to the city as a scene of boundless energy and modernity, a safe haven from every kind of persecution, not as the Waterloo of Western civilization. Once there, their very presence and bewildering diversity would make Mr. Sammler rueful and anxious.

On this apocalyptic note, our brief trajectory through New York writing must conclude. There are many competing postwar versions of New York that I cannot engage here: Frank O'Hara's chatty portrait of the city as a movie set and gossip mill inhabited by a few good friends, Pynchon's comic myth of the New York underworld in *V.*, or Donald Barthelme's postmodern New York of "The Balloon" and "City Life." Later we have Richard Price's rough but vital blue-collar New York; the frivolous punk New York of Tama Janowitz and the Lower East Side writers of *Between C and D*; the Yuppie New York of Jay McInerney's *Bright Lights, Big City*; the New York *noir* of Paul Auster's metaphysical detective stories, which take us back to the artist-fables of Poe and James; a late echo of Edith Wharton's New York in the engrossing social novels of Louis Auchincloss; and finally Tom Wolfe's insider reports on a city fractured by race and greed—trendy journalism disguised as fiction. And as many young writers such as Jonathan Lethem settle in Brooklyn, it becomes the setting for more and more New York fiction.

But recent novels can hardly match the ever-greater power of the movies to create and recreate the city, from *On the Town* and *The Naked City* of the late forties to the classic New York films of Martin Scorsese, Woody Allen, Sidney Lumet, Susan Seidelman, and Spike Lee. Since location shooting became the norm at the end of the sixties, New York has belonged more to the filmmakers than to the writers. Richard Price (in *Sea of Love* and *New York Stories*) became an adept screenwriter; Paul Auster, collaborating with director Wayne Wang, wrote improvisational Brooklyn movies like *Smoke* and *Blue in the Face*; and many New York novels today are simply embryonic movies. Oddly, Bellow's Juvenalian screed, which he later discounted for its excesses, was one of the few books that had the vehemence and violence to compete with those visual images. Unlike the work of the filmmakers and younger writers, Bellow's book alludes to the long literary tradition we've described here but is not nourished by it. Bellow's Sammler is a distant descendant of the *flâneur*, but the *flâneur* as an old man, out of touch, a wisdom figure who is cranky, brilliant, haughty, and dismissive. As Steven Marcus notes, his is a city that can no longer be read, though he reads it, insistently, through the lens of the most perverse modern authors.[3] Many other ethnic groups would follow Bellow's restless, haunted Jews in taking refuge in New York, but Mr. Sammler could only see them as a threat. In him the walker in the city has become virtually a blind man, whose urban text has turned into dark biblical prophecy and fierce social allegory.

[3] "Almost all the signifying messages have now become contradictory and cancel each other out. . . . The tendency of the whole is to collapse away from meaning (forget about systematic meaning) into incognizability and chaos." Steven Marcus, "Reading the Illegible: Some Modern Representations of Urban Experience," *Visions of the Modern City*, ed. William Sharpe and Leonard Wallock (1987).

THE SECOND CITY

After New York, the American cities that most inspired writers no doubt were Chicago and Los Angeles. In 1996, shortly before the Democrats were to meet in Chicago to renominate Bill Clinton, the Washington Post *asked me for some reflections on literary images of the Windy City. This is included here as a kind of appendix to my discussion of New York writers and a prologue to the essay on Upton Sinclair's* The Jungle.

AT THIS MONTH's Democratic convention, the city's first in twenty-eight years, Chicago will be like an old reprobate standing before the court of public opinion with a clean shave, a fresh haircut, and a new suit. Under the guiding hand of Mayor Daley the Younger, the city that once disgraced itself on national TV with policemen clubbing unarmed protesters will be working hard to reform its image. But will this spruced-up and well-behaved city be the real McCoy? One hundred and twenty-five years of history and literature since the Great Fire of 1871 tell us that the rowdy city of 1968 was the true Chicago—the rough-and-tumble frontier town that turned almost overnight, in the two or three decades after the fire, into America's great industrial colossus.

All the conditions that fueled this nation's runaway economic growth in those decades after the Civil War came together on the shores of Lake Michigan: a vast transportation network that turned Chicago into the railroad hub of America; technological breakthroughs like the elevator, which made the first skyscrapers possible, and the refrigerator car, which gave rise to a centralized meat-packing industry; the largely unregulated corporate monoliths created by men like Swift, Armour, and George Pullman, with their brutally antiunion labor tactics; an endless supply of cheap labor fed by waves of immigration; and huge retail emporiums like Marshall Field's, the temples of a new consumer culture.

These forces not only shaped the economy but led to explosive social changes, chronicled by novelists, journalists, and fascinated visitors, that transformed Chicago into a symbol of the new urban and industrial order. Chicago's precipitous growth made it a magnet not only for immigrants in search of work but for small-town Americans from all over the Midwest, from restless farm hands to aspiring poets, who were frustrated by the hardships of rural life, which offered them only hard work (if there was any work) and cold, dark nights, with little social or personal freedom. Among the migrants were writers like Theodore Dreiser, Sherwood Anderson, and Carl Sandburg, whose restless ambitions drew them to the great city. In company with keen social observers like Upton Sinclair and a legion of others attracted by the World's Fair of 1893, they reported brilliantly on Chicago and shaped its rough-hewn national image. When historian Henry Adams visited Chicago for the fair, he was sure he saw the blunt face of the future, the dynamic force that would dominate the twentieth century.

Even before the runaway success of muckraking books like Sinclair's *The Jungle* (1906), with its stomach-churning accounts of the slaughterhouses and meat-packing plants, conveying the pervasive stench and misery of immigrant workers' lives in Packingtown, Chicago's violent image was well established. Its sensational labor unrest included the Haymarket bombing of 1886, which led to the judicial lynching of several anarchist leaders, and the Pullman strike of 1894, in which federal troops fired on angry workers and helped crush a new railway union. The 1968 clashes between protesters and police—and the conspiracy trial that followed—belonged to a long, troubled history and were no doubt mild compared to the strife that preceded them, including the famous gangland battles of the 1920s that marked Chicago as the capital of bootlegging and organized crime during the Prohibition era.

The legendary career of Al Capone and the St. Valentine's Day massacre were immortalized in classic gangster films of the early 1930s like *Little Caesar*, with Edward G. Robinson; *The Public Enemy*, which ignited the career of Jimmy Cagney; and *Scarface*, written by the protean Ben Hecht. A Hollywood pro, Hecht was a veteran of the rip-roaring Chicago journalism scene, which he evoked in his hardboiled 1928 comedy *The Front Page*, written with Charles MacArthur. Decades later, he told the story straight in his juicy autobiography, *A Child of the Century* (1954). Growing up in Racine, Wisconsin, he took off for Chicago in 1910 at the age of sixteen and learned the newspaper trade from cynical, hard-bitten professionals. But what he really loved was the crude, irrepressible vitality of the city itself, the crowds on the streets, the con-men with their clever hustles, the sob stories he heard from the whores, the murder and mayhem among the lower classes, the greed and corruption among the ruling classes. Like other literate newspapermen, he admired and imitated H. L. Mencken, the Baltimore sage who skewered every sort of American humbug and, according to Hecht, "brought the sounds and smells of the street into his writing." (This is one thing Chicago journalists like Mike Royko and Studs Terkel kept doing.)

Mencken's favorite author was the man who created the subtlest literary image of Chicago, Theodore Dreiser. Unlike the muckrakers, Dreiser had little interest in exposing the city's corruption, pollution, or labor conflict, but he was enthralled by its spectacular growth, the constant flood of immigrants, the grid of new streets and street lamps stretching out into the prairie. The city was like "a giant magnet, drawing to itself, from all quarters, the hopeful and the hopeless," he wrote in his first novel, *Sister Carrie* (1900): "Its streets and houses were scattered over an area of seventy-five square miles. . . . The sound of the hammer engaged upon the erection of new structures was everywhere heard. Great industries were moving in."

Like Hecht, Dreiser was captivated when he arrived in the city at sixteen to make his fortune. He had lived there for a few months with his family three years earlier, and even then, he writes in his autobiography, "the spirit of Chicago flowed into me and made me ecstatic." Dreiser transposed onto his heroine, Carrie Meeber, his own excitement at first arriving by train in the great city, gazing at the flow of people in the streets and discovering the amazing array of merchandise in the new department stores. Through her eyes, as she looks at the finery and jewelry of the women and responds to the seductions of the men, the city comes to embody the mysteries of desire at the heart of urban life. When she loses her job, the thought of going back home strikes a chill into her heart.

Partly because he shared the viewpoint of the hungry outsider with her face glued to the plate-glass window, Dreiser became Chicago's canniest social historian. In later novels he exposed the intricate workings of its financial world. When Ben Hecht interviewed him about what the city had once been like, the detailed information he offered was so staggering that the young reporter despaired of ever becoming a novelist, for he felt "incapable of knowing anything so thoroughly." But there were many facets of the city that other writers knew more intimately than Dreiser. Sinclair, for example, gave a vivid sense of the helplessness of immigrant peasants trapped like cogs in the vast industrial machine—the packing plants, the steel mills—that would use them, grind them down, and cast them aside. Richard Wright, in *Native Son* (1940), described the desperation and violence of blacks trapped in the grim ghetto, objects of fear and hatred, cordoned off within a deeply segregated town.

Nearly all of Chicago's writers could agree in seeing the city as a raw, brute force, almost a condition of modern life, as reflected in the awesome power of the machine, the assembly line, the skyscraper, the railroad, the gigantic industrial enterprise, and the vast impersonal metropolis. It's hardly an accident that urban sociology was invented by men like Robert Park and Louis Wirth at the new University of Chicago, or that John Dewey's lab school and Jane Addams's Hull-House made the city a laboratory for educational and social experiment. Dewey and Addams, two of America's foremost progressive reformers, set out to repair some of the human damage in a city devoted to money, growth, and enterprise, just as the novelists set out to record it in harrowing detail.

Influenced by the ecological approach of the new urbanism, younger novelists would turn away from industrial scenes to probe the new ethnic communities, for Chicago was a city fractured into separate worlds. In "How 'Bigger' Was Born," a 1940 essay, Richard Wright attributes part of the inspiration for *Native Son* to the city itself, "the fabulous city in which Bigger lived, an indescribable city, huge, roaring, dirty, noisy, raw, stark, brutal; a city of extremes: torrid summers and sub-zero winters, white people and black people, the English language and strange tongues, foreign born and native born, scabby poverty and gaudy luxury, high idealism and hard cynicism!" In his great *Studs Lonigan* trilogy (1932–35), James T. Farrell, who had studied at the university, would give an encyclopedic account of the Archie Bunker world of lower-middle-class Irish Americans, just as Richard Wright would describe the fate of blacks who had migrated to Chicago from the rural South, as he himself had done in 1927. In his portrait of spiritual sterility, Farrell indicts the hypocrisy of the clergy, the narrow-mindedness of Lonigan's parents, the intellectual poverty of the schools, and the hollow masculinity of scrappy teenage boys hanging out on street corners and in poolrooms. Bigger Thomas in *Native Son* is a black Studs Lonigan, more violent, more frustrated, more hemmed in and bitter, and even more doomed to self-destruction. Where writers like Dreiser or Sandburg once celebrated the city's titanic energies, their successors, including Farrell and Wright, decried its human failures, its betrayal of the freedom and opportunity the migrants had come to find.

For postwar writers like Nelson Algren or Saul Bellow, Chicago was no longer an immigrant city, the city of enterprise that had built the skyscrapers and stockyards, that had raised the great Ferris wheel over the celebrated White City of the 1893 fair; it was a town of petty cons and hustlers, of grafters and fixers, a "city on the make." In novels like *Never Come Morning* (1942) and *The Man with the Golden Arm* (1949), Algren became the lyrical poet of the city's bottom dogs, the junkies and whores and petty criminals from Ben Hecht's Chicago, the flotsam of organized society.

Saul Bellow, on the other hand, grew increasingly detached from a city that had entranced him in his early work. (Like Algren he would eventually desert Chicago for the East.) In a 1950s story, "Looking for Mr. Green," his protagonist is a Depression-era intellectual down on his luck, delivering relief checks for the city, intrigued and thwarted as he tries to find his way around the elusive black ghetto, so different from the city he knew when he was growing up. The story eerily foreshadows today's debates over welfare but its real subject is less social, more symbolic. Bellow's surrogate never quite finds "Mr. Green," for he is like Ralph Ellison's invisible man, an anonymous everyman, standing not just for the black underclass but for a whole shadowy side of the city, a self-protective twilight world almost impenetrable to whites.

Three decades later, Bellow had grown more conservative, more ruminative but less generous. The protagonist of his novel *The Dean's December* (1982), a cultivated academic, is also drawn to the black underclass, but this time out of a sense of horror rather than real curiosity. Two gruesome murders lead him to reflect on the fate of civilization, the dark heart of man. "It was not so much the inner city slum that threatened us," he thinks, "but the slum of our innermost being." Chicago has become simply one of America's "half-demolished cities," all virtually indistinguishable. When Bellow's alter ego writes articles about the city for *Harper's*, as Bellow himself had tried to write a nonfiction book about his native city, many Chicagoans are offended, for he concludes that "Chicago wasn't Chicago anymore." Another character agrees: "I'm with you there. It's no longer a location, it's only a condition. South Bronx, Cleveland, Detroit, Saint Louis, from Newark to Watts—all the same noplace."

Is it possible that Chicago can welcome the Democratic convention at long last because it's no longer Chicago, only a generic American city with the usual share of civic boosters, commercial hucksters, and intractable problems? Whatever Mayor Daley's efforts to sanitize the city and repair the damage done by his father and his police force, it's hard to believe that Chicago's rowdy days are really over. In 1968, Norman Mailer, reporting on the Democratic convention, could still celebrate Chicago as the city of stockyards, by then almost gone, and of robber barons, who had long since become respectable patrons of the arts. Unlike cities that concealed their brutality behind a righteous facade, "in Chicago," says Mailer, "they did it straight, they cut the animals right out of their hearts—which is why it was the last of the great American cities, and people had great faces, carnal as blood, greedy, direct, too impatient for hypocrisy, in love with honest plunder."

UPTON SINCLAIR AND THE URBAN JUNGLE

VERY FEW WORKS of literature have actually changed the course of history, and critics have usually been suspicious of those that did. Compared to propaganda, literature usually influences our lives in subtle and indirect ways. It can alter our sense of reality and affect the climate of opinion; but books that create sensational controversies may well sacrifice the deeper purposes of literature to immediate effect, sometimes by appealing too cheaply to the reader's emotions. Upton Sinclair's *The Jungle*, first published serially in 1905 and in book form in 1906, has an unshakeable reputation as just such a work. It is remembered as a stomach-turning exposé of unsanitary conditions and deceitful practices in the meat-packing industry; as such it aroused the ire of a whole nation, from President Theodore Roosevelt on down, and it contributed enormously to the landmark passage of the Pure Food and Drug Act of 1906. (The book is said to have decreased America's meat consumption for decades.) Though *The Jungle* is still very widely read, in part as a historical document, few critics take the book or its author seriously anymore. Like *Uncle Tom's Cabin*, to which it has often been compared, *The Jungle* is considered agitation rather than art; its blunt naturalistic method, surfeited with sickening details, is considered crude even in comparison to the writing of Sinclair's immediate predecessors, unflinching realists like Dreiser, Norris, and Stephen Crane. These men went down in literary history as important novelists, even when their technique had gone out of fashion. Sinclair went down in history as a muckraker, a talented progressive journalist and reformer with no literary technique whatever.

This firmly etched picture needs serious revision, for it can't stand up to a careful examination of the book itself and it doesn't help us understand Sinclair's long and tumultuous career as a writer, agitator, and occasional political candidate. Sinclair himself always insisted that people had misread *The Jungle*: he had intended it less as an exposé of the meat industry than as an argument for socialism, to which he had recently been converted. ("I aimed at the public's heart, and by accident I hit it in the stomach.") For this misunderstanding he had only himself to blame, for the book made him a famous public figure overnight, and he cunningly played on its notoriety with all the wiles of a born publicist. Attacked by the big meat packers, he peppered the country with articles and statements supporting the details of his novel, nearly all of which were soon confirmed by independent investigation. Invited down to the White House by Teddy Roosevelt, he followed up his visit with a barrage of letters that left the president exasperated.

Though he sometimes fell for cranky and faddish ideas, such as fasting cures and mental telepathy, the irrepressible Sinclair continued to play this gadfly role for decades. He became something of an American institution, a one-man reform movement and radical crusader—a part quite out of keeping with everything in his earlier life. Sinclair was born in Baltimore in 1878, just two years before another hometown troublemaker-to-be, H. L. Mencken. His parents were impoverished Southern gentry, and along with his father's Virginia ancestry came longtime naval traditions and catastrophic Confederate loyalties. They moved to New York when Upton was eight or nine and lived in a succession of cheap rooming houses, as his father slowly destroyed himself with drink while his mother, feeling acutely her decline in status, gave her son heavy doses of religion and morality. A phenomenal reader with a quick, retentive memory, the boy had no formal schooling until the age of eleven, but by fourteen he entered New York's City College and soon afterward began to moonlight as a writer of jokes and pulp fiction. Before turning to serious writing he churned out a staggering quantity of juvenile potboilers, working with a fluency and prodigious energy that never abandoned him.

By 1900 Sinclair vowed to make his mark as an artist. He wrote several romantic and subjective novels that got little attention and left him desperately poor. The turning point in his life came when he joined the Socialist Party in 1904 and soon became one of its most vocal campaigners for social and economic reform. After it was founded in 1901 the party enjoyed more than a decade of extraordinary growth, which climaxed with the excellent showing of its candidate, Eugene V. Debs, in the presidential election of 1912. "Starting with 10,000 members in 1901," says historian James Weinstein, "the Party had grown to 118,000 by 1912, had elected some 1,200 public officials throughout the United States, and was publishing over 300 periodicals of all kinds." This socialist upsurge took place not primarily in the urban ghettoes of the East, under the influence of European ideologies, but in the vast American heartland, then undergoing the strains of industrialization. A great deal of rural populist strength fed into this Socialist tide. The deepest inroads were in states like Oklahoma that later became bulwarks of conservatism. Socialist mayors were elected in towns like Schenectady (New York), Butte (Montana), Granite City (Illinois), Davenport (Iowa), Lackawanna (New York), Berkeley (California), New Castle (Pennsylvania), and Flint (Michigan)—most often, as Weinstein notes, "in small or medium-sized railroad, mining, or industrial centers." (America's most powerful journalist, Walter Lippmann, began his career in 1911 as secretary to Socialist Mayor Lunn of Schenectady.)

Close to the center of all this Socialist activity was a rambunctious and spectacularly successful weekly newspaper out of Girard, Kansas, called the *Appeal to Reason*, which cost subscribers twenty-five cents a year and was written in the breezy muckraking style of Midwestern populism. In line with so much of the native American socialism that preceded the Russian Revolution, the paper avoided ideological factions and sectarian dogmatism. Like the Marxism of Upton Sinclair—for he was formed by this prewar climate—the socialism of the *Appeal* was less a science of history than a compound of moral indignation, quasi-religious fervor, and a set of simple truths about the social and economic system. The paper had a passion for social justice, the rights of labor, and the exposure of corruption. This formula, which was not far from folk wisdom, proved amazingly popular. Late in 1904, when the *Appeal*'s circulation was over half a million and heading upward, the editor sent Sinclair to Chicago to examine conditions in the stockyards. The resulting novel, based on seven weeks of intensive research, was serialized in the *Appeal* and achieved great notoriety even before it came out as a book.

Chicago in the summer of 1904 had been the scene of an unsuccessful strike against the huge meat-packing companies, the so-called Beef Trust. What attracted Sinclair was the raw industrial climate of the city, not the problem of adulterated meat. He signed on with the *Appeal* to tell the story of working men and women subjugated and finally ground under by vast monopolistic enterprises. But once there, he found that the product itself was as poorly regulated as the horrible conditions under which it was produced, that labor and consumer interests were identical and one could be used to draw graphic attention to the other. He discovered that the way to the public's heart was *through* its stomach, and thus he inadvertently became one of the fathers of the consumer protection movement. Whatever nostalgic hopes we may have for deregulation—a contemporary watchword for libertarians and conservatives—can scarcely survive Sinclair's portrait of laissez-faire industrial capitalism in its buccaneering phase. But his device was so effective, the picture he painted was so gruesome and unforgettable, that it obscured his original intention. Sinclair spiced his sociology with bits and pieces of a horror-film scenario, and, though it occupies relatively few pages, this was the putrid taste that people remembered.

The ultimate importance of *The Jungle* lies elsewhere. From the epic poems of Homer to the great novels of the nineteenth century, it's surprising how little literature or history is written "from below," from the point of view of the weak and dispossessed classes. Before the French Revolution—in Shakespeare, for example—servants, artisans, and peasants were usually portrayed without real dignity: as loyal retainers at best, or clownish rustics who were nimble figures of fun. The vaunted traditions of Western humanism rarely stooped to explore the inner humanity of those trapped by birth or occupation near the bottom of the social hierarchy. Even nineteenth-century novels that deal with revolutionary ferment, such as Flaubert's *Sentimental Education*, tend to individualize only middle-class characters, while treating the common people, as society itself treats them, as an undifferentiated mass, a volatile, incendiary crowd or mob. No doubt there were melodramatic explorations of the urban underworld by writers like Hugo, Dickens, and Eugène Sue. The industrial novels of mid-Victorian England, such as Dickens's *Hard Times*, were a significant breakthrough, but they often gave vague and idealized portraits of working-class characters. There were other precedents for what Sinclair was trying to do, including Zola's great novel about French miners, *Germinal*, and fellow Socialist Jack London's depiction of poverty in London's East End, *The People of the Abyss*. But Sinclair set out to propel "the workingmen of America," to whom he dedicated the book, into the center of the national consciousness. He aimed not merely to commiserate with them or to describe the conditions in which they worked but to call into question the basis of the system: the ethic of competitive individualism which turned the urban landscape into a savage place, a jungle.

This theme sounds almost too heavy for any novel, but only in the last four chapters does it threaten to turn *The Jungle* into a tract. The first two-thirds of the book are far more concrete and vivid. *The Jungle* is a protest novel, an exposure of intolerable working and living conditions in the city of Chicago at the turn of the century. But unlike most protest novelists, who push a thesis at the expense of a credible plot and lifelike characters, Sinclair is a natural storyteller. He commands a prose so readable and transparent that it offers little resistance to translators; this has helped make him one of America's most widely read authors abroad, where America is seen as a land of opportunity but also of unbridled economic savagery.[1]

Sinclair's other great gift is his sense of fact. In his research and interviews he was able to accumulate masses of clear information not only on working and living conditions but also about machinery, transportation, profit margins, sewage, hygiene, prisons, hospitals, the courts, the political clubs—all the institutions and apparatus needed to keep a modern city running. He shows not only how the meat industry and the steel industry operate but also how the machinery of power is greased, how the system of graft and patronage functions, how the bosses, the politicians, the contractors, the criminals, the magistrates, and the police work hand in glove.

Sinclair's method is too journalistic to make *The Jungle* a great city novel, but it is a very good one. From early on we notice that he is too willing to suspend his story while he takes his characters (and us) on a Cook's Tour of the meat-packing plant before they actually go to work. Later he contrives to get his hero, Jurgis Rudkus, a Lithuanian immigrant trying to support a large family, into every sort of job and every corner of Chicago life. By the end of the book, Jurgis has been drawn out into a pale Everyman, a transparent device to show us more and more about how this society functions. After losing his job with the packers Jurgis spends time in court, in jail, in the harvester works, in the steel works, as a hobo on the road, as a campaign worker, a union activist, a scab, a petty criminal, a beggar, a guest in the home of the big boss's son, a hotel porter, and finally a socialist convert who has found all the right answers.

---

[1] One clear example of Sinclair's influence can be seen in Brecht's early plays, such as *St. Joan of the Stockyards* and *In the Jungle of the Cities*, with their near mythical image of Chicago as a scene of bruising capitalist competition and exploitation.

The last third of the book has much less credibility than the terrible scenes that preceded it, largely because the central figure has been stretched too far. Once *The Jungle* leaves the stockyards it loses some of its grim intensity, which few novels could have managed to sustain.

Sinclair portrays the lower echelons of the industrial world as the scene of a naked struggle for survival, where workers not only are forced to compete with each other but, if they falter, are hard-pressed to keep starvation from their door and a roof over their heads. With the unions weak and cheap labor plentiful, a social-Darwinist state of nature exists, a Hobbesian war of each against all. (Apologists for laissez-faire capitalism made facile use of Darwin's notion of the "survival of the fittest," as if society could be seen as a human reflection of the struggle for survival in nature.) In the hierarchy of Durham's packing plant, "all the men of the same rank were pitted against each other; the accounts of each were kept separately, and every man lived in terror of losing his job, if another made a better record than he. So from top to bottom the place was simply a seething cauldron of jealousies and hatreds." When Jurgis is in bed with his first serious injury he is compared to "Prometheus bound," the helpless Greek Titan who first brought fire and technology to mankind, only to be deprived of his freedom. He is tormented by the idea that "he and all those who were dear to him might lie and perish of starvation and cold . . . that here in this huge city, with its heaped-up wealth, human creatures might be hunted down and destroyed by the wild-beast powers of nature, just as truly as ever they were in the days of the cave men!"

To convey this desperate vulnerability and isolation—which has slipped from our memories since the coming of the welfare state—Sinclair centers on an immigrant family whose economic problems are compounded by cultural dislocation. *The Jungle* begins with a powerful set piece, a traditional Lithuanian wedding feast for Jurgis and his sixteen-year-old bride Ona, which they can hardly afford, and which serves as a backdrop for the tremendous changes they have already begun to encounter in the new world.[2] Sinclair shows how capitalism creates disintegrating pressures that undermine family life, cultural ties, and moral values, despite the system's professed adherence to these traditions. Middle-class economics gives the lie to middle-class morality. With "literally not a month's wages between them and starvation," workingmen are under pressure to abandon their families, and women must sometimes choose between starvation and prostitution. Children must go out to work or to beg before they get much schooling, and once out of the house they quickly pick up the habits of the street and the values of the new society.

Immigrants with peasant backgrounds, and even migrants from America's own rural regions, are especially ill-equipped to survive in the urban jungle

[2] Michael Cimino borrowed this ethnic wedding-scene from Sinclair for the first hour of his Vietnam War movie, *The Deer Hunter*.

because of their stubborn individualism. Jurgis relies on his own strong back to carry his family, to cope with inhuman work; but he simply becomes a cog in the industrial machine, to be discarded as soon as he shows signs of wear. Jurgis and his family are desperate to own something, to be on their own; scarcely knowing the language, they are easily swindled when they put everything they have into buying a small house. Sinclair pays little attention to the kinds of support systems that were often available as safety nets for ethnic groups: mutual aid societies, religious institutions, credit unions, relief agencies. By painting the picture in stark colors he is trying to demonstrate, as Steinbeck would later do with his Okie family in *The Grapes of Wrath*, that peasant individualism is helpless before the new juggernauts of corporate power. He shows that isolation and self-reliance are formulas for weakness and self-destruction; only the solidarity of unions can give workers economic strength.

Though conditions were hard for workingmen then, one of the flaws of the novel is that Sinclair stacks the deck. Once things begin going bad for Jurgis, *everything* goes bad: there is a touch of the soap opera in this succession of tragedies. As in the fate-haunted novels of Thomas Hardy, the author cannot resist putting his finger on the scales, to make sure the plot conforms to his own pessimism. Worse still, as soon as Jurgis discovers socialism, everything goes almost miraculously right for him; he seems to be living in a different universe. Part of Sinclair's problem is inherent in the naturalist novel, with its deterministic outlook and its emphasis on the domination of individuals by larger social and biological forces. The great naturalists like Zola and Dreiser fortunately did not adhere too closely to their own pseudoscientific ideas. They recognized that novelistic characters cannot begin to exist without a modicum of freedom; they must have some capacity to surprise us, to reshuffle their lives, to say and do things that seem arbitrary and unexpected.

Sinclair's characters are conceived in more constricted terms, without condescension but without much human dimension. Again and again the omniscient author sees them "like rats in a trap," stalked by "fate" or riveted to their own "destiny," little more than "cogs in the great packing machine." Though the characters' lives are rich in credible detail, they can never quite bear the burden of all Sinclair wants their experiences to say. When the scales begin to fall from their eyes, when they see what their lives are really like, we feel the author behind them pulling the strings, giving Jurgis all his own understanding of the economic system. Jurgis does not have enough inner life to make his final conversion believable. Even in its powerful early chapters, the book demands a surprisingly narrow range of emotion from the reader. The more the characters are trapped by the system, the more they are transformed from agents to mere victims, and the principal feeling asked of us is pity—one of the most dehumanizing of all emotions, since it turns people into objects of our compassion rather than subjects in their own right.

This somewhat stunted humanity prevents *The Jungle* from being one of the truly great novels of city life, however accurate its social and economic framework may be. The Chicago of *The Jungle* is a city limned by a brilliantly articulate and observant journalist, who can lay bare all the gears of the machine and show where all the people fit in. The Chicago of Dreiser's *Sister Carrie*, on the other hand, published just a few years earlier, is not just a social and economic system but, like Balzac's Paris, a Roman arena of will and desire, a field of hopes and possibilities entirely outside the range of Sinclair's characters. Dreiser's characters too are limited creatures, mercilessly observed from a considerable distance by the author, and their plans often go awry. But they are never simply victims suffering against an urban backdrop; the city helps create their needs, fill out their minds, feed their hopes. Newly arrived from a small town, unable to find work, Carrie is poor as a church-mouse, but the finery she sees on people in the streets and in the shop windows inflames her with thoughts she could never have had back home. Walking through one of the new department stores, she sees "nothing which she could not have used— nothing which she did not long to own." Elbowed aside by women who can afford these things, she gets her first lesson in the reality of class. She looks down at her own clothes and realizes at once how much they reveal about her, how much they define and limit her. "A flame of envy lighted in her heart. She realized in a dim way how much the city held—wealth, fashion, ease—every adornment for women, and she longed for dress and beauty with a whole heart." Dreiser shows how class, identity, and personal passion are intertwined. He is determined to describe department stores for posterity, "should they ever permanently disappear," but interweaves his economic history with a tangled web of human desires. City life conditions his characters' every choice, their whole sense of reality.

The defining thing about Sinclair's people is that no such fanciful wishes can cross their minds. Frugal immigrants, they have no frivolous moments. They live too close to the edge of survival, ghettoed in Packingtown, cut off by language as well as by poverty, sacrificed to the industrial Moloch that dominates their existence. When they find sex they get no pleasure from it, and liquor gives them only the stupor of oblivion. "Four or five miles to the east of them lay the blue waters of Lake Michigan, but for all the good it did them it might have been as far away as the Pacific Ocean. They had only Sundays, and then they were too tired to walk. They were tied to the great packing machine, and tied to it for life." The machine that maims them physically also maims their humanity. But the novelist himself, sounding the clang of destiny for his characters, contributes to this amputation and enforces the condition that he pities. There is an accurate touch in what Sinclair describes: a life of grinding poverty in an urban ghetto is indeed cut off from the broader flow of city life— its parameters are narrow, its demands merciless. But it ought to include unpredictable and even joyous moments, which Sinclair's picture leaves out. His characters, like religious martyrs, relate to their environment only as exemplary sufferers, never as autonomous agents.

Sinclair's point is precisely that people who are "wage slaves" are not autonomous, any more than black slaves had freedom before the Civil War. From very early in the novel he compares his characters to the animals penned up and slaughtered every day in the stockyards, moved along on conveyor belts by machinery which cares nothing for their individual desires. In the monotonous killing of each of the hogs in chapter 3 ("as if his wishes, his feelings, had simply no existence at all"), Sinclair finds his key metaphor for the condition of the workingmen; a cold, efficient machinery assimilates them, a blind "Fate" swallows them up. A few of the men are even swallowed up literally when they fall into huge vats and emerge as "Durham's Pure Leaf Lard." (This was one of the few touches in *The Jungle* that could not be independently confirmed when the book appeared.) By and large it is the endless deadpan flow of concrete details, not the garish organizing metaphors, that gives the book its monolithic power. Sinclair shows precisely how wounded, diseased, and pregnant animals are turned into food under the same unhealthy conditions that soon leave healthy men wounded or diseased: "There was no heat upon the killing beds; the men might exactly as well have worked out of doors all winter. . . . On the killing beds you were apt to be covered with blood, and it would freeze solid; if you leaned against a pillar, you would freeze to that, and if you put your hand upon the blade of your knife, you would run a chance of leaving your skin on it." Grotesque injuries were inevitable, injuries for which the company would rarely take responsibility. While a man was laid up, his family could starve or freeze to death, and after a series of such injuries, if he survived, he would be too crippled to go on doing the work. When Jurgis is healthy and overflowing with life he gets a job immediately; when he becomes an empty husk of his former self he is reduced to beggary. And even among beggars he finds a jungle of savage competition, in which the truly needy are often at a disadvantage.

What enabled Sinclair's novel to have its sensational impact was his enormous dossier of irrefutable detail, straightforwardly presented and linked to an affecting human drama. Very few novels convey as much sheer information as *The Jungle*, information about the food the country was eating (which attracted most of the attention), but also information about the modern work process, about how the city functioned, with its complex mesh of graft and corruption, about the poverty and degradations of its slums, and, especially in its opening chapters, about the traumatic adjustment of recent immigrants to urban American conditions. If Sinclair himself had been a foreign-born writer, his book would quickly have been acknowledged as a pioneering treatment of the immigrant experience several decades before this became a fashionable literary subject.

Sinclair was one of the first native writers to deal with ethnic characters without condescension or disgust—with a sympathetic tolerance that unfortunately does not extend to racial issues. Blacks appear in *The Jungle* only as dissolute "scabs," used by the bosses for short periods and quickly discarded: "The ancestors of these black people had been savages in Africa, and since then they had been chattel slaves, or had been held down by a community ruled by the traditions of slavery. Now for the first time they were free—free to gratify every passion, free to wreck themselves. They were wanted to break a strike, and when it was broken they would be shipped away, and their present masters would never see them again." This is consistent with the theme of enslavement that runs through the whole book, but Sinclair makes no effort to see these hapless strikebreakers as human beings in their own right. They are simply an alien mass whose actions make solidarity harder to achieve, which was just the way many labor unions saw both blacks and immigrants. The prewar Socialist Party was good and prophetic on many modern social issues—including labor issues, women's issues, environmental concerns, welfare, health regulations, consumer protection, monopolistic business practices—but was divided and generally quiescent on racial issues. "Until the mass migration of Negroes into Northern industrial centers during the World War," says James Weinstein, "the Socialist Party paid little attention to the Negro."

The party declined sharply in numbers and influence after World War I. As in many other countries, a separate and more militant Communist Party was formed after the Russian Revolution, organized along Leninist lines. The old freewheeling utopianism and reformism of the prewar Socialists were replaced by a rigid adherence to whatever the current Soviet reading of Marxist dogma happened to be. But Sinclair, in his long career, remained generally faithful to the socialist spirit of the earlier period. His theoretical abilities were limited, but his energy and genteel combativeness were inexhaustible. *The Jungle* made him so famous that he became a political force in his own right. When he put the profits from the novel into founding a utopian colony in New Jersey, it became a subject for news and gossip. (It burned down after four and a half months.) When his troubled first marriage broke up, it caused a delicious scandal that he feared might damage the fortunes of socialism. Many times he used his enormous facility as an observer and writer to take on powerful private interests and explosive issues: the Rockefellers and the coal industry in *King Coal* (1917), the Teapot Dome scandal and the oil industry in *Oil!* (1927), and the Sacco-Vanzetti case in *Boston* (1928), all journalistic novels based, like *The Jungle*, on Sinclair's own arduous firsthand research. Between 1918 and 1927 he wrote a series of long polemical pamphlets on subjects like "the profits of religion," the state of journalism, and the educational system. (These deserve comparison to the personal journalism of I. F. Stone, the cultural criticism of Paul Goodman, and the muckraking of Ralph Nader in the 1950s and 1960s.) During the 1940s Sinclair applied the same glib talent to twentieth-century history in a series of eleven thinly fictionalized thrillers. Built around an agent named Lanny Budd, whose adventures are as fantastic and improbable as those of James Bond, this series made Sinclair one of America's most popular authors but it doomed his critical reputation once and for all. Typically, Sinclair's main point of pride was his accuracy. In his very genial and buoyant autobiography, published in 1962, he boasted that no one had yet corrected him on a matter of historical fact.

As a political figure Sinclair's most important moment after the initial impact of *The Jungle* came in California in 1934, when he left the Socialist Party and was nearly elected governor on the Democratic ticket, with a crusade to "End Poverty in California" (EPIC). Though he was defeated in a bitter mud-slinging campaign supported by the Hollywood studios and other moneyed interests, his bold platform helped push the national New Deal leftward. After World War II Sinclair gradually receded into obscurity, but for four decades he had been the epitome of the radical writer and activist. However old-fashioned he had begun to seem to younger writers between the wars, he had remained a figure of extraordinary authority for all those who experimented in a more socially oriented, more committed literature.

By the time Sinclair died in 1968, at the age of ninety, with some ninety books behind him, the sharp dividing line between fact and fiction, which he had never been willing to observe, had begun to break down. The social and political ferment of the 1960s gave rise to literary mutations such as the nonfiction novel, the novel as history, the documentary novel, the New Journalism (using fictional techniques), and finally novels like E. L. Doctorow's *Ragtime* that introduced real historical figures, often in an ironic vein. Rigid aesthetic demarcations, by which even Sinclair's best work was judged impure as fiction, gave way to a much greater willingness to mingle factual materials and fictional inventions. Earnest and sentimental as they could sometimes be, Sinclair's journalistic novels had foreshadowed this new turn of the wheel, but he was still remembered more as a muckraker than as a creative writer and socialist pioneer. At the age of eighty-nine he returned to the White House, where he had been the guest of both Theodore and Franklin Roosevelt, to watch Lyndon Johnson sign the Wholesome Meat Act of 1967. The wheel of food and drug regulation had come full circle, back to its prime mover, though it was not the wheel he had initially hoped to turn.

A RADICAL COMEDIAN

DURING THE 1920s, at the height of his fame and literary power, Sinclair Lewis was more than a best-selling author. Even more than Upton Sinclair, who was briefly his mentor and employer, he was an impetuous troublemaker, a disturber of the peace, whose novels were hotly discussed more as social criticism than as literature. Fiercely satiric works like *Main Street* (1920), *Babbitt* (1922), and *Elmer Gantry* (1927) were an important part of this raucous decade's self-examination. Americans recognized themselves in his books, which were at once iconoclastic and hugely entertaining, but some readers were outraged by their mocking portraits of ordinary citizens as comic types. The scandal culminated in 1930 when Lewis became the first American to win the Nobel Prize for Literature. His famous acceptance speech, later published as "The American Fear of Literature," was an attack on gentility and self-congratulation and a rallying cry for a younger generation of American writers, singled out by name, who were restless, disillusioned, and hungry for recognition.

Many people still recall the 1920s as a period of complacency and "normalcy," a time when the nation settled down from the traumatic bloodletting of the Great War and the fears and hopes inspired by the Bolshevik Revolution. During the war Germans were demonized as vicious rapists, antiwar publications like *The Masses* were suppressed, and civil liberties were threatened when universities fired pacifist professors while radicals were put on trial for sedition. Soon after the war there was a surge of intolerance directed against anarchists, communists, labor organizers, and immigrants. Initiated by A. Mitchell Palmer, Woodrow Wilson's attorney general, this "Red Scare" resulted in wholesale arrests and deportations. The governor of Massachusetts (and future president), Calvin Coolidge, gained national fame in 1919 by calling out troops to quell the Boston police strike. Prohibition went into effect in January. Shortly after *Main Street* was published in October 1920, Warren G. Harding was elected president of the United States, which put the final nail in the coffin of Wilsonian idealism and internationalism. The nation was in retreat or withdrawal: a puritan, conservative, small-town America was back in the saddle.

Or so it must have seemed. But 1920 was also the year when the census showed for the first time that more Americans lived in cities of at least 2,500 people than in rural communities. America's politics in the twenties would be deeply conservative, even isolationist, but its social fabric was changing inexorably, as Robert and Helen Merrell Lynd would show in *Middletown* in 1929 and Frederick Lewis Allen would chart amusingly in *Only Yesterday*, his popular social history of 1931. Not only was America growing more urban but its way of life was shifting under the pressure of rapidly spreading technology, from electricity, telephones, and labor-saving appliances to automobiles, radio broadcasting, and motion pictures.

Advances in technology also accelerated changes in values. Alarmed ministers preached against closed automobiles as "brothels on wheels," while movies and radio fueled a new hedonism with news and seductive fantasy about different lives in distant places. Celebrity cults grew up around film stars like Valentino, national heroes like Lindbergh, and athletes like Babe Ruth. Sports and leisure became big businesses in an expanding culture of consumption, pumped up by aggressive new techniques of advertising and public relations. Borrowing heavily from the jazz idiom of black artists, music and dancing became the liveliest expression of a much-debated youth rebellion. Behind Harding's return to "normalcy," the corruption of some of his cronies, the booming stock market, and the gnomic utterance of his successor, "Silent Cal" Coolidge ("the business of government is business"), America was being transformed by a quiet revolution of manners, values, and social yearnings.

Few individuals did more to prepare the ground for this upheaval than the cultural critics of the first decades of the century, including socialists like Jack London and Upton Sinclair, maverick academics such as John Dewey and Thorstein Veblen, realistic novelists like Theodore Dreiser, iconoclastic journalists like H. L. Mencken, and young radicals like Van Wyck Brooks and Randolph Bourne. In the half-century since the Civil War ended in 1865, America had undergone a period of enormous (and largely unregulated) economic growth, while assimilating the immigrants who had been coming in large waves since the 1880s. These writers, influenced by the ideas of Nietzsche, Marx, Shaw, Ibsen, and H. G. Wells, criticized American society for its disparities of wealth and poverty, the subtle poverty of its cultural and communal life, and its soulless materialism and conformity. They saw a country formally committed to personal freedom and Christian morality but actually living by the Darwinian values of the marketplace, a society that muffled individual expression and inhibited its own best instincts.

No novelist lent more ammunition to these criticisms or broadcast them more widely than Sinclair Lewis. He was born in 1885 in Sauk Centre, a raw Minnesota prairie town of three thousand people, still only a generation away from pioneer settlements and Indian encampments. (The first white child was born there less than twenty-five years before.) Lewis was the youngest of three sons of a prosperous local doctor, E. J. Lewis, a distant, unbending, and puritanical man; his mother died of tuberculosis when he was six. The boy was something of a misfit, ugly, awkward, bookish, and unpopular. He remained a loner as a student at Yale, where (according to one of his teachers, William Lyon Phelps) he "was regarded with amiable tolerance, as a freak . . . a complete and consistent individualist, going his own way, and talking only about things which interested him."

As an outsider who grew up feeling unhappy and unloved, who was never able to please the father he revered but also resented, Lewis was peculiarly susceptible to radical ideas. Thorstein Veblen, who grew up in a Minnesota farm family a generation earlier, observed the same tendency in intellectual Jews, who were alienated from their own tradition without fully accepting any other: "One who goes away from home will come to see many unfamiliar things, and to take note of them; but it does not follow that he will swear by all the strange gods whom he meets along the road." Veblen's self-portrait of the intellectual as a homeless skeptic has a particular resonance for the life of Sinclair Lewis, since *Main Street* is so focused on the theme of leaving home, the need to break away. Lewis himself remained a vagabond with few firm roots for the remainder of his life, yet insisted that his ashes be buried beside his father's in Sauk Centre.

It would be difficult to imagine American literature of the late nineteenth and early twentieth centuries without the displaced Midwesterners, from Twain and Howells to Willa Cather, from Sherwood Anderson to Hemingway and Fitzgerald, who came east to make their fortunes yet remained caught up in the world that produced and outraged them. In a famous article in 1921, the critic Carl Van Doren described this as "the revolt from the village," citing the influence of the biting narrative poems in Edgar Lee Masters's *Spoon River Anthology* (1915). The most famous example before *Main Street* was Sherwood Anderson's linked collection of stories, *Winesburg, Ohio* (1919), built around grotesque characters trapped in a small town—an ordinary annex of hell— isolated from each other, stranded in their own timidity, failing to live their lives. At the center of the book is a version of Anderson himself, a young man who learns all their stories and becomes the one who will escape to tell them.

At first *Winesburg, Ohio* didn't attract many readers, but its brooding poetic style, its warped and deformed characters, and ringing theme of personal liberation found an echo in many young writers, including Hemingway and Faulkner, who began their careers under Anderson's tutelage. Later novelists from Nathanael West and Carson McCullers to E. L. Doctorow would echo his work even more strongly. Lewis's work was harder to imitate. In five apprentice novels published between 1914 and 1919, he built up a solid reputation as a realist who had developed his own version of the need to escape the confines of provincial life. Even before he graduated from Yale, Lewis had been drawn to the bohemian world of prewar socialism, spending time as a janitor at Upton Sinclair's utopian community, Helicon Hall, and later at a California artists' colony in Carmel, where he came to know and work for Jack London (providing him with plots for stories).

Lewis held publishing jobs in New York from 1910 to 1915, but the moderate success of his first two novels enabled him devote himself full-time to his writing, which included a good deal of hackwork he churned out for magazines. As an undergraduate Lewis's literary output consisted mainly of Tennysonian romantic verse, but he had been incubating the idea for a novel based on Sauk Centre since 1905. By 1918 he was determined to write an honest, realistic book about small-town America, but his romantic and sentimental streak, now balanced by his sharp sarcasm, also helped shape *Main Street*. Carol Kennicott, the heroine, is a naive young idealist whose ardent desire to change the world, to make some kind of difference, mirrors the reforming spirit of the young radical critics of the 1900–20 period. She leaves her life as a librarian in St. Paul to marry a country doctor and return with him to Gopher Prairie, but the ugliness of the town and the intrusive philistinism of its people soon fill her with dread and disappointment. She feels caught in "a swamp of prejudices and fears." Her worst feeling is the sense of surveillance, of living constantly under judging eyes, as if she is "being dragged naked down Main Street." She hates being observed and talked about but also fears being cast out. "She wanted to hide in the generous indifference of cities," says Lewis.

Other writers had painted grim pictures of America's seemingly idyllic small towns, including Hamlin Garland in *Main-Travelled Roads* (1891) and Harold Frederic in *The Damnation of Theron Ware* (1896), pioneering works of American realism that helped inspire Lewis to write frankly from his own experience. Just as Flaubert said "Madame Bovary, c'est moi," Lewis put much of himself into Carol Kennicott. Her bluff husband, the reliable but unimaginative Dr. Will, whose favorite pastimes are hunting, motoring, and real estate deals, who adores Carol without really understanding her, is largely a portrait of his own father. But Lewis's marriage in 1914 to New York–born Grace Livingstone Hegger, whose cultural pretensions bordered on snobbery, also enabled him to see Sauk Centre and his family through the eyes of an outsider, an Easterner for whom the town would feel like an oppressive backwater.

Carol's disillusionment in her first walk along Main Street, her grating encounters with its leading citizens, color her whole life in Gopher Prairie. Never fully accepted, always feeling closely scrutinized, she spends the rest of the novel vacillating between her longing to escape and her despairing need to accommodate to things as they are. Along the way she repeatedly tries to bring Culture to the town, reading Yeats to her bored but patient husband and organizing fashionable parties, energetic outings, and amateur theatricals, each effort only driving home the futility of trying to change such a hidebound, self-satisfied world.

Like the small handful of other rebels and outsiders in Gopher Prairie (and like the discontented George F. Babbitt in Lewis's next novel), Carol is ultimately defeated by the town, brought to heel by social pressure, inertia, and her deeply ingrained wish to get along. But this is not what gives the novel its distinctive quality. Sinclair Lewis is a great satirist, one of the best America has produced, but *Main Street* is a more personal book, a love-hate letter to the world he came from. As satire *Babbitt* is wilder and more outrageous than *Main Street*. Its hero, far from being an outside observer, is himself the incarnation

of the shoddy business world around him, with its booster mentality, its Ro-
tarian atmosphere of 100 percent Americanism, its built-in social controls,
its joshing colloquial style of intolerance and intimidation. No one in *Babbitt* is quite human, and the hero's belated middle-aged crisis is a short-lived
rebellion easily put down. *Babbitt* is a brilliantly effective cartoon that looks
back toward Dickens and ahead to Nathanael West at their most slashingly
entertaining.

The townspeople in *Main Street* are also social stereotypes, and Gopher
Prairie is as much the epitome of small-town America as Babbitt is of the go-
getting American booster. Grounded in the oral traditions of Western humor,
Lewis's satire always aims at the type. But *Main Street* depends less on comic
exaggeration, much more on the range of emotions eddying through the heroine's mind, which reflect the writer's own very American dream of self-
improvement, uplift, and personal freedom. Edith Wharton, the great social
novelist to whom *Babbitt* was dedicated, told Lewis that she preferred *Main
Street*, despite the wonderful exuberance and energy of the later book:

> I don't think *Babbitt* as good a novel, in the all-round sense, as *Main Street*, be-
> cause in the latter you produce a sense of unity & of depth by reflecting Main
> Street in the consciousness of a woman who suffered from it because she had
> points of comparison, & was detached enough to situate it in the universe—
> whereas Babbitt is in and of Zenith up to his chin & over.

What Wharton commends here is more like a Wharton novel than a Lewis
satire: the focus on a single consciousness, an entrapped woman keenly aware
of her situation without being able to break out. Lewis wasn't really a novelist in Wharton's "all-round sense." But *Main Street* is a hybrid, a stinging satirical novel crossed with a more inward novel of personal discontent, longing,
and indecision. The Main Street side of the novel delighted H. L. Mencken
and ignited controversy by exposing the American town as stifling, mean-
spirited, and conformist. But *Main Street* was also a novel about a stultifying
marriage, a mismatch between Main Street values and neglected human
needs—a feminist novel to which many women responded strongly. "She was
a woman with a working brain and no work," Carol discovers soon after she
settles into Gopher Prairie. "I think perhaps we want a more conscious life,"
says Carol, too consciously echoing contemporary feminism. "We're tired of
drudging and sleeping and dying." This was Wharton territory: an ill-assorted
couple, thwarted aspirations, the theme of the unlived life, which Henry
James, D. H. Lawrence, and Sherwood Anderson had first explored. When the
trustees of Columbia University substituted Wharton's *Age of Innocence* for
Main Street after Lewis's novel was chosen by the jury for the Pulitzer Prize,
they were fleeing controversy yet honoring a work on exactly the same theme:
an unsatisfying marriage and the fear and social intimidation that hold it together. Both books studied marriage almost anthropologically, laying bare the

peculiar mores of inbred tribes and closed worlds, but at least Wharton's more oblique treatment was set safely in the 1870s.

As the Pulitzer judges recognized, the two strands of Main Street were a potent combination. Lewis's unsympathetic but insightful biographer, Mark Schorer, describes its appearance as "the most sensational event in twentieth-century American publishing history." Within a year it had sold 295,000 copies. It brought a critical view of American culture to a wide readership in a scabrously amusing form. "No reader was indifferent to Main Street," writes Schorer. "If it was not the most important revelation of American life ever made, it was the most infamous libel upon it. . . . America in general found that a new image of itself had suddenly been thrust upon it." This darker image of America was not confined to the kind of town Lewis grew up in, since America's rural communities were already giving way as he wrote his book. Lewis's inspiration was not simply to make "Main Street" a metaphor for small-town America but to make Gopher Prairie and the Kennicott marriage stand for everything rigid and dehumanizing about American life: the social intolerance, the crude architecture, the ugly public spaces, the disrespect for learning and art, the standardization imposed by modernity and the machine, the deep gulf between the sexes, and especially the middle-class woman's sense of uselessness.

Lewis's ideas were not new. Veblen, Mencken, and Van Wyck Brooks had been saying similar things for years. Shaw and Wells had been their prophets. But Lewis turned their coruscating observations and his own maladjustment into a folksy, concrete, ambivalent portrait of the American heartland. In America's Coming-of-Age (1915), Brooks had described a split between an unworldly idealism that went back to the Puritans and Transcendentalists and a bustling practical energy that joined the homespun Benjamin Franklin to the prodigious moneymaking and industrial growth since the Civil War. Ingeniously, Sinclair Lewis built this conflict into the strains in the Kennicott marriage and Carol's tensions with the good burghers of Gopher Prairie. The novel contrasts Carol's slightly ridiculous longing for beauty and uplift—mocked by Mencken, who said that "her superior culture is, after all, chiefly bogus"—with Will's down-to-earth practicality and the townspeople's iron resistance to Carol's elevating plans for them. Except for Will, they are small, limited, and mean; Carol, for her part, is ambitious, dreamy, and confused.

Lewis develops this contrast between practical wisdom and cultured idealism far too broadly. In one of his doctrinaire asides, he shows us American technology taking over the world—American industry, American kitchens and bathrooms, American standardization and uniformity. Against this mechanical uniformity he vaguely invokes the treasures of European art and culture, which he mentions with a naive awe. As Carol becomes a housewife in Gopher Prairie, her world shrinks; the can opener in her kitchen becomes "more pertinent to her than all the cathedrals of Europe." Lewis can't resist using his characters to pillory ignorance or preach the occasional sermon.

The characters themselves are sketched in the same black-and-white tones. At one extreme are the know-nothing Smails, Will's predatory kinsmen, who descend on Gopher Prairie halfway through the novel; also the widow Bogart, the Kennicotts' busybody neighbor, always sanctimonious in her "simpering viciousness," and her brutish son Cy. On the other side are the village rebels or aspiring artists, who are invariably ground down: Guy Pollock, the bachelor lawyer who loves poetry and is a prime victim of the "Village Virus," a death-like inability to live elsewhere; Carol's Swedish maid Bea and her husband Miles, the village atheist and radical, whom the good ladies of the town cruelly ostracize; the tailor's assistant, Erik Valborg, dandyish, slightly effeminate, culture-loving; and finally Fern, a vivacious young schoolteacher whose reputation, if not her virtue, is ruined by Cy Bogart. Lewis's mastery of speech and social detail never fails him—it gives this novel its tremendous power as a document of American life—but he conceives these people as animated caricatures, without the finer gradations of personality that would ever enable them to surprise us. Like many satirists, Lewis was a great observer, a superb mimic. But only Carol has an inner life that matters, a sensibility in which the author truly invests himself.

Main Street is defined less by Lewis's satire than by Carol's complicated longings and disappointments, her constantly shifting attitudes toward the town and her husband. If *Babbitt* succeeds as a comic tour de force, a barbed, illustrated social polemic, then *Main Street*, for all its superb documentation, is a more awkward, painful kind of book. Lewis places a three-dimensional character at the center of a two-dimensional landscape, a novel whose very dissonance of form conveys a menacing sense of enclosure and anxiety. A similar disparity between the sensitive protagonist and his or her absurd surroundings would later be used by writers as varied as Nathanael West (*Miss Lonelyhearts*, *Day of the Locust*), Mary McCarthy (*Memories of a Catholic Girlhood*), Joseph Heller (*Catch-22*), and Thomas Pynchon (*The Crying of Lot 49*), all of them dark satirists charting a journey of the soul among fools and knaves.

The more repugnant characters in Lewis's novel, the Smails and the Bogarts, do little but mock Carol, thwart her, and monitor her little deviations from the town's orthodoxies. The rebels, on the other hand, serve to echo her situation and provide cautionary lessons of what might happen if her heresies persist, or if she were not protected by her husband's social position. Even Vida Sherwin, who first appears as a soulmate, becomes little more than a crude Freudian case study in sexual repression, a frigid woman jealous of Carol's marriage. Only Will gives promise of being someone to match Carol's complexity, but in the end he's less a character than a vessel for Sinclair Lewis's own conflicts. At one moment he is simply a know-nothing—limited, obtuse, insensitive—a mouthpiece for reactionary clichés. At other times he is almost heroic: a humane, quietly conscientious doctor, unassuming in his professionalism, a forbearing husband, remarkably patient with his wife's emotional confusion, sexual withdrawal, and even physical absence when she goes off with their son to Washington to do war work.

Lewis identifies with Carol yet also, from the first paragraph of the book, when she is still a college student, derides her lofty cultural aspirations, which he sometimes shared. But her contradictory feelings about Will bring in something Lewis could not control: his own ambivalence toward Sauk Centre and his father. This forms the keystone of the book and contributes to Will's incoherence as a character. Nothing in the novel is more warmly imagined and beautifully written than the fifteenth chapter, in which Carol briefly feels the heroism of the doctor's daily routine and marvels at his steadfast behavior in an emergency. What Carol experiences as admiration and love, Lewis himself must once have known as a child's awe of his father's masculine strength. But his father's inaccessibility and rejection, along with the disapproval of the town, turned Lewis into a privileged misfit, like Carol. Yet Lewis himself *was* Sauk Centre, the provincial rube who had gone to Yale, who had married a lady. Soon Will's character shrinks again. Lewis's shifting feelings shape the novel; the often affectionate satire on Main Street is simply their outward expression.

Carol's sexual indifference to her husband is another striking feature of *Main Street*. She undresses behind a screen, moves to her own bedroom, and carries on a series of flirtations, first with Guy Pollock, until she grows weary of his "love of dead elegances," and then more seriously with Erik Valborg, stopping just short of actually sleeping with him. Lewis was not really interested (or courageous) enough to rewrite *Madame Bovary*, or Kate Chopin's powerful novel of adultery, *The Awakening*, or even Ibsen's *A Doll's House*, though a touch of Flaubert's Emma and Ibsen's Nora cling to Carol. Finally, his concern is more with Main Street than with these characters, more with America between 1912 and 1920 than with the "all-round" novel of personal relationships that Edith Wharton might have written.

As a sociological novelist Lewis had few peers. His prodigious travels, his research into American institutions, matched the journalistic diligence of his early mentor, Upton Sinclair. But he fictionalized his findings with quicksilver wit and brio, capturing the bright surfaces of American life and speech like few others before him. His characters do not live as people but they live as bywords and American myths. Main Street, Babbitt, the idealistic Martin Arrowsmith, and the lecherous, hypocritical Elmer Gantry belong to our national folklore and mythology rather than our stock of great fictional creations. The writers who just preceded him, James, Wharton, Willa Cather, and those who arrived just after him, Faulkner, Hemingway, and Fitzgerald, were much more careful craftsmen, close students of human consciousness in its social setting. *Main Street* comes closest to their kind of novel, since much of it flows through Carol's half-formed mind. In a touching memoir published shortly after his death, his first wife, Grace Hegger, acknowledged that he "created no school of writing as have Hemingway and Faulkner, Henry James and Flaubert. He influenced public thinking rather than public writing."

Though later social novelists, from J. P. Marquand to John Updike, showed their debt to him, his real successors were widely read sociologists like David Riesman and William H. Whyte rather than modern writers. Lewis belongs to a tradition of social observation that extends from Tocqueville, who explored "the tyranny of the majority" in America, to Riesman's "other-directed" personalities and Whyte's organization men. Like Lewis, all of these students of American society were concerned with individuality and conformity, the process by which we shape ourselves to other people's views. This issue went back at least as far as Emerson's essay "Self-Reliance," with its prescient attack on conformity and its argument that "whoso would be a man, must be a nonconformist." Riesman and Whyte saw the social controls of Lewis's small towns recreated in the "togetherness" of the new suburbs. The "thick description," the astonishing abundance of detail that dominates Lewis's novels, goes far beyond any Emersonian manifesto; it belongs more to a sociological tradition than to a literary one.

Rarely has a ferment of social criticism and private feeling permeated a novel as effectively, and with such immediate public impact, as in *Main Street*. Out of painful memories of his own upbringing and his grasp of a rapidly changing world, Sinclair Lewis fashioned a portrait that resonated strongly for readers of the 1920s. In projecting his own conflicts onto a wider screen, Lewis gave Americans a keen sense of themselves as a people in transition, caught between the town and the city, between commercial values and a cosmopolitan sense of art and culture, between the rude West and the refined East, between women as homemakers and women as independent beings, and between the older demands of family and community and the new stress on self-fulfilment. In Washington near the end of the novel, Carol at last feels "no longer one-half of a marriage but the whole of a human being." But she has also become a face in the crowd, a little shocked at her new urban anonymity, and eventually she allows herself to be drawn back home. In Carol's unresolved conflicts with her adopted town, her stolid husband, and her own self, *Main Street* becomes both a caustic farewell to small-town America and a lively prologue to the cultural divisions of America's first genuinely modern decade.

THE MAGIC OF CONTRADICTIONS:
WILLA CATHER'S LOST LADY

FIRST PUBLISHED IN 1923, when Willa Cather was almost fifty years old, *A Lost Lady* occupies a special place in her rich and varied body of work. Though it never gained the wide popular appeal of *My Ántonia* or *Death Comes for the Archbishop*, which became staples of the school curriculum, it has long been a work that critics admire extravagantly and ordinary readers remember with passionate enthusiasm. The early reviews were laudatory but a little condescending, for Cather's "portrait of a lady" is barely longer than a novella and centers on a single character. To Edmund Wilson it was "a charming sketch performed with exceptional skill." Joseph Wood Krutch found it "short and slight," not "a great novel" but "that very rare thing in contemporary literature, a nearly perfect one." But the tide was turning by 1937 when Lionel Trilling, not Cather's greatest admirer, described it as "the central work of her career. Far from being the delicate minor book it is often called, it is probably her most muscular story." Later critics, including Alfred Kazin in *On Native Grounds* (1942), followed Trilling in seeing *A Lost Lady* and its even darker successor, *The Professor's House* (1925), as Cather's pivotal works, affecting, powerfully imagined, and strikingly modern even in their recoil from modern life.

The early readers who described the book as a character sketch saw only the brilliance of Cather's portrayal of Marian Forrester, the high-spirited wife of one of the great pioneers and railroad builders. They were less attuned to the historical implications of Cather's fable and missed the enigmatic, ambiguous elements in Mrs. Forrester's portrait. On the surface Marian Forrester belonged to Cather's long line of restless, magnetic, intelligent women like Alexandra Bergson, who grows wealthy farming the virgin land in *O Pioneers!* (1913); Thea Kronborg, the Swedish girl who becomes a famous opera singer in *The Song of the Lark* (1915); and Ántonia Shimerda, the heroine of *My Ántonia* (1918), who survives tragedy and abandonment to become the mother of many children, "a rich mine of life, like the founders of early races."

These earlier heroines were all immigrants, but Cather herself had grown up among the farms and small towns that shaped their lives; many of their experiences were also her experiences, and she loved the irrepressible hunger for life she saw in them, which mirrored her own fervent ambition to live boldly. At a time when immigrants in literature were usually treated as comical figures with silly accents or as piteous social victims, when women characters were expected to find happiness only in love or marriage, Cather portrayed forceful women who tilled the soul, balanced the books, negotiated an alien culture,

navigated new worlds in literature and the arts, showed adventurous, independent minds, and, above all, had a tremendous spark of emotional and physical
vitality that Cather admired as the very sap of life. At the end of My Ántonia,
we learn that the heroine's "inner glow" has not faded: "Whatever else was
gone, Ántonia had not lost the fire of life."

A Lost Lady is a brilliant epilogue to Cather's famous pioneer novels but it has
a different tone, not heroic and optimistic like the Whitmanesque O Pioneers!
but bittersweet and retrospective in the vein of Edith Wharton's autumnal Age
of Innocence. O Pioneers! is a fertility myth in which the golden land yields lovingly to the plough, the women are almost magically in tune with the rhythms
of the soil and the seasons, and death is simply the moment of being gathered
back into the larger whole, the vibrant heart of nature. This sense of the inevitable is brought home to us by the stately, almost biblical nobility of the
book's style. Even in My Ántonia, which builds up a harsher picture of the struggles of an immigrant farm family—beginning with unspeakable poverty, miserable living conditions, depression, and even suicide—a stirring sense of progress
gradually emerges, all thanks to hard work and the fecundity of the land. "The
windy springs and the blazing summers, one after another, had enriched and
mellowed that flat tableland; all the human effort that had gone into it was coming back in long, sweeping lines of fertility," says Jim Burden, the narrator, who
has been away in the East. "The changes seemed beautiful and harmonious to
me; it was like watching the growth of a great man or of a great idea."

Willa Cather's recollections of pioneer life had not always had this amber glow
of fruition. The best stories in her first work of fiction, The Troll Garden, were
written under the influence of Hamlin Garland's Main-Travelled Roads, with its
tales of back-breaking labor and dreary poverty on Western farms. The early
Cather, like Garland, identified the West with small-mindedness, boredom, and
conformity, the East with escape, personal development, and a rich artistic culture. In one of Cather's fiercest stories, "The Sculptor's Funeral," the nasty back-
biting that surrounds the funeral of a native son, who had made his reputation as
an artist in the East, exposes one Western town as a "dung heap," a "borderland
between ruffianism and civilization." The reverse occurs in "A Wagner Matinée." A farm wife, turned old, dull, and shapeless by her labors, long deprived
of any real stimulation, visits Boston, where she discovers, with a terrible pang of
recognition, the musical life she left behind long ago. After attending a concert
with her nephew, she bursts into tears and hates to leave the empty hall:

> For her, just outside the door of the concert hall, lay the black pond with the
> cattle-tracked bluffs; the tall unpainted house, with weather-curled boards; naked
> as a tower, the crook-backed ash seedlings where the dish cloths hung to dry; the
> gaunt, moulting turkeys, picking up refuse about the kitchen door.

These carefully etched details, recorded by the young man who witnesses her
misery, anticipate the way Cather would use her precise memories of growing

up in Nebraska to write her prairie novels. Willa Cather was born in the Shenandoah country of Virginia in 1873, but when she was nine her parents pulled up stakes and joined the rest of the family on a farm in Nebraska. Initially Cather felt she had fallen off the edge of the world. "There seemed to be nothing to see; no fences, no creeks or trees, no hills or fields," her narrator writes near the beginning of My Ántonia. "There was nothing but land: not a country at all, but the material out of which countries are made. . . . I had the feeling that the world was left behind, that we had got over the edge of it, and were outside man's jurisdiction." Her early sense of dislocation undoubtedly heightened the empathy she felt for immigrants and exiles.

A year later she moved with her family to Red Cloud, a town barely ten years old, where she encountered a world quite different from the farm. As a mischievous tomboy, a hungry and eager reader, yet also someone who lived at the tip of her senses, she felt stifled by the atmosphere of respectability that weighed more heavily on girls than on boys, on "Americans" more than on immigrants. Yet it was here and on nearby farms over the next six years—among brothers, sisters, aunts, uncles, and grandparents, among sympathetic neighbors who fed her books and stories, and especially among the bright, enterprising "hired girls" who were helping to support their immigrant families—that Cather absorbed the vivid impressions that would carry her through most of her writing life. "I was all over the country then, on foot, on horseback and in our farm wagon," she later recalled. "My nose went poking into nearly everything. It happened that my mind was constructed for the particular purpose of absorbing impressions and retaining them."

Cather loved the ordinary rhythms of rural life but grew up with a hatred of the routine, the commonplace, "the homilies by which the world is run" (as she described it in "Paul's Case," her best-known story, about someone who is different, an aesthete, implicitly gay, and soon ground under). Among those in Red Cloud who lent a touch of romance and distinction to Cather's early life was Silas Garber, a former Union Army officer who had founded the town in 1870 and was elected governor of Nebraska four years later. He had a much younger wife, whose elegance and vivacity made a strong impression on the young Cather. Living amid a beautiful grove of cottonwood trees at the edge of town, the Garbers were the nobility of Red Cloud, their lives a window onto the pioneer days when the town was settled. Cather based her account of the Forresters in A Lost Lady on her warm memories of the Garbers, which came flooding back when she read of Mrs. Garber's death in 1921.

What Cather felt she needed was a point of view to register the effect of the Forresters, especially the lovely Mrs. Forrester. "I had to have something for Marian Forrester's charm to work on," she remarked. "You can't talk about beauty for pages and pages." In "A Wagner Matinée," Cather had observed the miserable life and appearance of an overworked farm woman through the eyes of her young nephew, now living far from her world, who serves as embarrassed spectator to his aunt's unhappiness. In *O Pioneers!*, the work in which she found her true voice, Cather had dispensed with such an onlooker; his "culture" and detachment had clouded her lens, and his style—which was hers at the time—was too Jamesian, too literary, and therefore condescending. Cather's early stories were inflected by her own need to get away, and by the long road she had traveled from Red Cloud. With *O Pioneers!* she was reunited with her past. Following the advice of her mentor, the New England writer Sarah Orne Jewett, to write from the heart, she tapped directly into her recollections in a style of almost epic simplicity. But Cather could not honestly sustain such an impersonal viewpoint; these were *her* memories yet she *had* moved away; her life had gone in a different direction. Moreover, they were a young person's experiences, sometimes little more than a child's impressions; they involved people she could not fully understand, people who were at some level unknowable to her.

Cather solved this problem in *My Ántonia* by handing the story off to a surrogate, Jim Burden, whose early life resembled her own. This is *his* Ántonia: we see her by fits and starts, episodically, through his eyes. Ántonia is absent from the novel for long periods, and when Jim goes away for twenty years, as Cather too had gone away, Jim catches up with the changes in her life through other people's reports, before he sees her again. Cather's solution isn't wholly successful: Jim Burden wavers between being a full-fledged character and a mask for the author, and since he is said to be male, we never understand why his relationship to Ántonia and other women never fully develops. (It falters, lesbian critics suggest, because of Cather's own masked and obstructed sexuality, but to Cather herself it simply reflected what she really was, an observer.) Yet the narrator furnishes Cather with something very valuable, a precisely situated viewpoint on the world of her youth. Forsaking the novelistic contrivances of a unified plot and omniscient knowledge, Cather organizes her book around the act of remembering, with its gaps of time and recollection, its moments of transcendence, its privileged glimpses of a long-buried world: simple images fraught with strong feeling.

The casual, lifelike pattern of memory in *My Ántonia* foreshadows something decisive for *A Lost Lady*, a sense of character as mystery, a Wordsworthian way of seeing by glimpses that respects the "burden" of the mystery. Cather deliberately avoided telling us too much about a character; she believed in *withholding* character, as she once said in a letter to her friend Dorothy Canfield Fisher. The story of Mrs. Forrester's life preceding her marriage comes so late in the novel, and is so condensed and improbable, that it's almost a satire on our need to know, a deliberate piece of "fiction." The original Mrs. Garber was not one of Cather's contemporaries, like Ántonia, but a kind of Lady Bountiful to the young people of the town. We see Marian Forrester from young Niel Herbert's angle: he is at first adoring, then bitterly disenchanted, and at last grudgingly reconciled to her complex nature. Her impact on him is the heart of the novel, the key to its effect on the reader.

Niel is not actually the narrator, since Cather needed to put things in the story that he could not have witnessed (and could not abide), but through him Cather evokes all that these people meant to her as a girl in Red Cloud, the town here called Sweet Water.

For many years critics saw Niel simply as a window on the Forresters' world. Cather's first biographers, E. K. Brown and Leon Edel, wrote that Niel was "simply Jim Burden from *My Ántonia* renamed"; a later critic, Philip Gerber, carelessly described him as "the narrator of the novel," adding that "Niel exists chiefly to represent the author and her attitude." Cather herself once said in an interview that "he isn't a character at all; he is just a peephole into that world. . . . he is only a point of view." But some recent critics have argued that because of his horror at Mrs. Forrester's adultery and his disgust at her refusal to "immolate herself" after her husband's death ("she preferred life on any terms"), Niel's point of view cannot be fully trusted. The question can be simply posed: Is Mrs. Forrester truly "a lost lady" after her husband's death, "like a ship without ballast, driven hither and thither by every wind," as Niel thinks; or is she simply lost *to him*, because, like an unhappy adolescent robbed of his innocence, he cannot bear the sexual form of the vitality that first enthralled him. "Lilies that fester smell far worse then weeds," he mutters to himself, echoing the disillusionment of Shakespeare's ninety-fourth sonnet, with its lament that "sweetest things turn sourest by their deeds."

This issue can never be resolved, for what makes *A Lost Lady* such a rich and resonant work, as enchanting as its heroine, as ambiguous as its title, is that Cather has it both ways. She uses Niel as a delicate sensor to register the impact of Captain Forrester as a survivor of the frontier generation and of his wife as a beacon of graciousness, elegance, and beauty for Sweet Water. "A Lost Lady was a woman I loved very much in my childhood," Cather said in the same interview. "I wasn't interested in her character when I was little, but in her lovely hair and her laugh which made me happy clear down to my toes." *A Lost Lady* conveys the magic of an impressionable child's point of view but also its inevitable limitations. The Captain himself pointedly rebukes Niel's implicit judgment of his wife; he makes it clear that he's aware of her affair and understands the complexity of her character, including her sexual needs, as Niel cannot; he makes Niel see how much he values her.

Yet Niel *is* a character, in part because he grows up in the course of the book, fired up at first by what the Forresters represent ("a different world from any he had ever known"), but eventually educated by the troubles they undergo, the painful reverses that complicate their lives in a way he can only fathom as an adult (and barely even then). Cather drew inspiration from Flaubert's *Sentimental Education*, in which a young man is drawn by the beauty and charm of an older woman, only to find how disappointing, how commonplace life can turn out to be; he is left in the end with little more than a few early memories. But Cather colored this picture with touches from *Hamlet*, where another young man recoils from a woman's middle-aged sexuality, her insistence on surviving her husband and living life "on any terms."

The novel's epigraph is from the disconnected ramblings of Ophelia, truly a lost lady. But the title phrase appears in the novel only as "his long-lost lady," with her "long-lost lady laugh," suggesting that despite the reverses in her life, she is lost only to Niel, who cannot keep from condemning her. But in the end, we hear, "he came to be very glad that he had known her, and that she had had a hand in breaking him in to life." After the idealizations that lit up his childhood, after his own failure to find the happiness her bright laughter had promised, he learns something about the mixed, ambiguous nature of the adult world.

If Niel's education were the whole story, the novel would be a sketchy example of the bildungsroman, the novel of personal development. If Marian's adultery were the whole story, A Lost Lady would be a minor offshoot of works like Flaubert's Madame Bovary, Tolstoy's Anna Karenina, or Kate Chopin's The Awakening, which Willa Cather reviewed caustically when it appeared in 1899. Like My Ántonia, A Lost Lady is a memory novel: by focusing on what the Forresters once meant to Niel, it conveys Cather's darkening sense of how the West has changed since she grew up. The settlers of O Pioneers! and My Ántonia were homesteaders taming the land and making it fruitful by sweat and labor. But Daniel Forrester represents another kind of pioneer, the adventurer and entrepreneur; he and his powerful friends belong to the railroad aristocracy of "the road-making West." They "dreamed the railroads across the mountains," says the Captain, "just as I dreamed my place on the Sweet Water." They were the "men who had put plains and mountains under the iron harness."

There is a curiously abstract quality to Cather's reminiscence of the pioneer days in A Lost Lady. It feels disembodied, like a fairy tale of long ago. Where My Ántonia, written only five years earlier, gave us a graphic sense of the hardships of frontier life, in this novel the pioneers are remote figures, reduced to brilliant metaphor: they dreamed the railroads across the mountains, they put the plains and mountains under the iron harness. Those who built the railroads were not simply bold and hardy dreamers, as they appear here, but Gilded Age buccaneers, venturesome capitalists supported by cheap labor and vast federal subsidies. Here the Forresters and their friends take on the fabric of legend. "It had already gone, that age; nothing could ever bring it back. The taste and smell and song of it, the visions those men had seen in the air and followed,— these he had caught in a kind of afterglow in their own faces,—and this would always be his." These people and their stories added color, dash, and dreamy aspiration to Cather's childhood.

A Lost Lady weaves an elegiac myth about "the end of an era, the sunset of the pioneer," for Cather saw such people not simply as entrepreneurs and fortune-builders, not even as discoverers and nation builders, but as a local aristocracy of manners and moral responsibility. Now they are being replaced by new men whose conscience is not so fine, who cheat Indians out of their land and small bank depositors out of their savings. When a bank in which he has a major interest fails, Forrester impoverishes himself (and later his widow) by making good on every dime. "That was what a man of honour was bound to do," explains Niel's uncle, another man of the old school. Captain Forrester's "clumsy dignity covered a deep nature, and a conscience that had never been juggled with."

Despite the seeming casualness of the narrative, which at first appears to be no more than random memories punctuated by gaps and elisions, A Lost Lady is the most tightly organized novel Cather wrote, with hardly a spare word. The themes I've touched on here, the education of a young man and the dignity of the old order, are foreshadowed from the opening pages. The first two chapters form a prologue, set seven years before the main action begins, that shows us the Forresters' world at its zenith, when both their marriage and the town are still thriving. The story begins like a fairy tale, on "a summer morning long ago, when Mrs. Forrester was still a young woman, and Sweet Water was a town of which great things were expected." The Forresters' house "would probably have been ugly enough" but is made special by its lovely setting and the way of life of those who inhabit it. The prologue evokes the heyday of the pioneers, when Sweet Water was an important division point on the Burlington Railroad, and the house, set on a beautiful Indian site, was the place the railroad barons stopped to pay their respects and be graciously received. But now it has become a vestige of that earlier time. Mrs. Forrester extends her hospitality even to the boys of the town, including Niel (age twelve), who fish and hike and play on the land.

The snake in this garden is an older boy named Ivy Peters—nicknamed Poison Ivy—who specializes in poisoning dogs and torturing birds. When Niel climbs a tree to put a blinded bird out of its misery, he falls and breaks his arm, and gets a luxurious taste of Mrs. Forrester's loving care. "He was in pain, but he felt weak and contented. . . . The little boy was thinking that he would probably never be in so nice a place again." Ivy Peters, Niel's opposite number, is already the young upstart, the new man who feels that "I'm just as good as she is." For now he is expelled from the house by her "imperious courtesy." But eventually he will take revenge by draining the Forresters' lovely marsh, which stands not only for the children's Eden but for the kind of impractical, unproductive beauty cultivated by the old order. As a young lawyer who amasses wealth by cutting corners, Peters will condescend to the Captain and, after the old man's death, have an affair with his wife and eventually take over her property.

All this is anticipated in the opening chapters. The Forresters, with their Sherwood Forest style of generosity, will give way to the Ivy Peters of the world, "this generation of shrewd young men, trained to petty economies by hard times," who exploit the fruits of the world the pioneers made. Ivy Peters is the great flaw in Cather's parable. Not only pragmatic but dishonest, disrespectful, gratuitously sadistic, he helps us notice how Cather idealizes the old order and demonizes the forces that shaped the modern world. Stepping outside the frame of her story, she cannot resist blazing out at all he represents when he drains the Forresters' marsh and puts their land to prosaic use:

> The Old West had been settled by dreamers, great-hearted adventurers who were unpractical to the point of magnificence; a courteous brotherhood, strong in attack but weak in defence, who could conquer but could not hold. Now all the vast territory they had won was to be at the mercy of men like Ivy Peters, who had never dared anything, never risked anything. They would drink up the mirage, dispel the morning freshness, root out the great brooding spirit of freedom, the generous, easy life of the great land-holders. The space, the colour, the princely carelessness of the pioneer they would destroy and cut up into profitable bits, as the match factory splinters the primeval forest.

In her next novel, *The Professor's House*, Cather would stay clear of the cardboard villainy of Ivy Peters and create a more nuanced fable of decline, with the professor's student, Tom Outland, as the pure adventurer, who luckily dies in the war before he can fall into compromise, and the professor's son-in-law, the charming and ingratiating Louie Marsellus, as the enterprising Jew who knows how to market Outland's discoveries. Cather will build the story not around a single house, as in *A Lost Lady*, but around a series of houses, from the ancient cliff-dwellings of New Mexican Indians to soulless homes with all modern conveniences. Yet even in *A Lost Lady* Cather qualifies her moral when she describes the pioneers as "dreamers" and Ivy Peters as the man who "would drink up the mirage, dispel the morning freshness," or when she tells us that the Captain, having no children of his own, is a man who "could afford to humour his own fancies." Dreams, mirages, fancies, and the morning dew are things that are inevitably dispelled: they evaporate of their own nature. Cather turns the rugged pioneers into myth, the antithesis of all she finds detestable in the new, more utilitarian West. But her tone signals that she's idealizing them, reifying a lost world as she remembers it from childhood. In Niel's painful disillusionment with Mrs. Forrester, Cather takes the full measure of this disabling idealization.

"Life began for me," Willa Cather once said, "when I ceased to admire and began to remember." This is a shift Niel cannot fully make, for he clings to his childhood image of the Forresters and his disgust at how their lives and the world have changed. Much of this undoubtedly reflects Cather's own burnished memories: the courtliness and dignity of the Captain, his wife's "soft, musical laugh which rose and descended like a suave scale." Yet Cather's fable takes on a life of its own that subtly separates us from Niel's viewpoint. Though Cather maintained that Niel was no character, she nevertheless gave him a history that begins and ends in unhappiness. For Niel as a child, "home was not a pleasant place to go to; a frail egg-shell house, set off on the edge of the prairie where people of no consequence lived." His mother had died when he was five, and his agreeable father was not a success. A poor relation keeps house for them in a slovenly way that Niel despises. Except for his uncle, the Judge, one of the town's old grandees, "Niel felt there was an air of failure and defeat about his family." For a boy like this, who aspires to something finer, the Forresters are royalty, their way of life magical.

When the town's economy falters and Niel's father leaves for Denver, Niel lives "with monastic cleanliness and severity" behind his uncle's law offices; this brings him into greater contact with the Forresters just as their world is beginning to unravel. They give him a thrilling intimation of another, more elegant life. He has seen fashionable women but "had never found one so attractive and distinguished as Mrs. Forrester. Compared with her, other women were heavy and dull; even the pretty ones seemed lifeless,—they had not that something in their glance that made one's blood tingle."

Niel is now nineteen, yet his attraction to Mrs. Forrester is not primarily sexual; it comes from her association with a bygone age. Cather remarks how strange this is: "Curiously enough, it was as Captain Forrester's wife that she most interested Niel, and it was in her relation to her husband that he most admired her. Given her other charming attributes, her comprehension of a man like the railroad-builder, her loyalty to him, stamped her more than anything else." Yet this rather dry admiration is belied by the excitement Niel actually feels in her presence. "Where Mrs. Forrester was, dulness was impossible, Niel believed." She is vivid and witty and has an artist's keen powers of attention and self-projection. "One could talk with her about the most trivial things, and go away with a high sense of elation."

Niel's extreme reaction to his discovery of her affair is more like a lover's or a son's jealousy than a young admirer's disapproval. Long before Niel knows anything of this liaison, he feels repelled by Frank's Ellinger's very presence, by his masculine sexual energy: "His whole figure seemed very much alive under his clothes, with a restless, muscular energy that had something of the cruelty of wild animals in it. . . . [Niel] didn't know whether he liked him or not. He knew nothing bad about him, but he felt something evil." Frank's energy is contrasted with the Captain's mountainous and dignified immobility, which Niel cherishes. Cather had begun *A Lost Lady* with Niel as narrator, but soon rewrote it in the third person, heightening the ambiguity by detaching the reader from Niel's outlook. First *we* learn of the affair, then the adoring young Adolph Blum, who is in awe of her. ("With Adolph Blum her secrets were safe. His mind was feudal; the rich and fortunate were also the privileged.") Only later does Niel find it out himself, in what only can be seen as a lover's fancy gone awry, or the primal scene of a child witnessing his mother's violation.

This is how it happens. With Frank in town and her husband gone, Niel is determined to call on her early one morning, when the marsh is "globed with dew" and there is "an almost religious purity about the fresh morning air," when the day is "still unsullied, like a gift handed down from the heroic ages."

He would make a bouquet for a lovely lady; a bouquet gathered off the cheeks of morning . . . these roses, only half awake, in the defencelessness of utter beauty. . . . —and they would perhaps give her a sudden distaste for coarse world-lings like Frank Ellinger.

Instead, outside her bedroom window, he overhears the lovers laughing to-gether. In disgust, he throws the roses into "a mudhole the cattle had trampled under the bank of the creek," a spot that suggests his view of their lovemaking, perhaps of sex in general. To Niel his lovely lady, exalted and unreachable like the heroine of romance, has suddenly become a lost lady. His reaction is melo-dramatic, despairing. He feels that his sense of reality has been altered forever, that purity and freshness and trust have been banished from the world. "In that instant between stooping to the window-sill and rising, he had lost one of the most beautiful things in his life. Before the dew dried, the morning had been wrecked for him; and all subsequent mornings, he told himself bitterly."

It's conceivable that Cather herself would have shared Niel's repugnance. As Blanche Gelfant showed in an essay on My Ántonia in 1971, Cather's work repeatedly associates sex and marriage with dissolution and death, as when the thwarted young lovers in O Pioneers! are murdered by the woman's deranged husband just moments after they fall into each other's arms. Cather's male nar-rators may have been a mask for her own attraction to the vibrant women she writes about. Or she may simply have felt that true friendship, intellectual companionship, and a consanguinity of souls—like the lifelong bond between the two priests in Death Comes for the Archbishop—made for a more enduring connection than sex. Throughout her life she had intense friendships with other women, and when her closest companion, Isabelle McClung, decided suddenly to marry in 1916, Cather was visibly shattered. (As if to override her ambivalence, Cather dedicated both A Lost Lady and The Professor's House to McClung's husband, a Canadian-Jewish violinist named Jan Hambourg.) Whatever her own feelings about sex, the story takes on a logic of its own, and Cather makes it impossible for the reader of A Lost Lady either to identify fully with Niel's reaction or to disengage from it. This paradoxical quality makes the novel itself as fascinating and elusive as its main character, of whom we are told: "She mocked outrageously at the proprieties she observed, and inherited the magic of contradictions."

As Cather portrays it, there's a childish petulance and disenchantment about Niel's response to Mrs. Forrester's fall, which reveals how much he has put her on a pedestal. But she refuses to play the courtly lady, and tries to serve her own needs while remaining impeccably devoted to her failing husband. Not only does the Captain show Niel how well he understands her, but Cather allows her to defend herself passionately against Niel's disapproval. Niel would have her live on grace and style alone, but even he acknowledges that she must have money and people and sexual attention to carry on. ("He dreaded poverty for her.") As the Captain's declining health and income deprive her of the social stimulus she desperately needs, her hunger for life becomes even stronger: "Perhaps people think I've settled down to grow old gracefully, but I've not. I feel such a power to live in me, Niel. . . . I wanted to see whether I had anything left worth saving. And I have, I tell you!"

Niel believes she's worth saving in a different sense: he wants to save her from herself. He cuts the telephone cord with a pair of shears as she is berating her lover for abandoning her—an aggressive stroke we would expect more from Ivy Peters than from Niel. "For once he had been quick enough; he had saved her," he imagines. As when he tried to "save" the blinded bird, it proves to be a futile gesture; the town gossips hear of it anyway, and this was not how she had wanted to be saved. Finally, when the Captain's health deteriorates further, when she loses her grip and commonplace people invade their house, delighted to see how ordinary it is, Niel gives up a year of school in the East to become the family nursemaid, the devoted son. This gives him deep satisfaction—he finds "a kind of solemn happiness in his vigils"—for he has the illusion that he can stop time. He clings to the idealized family he never had, trying to hold on to a vanishing world. Niel's contentment is as revealing as his distress over her affair. "He had the satisfaction of those who keep faith. He liked being alone with the old things that had seemed so beautiful to him in his child-hood. . . . No other house could take the place of this one in his life."

There is a great deal of Cather herself in these words. Her attachment to old houses, her anguish at leaving them behind, was legendary, and in *The Professor's House* she even made a beloved and familiar old house the linchpin of a novel, the symbol of her character's depression and resistance to change. She felt that her rediscovery of "the old things"—and people—of her childhood had marked her real beginnings as a writer. She was proud that, like Virgil, she had brought the muse to her native region. Her growing attraction to the Southwest (in *The Song of the Lark*, *The Professor's House*, and *Death Comes for the Archbishop*) is rooted in the appeal of the "old things" of culture itself, a timeless realm that an-tedates the changes she had celebrated in her early pioneer novels.

Even *My Ántonia*, a much less autumnal work, had reached for certain emblematic moments of vision that would become indelible memories: the image of a plough in the sunset, or of the sun and moon together creating a "singular light." At the second of these scenes, Jim Burden dissolves: "I felt the old pull of the earth, the solemn magic that comes out of those fields at nightfall. I wished I could be a little boy again, and that my way could end there." He gazes hard at Ántonia's face as if to memorize it. She herself finally becomes a series of visionary moments for him: "she had always been one to leave images in the mind that did not fade—that grew stronger with time. . . . She lent herself to immemorial human attitudes which we recognize by instinct as universal and true." This is the monumental Ántonia, fixed in time, not the irreverent, irre-pressible Ántonia of the novel's early pages.

In *A Lost Lady*, Cather stripped away the lyricism that lends eloquence to *My Ántonia*; we see the lady from Niel's viewpoint yet see around and beyond it. Though adept at playing every part demanded of her, she refuses to be hemmed in by his nostalgic myth. Niel loves her house for what it meant to him, but she feels suffocated by it. She feels trapped and buried by her old life. He is aghast that she is "finding new friends among the young men," strenuously animating them with her vitality, and he even discourages one of the Captain's old friends from helping her. Niel imagines that "the right man could save her, even now. She was still her indomitable self, going through her old part." But "her old part" is not the one she now wishes to play.

Cather not only allows her to make a case for herself, to assert her right to live on as she pleases, but refuses to punish her by killing her off—the inevitable consequence of adultery in the nineteenth-century novel. Instead she remarries, and Niel is glad to learn "that she was well cared for, to the very end." There may be a trace of bitterness in the way he says this, and something tawdry in what we hear of her life in Buenos Aires, which tartly reflects on her earlier concern about money and her need to carry on, no matter what. She is made to seem like a kept woman, desperately holding time at bay with her dyed hair and too much make-up. But she does not immolate herself, as Niel wishes. She is not consumed by guilt and regret.

If Cather, with her own love of the past, shares some of Niel's censure of Mrs. Forrester, she also underlines the element of pathology in his reaction, his outrage at the compromises she makes, his need to imprison her in the role that once delighted him. There's a Swiftian horror to his recoil from her affair and a snobbish aura about his disapproval of her widowed life, her determination to live "on any terms." In the spirit of Swift and Orwell, Niel wonders whether the "brilliancy" of beautiful women is "always fed by something coarse and concealed." Jim Burden in *My Ántonia* had realized the intimate link between the carefree laughter of farm girls and the poetry of Virgil ("if there were no girls like them in the world, there would be no poetry"). But Niel's mind is troubled by the sexual source of a woman's high spirits, style, and vitality. He feels haunted by some dark knowledge and uncertainty:

> Would that chilling doubt always lie in wait for him, down there in the mud, where he had thrown his roses one morning?
>
> He burned to ask her one question, to get the truth out of her and set his mind at rest: What did she do with all her exquisiteness when she was with a man like Ellinger? Where did she put it away? And having put it away, how could she recover herself, and give one—give even him—the sense of tempered steel, a blade that could fence with anyone and never break?

This is the unsettling riddle of culture itself, the connection between high and low, as Freud would describe it in *Civilization and Its Discontents*, as Hamlet, Othello, and Lear had obsessed about it in Shakespeare's tragedies.

Like its immediate successors, *The Professor's House* and *My Mortal Enemy*
(1926), *A Lost Lady* is unquestionably a novel of decline, reflecting both an
obscure emotional crisis in Cather and a deep new streak of cultural pessimism.
Willa Cather was withdrawing from the modern world, but announcing it in a
strikingly modern way. The triumphs of Alexandra, Thea, and Ántonia give way
to the bitter disappointments of Marian Forrester, Professor St. Peter, and finally
Myra Henshawe, who once ventured all for love but goes to her grave wondering, "Why must I die like this, alone with my mortal enemy?" A rueful aura of
defeat and disintegration hangs over all three novels, despite the warm elegiac
tone of *A Lost Lady*.

In her prefatory note to a collection of essays, *Not Under Forty*, Cather famously remarked that "the world broke in two in 1922 or thereabouts," leaving
her and her subjects on the far side of a vast cultural divide. That was the year
Cather was writing *A Lost Lady*, the year *The Waste Land* and *Ulysses* broke
upon the world, the year her war novel *One of Ours* was trashed by serious critics. She was still in pain from the defection of Isabelle McClung. She had
always felt a great piety toward the past, though in works like *Death Comes for
the Archbishop*, written soon afterward, it began to dominate her work in a new
way. There, with an emphasis on serenity, resignation, and renunciation, she
created a perfect past from which all passion and conflict had been exorcised.

Cather was sufficiently distressed by the effects of her remark about how
"the world broke in two" to erase it from a subsequent edition. Whatever the
sources of her malaise, it proved surprisingly beneficial for her work. Her personal crisis made her writing hard as a diamond. In an essay called "The Novel
Démeublé," also written in 1922, Cather made her case for the kind of pared-
down, allusive writing exemplified by *A Lost Lady*. It called on novelists to
replace journalistic documentation and Balzacian realism with oblique emotional suggestion. "Whatever is felt upon the page without being specifically
named there—that, one might say, is created." In a famous phrase, she said
that great fiction, like poetry, is marked by this "inexplicable presence of the
thing not named." Hemingway, who dismissed her war novel, would later
make this a basis for his aesthetic.

A Lost Lady is the overture to Cather's middle years, when exceptionally
spare writing and tragic themes replaced the lyricism of *O Pioneers!* and *My
Ántonia* and the circumstantial detail of *The Song of the Lark*. Since she turned
away from the analytic style of Henry James, Cather had always tried to write
simply and resonantly. Her writing had the solid architecture of brick or stone.
In a brief 1920 essay, "On the Art of Fiction," she decried writing that dazzled
the reader with "sharp photographic detail" and "taught us to multiply our
ideas instead of to condense them." Summing up, she says: "Art, it seems to
me, should simplify."

When Jim Burden describes his grandfather's prayers in *My Ántonia*, he
notes: "He had the gift of simple and moving expression. Because he talked so

little, his words had a peculiar force; they were not worn dull from constant use." In a tribute to the short-story writer Katherine Mansfield in *Not Under Forty*, Cather described the writer's way of approaching "the major forces of life through comparatively trivial incidents. She chose a small reflector to throw a luminous streak out into the shadowy realm of personal relationships." Such oblique, miniaturizing effects intensify the mystery and impact of Marian Forrester's sketchy history in *A Lost Lady*.

The Mansfield essay, first published in 1925, provides an especially good gloss on the tragic themes of the middle-period novels. It contrasts "the group life" of any family with "another—secret and passionate and intense—which is the real life that stamps the faces and gives character to the voices of our friends." In this interior life, she says, each of us

> is escaping, running away, trying to break the net which circumstances and his own affections have woven about him. One realizes that human relationships are the tragic necessity of human life; that they can never be wholly satisfactory, that every ego is half the time greedily seeking them, and half the time pulling away from them.

This is as true for Niel Herbert as for Marian Forrester, for Professor St. Peter as for Myra Henshawe. In the end they are all mismatched, disappointed. Life's bright romantic promise has not panned out for them. Cather was not one of Freud's admirers, but she came to share his view of the tragic conflict between the inner child, with its illimitable needs, and the social self—what St. Peter thinks of as "the secondary social man," which he has begun to slough off.

The clash between the unbounded horizon of desire and the limits of actual life was a subject not only for Freud but for the English Romantic poets who were among Cather's favorite reading. It was the theme of Wordsworth's most powerful poems, including "Tintern Abbey" and "Ode: Intimations of Immortality" and it recurs everywhere in Keats and Shelley. The spirit of Keats especially broods over *A Lost Lady*. From his earliest poems to his late letters to Fanny Brawne, Keats too went from idealizing women to lashing out at them. The elusive women, half-temptress, half-goddess, in works like Keats's *Lamia* or "La Belle Dame Sans Merci" are wonderful examples of "the magic of contradictions," but also of male ambivalence toward woman's nature. Niel Herbert is first intoxicated with Marian Forrester, then bitterly disenchanted with her, and finally baffled by her. At the end he wonders whether her bright vitality represented life's genuine promise or was simply an illusion, an effect of artifice and stagecraft.

In "her best days," he recalls, "her eyes, when they laughed for a moment into one's own, seemed to promise a wild delight that he has not found in life." He imagines conjuring her up as a young woman, so that he can "demand the secret of that ardour; ask her whether she had really found some ever-blooming, ever-burning, ever-piercing joy, or whether it was all fine play-acting." The

very language here—the ardor, the skepticism, the longing for permanence—
is Keatsian to the core. So is the question Niel dreams of asking, which the
novel itself does ask, without imagining that it can be answered.

F. Scott Fitzgerald was so taken with *A Lost Lady* that he feared it would
look like he had plagiarized it in his portrait of Daisy in *The Great Gatsby*.
Cather graciously brushed aside his concern. In fact both writers were devoted
readers of Keats and intuitively grasped the real spirit of Romantic poetry,
which was less the celebration of nature in *O Pioneers!* or the Virgilian pastoral
of *My Ántonia* than the divided consciousness of Keats's odes, charged with
questions rather than affirmations. *A Lost Lady* combines Cather's plangent
sense of the past with her ambiguous, skeptical feeling about life's possibilities.
The novel conjures up the shade of the young Marian Forrester just as Keats
plumbs the mystery of the Nightingale or the Grecian Urn with queries they
cannot answer. Niel tries to cordon off the past, to arrest it in its flight; in his
great odes, Keats's speakers confront an image of their desire as its ecstatic energy slips away from them.

> Was it a vision, or a waking dream?
> Fled is that music:—Do I wake or sleep?

A DIFFERENT WORLD

From Realism to Modernism

THE AUTHORITY OF FAILURE

It felt strange indeed in the fall of 1996 to mark the centennial of the birth of F. Scott Fitzgerald, a writer whose work feels so fresh, who died young and seems perpetually young, like Keats, the poet he most loved. Fitzgerald scholars and enthusiasts met at Princeton to celebrate his life and work, and on his actual birthday I found myself speaking about him at the Great Neck Public Library on Long Island, in the very town where he conceived *The Great Gatsby* and began writing it in 1922 and 1923. Great Neck was then a fashionable new suburb beloved by show business types like Eddie Cantor. But it was also the place where Fitzgerald and his wife threw themselves into the wild, sad, drunken parties he portrayed with satiric gusto, yet also a tragic edge, in *Gatsby*, parties that mean as little to Gatsby himself as to the guests who sponge off him.

Fitzgerald's Great Neck years were not the happiest time of his life, though he seemed, like Gatsby, to be sitting on top of the world. He had only one writer friend there, Ring Lardner, who drank even more than he did. Fitzgerald himself tended to go off on benders for two or three days in New York. It was there he wrote his only play, a political fantasy called *The Vegetable*. He hoped it would make his fortune, but it died in Atlantic City in November 1923, on its way to a Broadway staging that never took place. This was a taste of failure he never forgot. "I worked hard as hell last winter," he later wrote, "—but it was all trash and it nearly broke my heart as well as my iron constitution." He was only twenty-seven years old.

Many people would have been surprised at the sad note of waste and decline that seeps into this comment—partly because his best work was still before him, but also because Fitzgerald and his young wife, Zelda, were just then the very embodiments of youthful energy and style for fashionable America. But our continuing sense of Fitzgerald as a poet of lyrical longing and dreamy aspiration can easily obscure the darker, more somber side of his work. Like his friend Hemingway, Fitzgerald was not simply a writer but a figure, a cultural icon who would always remain linked in the popular mind with the fizz and exuberance of what he himself dubbed the Jazz Age.

A key element of the Fitzgerald myth, especially that sense of his perpetual high spirits, began with his connection to Princeton. Much to his embarrassment, he never graduated, but in a sense he graduated posthumously when the university became the much-visited haven for his voluminous papers. When Fitzgerald arrived in 1913, Princeton was in many ways far from a serious university, though it had become more serious under its most recent president,

Woodrow Wilson, who had gone on to become governor of New Jersey and, earlier that year, president of the United States. It was a very white, very male university, hardly expensive by today's standards but accessible mainly to the children of the rich, those from "good" families who had gone to the elite boarding schools. While Fitzgerald's friend and classmate, Edmund Wilson, later America's leading literary critic, managed to get a splendid education there, for many others the gentleman's C was a way of life, and there was a long tradition behind it. You could get by quite well without cracking a book. Most Ivy League colleges were so frivolous that the more thoughtful under-graduates, Fitzgerald included, later believed they had gotten their education only after they left school.

As a Midwestern boy, Fitzgerald felt like an outsider, not one to the manor born. But *as* an outsider he came to love everything about the school: the dating rituals, the drunken sprees, the football games he never managed to compete in, the varsity shows he helped write with his friend Wilson, which became the high points of his college career. A few years later, in the spring of 1920, he published *This Side of Paradise*, a thinly disguised version of his college experiences; to everyone's surprise, it became an overnight sensation. Like Lord Byron in 1812, he awoke and found himself famous. His commercial and literary careers were launched. Soon afterward, in a grand ceremony in St. Patrick's Cathedral, he married the belle of Montgomery, Alabama, Zelda Sayre, a daffy and beautiful young woman who had once broken off her engagement to him because his financial prospects looked so dim.

With the wild success of the book and the brilliance of their marriage, Scott and Zelda embarked on a decade-long odyssey as the shining young couple whose beauty, charm, and sense of fun embodied the devil-may-care spirit of the new postwar generation. Whether they were living among theater people in Great Neck, swimming with other expatriate Americans along the Riviera, or writing amusing little stories and articles about each other for stylish popular magazines, Scott and Zelda came to personify the youth culture of the Jazz Age, when life seemed like a drunken lark and a good part of privileged young America went on a big hedonistic spree.

Living in the public eye, always furnishing good copy, Scott and Zelda helped write the script that cast them as legends. This was the beginning of the media age, with its emphasis on personality, novelty, showmanship, and style. The best one can say about Fitzgerald's role as a celebrity was that, unlike Hemingway, he never believed his own clippings and always kept a good deal of himself in reserve. He had a sense of being answerable to posterity rather than to the newspapers.

Part of Fitzgerald's problem came later, during the Depression, when his name remained associated with his portraits of the rich; this in turn was mistaken for admiration, approval, and envy of their fashionable lives. But Fitzgerald, though fascinated by the manners and morals of the rich and intrigued by the freedom that came with their money, nourished a burning ambition to be a serious writer, someone whose work would matter to people fifty years later. Among the rich he never forgot that he was an outsider, but Fitzgerald also proved to be a wickedly percipient yet empathetic observer. He took note of how much and yet how little their money could do for them—how much freedom and style it gave them, but how little protection it furnished against disappointment and unhappiness, as he himself would later discover.

Fame is famously fickle. Soon after the crash, everything from the 1920s seemed like ancient history, a tale of sound, fury, and innocence before the fall, and Fitzgerald's shallow celebrity was no exception. Within a few years Fitzgerald would be an icon of a different kind: once a byword for youth, elegance, and exuberance, he would become an emblem of failure, a back number. Once again, with a vengeance, the myth would obscure the writer and come close to obliterating him. This remains the lesser-known Fitzgerald, the gifted but chastened Fitzgerald of the 1930s. The legend of his decline, which he helped broadcast—everyone who met him during his last years in Hollywood heard it—continues to haunt his reputation today.

Perhaps the worst moment in this unhappy story comes in the fall of 1936. F. Scott Fitzgerald is about to turn forty, no easy transition for someone whose life was once identified with the passion and promise of youth. Things had long since begun to sour for him. In 1930, Zelda, increasingly desperate to find herself as a writer, a dancer, or simply someone who had a life in her own right, had suffered a nervous breakdown, and since then she had been in and out of hospitals. Scott himself had had a critical success in 1925 with *The Great Gatsby*, a book admired by writers as different as Edith Wharton and T. S. Eliot, but commercially it was a disappointment compared to his apprentice novels and widely read short fiction. His effort to storm Broadway had failed. Once he had had an almost golden facility; his prose had a spontaneous poetry all its own. But he struggled for nine years to finish his next novel, *Tender Is the Night*, which got a mixed reaction from critics and public when it finally appeared in 1934. Reviewers were puzzled and ambivalent; sales again fell short of expectations. Fitzgerald had become a chronic alcoholic, and the failure of his most ambitious book sent him over the edge. But he did more than abuse his health and break down: in the spring of 1936, in a shocking series of articles for *Esquire*, he wrote about his problems in a harsh, unsparing, confessional vein—something familiar to us today from memoirs and talk shows, where dysfunction has gone public, but completely unheard-of in those more reticent and buttoned-up times.

In these articles Fitzgerald hardly came clean about either his marital problems or his drinking, but he described in surprising detail his loss of confidence and vitality, his failure to take care of his talent, his waste of energy on simply being a celebrity—on his need to be liked, to be charming and personable, to be all things to everyone he knew. This was not yet a therapeutic culture, though Dale Carnegie was just then making his auspicious debut. Hemingway, his friend and cruel rival, who would spend a lifetime burnishing his own myth, was aghast that Fitzgerald would expose himself in this way. Their mutual editor, the legendary Maxwell Perkins of Scribner's, a man of infinite discretion, was saddened and disapproving. Another friend, John Dos Passos, couldn't imagine how anyone could waste his energy on merely personal problems when the whole world was coming apart. But these poignantly written articles brought Fitzgerald's name before the public again, as it had not been for a long time.

Into this picture came a reporter for the *New York Post*, perhaps not so different then from the Murdoch-driven paper it is today, a reporter with the ominous name of Michel Mok, to interview Scott for his fortieth birthday. There was a scent of blood in the water. Fitzgerald was under a nurse's care at an inn in Asheville, North Carolina, but he was still drinking, and the reporter described in wretched detail how he kept popping up for a thimbleful of gin from the makeshift bar, how his face twitched and hands shook as he described his life and made the usual drunkard's rationalizations.

The front page of the *Post* the next day told the whole story: "The Other Side of Paradise / F. Scott Fitzgerald, 40, / Engulfed in Despair / Broken in Health He Spends Birthday Re- / gretting That He Has Lost Faith in His Star." What had been eloquent if not wholly frank in Fitzgerald's own articles became pathetic in the tabloid version. *Time* picked up the story and gave it much wider currency. The effect on Fitzgerald was catastrophic. He thought he was ruined and took an overdose of morphine, but luckily vomited it up. He felt his credibility as a writer and a serious man was gone. The *Post* interview was perhaps the lowest point he reached in the decade, but it fixed his image as a washed-up, self-pitying writer, a miserable caretaker of his talent, the relic of a distant and unlamented era. (Even a decade later, when reviewers like Lionel Trilling wrote about *The Crack-Up*, Edmund Wilson's collection of his late friend's articles and letters, they would still point to the effects of the *Post* story on Fitzgerald's waning reputation.)

In a limited sense this image endures even today. No one, of course, thinks of Fitzgerald as a pathetic drunk—a "rummy," as Hemingway called him. In fact, Fitzgerald's reputation bounced back amazingly after the war, and *The Great Gatsby* is secure as one of the most widely taught of twentieth-century American classics. But most people still think of his life in the 1930s as the melancholy aftermath of his brilliant decade, a time of decline and failure as vividly portrayed by the man himself. There is no doubt how much he really *did* suffer during this period, when his golden marriage was all but over, when drink and disappointment often made him behave strangely, when his stories were no longer welcome in the magazines that had provided most of his income, when even Hollywood could find no real use for his talents. In the popular mind today, he remains the chronicler of the Jazz Age, the flapper era, the frivolous youth culture, and the more flagrant excesses of the American Dream.

To the socially minded critics of the Depression years he was simply irrelevant, and this view has curiously been resurrected among some scholars today, who have repeatedly drawn attention to neglected black, proletarian, or women writers of the period. It would be an exaggeration to say that an interest in Zora Neale Hurston, Langston Hughes, or the Harlem Renaissance has been purchased at the expense of, say, *The Great Gatsby*, *The Sun Also Rises*, or *As I Lay Dying*. Making space for the rediscovered books of Hurston or Nella Larsen doesn't undercut Faulkner and Fitzgerald: the literary canon isn't a zero-sum game, even if the syllabus may be limited. But to many professors Fitzgerald has simply become one of the dead white males, more a burden than a revelation.

Actually, Fitzgerald's work has weathered the politics of multiculturalism reasonably well. Students today still respond passionately to his books, especially *The Great Gatsby*, even if their teachers have gotten bored with connecting it to the American Dream, and perhaps have passed some of this boredom on to their charges. There are scholars who feel that Fitzgerald deals with much too narrow a class of privileged Americans. This echoes the widespread disapproval of his work last heard during the Marxist thirties, when proletarian critics grew tired of reading about the Lost Generation and the emotional entanglements of wealthy expatriates on the Riviera in the 1920s. As the young critic Philip Rahv wrote in the Communist *Daily Worker*, reviewing *Tender Is the Night* when it appeared in 1934, "Dear Mr. Fitzgerald, you can't hide from a hurricane under a beach umbrella." The hurricane, of course, was the Depression, which exposed the failure of capitalism and drew attention to the class antagonisms that Americans had usually tried to soften and blur.

To his credit, Rahv understood that Fitzgerald's most complex novel, with its assortment of wealthy and idle characters, was a fierce yet subtle indictment of the rich, not a sycophantic tribute to them. But the interests of readers and critics alike had turned elsewhere; the language of fiction, partly under Hemingway's influence, had grown simpler and more plebeian, and Rahv felt that Fitzgerald's celebrated style obscured his harsh theme, "transforming it into a mere opportunity for endless psychologizing." Psychology was generally seen as self-indulgence by thirties Marxists, for it drew attention to personal problems—a bourgeois luxury—rather than the social structures of exploitation and injustice. The *New Masses* reviewer of Henry Roth's *Call It Sleep*, published the same year, had mocked the young protagonist as a "six-year-old Proust" and lamented that "so many young writers drawn from the proletariat can make no better use of their working class experience than as material for introspective and febrile novels." The same buzzword, "introspective," appears in Rahv's review of Fitzgerald when he complains of the novel's "delicate, introspective wording . . . its tortuous style that varnishes rather than reveals the essential facts."

It's certainly no news that Marxist critics of the 1930s were none too fond of introspection or stylistic elaboration. They thought they already knew all "the essential facts" about our society, and they preferred a more hard-boiled manner to reveal the unvarnished truth as they saw it. Ironically, Fitzgerald's own style did become more spare and direct as his life went downhill after 1929 and 1930. The content of his work changed as well, for he was struck by the eerie parallels between his own change of fortunes and the fate of Americans at large, who had prospered in the twenties when he was at the peak of his fame, then broken down just as Zelda had her first nervous breakdown in 1930, and suffered deeply as he himself came apart after the relative failure of *Tender Is the Night.* "My recent experience parallels the wave of despair that swept the nation when the Boom was over," he wrote in the last *Esquire* piece. Fitzgerald felt he had experienced the Crash in personal terms.

In short, it was an already deeply wounded man who was mocked in the *Post* in 1936 but, oddly, someone who had become more of a Depression writer than his critics realized, a writer whose own reverses made him more sympathetic to the failure and misery of others. There's the irony here: like another great figure from the 1920s, the seemingly mandarin poet Wallace Stevens, Fitzgerald was attacked by the camp which, in his own fashion, he was actually trying to join. (The Depression and its new literary culture had provoked and invigorated Stevens after years in which he had written no poetry.) Still, as Fitzgerald began to see himself not as the favored child of fortune, the young prince in the fairy tale, but as a representative man, his work became *more* introspective, not less. In the 1930s, taking stock of his own problems, trying to salvage something out of his losses, Fitzgerald virtually invented the confessional mode in American writing. Later works like Mailer's *Advertisements for Myself* or Robert Lowell's *Life Studies* (both published in 1959) would have been impossible or quite different without the much-maligned example of the "Crack-Up" essays. This suggests that it may not be the lyrical, romantic Fitzgerald of the 1920s who most claims our attention today but the shattered, disillusioned Fitzgerald of the 1930s; not the poet of early success, romantic possibility, and nostalgic regret but the hard-edged analyst of personal failure and irretrievable loss, the man who redeemed in his work what was slipping away from his life, who achieved a hard-won maturity even as he described himself as a failure, an exhausted man, a spent force.

This is the final irony—that the dark image of Fitzgerald in the 1930s came from Fitzgerald himself, not from the malicious pen of Mr. Mok and the *Post* headline writers. Starting with stories he wrote in 1929 and 1930, long before the "Crack-Up" articles, Fitzgerald gave an unsparing account of what was going wrong in his life. More than that, he made creative use of it to take his work in a daring new direction. As in the 1920s, *he* was the source of the myths that circulated around him, but unlike Hemingway he saved them for his own work, not for the gossip columns. This points to a great difference between a writer who breaks down and cannot work and one who uses his frustrations and disappointments as new material, producing work that shows a quantum leap in human understanding.

In one sense his writing after 1929 or 1930 became the opposite of everything that preceded it. He became the poet of failure and decline rather than of youthful, romantic inspiration. With each revision of the book that became *Tender Is the Night*, the expatriate life of his initial models, Gerald and Sara Murphy, gave way to the troubled history of Scott and Zelda, including her breakdown and his sense of creative blockage and diminished promise. Yet in other ways this was a clear development from things he had already written. In "Early Success," an essay written in 1937, when such success was long behind him, he recalled how everything seemed to go awry for his young heroes. "All the stories that came into my head had a touch of disaster in them—the lovely young creatures in my novels went to ruins, the diamond mountains of my short stories blew up, my millionaires were as beautiful and damned as Thomas Hardy's peasants." Fitzgerald came to realize there was always a kernel of tragedy, a dose of melancholy in these stories, a backdrop of dark clouds that he had not yet, when he wrote them, encountered in his own life. But it was all bathed in a romantic glow, a poignant sense of thwarted possibility, loss, and regret.

One of my favorite examples is a 1922 story called "Winter Dreams"—Fitzgerald himself said it was a rehearsal for *The Great Gatsby*. The very title embodies the story's contradictory moods of hope and frustration, dream and denial. The young hero, with the slightly foolish name of Dexter Green, has invested *his* winter dreams in a young woman with an even more banal name, Judy Jones— a forerunner of Gatsby's great flame, Daisy Buchanan. By the end, after she has toyed with him for years, he learns that Judy Jones has married a man who mistreats her and, worse still, that she has lost her looks, has become commonplace. This is a shattered dream rather than one that is simply unfulfilled: "The dream was gone. Something had been taken from him." He thinks of

> her mouth damp to his kisses and her eyes plaintive with melancholy and her freshness like new fine linen in the morning. Why, these things were no longer in the world! They had existed and they existed no longer.
>
> For the first time in years the tears were streaming down his face. But they were for himself now. He did not care about mouth and eyes and moving hands. He wanted to care, and he could not care. For he had gone away and he could never go back any more.

No one can fail to be moved by the tender simplicity of these lines, which combine a plaintive feeling of loss with a hard-nosed sense of inevitability: these things once seemed possible, but now they are not to be. In his early work Fitzgerald was a dreamer, but not someone who believed that dreams could be realized. Already in the 1920s, his work had a tragic and elegiac cast, yet he still valued his heroes, like Gatsby, for their generous illusions, for the glow of possibility that surrounded them. *The Great Gatsby* is a novel about a self-made man, about the grandeur and failure of our dreams, but also about all that distinguishes them from reality. Think of Nick Carraway's harsh judgment of Daisy Buchanan and the illusions Gatsby has fabricated around her. But think also of Nick's surprisingly warm farewell to Gatsby himself, to whom he alone remains loyal. With his impetuous faith in people, Gatsby is the kind of creature Emily Dickinson had in mind when she wrote, "I dwell in Possibility—/ A fairer House than Prose."

This poetic glow of possibility was precisely what diminished into prose for Fitzgerald after 1929 or 1930, starting with some harsh stories about the disintegration of a marriage—"The Rough Crossing" (1929) and "One Trip Abroad" (1930)—stories he never reprinted because they were too close to the material he was developing for *Tender Is the Night*. Both stories, like the novel, are about Americans abroad; both use travel and even bad weather as metaphors for what distracts people from each other, wears them out, and shows up the fault lines in their marriages; and both make disillusion and disappointment their central theme. While "The Rough Crossing" centers on a single bad trip, "One Trip Abroad" follows a couple through years of aimless wandering as they move from one hollow niche of "Society" to another. Now broken in health, they have finally landed in a sanitarium in Switzerland, "a country where very few things begin, but many things end." There they see another couple and, in a melodramatic flash of lightning, realize that the pair are their younger selves as we saw them at the beginning of the story, not yet tired, ill, decadent, and out of tune with each other. Despite its unusual Gothic touches, "One Trip Abroad" is a schematic miniature of *Tender Is the Night*—its heroine is even called Nicole—in much the same way "Winter Dreams" contains the seed of *The Great Gatsby*.

But "One Trip Abroad" also connects directly with Fitzgerald's next important piece of fiction, one of his most resonant and enduring stories, "Babylon Revisited," first published in 1931—probably the only work of his as widely taught as *The Great Gatsby*. "Babylon" also has its nonfiction parallel in an oft-quoted essay written around the same time, "Echoes of the Jazz Age," which has always been a staple for historians writing about the 1920s. The essay debunks the very period with which Fitzgerald's name is associated; by 1931, less than two years after the stock market crash, the twenties already felt like ancient history. ("Only Yesterday," as Frederick Lewis Allen put it in the title of his famous social history, also published in 1931.) Fitzgerald sees the period somewhat nostalgically, with mock horror, as his own and the culture's "wasted youth," a "flimsy structure" built on "borrowed time," that came tumbling down when the players lost all their confidence. But whatever elegiac glow could be found in the essay was ruthlessly excised from the story, where there is almost nothing of value to redeem the old way of life.

Charlie Wales returns to Paris, the scene of many a debauch in the 1920s, to reclaim his daughter from the fierce sister-in-law to whom he had been forced to surrender custody. His wife had died under circumstances for which he bears some responsibility; his own health had broken down under the weight of his drinking; but now, like Fitzgerald himself in "The Crack-Up," he has somehow managed to paste it all together. Sober and serious for the first time in years, he wants his daughter back before her childhood has completely passed him by, before she no longer really knows him. Much of the story is taken up with his reflections on his former life. "He suddenly realized the meaning of the word 'dissipate' [a word that had also figured significantly in "One Trip Abroad"]—to dissipate into thin air; to make nothing out of something." "He remembered thousand-franc notes given to an orchestra for playing a single number, hundred-franc notes tossed to a doorman for calling a cab." This had once seemed insouciant, carefree, impulsive. "In retrospect it was a nightmare."

His high-strung sister-in-law blames him unfairly for her sister's death, but much as she dislikes him, she is beginning to relent. She can see that he's a changed man, a man who desperately wants his daughter, his future, restored to him. But into this volatile mix comes a blundering, drunken couple from his earlier life—"sudden ghosts out of the past," revenants like the couple in "One Trip Abroad"—the worn remnants of a time when they all lived for pleasure, for the moment. After one particularly jarring intrusion, Charlie's sister-in-law pulls back, refuses even to see him. The doppelgänger couple, with their ill-timed reminder of how he used to live, has done him in, ruined him all over again. Fitzgerald had once focused lovingly on characters who dreamed a life for themselves, imagined an idyllic or romantic future. Now he writes about people who have learned that the past cannot easily be set aside: our actions have consequences, and the ghosts of our earlier selves will continue to haunt us, without a trace of their old romantic blush.

Elements of Fitzgerald's new hard-edged, almost tragic outlook can be found in virtually every significant piece of writing he did in the 1930s—in stories like "Babylon Revisited" and "Crazy Sunday," in the essays, letters, and journals collected in Edmund Wilson's landmark edition of *The Crack-Up* (the book that helped restore Fitzgerald's reputation after the war), in novels like *Tender Is the Night* and the unfinished *Last Tycoon*, and even in commercial formula fiction like the seventeen Pat Hobby stories he wrote for *Esquire* in the last year of his life, which continued appearing month after month after Fitzgerald's death in December 1940.

These terse and brutally satiric stories, written mainly for money, give us Hollywood through the eyes of a hack writer, not Fitzgerald himself but the kind of facile mediocrity who drove him crazy while he was trying to learn screenwriting as a serious craft. As his name suggests, Pat Hobby is the sort of talentless fellow who knows all the little tricks, tricks so old they don't even work anymore, who steals ideas and connives for screen credit but wouldn't dream of actually reading the books he's supposed to adapt. According to the neat formula Fitzgerald evolved, Pat Hobby gets his well-deserved comeuppance in every story.

Fitzgerald could never write about people entirely from the outside, without insinuating something of himself into them, seeking some authentic core of emotion in their character. The mildly despicable Pat Hobby is washed up, an ineffectual remnant of the silent-film days, hanging on by a thread. So Fitzgerald injects some of his own sense of failure into this man, just as he had invested it, much more subtly, in the inexorable decline of his more obvious alter ego, Dick Diver, in the second half of *Tender Is the Night*. Pat Hobby has always been a hack, even when the little tricks still came off, but Dick Diver was once a serious, promising, brilliant man, a psychiatrist who made an unfortunate marriage to one of his former patients and, though he was acutely aware of the risk of being bought, gradually allowed himself to be taken over by her wealthy family as a private nursemaid. But this is only one of many reasons that his life goes awry. Diver's decline has no single, definite cause; it has too many causes. Fitzgerald may have modeled it on the vague disintegration of the ambitious and idealistic young minister in one of his favorite novels, Harold Frederic's *The Damnation of Theron Ware* (1896). Diver's fate rivals the precipitous descent of Hurstwood in Dreiser's *Sister Carrie* as the greatest failure story in American literature. Like the gifted but flawed protagonist of Santayana's 1936 novel *The Last Puritan*, Diver is a man who simply "peters out."

This focus on failure is what makes the last phase of Fitzgerald's career resonate so strongly with the Depression for us in ways that contemporary readers failed to register. The critics who attacked him for still writing about the rich were as misguided as the friends who accused him of wallowing in self-pity. Fitzgerald had always worked not simply by investing himself in his characters but by mythologizing himself, heightening his dreams and disappointments into representative moments, carrying much of the culture on his own back. Now, as the culture tried to forget him, to relegate him to the past, he had turned the miseries of his life into confessional fables, becoming again a symbol of the age, this time an unwelcome one, a reminder of how much America had lost. Comparing himself as usual to Hemingway, he wrote in his notebooks: "I talk with the authority of failure—Ernest with the authority of success." The operative word here is "authority," not simply "failure": *Something broke in me, but I speak with the weight of experience. I am a different animal, someone who has gained a hard-won awareness.* In Whitman's famous words from "Song of Myself," "I am the man, I suffer'd, I was there." He lived it, but rather than buckling under its weight, he also wrote it, transforming it into a story he'd never told before.

Eventually, *Tender Is the Night* grew on readers who had disliked or misunderstood it when it first appeared. Hemingway, though he later came grudgingly to admire the book, at first objected fiercely to the touches of tragedy in the novel. His own view was more stoical, fatalistic. "We are all bitched from the start," he wrote to Scott. "You see Bo, you're not a tragic character. Neither am I." A few years later Fitzgerald set out to write a tragic novel about Holly-wood at exactly the moment he was satirizing it in his stories. The source was not self-pity, as Hemingway mistakenly imagined, but something richer, harsher, deeper—a sense of deprivation and loss that alters one's outlook, a new maturity that comes through in every line of "The Crack-Up," *Tender Is the Night*, and the unfinished text of *The Last Tycoon*.

My emblem for this last phase of Fitzgerald's work is a little-noted passage in his 1932 essay "My Lost City," one of the greatest tributes ever written to New York. Near the end, Fitzgerald does what many New Yorkers did that year, just as the Depression was approaching its darkest point: he goes up to the top of the Empire State Building, then newly built, and finds that instead of scal-ing the heavens, as he might have hoped to do, he gets a better perspective on the terrestrial world below:

> Full of vaunting pride the New Yorker had climbed here and seen with dismay what he had never suspected, that the city was not the endless succession of canyons that he had supposed but that *it had limits* [his italics]—from the tallest structure he saw for the first time that it faded out into the country on all sides, into an expanse of green and blue that alone was limitless. And with the awful re-alization that New York was a city after all and not a universe, the whole shining edifice that he had reared in his imagination came crashing to the ground.

On one level this passage is a little joke on the provinciality of New Yorkers, much like Saul Steinberg's celebrated cartoon of the contracted world west of the Hudson as seen from Manhattan. But something more serious is also hap-pening here. The "country on all sides," the "expanse of green and blue that alone was limitless," is clearly an allusion to the great climax of *The Great Gatsby* when, before the narrator's very eyes, "the inessential houses began to melt away until gradually I became aware of the old island here that flowered once for Dutch sailors' eyes—a fresh, green breast of the new world." There, in Fitzgerald's grandiose leap of imagination, man had come "face to face for the last time in history with something commensurate to his capacity for wonder." Here, in "My Lost City," that dreamy, utopian capacity for wonder, the whole imagined sense of possibility, crumbles before a new sense of limits.

The *Gatsby* passage, though hedged with subtle qualifications, speaks for the poetic, expansive Fitzgerald of the 1920s; this new version, with its tone of mockery and humility, speaks for the chastened Fitzgerald of the 1930s, a writer who accords far better with our own painfully acquired sense of limits. What was the watchword of social policy and political frustration in postsixties America if not a sense of dashed hopes and more limited goals? This is the clear-eyed, un-self-pitying mood that underlies every Fitzgerald text of the Depression decade, most patently in "The Crack-Up," which his contemporaries misread and undervalued, though it should have been as congenial to hard times as it is to our own postutopian era.

This was the mood of the great Romantic crisis poems, which formed Fitzgerald's sensibility long before he fully understood them, before he actually experienced their peculiar mixture of elation and regret, loss and renewal, crisis and resolution. This was the disintoxicated mood of the last stanza of Keats's Nightingale Ode, a poem Fitzgerald could never read aloud without tears. On the surface it appears that Fitzgerald goes from being a pie-eyed romantic in the twenties to a disillusioned realist in the 1930s, except that this very disintoxication is a crucial moment of the Romantic imagination. It's the moment of clarity when the dreamer, the visionary, is humanized by loss, by suffering, by fellow feeling—when the mental traveler, no longer adrift in "faery lands forlorn," turns homeward, in Keats's words, to the "sole self," the self without romantic illusions.

All these poems proceed from a sense of visionary possibility, through a maelstrom of inner crisis and loss, and finally to a modest rededication to new beginnings, exactly as Fitzgerald does in the "Crack-Up" essays. This was the itinerary of both "Tintern Abbey" and "Ode: Intimations of Immortality," but perhaps Wordsworth put it best in his "Elegiac Stanzas" of 1805, written after his beloved brother John had been lost at sea. He gazes at a turbulent seascape painted by a friend and thinks how he would once have added some calming touch, a romantic glow—in Wordsworth's famous phrase, "the gleam, / The light that never was, on sea or land." (How much like the shimmer of iridescence Fitzgerald provided at every turn in his early stories, even the sad ones.) But Wordsworth tells us he can do this no longer. His sense of reality has been altered by his brother's unexpected death. Nature now seems anything but benign:

> So once it would have been,—'tis so no more;
> I have submitted to a new control:
> A power is gone, which nothing can restore;
> A deep distress hath humanised my soul.

These troubled but grimly hopeful lines, stark yet consoling, could serve as a motto for all the neglected writing of F. Scott Fitzgerald's last decade, when the lyrical dreamer gave way to the damaged but undaunted survivor, transfigured by misfortune and a new sense of maturity. With its sober and sobering vision, this may be the work of Fitzgerald's that makes the deepest claim on us today. Even Hemingway, ever competitive, came around in the end. "Scott's writing got better and better, but no one realized it, not even Scott," he told his son Gregory. "The stuff he was writing at the end was the best of all. Poor bastard!"

EDMUND WILSON: THREE PHASES

As WE GROW remote from the cultural situation in which they worked, even great critics are more likely to be forgotten than reconsidered. Unlike literature, criticism actually develops from one generation to another as critics build on their predecessors by exploding or assimilating them. Unless it survives on style alone, criticism, as a timely mediation between writers and readers, quickly grows dated. Edmund Wilson's work, however, is a notable exception. It tells us a good deal that we can go back to his first reactions to Hemingway or Fitzgerald in the twenties and still respond strongly to his fresh treatment, despite the deluge of criticism and biography that now surrounds those authors.

Wilson himself has also been enveloped in posthumous information, much of it coming from his own hand. In the past few years we've learned a great deal, perhaps too much, about Wilson the man. There have been seven volumes of diaries, a large and very readable selection of letters, a separate edition (recently enlarged) of his correspondence with Vladimir Nabokov, a number of biographies and memoirs by and about Mary McCarthy in which Wilson figures chiefly as the villain, and a widely reviewed biography by Jeffrey Meyers. A comprehensive life of Wilson by Lewis Dabney should soon follow. While Meyers is respectful of Wilson the writer, and tries hard to imagine the marriage to McCarthy from Wilson's point of view, his book focuses perhaps too much on Wilson the almost clinical lover, the difficult husband, the distracted, intermittent father, the imperious personality. What we surely need is a detailed intellectual biography, which Meyers's work does not pretend to be. It's not entirely without interest, if true, that Wilson and his friend John Peale Bishop once shared the body of Edna St. Vincent Millay—I forget which one took the upper half and which the lower—but it's hard to see what it adds to our understanding of Wilson the writer. Wilson's curious attitudes toward sex had already been clear from his fiction, especially the story "The Princess with the Golden Hair" (from the once-banned novel *Memoirs of Hecate County*), and from his published journals. We need to go back to his work—to ask searching questions about how he still engages us as contemporary readers, and to explore the range of his manifold connections to the cultural and political life of his times.

We can think of Wilson's career as an itinerary in three phases, as he himself once tried to do in some notes for an autobiographical novel. (These can be found in his truncated journals of the 1940s.) He was a commanding figure from the early twenties, when he began writing for *Vanity Fair*, to the early seventies, when he died; and only H. L. Mencken has been as posthumously prolific. I'm struck by the extraordinary variety of Wilson's huge body of writing, from the drama and fiction and poetry at which he was not very successful to the travel writing that supports much of his later work. His early criticism, itself enormously varied, offers a good point of departure. Besides introducing an often puzzled audience to the new American writers of his generation and to the difficult modernists—he wrote some of the first articles about them to appear in the American press—he also wrote about Chaplin movies, popular culture, vaudeville, and the Ziegfeld Follies. In its freshness and abundance, *The Shores of Light* is surely the best collection of his journalism: ninety-seven articles from the twenties and thirties, full of the excitement of discovery, yet only a selection of what he published then. It would be hard to imagine a more spirited literary chronicle of the era.

Nothing illuminates the conditions under which Wilson worked better than these weekly pieces, written under deadline yet always alert to new subjects. Today we no longer have a steady critic writing weekly essays for a magazine like *The New Republic*, Wilson's main forum during the period. His protégé Malcolm Cowley followed him in this chair, and Wilson went on to write less regularly but at greater length for *The New Yorker*. His old nemesis, Stanley Edgar Hyman, who had once dismissed him as a mere journalist, was perhaps the last to occupy such a critical perch, taking on every important new novel for *The New Leader* in the 1960s. Perhaps the vigorous literary journalism of John Updike and Gore Vidal has come closest to Wilson's in scope, though without his daunting critical authority; their collections of essays provide a highly readable record of the literary culture for at least two decades following Wilson's death in 1972. Today, the weekly book columnists in the *Washington Post*, Jonathan Yardley and Michael Dirda, still cover a wide range of subjects reflecting their own idiosyncratic curiosity, but this is at best an echo of the earlier role of the strategically placed critic monitoring the culture as a whole.

The young Wilson tried his hand at everything. From the very beginning, his was a nineteenth-century approach to criticism: the generalist as man of letters—judicial, didactic, authoritative—within a much more book-oriented culture than we have today. Unlike his Victorian predecessors, he was often playful as well, doing comic turns and writing imaginary dialogues between very different authors and critics. In one anonymously published twenty-page piece called "The All-Star Literary Vaudeville," he offered a sweeping yet entertaining account of virtually every writer on the scene. Like an expert tour guide, he takes on these writers with a no-nonsense directness that would become his hallmark and a remarkable self-assurance about what he thinks of each one of them. These really are encounters, a favorite word of his during the period. And even when he is wrongheaded or rudimentary, he engages the writers, some of them quite difficult, with the full weight of his own experience and sensibility. If a case can be made against the Wilson of *The Shores of Light*, it is that his almost perfect pitch for prose fiction deserts him when he turns to poetry. At one of the great moments in American poetry, he favors friends like Elinor Wylie or Millay while doing scant justice to major figures. like Robert Frost, Wallace Stevens, Hart Crane, or William Carlos Williams. More a socially oriented critic than a technical one, he excels at connecting writers to their milieu, an approach more suited to the social and biographical texture of fiction than the more self-enclosed linguistic density of poetry.

Despite this limitation, *The Shores of Light* brings back the glory days of Wilson as a critic, wonderfully in tune with new literary movements, responding to a great creative surge as yet unappreciated by the world at large. Wilson once confessed that he loved talking about writers to people who hadn't yet read them—exactly the opposite of the academic critic who writes only for the initiated. And this love of introducing a writer to an audience, in print or in conversation, enabled Wilson to give free play to the narrative gifts never fully realized in his fiction. When he writes about Proust and Joyce in *Axel's Castle*, he actually sets about to recreate their work—not simply to retell the story, but to convey it in terms so nuanced with interpretation, irony, and judgment that it becomes something new, a redaction that is itself novelistic.

What makes the pieces so impressive when you reread them is not only his range and style but the supple agility of his dealings with different kinds of authors. In the middle of the book he even slips in a manifesto called "The Critic Who Does Not Exist," in which he maps out the warring critical and literary schools of the time, each propagating its own doctrine with little attention to other viewpoints, and with no genuinely disinterested critic ("that is, a writer who is at once first-rate and nothing but a literary critic") prepared to challenge them. This pointless warfare sounds a little like the theory-driven scene of recent academic criticism. Amid these political factions and rival methodologies, Wilson saw himself as just that kind of critic, someone moving easily among many kinds of writers, constrained by no dogma or party spirit, committed to literature itself in all its protean variety.

Assembling his articles long after they first appeared—*The Shores of Light* did not come out until 1952, as a sequel to the collection of more recent work called *Classics and Commercials*—Wilson dramatizes his critical stance with a witty juxtaposition, setting a piece on H. L. Mencken alongside one on Woodrow Wilson's tenure as president of Princeton. We would normally think of Mencken and Woodrow Wilson as polar opposites: Wilson so moralistic, impassioned, rhetorical; Mencken ever the iconoclast, eagerly deflating moralistic cant. But the young critic presents them to us as two rigidly determined minds, repetitious, predictable, and inflexibly themselves. A part of Wilson's sensibility is drawn to this kind of stubborn conviction: it helps explain his lifelong interest in the effects of New England Puritanism on later American culture. At the end of each piece he does a dialectical turn, showing how Mencken's dogmatic quality gives him power as a satirist, and honoring Woodrow Wilson's unbending idealism, which would cause him so much trouble in his conflict with the U.S. Senate.

Edmund Wilson had a streak of sympathy for both positions, especially the idealism, which was in short supply during the Coolidge years when he wrote his piece. But the critical temperament, as he understood it, was just the opposite of what these men possessed, for they were strongly defined personalities who always knew exactly who and what they were. The later Edmund Wilson would become quite magisterial, but the young critic was gifted with a Keatsian negative capability that opened him up to very different literary experiences. And the innovative, devil-may-care spirit of the 1920s was exactly the setting for such a critic.

The twenties concluded for him with the publication of *Axel's Castle* in 1931, which set the pattern for the later stages of his career. If the reviews collected in *The Shores of Light* show Wilson as the working critic, the writer in the trenches taking each new book as it comes, then *Axel's Castle* is the synthesis that rounds off the whole period, the longer view with which he took leave of each phase of his literary life. Wilson reached for permanence in the same way with *To the Finland Station* (1940), which provided a coda for his Marxist adventure in the 1930s, and *Patriotic Gore* (1962), the enduring result of his return to American culture and to his own origins during the 1940s and 1950s.

It's characteristic of these longer, more ambitious projects that Wilson, conscientious puritan that he was, persisted and carried through with them long after he had outlived the original impulse to write them. He had already converted to socialism by the time he completed his book on the modernists, just as he'd grown disaffected with Marxism and the Soviet Union when he put the finishing touches to his account of the revolutionary tradition from the 1790s to 1917. This is a tribute to Wilson's work ethic—he started and he was damn well going to finish—but it gives these books a slightly odd character, even a certain incoherence. In *Axel's Castle*, for example, the great chapters on Proust and Joyce portray them not simply as formal innovators but as social observers deeply involved with the life of their times. But by the end of the book he comes close to condemning them for retreating to a symbolist castle, an impenetrable fastness of art for art's sake—exactly what he had already shown they had *not* done.

Wilson's own shifting views created a fissure within the book, as Malcolm Cowley later observed. They also led to his active political commitments of those years: the unsigned 1931 manifesto in which he urged liberals, radicals, and progressives to "take Communism away from the Communists"; the Depression journalism and travel writing collected in *The American Jitters* (1932) and *Travels in Two Democracies* (1936); and finally, his masterpiece, *To the Finland Station*. This book was the result of his conversion to radicalism, which led him initially to take to the road for *The New Republic* to cover the local and human effects of the Depression, doing real reporting, not simply literary journalism. Wilson would always insist that the Depression had hit America with the impact of a flood or earthquake, a vast cataclysm that altered the whole landscape. Like many young intellectuals, he himself had already been skeptical of the booming business civilization of the 1920s; for them, as he later said in "The Literary Consequences of the Crash," written especially for *The Shores of Light*, "these years were not depressing but stimulating. One couldn't help being exhilarated at the sudden unexpected collapse of that stupid gigantic fraud. It gave us a new sense of freedom."

Wilson's work in the early thirties was not reviewing but traveling, interviewing, social reporting. Like so many other newly radicalized writers, he set out to record how ordinary Americans were coping with hard times. But gradually he conceived the project of writing a biographical history of the whole revolutionary tradition—an unlikely enterprise for someone with little economic or political background. *To the Finland Station* holds up today, I think, as his greatest book, not so much as intellectual history—he always remained skeptical about the intricacies of Marxist dialectics—but as sheer human drama, with an immense sweep that carries us along even in postutopian times. Putting aside the sectarian polemics and scholastic debates so often fatal to radical intellectuals, he was able to bring something unique to bear on Marxism: the same critical sensibility and vital human interest he had brought to modernism. He examined Saint-Simon and Marx with all the restless curiosity he had just trained on T. S. Eliot and Gertrude Stein.

Many years later, V. S. Pritchett described it as "perhaps the only book on the grand scale to come out of the Thirties—in either England or America. It contains, to a novel degree, the human history of an argument." *To a novel degree*: this is a finely phrased remark. It's ironic, in the light of Wilson's own limitations as a novelist, which he acknowledged when he compared himself ruefully to Fitzgerald, that *To the Finland Station* has many of the qualities of great fiction—a bold narrative thrust, for example, and striking, larger-than-life characters—seasoned with a mixture of irony and empathy toward the eccentric figures who made up the Marxist tradition. Above all they are intellectuals, caught up, as Wilson then was, in a passion for changing the world, for actually altering and affecting history. In "The Revolutionary Personality," a review written for *Partisan Review* in 1940, Meyer Schapiro described how Wilson's portraits "impose themselves by their concreteness, finesse, and sympathy . . . like the great fictional characters of literature." But he also pointed out the connection to Wilson himself by noting that in this book "the conditions of intellectual work become as concrete, as unforgettable, as the moments of action." Wilson put flesh and blood on the revolutionary tradition without silencing his own critical voice.

Denis Donoghue has suggested that Wilson was not really a literary critic because he didn't exert interpretive pressure on a writer's language, but there are different ways to be sensitive to language, as there are different kinds of critics. Always the portraitist, the historian of motive and behavior, in books like *To the Finland Station* and *Patriotic Gore* Wilson bears down on language as a key to individual temperament. He looks closely at Marx's writings, including his early poetry and student writings, scrutinizing his imagery to grasp the configurations of his mind. This approach was certainly original in the 1930s, when Marxism was invariably debated as doctrine and ideology, not as the written traces of an individual mind. (Perhaps the closest parallel was Kenneth Burke's pioneering 1939 essay on the rhetoric of *Mein Kampf.*) Later Wilson would closely inspect General Grant's letters and memoirs, for he was interested not only in style but in language as the basis for a social or psychological portrait, as if he were shaping a character in fiction.

This brings me to Wilson's third major project, *Patriotic Gore*, his book about the literature of the Civil War. This book emerged from his enormous dissatisfaction with contemporary America after 1940, which led to his withdrawal to the country, his turn toward autobiography, a fascination with his own family background, and a gradual disengagement from the current critical scene. *Patriotic Gore* is preceded by a notorious introduction that sees nations in biological terms, devouring each other like "sea slugs." This is often seen as arbitrary and unconnected to the book—some of Wilson's friends tried to convince him to remove it—but it's intrinsic to the mood in which he wrote the work as a whole. *Patriotic Gore* demonstrates not only his recoil into the American past but his attraction to those qualities—essentially qualities of republican virtue—that he could not find in the public world of the American present.

If *To the Finland Station* is about personality, as revealed in the youthful passion to change the world, then *Patriotic Gore* is about character, as reflected in traits like stoicism, persistence, fortitude, skepticism, and clarity of mind. Wilson's new heroes are no longer intellectuals but aging warriors like Grant, Lee, Sherman, and that staunch ex-warrior, Justice Oliver Wendell Holmes. The book begins with an unlikely revolutionary, Harriet Beecher Stowe, whose extraordinarily *humane* exposure of the Southern slave system derived from her close reading of the character of its participants and her appeal to cherished family values, which were undermined when the families of slaves were cruelly separated. But Wilson's book finds its center in the unflappable figure of Grant—in battle utterly unconscious of danger; then, as a dying man, stoically completing his memoirs in the teeth of great suffering, to provide for his family after his death. "In what Grant did and in what he wrote," Wilson finds "something of the driving force, the exalted moral certainty, of Lincoln and Mrs. Stowe." Wilson admires Grant not only as a man but also as a plain stylist, expressing exactly what he wanted to say with strength and simplicity "in the fewest well-chosen words." His Grant was the writer whose prose intrigued both Matthew Arnold and Gertrude Stein. "These literary qualities, so unobtrusive," says Wilson, "are evidence of a natural fineness of character, mind, and taste."

So this, I think, is where Wilson himself came to rest, as an old man no doubt identifying with Grant's infirmities as well as his temperament, admiring "the dynamic force and definiteness of his personality." This is Wilson as a rock-ribbed American character, no longer the Keatsian seismograph of the cultural and political scene but withdrawn, like his father before him, into "a pocket of the past." Wilson could be immensely eloquent about this "old fogeyism," as he liked to describe it. At one point he called himself a man more or less of the eighteenth century, at other times a man of the 1920s, two periods of relative civility that preceded times of political crisis. But for all of the diversity of his interests in his last years—he explored Russian literature, learned Hebrew and wrote about the Dead Sea Scrolls, went to Haiti, studied Hungarian—in the end he became something of a nativist, whose fundamental values were invested in a Roman and republican ideal he linked to people like Grant and Holmes. In the peroration to *Patriotic Gore*, after some eight hundred pages, he describes the aged Holmes as "perhaps the last Roman," and as "a just man, a man of the old America, who having proved himself early in the Civil War, had persisted and continued to function through everything that had happened since, and had triumphed in remaining faithful to some kind of traditional ideal."

What an odd yet moving place for Edmund Wilson to settle down: the free-living modernist of the 1920s has been transformed into the quintessential American of an earlier era; the critic gifted with a Keatsian receptivity has become the eccentric Johnsonian figure we can still recall from Wilson's later years. So we conclude where we began, with Wilson's bristly personality forming a barrier between us and his work. It may well be that the more we learn about Wilson, the less we like him. This certainly happened to me when I first reviewed his journals of the 1930s, with their detached, almost clinical record of his sex life. But he lived his writing life on a heroic scale.

As a reader he remained omnivorous to the end. In his last years he was rediscovering minor American realists like Harold Frederic and Henry Blake Fuller. His passion to record his life and thinking never abated; he can be compared to the great Victorians in his plenitude and persistence, in the strength of his work ethic and the moral calling he brought to the practice of criticism. His curiosity, his gift for languages, kept him from turning provincial. At a time when other critics grew enamored of technique, he used everything from social history and biography to psychoanalysis to hold fast to the elusive human dimension of literature. He saw reading and writing as encounters colored by sensibility, style, personal history, and social practice. He never lost confidence in his own power to make sense of his impressions, to translate other people's language into limpid, terse, and resonant language of his own. As his large personal presence fades, the real Edmund Wilson, the one who matters most, survives in his books.

A GLINT OF MALICE

FOR AT LEAST a quarter of a century, from the late 1940s to the early 1970s, Mary McCarthy was more than an author, more than a cultural figure. To the savvy, college-educated young of that time she was a byword, a role model: the bad girl who got away with it, the wicked satirist who held everyone up to ridicule, the Vassar girl who instructed us in worldliness and sexual sophistica- tion, the brilliant critic and essayist whose work exploded the stereotypes of feminine sensibility—in short, the fastest gun in the intellectual world, dar- ingly sexual yet sharply intelligent.

This formidable literary personality was very much on my mind when I found myself teaching in Paris in the fall of 1980, a figure compounded from innumerable essays and interviews; from the barbed stories in her first book, *The Company She Keeps*, and the more condescending mockery of her best- selling novel *The Group*; from her trenchant Vietnam reportage of the late six- ties, but also my vivid memories of a recent summer spent in Italy with *The Stones of Florence* as an indispensable guide. But this treasured mental image of mine had no resemblance to the dignified, grey-haired lady I finally met in January 1981, shortly before I returned to New York. I had called her at the suggestion of a mutual friend, and she invited me first to tea, then to a larger party at her comfortable flat on the rue de Rennes. There she played the role of Mrs. James West, the perfectly correct wife of a recently retired foreign ser- vice officer.

At first our conversation was flat and formal. I had no real reason for visit- ing with her except to meet an icon of my youth, a writer I had intensely ad- mired who was now our last well-known expatriate author in Paris. But how long could we go on talking about the names for different fish in French and English? After three-quarters of an hour things took a different turn when I happened to mention the recent adventures, sexual and political, of some of her old friends in New York. A glint of malice lit up her eyes. She was hungry for details. "Oh, that would make a wonderful story," she said more than once. Not quite, I thought: a wonderful Mary McCarthy story, something quite spe- cial and different. Soon we were getting on so famously that McCarthy invited me to a party the following week, a few days before my departure from Paris. There I encountered a cross-section of the expatriate scene of the 1980s: the aging children of Russian émigrés from the 1920s, dowager countesses out of Henry James, wealthy American bachelors who clipped coupons and followed the affairs of *vedettes* of the Paris Opera and young dancers in the ballet troupes. There was a delicious taste of decadence in the air. To my great sur- prise, McCarthy's French pronunciation was appalling, though she knew the language well and had even done translations. I was struck by how American she still seemed after decades in Paris. The word among her friends, as I was told after her death in 1989, was that "Mary spoke French so badly that you could understand every word."

Later, during the 1990s, after reading and rereading her work over a period of several months, I could better understand who Mary McCarthy was, what kind of stories she had written, and why she had disappeared into the grey-haired lady, to burst forth only when our talk turned to the wayward New Yorkers whose foibles had once fed her imagination. Her last two novels, *Birds of America* and *Cannibals and Missionaries*, had been grave, ponderous affairs, with little of the clever, malicious wit her friends feared and other readers savored. She told interviewers she had given up fiction—she said she lacked the social information. But even the memoirs she went on to write seemed lamely matter-of-fact, even trivial at times, compared to *Memories of a Catholic Girl-hood* and such dazzling autobiographical essays from the midfifties as "Artists in Uniform," about an unsettling encounter with an anti-Semitic colonel, and "My Confession," which traced her political initiation and concluded with her credo as a historical observer.

McCarthy's work always had its detractors, such as Alfred Kazin, who said she had "a wholly destructive critical mind," and Randall Jarrell, who famously lampooned her in his brisk roman à clef, *Pictures from an Institution*, which is almost a second coming of her own wicked academic satire *The Groves of Academe*. Even William Barrett in his memoir of life among the New York intellectuals, *The Truants*, who describes McCarthy in larger-than-life terms as one of the most extraordinary women of our time, observes that her novels and stories had "wit, sharp observation, extraordinary intelligence, an unflagging brilliance and elegance of language," but lacked "the simple virtue of feeling."

Those who did not know McCarthy in her prime could be less generous. For younger readers who saw her only as the sharp-tongued woman embroiled in a gratuitous lawsuit with Lillian Hellman, the McCarthy mystique had little meaning. Feminist critics, who have exhaustively promoted and analyzed nearly every other woman writer, have shown remarkably little interest in her. If we could understand why her work has faded, we might learn a great deal about why it mattered so much in the first place.

The first problem with Mary McCarthy's fiction is that not much happens in it. This above all has kept most of her books from gaining a wide readership. Also, it's often said that her characters are little more than intricately described specimens, pinned and mounted like butterflies but incapable of growth or change. Her own reply, apropos of her best-selling novel *The Group*, is that they are "all essentially comic figures," and hence "it's awfully hard to make anything happen to them." But this dictum is belied by comic novelists from Fielding and Jane Austen to Evelyn Waugh and David Lodge. Like those writers, McCarthy is essentially a novelist of manners, but she lacks much of their gift for mixing flat and round characters—comic stereotypes and three-dimensional beings who can develop by undergoing real experiences.

In satiric works like *The Oasis* and *The Groves of Academe*, McCarthy is wonderful at setting the stage and inserting the actors as comic props. She has the born essayist's gift for describing a world but not the novelist's power to make it move, or make it moving. Her strength is less for emotion than the anatomy of emotion, less for personality than the tics of personality. Like Waugh she has a nose for society—not unconnected with snobbery—and an unerring sense of the ridiculous. Her easily recognizable caricatures achieve a crushing accuracy of outline by flattening her characters' human density. But having laid them out she has no idea of what to do with them, not from lack of talent but out of a dark view of human possibility.

At the end of "Portrait of the Intellectual as a Yale Man," the longest, most ambitious story in *The Company She Keeps*, the blithe, vapid Jim Barnett, who had always skimmed across life's surfaces, has lost his old ease and innocence. He had flirted casually with politics and ideas as he flirted with women. He had given a convincing imitation of serious purpose. But his brief infatuation with Meg Sargent, who is McCarthy's surrogate in these stories, has disrupted his smooth life, sexually as well as ideologically, and left him badly frightened and "professionally bewildered," convincing him "that he must keep down his spiritual expenses—or else go under." After the charade of being a serious man, he recoils into his convenient marriage and convenient job. "It was self-knowledge [Meg Sargent] had taught him; she had showed him the cage of his own nature. He had accommodated himself to it, but he could never forgive her."

Here for once McCarthy's analytic touch works beautifully. She is essentially a *moraliste*, a dry, lucid anatomist of human nature in the tradition of Montaigne, La Rochefoucauld, and Benjamin Constant, whose great love story *Adolphe* is one of the most acutely analytical novels ever written—about passion, no less. For McCarthy, self-awareness and lucidity, the very things that descend like a plague on Jim Barnett, are nearly absolute values—and, as we all know, her prose is astonishing for its clarity and precision. But far from being healing and therapeutic in the manner of popular fiction, this bolt of self-knowledge brings us harsh news of our own limitations, the iron cage of personality. For Jim Barnett this news is deadly. "In some subtle way, Jim had turned into a comfortable man, a man incapable of surprising or being surprised. The hair shirt he wore fitted him snugly now."

McCarthy's critics might say that the decline of Jim Barnett into a rather seedy alcoholic and sell-out reveals less about the intractability of human nature than about her superior attitude toward her characters, especially since it is her own alter ego, Meg Sargent, who shows Jim "the cage of his own nature."

McCarthy's good friend Dwight Macdonald, who (like John Chamberlain and Malcolm Cowley) may have been one of the models for Jim Barnett, and who certainly sat for the boisterous and obtuse Macdougal Macdermott in *The Oasis*, would have been sympathetic to the anti-Stalinist polemic of the "Yale Man." But he wondered privately about *The Groves of Academe*:

> Why does she have to be so goddamned snooty, is she god or something? You begin to feel sorry for her poor characters, who are always so absurd or rascally or just inferior and damned—she's always telling them their slip's showing. She doesn't *love* them, that's the trouble, in the sense of not feeling a human solidarity or sympathy with them—can't create real characters without love, or hate which is also a human feeling; she had just contempt and her poor puppets just wither on the page. . . . The trouble is she is so damned SUPERIOR to her characters, sneers at most of them and patronizes the rest.

This is as shrewd a comment as any later critic would make, exaggerated perhaps, but not unfair to the brittle writing and impoverished human atmosphere of weaker novels like *The Groves of Academe* and *The Group*. This is why McCarthy needs the autobiographical protagonist, why *The Company She Keeps* and *Memories of a Catholic Girlhood* are much better than the satiric books. McCarthy needs a character she can't feel superior to, someone who can convey not only her wit and cleverness but her weakness and sense of vulnerability, her second thoughts, misgivings, and mistakes. And she herself was the only candidate.

What McCarthy's work badly needed was the "unfinished woman" that Lillian Hellman evoked, the woman before she became a duchess, a princess among trolls who so emphatically knew her own worth. Just before sitting down with Mary McCarthy, I reread several volumes of Leon Edel's biography of Henry James. I was most struck, especially in the second volume, by the tremendous drama of James before he became Henry James, when he was a struggling journalist just learning to write novels, churning out copy to make ends meet, trying to interest editors in his work and gain a toehold in the social world that would become his subject.

In her two best books, especially *The Company She Keeps*, McCarthy is an unformed character in search of a self, wrestling with knaves and naifs who are not really her equal. Yet she is also troubled, put upon, ambivalent. Always an autobiographical writer, McCarthy needed her personal history to furnish her with a character she would never fully understand and with a ready-made story that would intrigue and challenge her. Her own story gave her the pieces of a plot she wasn't good at inventing and a character to whom she *can* make things happen.

From the time she wrote her first book Mary McCarthy set out to shock, and with the celebrated story "The Man in the Brooks Brothers Shirt" she fully succeeded. She was after all the *shiksa* in a group of largely Jewish intellectuals, a scarlet woman in a decade that thought itself more proper and serious than the 1920s. Innocently enough, she needed a slight aura of scandal to set her creative juices flowing. When I first read "The Man in the Brooks Brother Shirt" twenty years later, this account of Meg Sargent's casual seduction in a Pullman compartment was still a byword for sexual daring and sustained wit and brilliance. For its time, the heroine's intransigent intellectuality was as original a literary creation as her casual (though easily embarrassed) sexual adventuring. Every charge that would later be leveled at McCarthy—her snobbishness, her undue care for social niceties, her wobbly moral compass, her traffic in gossip, her sense of superiority—was not only showcased in this story but became part of its theme as the protagonist constantly questions her own behavior.

If feminist critics show no interest in *The Company She Keeps*, it may be because Meg Sargent is neither a victim nor a role model. The company *she* keeps is entirely male. Her only relationship with other women—including the wives of the men she sleeps with and the women in her own radical bohemian milieu—is competitive and dismissive. The wives are caricatures of middle-class respectability; the others offer little competition. "It was not difficult, after all, to be the prettiest girl at a party for the sharecroppers."

Meg is completely oriented toward men yet intensely critical of them. Only they can give her the stage on which to shine, the platform from which she can look down on them. Nearly every one of the stories is about the Gifted but Confused Woman who gets embroiled with the Unsatisfactory Male, beginning with the husband and the lover in her first story, "Cruel and Barbarous Treatment," and winding up with her psychiatrist and her second husband in "Ghostly Father, I Confess." The Brooks Brothers man, who seems impossible to begin with—a "self-made man," a Babbitt—turns out to be the least unsatisfactory male in the book, though he shares one trait that disqualifies several other men: he is simply too nice to her, and horribly claims to see the sweet girl concealed inside her.

But in her whirl of projections—and much of the story is the quicksilver flow of her imaginings, her rationalizations—she turns even his vulgarity to advantage. If he is not an intellectual, as she is, then he must somehow represent Ordinary Life, with which intellectuals are always in danger of losing touch. Leapfrogging from one fantasy to another, she imagines she sees in him what she misses in all the men she knows in New York, "the shrewd buyer's eye, the swift brutal appraisal." Of the men she had been with, she feels,

> In one way or another they were all of them lame ducks. The handsome ones, like her fiancé, were good-for-nothing, the reliable ones, like her husband, were peculiar-looking, the well-to-do ones were short and wore lifts in their shoes or fat with glasses, the clever ones were alcoholic or slightly homosexual, the serious ones were foreigners or else wore beards or black shirts or were desperately poor and had no table manners. Somehow each of them was handicapped for American life and therefore humble in love.

This brilliant inventory, like the rest of the story, highlights the way Mc-Carthy's judgments—for all her confessional intensity, sexual bravado, and intellectual arrogance—were neither religious, moral, nor political but rather social: they were judgments about class, taste, style, and, above all, appearances. As the love interest of such men, she felt somehow devalued. When she left her lover Philip Rahv to marry Edmund Wilson, as she explained in her posthumous *Intellectual Memoirs*, it was important that he "came from the same stock, Anglo-Saxon, Presbyterian." After years among actors, bohemians, and Jews, "there was a certain feeling of coming home, to my own people." Yet in dealing with the New York intellectual world of the 1930s in this last, unfinished book, McCarthy's writing comes alive again, just as her conversation did at our first encounter.

Meg Sargent hasn't the least *moral* qualm about the prospect of being seduced by Babbitt on the train. "Still," she thinks, "the whole thing would be so vulgar; one would expose oneself so to the derision of the other passengers." In *Memories of a Catholic Girlhood*, McCarthy recalls how, as a schoolgirl, her desire to shine was replaced by the "fear of appearing ridiculous" as a "governing motive" of her life, a motive that no doubt contributed to her lifelong need to highlight the ridiculous in other people's behavior.

But with "The Man in the Brooks Brothers Shirt," surprisingly, the romantic side of McCarthy, her tenderness, overcomes this fear, overcomes even her social and intellectual scruples. "For the thing was, the man and the little adventure of being with him had a kind of human appeal that she kept giving in to against her judgment. *She liked him.*" For once she is unguarded, pleasantly embarrassed, entirely without cunning. Meg Sargent's gloriously tacky adventure on the train is also Mary McCarthy's self-transcendence as a writer. Here she dramatizes and overcomes the defects attributed to her fiction: that she is too judgmental and superior, that she doesn't love any of her characters, that, as Kazin insists, she reserves indulgence only for herself.

McCarthy could not really keep up the benign vein of this story. Malice, mockery, and witty derision would remain central to her fiction, as in the often inane world of *The Groves of Academe* and *The Group*, where she expertly puts the puppets through their paces. At her best in these books, as in her nonfiction, she could be an amusing satirist and an entertaining reality instructor, enclosing a barbed essay on progressive education in the first book and a daring brief on sexual initiation and contraception in the second. But few readers took much notice when she pursued the other vein of *The Company She Keeps*, her sense of the confusion, passivity, insecurity, and entrapment that lay just beneath her heroine's brash confidence. Her tempestuous marriage to Edmund Wilson brought her face to face with these feelings.

Wilson, who figures as Meg's second husband, Frederick, in "Ghostly Father, I Confess," which deals with her analysis, and who reappears under another name in McCarthy's next important story, "The Weeds" (1944), apparently treated her with none of the gentle indulgence that Meg despised in the men of *The Company She Keeps*. These two grim stories—the second dealing with her failure to leave Wilson—serve as a bridge from the buoyant sexual comedy of *The Company She Keeps* to the harsh Dickensian coming-of-age portrayed in *Memories of a Catholic Girlhood*, which she began writing immediately after "The Weeds," just as her unhappy marriage to Wilson was disintegrating.

McCarthy always conceded that Wilson turned her into a "creative" writer by sitting her down in a room—just as Colette's husband had done to her— and telling her, with the authority not just of a husband but of America's leading critic, that she had a talent for imaginative writing. In her final, unfinished memoir she acknowledged this again, but with a surprisingly ambivalent and bittersweet edge: "If he had not shut the door firmly on the little room he had shepherded me into . . . I would not be the 'Mary McCarthy' you are now reading. Yet, awful to say, I am not particularly grateful."

But the harshness she ascribed to Wilson made her a writer in an even deeper way, for it brought back the vulnerability she had tried to put behind her. In "Ghostly Father, I Confess," Meg Sargent begins by confidently skewering her analyst: his taste is vulgar, his intelligence scarcely matches hers. "She had enjoyed doing that malicious portrait," she thinks. When he questions her about it, she says simply, "I've got a good eye for social types, and I've had a lot of practice." But what she's really doing, it turns out as the story goes on, is resisting the reflux of her melodramatic past, the burden of a miserable childhood and an unhappy self that she had suppressed until marriage to Wilson made her feel helpless and imprisoned.

Mary McCarthy's parents had both died in the flu epidemic of 1918, when she was six, and until she was rescued by her grandparents, she and her brothers were raised by cold, strict, comically sadistic guardians out of *Nicholas Nickleby*. But this was material for just the kind of Victorian novel she would never dream of writing. "I reject the whole pathos of the changeling, the orphan, the stepchild," thinks Meg. "Her peculiar tragedy (if she had one) was that her temperament was unable to assimilate her experience; the raw melodrama of those early years was a kind of daily affront to her skeptical, prosaic intelligence." Though a lapsed Catholic, McCarthy felt that confession was good for the soul, even confession to an analyst she loathed as her husband's surrogate. Her first story inspired by the marriage to Wilson, "Ghostly Father," was also the first story in which she could grapple with her orphaned, emotionally deprived past, and it became a prologue to all her later autobiographical writing.

"Ghostly Father" and "The Weeds" intimate that the humiliation and misery she felt as Wilson's wife brought her close to a breakdown, but also tore down her defenses and gave her access to the vulnerable child behind them. Graham Greene said that an unhappy childhood is a writer's capital for life, but McCarthy drew on this legacy only under the greatest stress. *Memories of a Catholic Girlhood* had the kind of Dickensian plot and characters to be found nowhere else in McCarthy's work. But this dry and preternaturally clear book is anything but Victorian melodrama. In her concern with getting the facts right, a dominant motif in her work, and in the give and take between the individual chapters and her interpolated comments and corrections, McCarthy managed to make her improbable past accessible to her skeptical, prosaic intelligence.

Memories was the last book in which McCarthy was fully able to strike this balance between tenderness and intelligence, between "the facts" and the feelings. Some of this can also be found in the essays collected in *On the Contrary* and in her wonderful book on Florence, and it reappears sporadically in her late memoirs and the deeply felt obituary tributes she wrote for her friends in her last years. McCarthy's cool wit and sophistication proved bracing for more than one generation, as her wicked satirical eye influenced writers as different as Philip Roth (in his first collection of stories) and Wilson's friend Nabokov (in *Lolita*).

But she was at her best when her intelligent mockery wasn't merely mocking, when she herself was implicated in it. Scornful satire may have been McCarthy's defense against feeling, but at her best the vulnerable woman could be seen behind the highbrow scold. Satire was her vehicle for social observation and the kind of sexual comedy that meant so much to my generation, the generation that came of age just before the Pill, just before the sexual and behavioral revolutions of the sixties took hold.

For us McCarthy was the chronicler not only of a hard-won sexual freedom— "Get yourself a pessary," she says, in the opening line of the best-known chapter of *The Group*—but also of social discomfort and sexual embarrassment: the foolish display, the drunken seduction, the safety pin on the underwear. Her best heroines were those who not only flouted conventions but had a hard time getting away with it, who did things against their better judgment and often found themselves in tight situations largely of their own making. It would be too simple to say that the Pill did her in by altering sexual mores forever, that she lost her subject and her audience when these matters became too easy, too free of conflict and misgivings. In truth, they are never easy; life always provides us with rich sources of embarrassment.

Only comedy can assuage the complications that intelligence can never fully control. Especially for a Catholic, comedy hints at forgiveness, implies an act without serious consequences. Meg Sargent's misgivings over the episode on the train only ease up when she can see it as farce rather than high drama, vulgar or tender seduction rather than her own self-betrayal. For, as she says, "The world of farce was a sort of moral underworld, a cheerful, well-lit hell where a Fall was only a prat-fall after all."

SILENCE, EXILE, CUNNING

The Modern Writer as Exile

There have been writers in exile for almost as long as there have been any writers at all. Sometimes they have served as the articulate voice of masses of people, even whole nations, that had been cast out of their land. Surely the most eloquent example was the anonymous author of Psalm 137, which begins with the plangent sound of mourning ("By the rivers of Babylon, / there we sat, / sat and wept, / as we thought of Zion") and with a firm refusal to make music for his captors ("How can we sing a song of the Lord / on alien soil"), then continues with a pledge of faith ("If I forget you, O Jerusalem, / let my right hand wither; / let my tongue stick to my palate / if I cease to think of you"), and finally concludes with a bloody curse on Israel's enemies:

> Fair Babylon, you predator,
> > a blessing on him who repays you in kind
> > what you have inflicted on us;
> > a blessing on him who seizes your babies
> > and dashes them against the rocks!

But the psalmist was only one of the voices of Israel in its Babylonian exile. Much of biblical prophecy is bound up with the theme of exile and redemption. Prophets like Isaiah, Jeremiah, Ezekiel, and Zechariah either warn Israel of impending disaster, look for explanations for the catastrophe that has already occurred, or console the people with the promise of God's renewed favor and a return to their homeland. In the hands of the astonishing poet or poets whom scholars have labeled the Second Isaiah, this theme of exile and repatriation is gradually spiritualized into a vision of messianic redemption that would sustain Jews through the centuries. First God sends Cyrus of Persia to restore the people, their city, and its holy temple. "He shall rebuild My city / And let my exiled people go / Without price and without payment" (45.13). But by the end the prophet describes the city as an eternal one, giving us a vision of the end of days:

> For behold! I am creating
> A new heaven and a new earth;
> The former things shall not be remembered,
> They shall never come to mind. . . .
> For I shall create Jerusalem as a joy,
> And her people as a delight;

And I will rejoice in Jerusalem
And delight in her people.
Never again shall be heard there
The sounds of weeping and wailing. (65.17–19)

As far back as the book of Exodus, the Hebrew Bible had introduced the theme of exile and redemption into the lexicon of Western thought, where it would become a potent strand of religious vision and utopian social hope. For the Jews themselves the Bible, the hopes that sprang from it, and the many commentaries upon it were essential in preserving their nationhood during their long sojourn in the diaspora. But these ideas deeply infused other traditions as well. We have only to think of the Hebraic strain in British working-class radicalism, which found such inspiration in Blake's "Jerusalem," with its idea of building God's city in "England's green and pleasant land," or the redemptive motif in the culture of African-American slavery and oppression, as crystallized in poignant spirituals like "Go Down, Moses," with its refrain of "Let my people go."

But there is another kind of exile to which writers have always been subjected: as banned individuals, out of favor with authority. With his cult of personality, the Roman emperor Augustus was the archetype of the modern dictator, as he showed when he banished the cynical and amusing Latin poet Ovid to distant exile on the Black Sea, in part for the indiscretions of his *Art of Love*. If Ovid was a malicious wit who overstepped the bounds of Roman decorum, Dante was a political animal who was banished when his faction, the Guelphs, lost out in the civil strife that raged in Florence at the turn of the fourteenth century. In writing his *Divine Comedy* he paid back some of his enemies, consigning them to horrendous and humiliating punishments. But the poem also gave the fate of individuals a cosmic dimension, turning his longing for home into a spiritual journey and a road map to paradise.

As the fate of Ovid and Dante shows, not every exiled writer had his tongue ripped out. Unhappy as the man himself might be, the writer may thrive in exile. Writers often compensate for their powerlessness by escalating their verbal power, perhaps by addressing posterity when they cannot reach their own countrymen, or by transcending factional polemic with a larger, more embracing vision, or by becoming the kind of stringent critical mind that only an outsider can be. Ovid and Dante experienced their banishment as a personal catastrophe and never ceased to hope for a return. But Voltaire in his long exile from Paris, like Solzhenitsyn in rural Vermont two centuries later, became virtually a rival center of authority, a model of intellectual freedom and moral courage that could not be intimidated. The tumultuous welcome Voltaire received on his return to Paris in 1778, which may have hastened his death, was a prophetic omen that foretold the collapse of the Old Regime. As Solzhenitsyn would put it, the free mind of a writer is like an independent government in his

own country, something that can be silenced but not really suppressed. "Manuscripts don't burn," said another suppressed Russian writer, Mikhail Bulgakov.

The challenge of the exiled writer as gadfly and outsider runs all through the
nineteenth century, from the voices of Byron and Shelley in Italy, mocking
post-Napoleonic England as a land of political repression and moral hypocrisy,
to the cynical wit of Heine in Paris, the revolutionary writing and agitation of
Marx in London, and the rivers of verse and political satire that came streaming from Victor Hugo on the Channel islands of Jersey and Guernsey, where
he had taken refuge from the dictatorship of Napoleon III. But from the viewpoint of our own bloody century, the fate of these writers, like the changing
fortunes of their countrymen, seems remarkably benign. In exile they became
titanic figures, rival centers of power, separated from their compatriots but per-
forming on a much larger stage. The twentieth century tells a far darker story.
Our century didn't invent mass murder or ethnic cleansing; governments had
uprooted and destroyed large masses of people before. But now they found remarkably efficient methods for doing so, and discovered too that it could be
more effective to imprison and even kill writers than to exile or silence them.
Compared to modern totalitarian regimes, the autocracies of the eighteenth
and nineteenth centuries seem careless and benevolent.

Besides killing or intimidating large segments of Russia's own population,
Stalin's secret police murdered some of its greatest writers, including Osip
Mandelshtam and Isaac Babel. Stalin's successors reverted to more traditional
methods, packing Solzhenitsyn off to America, Andrei Sakharov to a closed
city off-limits to Westerners, and other dissidents to Siberian labor camps. On
the other hand, many German writers escaped the clutches of Hitler, since
they were among his first targets when he assumed power in 1933. The transfer of literary and scientific talent from Germany and Austria to America in
the 1930s was one of the great intellectual migrations in the history of
mankind. Its effects on the film industry, on psychoanalysis, on music and the
fine arts, and on many fields of research and scholarship in American universities were incalculable. In Los Angeles alone the émigré community at one
time included Thomas Mann, Bertolt Brecht, Bruno Walter, Billy Wilder,
Theodor Adorno, Fritz Lang, Arnold Schoenberg, and many lesser lights.

Other centers of genius in exile could be found at the New School for Social Research, with its amazing concentrations of European talent; among Yiddish writers in New York, who spoke for a large immigrant population; among
the New York painters, who were so receptive to the styles that Hitler had
banned, from expressionism and surrealism to abstraction; or around Einstein
in Princeton. Younger figures like Hannah Arendt rose from anonymity to
exert a huge influence. Most but not all of these refugees were Jewish; some
were Communists, like Brecht, or married to Jews, like Thomas Mann, or simply desperate to breathe free air after their books had been burned and their art
banned. All of them suffered tremendous linguistic and cultural dislocation.

They were cut off from their language, separated from the world that had nurtured them, face to face with an American public whose taste and judgment seemed not only alien but often unfathomable.

As moving and momentous as the story of these political refugees might be, they are not primarily the ones I have in mind in describing the modern writer as an exile. Many of these writers, artists, and scientists left Europe when their careers were already launched. It was precisely their fame that protected them from the Nazis and enabled them to find refuge more easily. Mann and Brecht remained German writers, whether they stayed here or returned. Ill and exhausted, Freud took refuge in England only at the end of his life, when his work was nearly behind him. None of these established figures tried writing in English. Meanwhile, émigré painters and musicians spoke an international language that needed no translation. The writers and artists who concern me here were not basically political outcasts fleeing their country for fear of their lives. In most cases they were expatriates: their exile (or emigration) was self-chosen, however deep were the pressures that made it necessary. Whether they continued writing in their own language or, with stupendous difficulty, mastered another, they each created a new idiom, a more modern idiom, that was the verbal expression of their dislocation and expatriation.

Taken together or separately, these modernists, with their own lives in upheaval, devised striking new modes of understanding, for they were intensely alert to a world in almost constant upheaval. But they had other things in common. To a remarkable extent their loyalty was to art rather than to any nation-state. They saw art as a way of developing new forms of consciousness that could register the seismic shocks of modernity. MAKE IT NEW was the premise of all they said and wrote. And they felt they *had* to leave home, not because they had chosen to be rootless wanderers, but largely to fulfil their sense of individual destiny and personal vision. Though many of them remained caught up in the world they had left behind, recapturing it in minute detail from their distant perch, their exile was something deeper than Voltaire's, deeper than Solzhenitsyn's. Those political exiles, as critical as they were, remained so deeply embedded in their own culture that they seemed never truly to have left home.

The modernists were exiles of the spirit rather than of the body politic, though a few of them (like Nabokov) were political fugitives as well. For American culture the first large example of the spiritual expatriate is Henry James, followed closely by T. S. Eliot and Ezra Pound, who were alert to his example. We have spoken so far of autocracies and dictatorships, of murderous regimes that saw the writer as a dangerous threat to their power. It might seem strange that so many writers should flee America just when millions of immigrants were seeking it out, indeed, were transforming it in ways that motivated some of these writers to look abroad. When James and Eliot and Henry Miller left America, when D. H. Lawrence abandoned England, when Joyce and Beckett took off from Ireland, they were trying to escape not a monolithic political system, not outright tyranny, but something they found equally insidious: a small-minded, provincial mentality, a lack of privacy, a leveling equality, a constricting puritanism, a tiresome set of family quarrels, an oppressive nationalism, a miasma of conventional religion and morality, a philistine hatred, fear, or incomprehension of art. At first they left small towns for big cities, giving up jobs they hated for creative lives of uncertain promise. But just when immigrants poured into America in search of opportunity, the expatriates sailed away to seek deeper cultural roots.

Classic American writers like Emerson, Whitman, and Thoreau were exhilarated by the sense of belonging to a new nation, freed from the heavy hand of outworn traditions. But other writers felt just as oppressed by the thinness of American life, its tenuous connections to earlier culture, including the whole history of literature and art. (This, at least, was how Henry James put it in his 1879 biography of Hawthorne, where he listed all the things American society did *not* offer the novelist.) If some writers like Whitman rejoiced in America as a rough-hewn community, an escape from hierarchy and class, others (like James) sought out Europe precisely because of the density of its social distinctions and cultural traditions. They never truly became European but they were fascinated by the contrast between our world and theirs. James saw the clash of mores between Americans and Europeans through the eyes of an increasingly refined sensibility that had largely lost its national accent. He was less an exile than the first truly international American writer, at home everywhere and nowhere. By the time he revisited America in 1904, for the first time in more than twenty years, he had become the proverbial visitor from Mars, and the land of his birth had grown ineffably strange to him.

Though they were poets rather than novelists, T. S. Eliot and Ezra Pound created their literary personalities, even lived their lives, in the shadow of Henry James—not simply of his expatriation but of his fierce devotion to art, his recoil from American provinciality, and his cosmopolitan sophistication. His famous advice to the young novelist was to be someone on whom nothing was lost; his whole life was devoted to the enlargement of consciousness, to being aware of everything in a world alive with signs, shimmering with meaning. For James the life of the outsider heightened the intensity of consciousness, the acute perspectivism, that was part of his legacy to modernism.

If James shaped his own world out of the international present, Eliot and Pound created idiosyncratic traditions out of the European past. Eliot's internationalism seems at first to be backward-looking, rooted in a hatred of modernity, but in other ways it was prophetic of the transnational world that was just then coming into being, whose full flowering we can see around us today. Delmore Schwartz noted this and more in a shrewd essay of 1945 called "T. S. Eliot as the International Hero," which is not about Eliot's relation to America or Europe but his relationship to modern life. Echoing lines from *The Waste Land*, he writes that "the reader of T. S. Eliot by turning the dials of his radio can hear the capitals of the world, London, Vienna, Athens, Alexandria, Jerusalem."

Schwartz is writing at the end of the war, just when radio listeners, also creatures of modern life, could hear grisly and bloody reports from such capitals almost every day, much as we, their successors, also do when we tune in to CNN. But our relation to this new global order, which reaches us through the tentacles of the media, is both very close and very distant. Much more than Henry James, Eliot is a prophet of our deracination, a deracination that lies at the heart of modernism. Delmore Schwartz is not fooled by the Eliot who calls himself Anglo-Catholic, royalist, and conservative. The critic sees these traditional allegiances as desperate ploys of the deracinated man, the spiritual exile. Here is the sonorous, rhetorical, but poetically precise conclusion of Delmore Schwartz's essay:

> Modern life may be compared to a foreign country in which a foreign language is spoken. Eliot is the international hero because he has made the journey to the foreign country and described the nature of the new life in the foreign country. Since the future is bound to be international, if it is anything at all, we are all the bankrupt heirs of the ages, and the moments of crisis expressed in Eliot's work are a prophecy of the crises of our own future in regard to love, religious belief, good and evil, the good life and the nature of the just society. *The Waste Land* will soon be good as new.

Today we no longer take Eliot's work at face value as the gospel of modernity, with the man himself as its high priest, as Delmore Schwartz's generation did. Instead we see how sharply Eliot's vision emerged from his own troubled and dislocated personality, as well as his recoil, like James's, from how his native land had changed. Yet Schwartz, who was himself a famously troubled Jewish poet and critic, endlessly musing about the paradoxes of his own identity, here puts his finger on something essential. Exile is not crucial to modern writing simply because so many of its leading figures happened to leave home; rather, they left home because they saw modern life itself as broken, dislocated, discontinuous with the past, as something that could not be understood through old, firmly rooted national traditions. Schwartz's comments help us understand why a writer like Kafka, who almost never left home, felt even more homeless and rootless than Joyce, Beckett, and Nabokov, who, like millions of ordinary immigrants before and after them, left home forever.

When we think of the modern writer as exile, Joyce is inevitably the first name that comes to mind. It was he who seemed to make expatriation the core of the writer's being, the heart of his devotion to art and his war with society. Joyce first left Ireland when he was barely twenty, in 1902, returned the following year when his mother was dying, and then left definitively in 1904 with the woman he had just met, Nora Barnacle. But there is no room for any travel companion in the famous concluding chapter of his *Portrait of the Artist as a*

Young Man, where Stephen Dedalus explains that only on his own, free of all entangling loyalties and attachments, can he become what his destiny demands. "You talk to me of nationality, language, religion," he tells a friend. "I shall try to fly by those nets." Shortly before his departure from Ireland, he says: "I will not serve that in which I no longer believe whether it call itself my home, my fatherland or my church: and I will try to express myself in some mode of life or art as freely as I can and as wholly as I can, using for my defence the only arms I allow myself to use—silence, exile, and cunning." Not long after this he sets off "to encounter for the millionth time the reality of experience and to forge in the smithy of my soul the uncreated conscience of my race."

The criticism of recent decades, inspired by the surviving fragment of an earlier version of this book, plays down Joyce's identification with these lines. But even if Joyce is having fun at the expense of an earlier self, even if he finds Stephen's sentiments a little callow and rhetorical, it is hard to find anything here that doesn't speak for Joyce himself, who also was ready to sacrifice the ordinary attachments of life to the higher pursuit of art. For Joyce, who had already described the paralysis of Irish life in his collection of stories, *Dubliners*, whose only play would be an Ibsenite drama called *Exiles*, alienation and homelessness were indispensable weapons in the writer's war against routine, mediocrity, narrow-mindedness, and cant. Stephen's words take us back to the Romantic idea of the loner, the isolated artist, the figure of the wandering Jew.

Although Joyce in his next novel, *Ulysses*, portrays Stephen as something of a stiff and a prig, someone too cerebral ever to become a great artist, he takes as his new hero another exile, a workaday modern example of the wandering Jew, that man of the diaspora, Leopold Bloom. A network of associations, beginning with the title, connects Bloom's itinerary through Dublin to Homer's *Odyssey*, but Joyce includes other references, to the Passover Haggadah and to free-thinking Jews like Mendelssohn, Marx, and Spinoza, that bring the whole subject of exile back to where it began. If the Nazis would soon attack the Jews as rootless cosmopolitans, Joyce saw them as historical antecedents of his own restless quest. Yet late in life, asked if he might ever return to Ireland, he said, "Have I ever left?"

Two of the writers most influenced by Joyce—Beckett and Nabokov—came from different ends of Europe, converging on Paris in the late 1930s, just before Joyce himself fled back to Zürich. Beckett, from the time he first left Dublin for Paris in 1928, served informally as Joyce's secretary, taking dictation, doing small errands, and writing a semiofficial commentary on the Master's new work in progress. In many ways he modeled his career on Joyce's, at first exploiting some of the same learned wordplay, ecclesiastical casuistry, and dry, scatological Irish humor. But Beckett, like Nabokov, was also influenced by Joyce's most imposing contemporary, Franz Kafka, whose work, almost all of it published posthumously, cast a huge shadow over the young writers who came of age in the 1930s. When Joyce in 1938 asked his young protégé if they were still reading *Ulysses* in Dublin, Beckett named a few names. "But they're all Jews," Joyce remarked. Beckett then told him that many intellectuals were turning to Kafka, a German-speaking Jew from Prague who had made exile and homelessness an even more central theme in his life and work than Joyce had done.

If Joyce was alienated from the Dublin world he so intimately knew, Kafka felt triply cut off: from the Czech majority as a German, from the Germans as a Jew, and even from Jews as a brooding, solitary temperament, ill at ease in his own skin, who only discovered traditional Judaism, Eastern European Yiddish culture, and Zionist nationalism quite late. Kafka grew ever more fascinated with these curious bonds of community that had played no part in his upbringing, but he never overcame his ingrained ambivalence, his sense of estrangement from ordinary life. "What have I in common with Jews?" he once wrote in his diary. "I have hardly anything in common with myself." Yet he became the friend and patron of a group of Yiddish actors stranded in Prague, and later he fantasized about emigrating to Palestine, working in a library in Jerusalem or even as a waiter in Tel Aviv, where he might at least feel connected to *something*. He was strangely drawn to the characters his Yiddish actors portrayed, "people who are Jews in an especially pure form because they live only in the religion, but live in it without effort, understanding, or distress."

For a few years after the first world war, triumphant Czech nationalists turned angrily on both Germans and Jews. After seeing a day of looting in Prague, Kafka wrote to his brilliant Czech translator, Milena Jesenská, "I've spent all afternoon out in the streets bathing in Jew-hatred. *Prašive plemeno*— filthy brood—is what I heard them call the Jews. Isn't it only natural to leave a place where one is so bitterly hated? (That doesn't even take Zionism or feelings of national pride.) The heroism involved in staying put in spite of it all is the heroism of the cockroach, which also won't be driven out of the bathroom." As he saw the mounted police wading into the screaming mob, he felt "the ugly shame of always having to live under protection."

Kafka's feelings of estrangement went far deeper than the matter of national loyalties or even the shame of persecution. He felt exiled from no place he could begin to imagine as his real home; the ultimate modernist, he felt exiled from life itself. Caught in a life and death struggle with his utterly conventional father, he could not even begin to conceive of belonging to a family. His best stories, beginning with "The Judgment" and "The Metamorphosis," are all about being expelled from the pitiless magic circle of family life. Kafka's insecure heroes long for acceptance but feel condemned to self-immolation, to being outcasts even from their own loved ones. To his new fiancée, Felice Bauer, he writes in 1913, "I lack all aptitude for family life except, at best, as an observer. I have no family feeling and visitors make me almost feel as though I were maliciously being attacked."

In isolation he finds at least some kind of negative integrity: "In me, by myself, without human relationships, there are no visible lies. The limited circle is pure." Nine years later, with the engagement long since broken off, his ambivalence has fiercely reasserted itself. As he writes in his diaries: "Without forebears, without marriage, without heirs, with a fierce longing for forebears, marriage, heirs. They all of them stretch out their hands to me: forebears, marriage, and heirs, but too far away from me."

This intense experience of isolation—of being cut off from the expectations of ordinary life—is exactly where the young Beckett takes up the torch of modernism. Beckett worshiped Joyce for the integrity of his commitment to art. But where Joyce, through Leopold Bloom, somehow immersed himself in the concrete round of daily experience, Beckett, even more than Kafka, found it immensely difficult to connect with people. Infinitely resourceful at indicting himself, Kafka was always intensely verbal. But Beckett's closest friends could spend long hours with him in almost complete silence, as if he had taken Joyce's prescription of "silence, exile, and cunning" more literally than the master. Joyce's later books grow more garrulous but Beckett's work, full of gaps and silences, seems to reach out beyond language. Beckett could correspond with children, could lose himself in sports, but he had a bleaker, more diffident, more depressive temperament than Joyce. Where Joyce in *Dubliners* saw moral paralysis, Beckett in *Molloy*, *Malone Dies*, and *Endgame* described physical paralysis, a world static in every way. Where Joyce's humor was warm and earthy, even occasionally pornographic, Beckett's humor is poignant and farcical, at times laced with disgust, confirming, not alleviating, his own deep sense of hopelessness. In spite of this humor, his vision is perhaps the darkest of any modern writer, Kafka included.

In Beckett, as in Kafka, exile is not a matter of losing one's place but of having no place to begin with. At first a rather derivative writer, Beckett didn't begin to come into his own until long after Joyce's death in 1941. His breakthrough came about when he did what few other transplanted writers had as yet attempted: he began writing in his second language, French, which freed him in one stroke from Joycean wordplay and from the dense network of literary associations that, for him at least, saturated the English language. The Swiftian concreteness of English had bound him, as it did Joyce, to what he could see, feel, and even smell; the Cartesian abstractness of French, on the other hand, lent a piercing clarity to his sense of isolation and hopelessness. Leavened only by a sly vaudevillian humor, his work became a series of crystalline monologues set in a void, a world in which there is no progress, only repetition, in which life itself is little more than a brief commotion, an anteroom of death.

Kafka and Beckett are the most extreme examples of what Delmore Schwartz saw in the poetry of T. S. Eliot: modern literature as an expression of exile from life itself. This is by no means the whole story of modernism, but it is an important part of the story. Schwartz saw Eliot as a voyager, an adventurer, a Marco Polo exploring a distant land. But Beckett's and Kafka's work is all about not getting anywhere, not being admitted—the necessity and yet the futility even of trying; it's all about exclusion and entropy, life ceaselessly running down. Think of the endlessly frustrated petitioner in *The Trial*, spending a lifetime trying to gain admittance to the Law, or of K., the land surveyor, using all his wiles to get the Castle to acknowledge that it has summoned him to take up a position, or of the Hunger Artist, fasting in his cage until he is little more than a wraith lost among sticks of straw.

Beckett's two greatest works follow Kafka's pattern closely. The postapocalyptic landscape of *Endgame* is his *Trial*, his account of waiting for death, inspired in part by the months he spent at the bedside of his dying brother. On the other hand, the flickering hopes of *Waiting for Godot*, never encouraged but never quite extinguished, may be seen as his version of *The Castle*, with its endless struggle to gain at least acknowledgment from some distant power. This is not to say that Kafka's or Beckett's works can be reduced to allegories of exile, or allegories of anything, only that at their best they convey the tremendous sense of displacement, exclusion, or futility that is close to the heart of one form of modernism. Nor is it always so dark an experience. I've spent many hours trying to convince students of the comic dimension of these writers, which the writers themselves often stressed. Kafka's friends have described his peals of laughter as he read aloud from the somber pages of "The Metamorphosis." There is grisly humor too at the end of "A Hunger Artist": with his dying words, the hero mocks his own vanity: "I always wanted you to admire my fasting," he says, but his final spin on the story is less romantic. He fasted only "because I couldn't find the food I liked," a punch line if I ever saw one, but my students rarely bought it.

Other modern writers strike an even more blatantly comic note. They see their exile not as an exclusion or a deprivation but as a wellspring of freedom and a source of exhilaration. For Henry Miller, the Paris of the Depression years was anything but depressing; it was the Land of Fuck, where conscience or remorse could be left behind. Exiled to America, Vladimir Nabokov finds his adopted land an overflowing source of comedy. Like Beckett, he does his best work when he switches in midcareer to a new language. But where Beckett grows spare and minimal, Nabokov explodes into lexical abundance, a plenitude of proliferating puns, arcane allusions, and Proustian leaps into lyricism. But it is hard not to see this abundance as in part a compensation for a deep sense of loss—the loss of the parental homeland and its literary tradition, as described in his autobiography, *Speak, Memory*; the loss of a familiar culture and way of life, as evoked in the strange world of the elderly émigré, Pnin; or the loss of "my natural idiom, my untrammeled, rich, and infinitely docile Russian tongue," as he himself says in the afterword to *Lolita*. The whole phenomenon of "the perilous magic of nymphets," of unspoiled young girls at the very beginnings of adolescence, focuses upon such a transient stage of life that it too becomes an evocation of loss. Humbert Humbert's fixation on Lolita attaches him to a love that cannot last, a mixture of innocence and corruption that must pass quickly into the intolerable blandness of growing up. In these terms, all exile recapitulates the universal loss of the Edenic world of childhood.

In the kinky, extravagant affections of Humbert Humbert, who is as incurable a romantic as he is a child molester, Nabokov gives us his most devastating portrayal of the émigré personality. Humbert's wealth of language is part sarcasm, part ecstasy, and part Proustian nostalgia for a lost innocence that can be described but never really recaptured. But it is also a modernist hall of mirrors, a world in which "reality" is always enclosed in quotation marks. In the rich artificiality of his language, in its surface virtuosity, Nabokov reenacts the shock of alienation as strenuously as his more downhearted predecessors did.

There have been many exiled writers since Kafka, Beckett, and Nabokov—the great Polish poet Czeslaw Milosz; refugees from the Prague Spring, like Milan Kundera; writers expelled from the Soviet Union, including Solzhenitsyn and Joseph Brodsky; even writers who lived for years with a price on their head, like Salman Rushdie—but none who have given us as deep a sense of estrangement and dislocation. Perhaps the black writers who left America after the war, such as Richard Wright, Chester Himes, and James Baldwin, came the closest. They were deeply American but could never quite shake off their sense of horror at the racially divided world they had abandoned. No matter how well the writer adjusts to life in a new land, or settles into that other homeland, the kingdom of art, the modern writer remains a displaced person, unhappy at home yet always something of a stranger abroad. The writers we remember are those who somehow used it to their advantage, turning exile and alienation into a privileged vantage point, a more penetrating way of interpreting the world around them.

Through the incessant shocks of the twentieth century, millions of people migrated; others were forcibly uprooted, tortured, or arbitrarily killed; and many millions more, without changing their address, saw the world transformed around them. There were also legions of immigrants who simply sought a better life, leaving it to their children to take imaginative hold of the shock of their journeys and the fault lines between their old and new identities. In truth, thanks to horrendous wars, vast movements of populations, the explosion of technology, and a myriad of demographic and economic changes, we were all catapulted into a brave new world. Whether our great writers sought exile to free up their imagination or simply had it thrust upon them, the results were the same: a new language to convey the bruising effect of modern life as the rest of us have dumbly experienced it. At those higher frequencies, they still speak for us.

An Outsider in His Own Life

It is not hard to guess why Samuel Beckett's biographer, Anthony Cronin, portrays him in the subtitle of his 1997 book as "the last modernist." When *Waiting for Godot* opened in London in 1955, Kenneth Tynan wrote: "It has no plot, no climax, no *dénouement*; no beginning, no middle, no end." If modernism liberated the writer from conventional storytelling and circumstantial realism, Beckett's novels and plays took modernism just as far as it could go. But *Godot* was an evening's entertainment compared to what followed. Beckett's work grew ever more minimal and austere, halting just before the vanishing point, like the anorexic sculpture of his friend Giacometti, while retaining much of its hypnotic power. Like the man himself, whose gaunt figure, courteous mien, and aversion to publicity became legendary, Beckett's writing took literature as close to silence as anyone can imagine.

Though Beckett lived until 1989, he belongs chronologically (and spiritually) to a much earlier era. Born in 1906, he fits in easily with writers such as Nabokov, Faulkner, Henry Miller, Witold Gombrowicz, S. Y. Agnon, Jorge-Luis Borges, Henry Roth, Nathanael West, and Céline. They were all second-generation modernists who arrived on the scene in the late twenties or early thirties, shortly after Eliot, Joyce, Kafka, and Proust had written their major works. Caught between the anxieties of influence and the uncertainties of political and economic crisis, they often turned to a dark, acrid, and mocking humor that became one of the great literary vehicles of the Depression years.

Beckett seemed like the last of this generation, for he not only carried on so long but was late in finding his own voice. It was not until after the war that he made his wholly original synthesis of Proust's explorations of memory, Joyce's linguistic virtuosity and learned whimsy, the surrealists' fascination with dream logic, and Kafka's and Eliot's profound sense of sterility and blockage. These writers were in the air in 1928 when Beckett arrived in Paris and quickly attached himself to the circle around Joyce and *transition*, Eugene Jolas's avant-garde magazine. Certain elements of Beckett's vision could already be found in his grim little 1931 book on Proust, where he evoked the deadening effect of habit as the only defense against time and mortality. He arrived early at an extremely bleak view of life and a sense of the strangeness of his own detached and morbid temperament. But the fiction and poetry that followed were too cerebral yet also too directly autobiographical to make much of an impact. He probably accumulated more publishers' rejections than any great twentieth-century writer. Had Beckett died by 1945 like some of his colleagues in the French Resistance, his early work would have been among the minor curiosities of Irish literature.

Anthony Cronin's work arrived hard on the heels of James Knowlson's *Damned to Fame*, an exhaustive biography authorized by Beckett himself, which profited from five months of revealing interviews shortly before the subject's death. But if *Damned to Fame* was a definitive piece of scholarship by a leading Beckett authority, Mr. Cronin's underrated book proved to be a work of real novelistic flair by an Irish writer who knew both Beckett and his Dublin background, including intimate friends like the poet Tom MacGreevy and favorite actors like Jack MacGowran and Patrick Magee, for whom Beckett wrote *Krapp's Last Tape*. Of Magee, Cronin writes: "He was grey-haired but ageless and could combine debility with menace, as Beckett characters with their suppressed violence often do." Beckett's Irish milieu—the family dynamics and old friendships, the educational scene, the social and moral attitudes, the physical setting—comes through strikingly in these pages.

Where Knowlson usually writes as Beckett's advocate, seeing his life in hindsight as a steady advance toward a great literary career, Cronin, relying heavily on Beckett's letters and early fiction, remains more attentive to the byways, hesitations, and failures as they were experienced at the moment. Between these two illuminating biographies, Knowlson's matchless sources sometimes give him the advantage. Thanks to the chance discovery of a previously unknown cache of letters, he shows how the mainsprings of *Endgame* lay in the agonizing months Beckett spent at the bedside of his dying brother. But Cronin's vigorous narrative, deft characterization, and fine flashes of critical insight make Beckett more accessible to the general reader.

One virtue of Cronin's biography is its shrewd and perceptive portrayal of the many stages of the writer's transformation from a quirky, self-conscious regional writer to a more universal one: from a genteel upbringing in a Protestant suburb of Dublin to the beginnings of an academic career as a French teacher at Trinity College; from his early years in Paris attending upon Joyce to his wanderings and frustrations in the 1930s; from the wartime escape to Roussillon, the village in the Vaucluse where he wrote *Watt*, to, finally, his creative breakthrough in a few intense years of writing immediately after the war.

Externally Beckett's life was uneventful. His temperament was phlegmatic—one of his lovers, the mercurial Peggy Guggenheim, called him Oblomov, a byword in Russian literature for inertia. Even his courageous work for the Resistance in Paris and Provence, for which he was awarded the Croix de Guerre in 1945, seems to have demanded little concrete action, though in Paris at least he was in grave danger just before he fled. (Many members of his group were denounced and arrested, and barely twenty out of eighty survived the war.) Beckett's surprising Resistance activities and his affair with Peggy Guggenheim were first explored in an earlier biography by Deirdre Bair. But the drama of his life was elsewhere, in the struggle with his inner demons: his Swiftian ambivalence toward the body, his obsession with decline and incapacity, and his sense of utter isolation. The very act of writing stirred deep conflict, which he once described as the paradox of the artist for whom "there is nothing to express, nothing with which to express, nothing from which to express, no power to express, no desire to express, together with the obligation to express." In the closing words of *The Unnamable*, his most intransigent novel, Beckett put this paradox more succinctly: "you must go on, I can't go on, I'll go on."

Depressive, uncomfortable in his skin despite early success as an athlete, ill at ease with all but a handful of people he trusted, Beckett had a sense of being his own double, an outsider in his own life. He was haunted by a feeling of absence, intrigued by the notion of never having been born, which he picked up from a lecture by C. G. Jung. In the midthirties, a host of psychosomatic ailments drove him into almost two years of analysis, a surprising turn for a writer whose temperament was so little given to explanation. Few writers have achieved such purity of expression within so limited a range. Right from the beginning, he saw birth and death as part of a single continuum, with life itself as little more than a futile stay of execution, a long day's dying. "They give birth astride of a grave, the light gleams an instant, then it's night once more," says Pozzo near the end of *Godot*. Vladimir echoes him: "Down in the hole, lingeringly, the grave-digger puts on the forceps." Yet Beckett could make light of his own dark disposition, as when someone at a cricket match described it as "the sort of day that makes one glad to be alive," and he demurred: "Oh I don't think I would go quite so far as to say that."

This was the positive side of Beckett's detachment, the residue of Irish humor that enabled him to see himself as a character, uncompromising, unworldly, a modern Cassandra wary of all consolation. Beckett's earliest fiction, full of learned allusion, was transposed from his own seemingly directionless life. He stumbled under the weight of his own erudition. His breakthrough was the discovery of how much he and his characters did *not* know, how little they could understand or explain. After 1945, as Anthony Cronin shows, Beckett moved beyond self-portrayal to a modernist impersonality, devising abstract identities that "could be revelatory without being self-revealing." Just as Prufrock stood in for Eliot, Beckett himself was replaced by a shifting surrogate, the "Beckett man," Cronin calls him, more a voice than a fleshed-out character, on which he performed endless variations. Molloy, Moran, and Malone in his fiction, Vladimir and Estragon in *Waiting for Godot*, Hamm and Clov in *Endgame*, Krapp in *Krapp's Last Tape* were masks remote from his actual life, remote from any life as we know it, but closer to his inner experience, especially the feelings of forlorn hope, bitter regret, unresolved need, and inexorable decline. Even his turn to writing in French was another hair-shirt, a daring simplification, a way of escaping the allusive manner of Joyce and distancing himself from his rich linguistic grounding in English. "You couldn't help writing poetry in it," he said of his native language.

But as Beckett's genius emerged, there was a world of difference between the interminable first-person monologues of his fiction, which played into his solipsism, and the crisp antiphonal patter of his plays. Even at their breathtaking best, as in *Molloy*, the desolation of the novels will always be hard to get down. The clownish figures in *Godot* are no less thwarted than Molloy, crawling through a nameless town in search of his mother; the foursome in *Endgame* are no less terminal than Malone on his deathbed, scrawling the words we read. But the characters in Beckett's plays have a mesmerizing vitality and low humor despite their stripped-down lives. ("Nothing is funnier than unhappiness," says Nell in *Endgame*.) Quoting a donnish early poem, the critic Hugh Kenner wrote: "these are intense but facile despairs. It is when the clown imitates them that they leap into elegance." Beckett's tramps descend from vaudeville routines; their timing, their physical business, even their silences come from silent comedy. These bickering couples are acting out rituals of dependency and disconnection that, as both biographies show, had deep roots in Beckett's life, especially his relations with a series of women he could neither live with nor live without, starting with his censorious mother and continuing with his wife, Suzanne.

Beckett's ability to write sustained fiction deserted him as he was struggling to complete *How It Is* in 1960, though there are some later prose pieces of astonishing beauty, like the autobiographical *Company* (1980). His plays came more and more to resemble the desolate monologues of his fiction, with only one speaker, sometimes only one actor *not* speaking but simply listening to a disembodied voice, on tape or in his mind. The slowly fading image of Billie Whitelaw rocking herself to death in *Rockaby* (1980), accompanied only by the sound of her own recorded voice, remains indelible. In *Not I* (1972), one of the most terrifying of these late plays, the speaker is designated as a "Mouth," pouring out a torrent of jagged memories to a silent, helpless "Auditor." When the incomparable Whitelaw first performed in this play, she was so tense and overwrought that the director was forced to clamp her head in place to keep it from moving, a perfect metaphor for Beckett's own Bartleby-like descent into immobility, combined with his absolute need for control. "Oh Billie, what have I done to you," Beckett said when she collapsed from emotional exhaustion at a rehearsal.

As a man Beckett seems to have been the soul of kindness, generosity, and personal loyalty, but as a writer he kept faith with the obscure corners of his mind. His gallows humor was as medieval as it was modern. His work had what Cronin calls a "strange élan in the midst of despair," a "fierce joy in knowing and saying the worst that can be said about human existence." Given his vision, the sterility of Beckett's later years is easier to understand than the great outpouring from the late forties to the late fifties. Hugh Kenner, who knew him well, was struck by the contrast between the Irish and French Beckett, between "the gentle comedian" and "the morbid solipsist." Anthony Cronin tries to normalize Beckett, to make him more imaginable, even more ordinary, but he is also attuned to the essential strangeness of his personality. Beckett's work was so parsimonious and spare, his whole way of life so ascetic, that it comes as a shock, in all these books about him, to see him surrounded by so many words, enveloped in a cascade of biographical detail. The particulars of his life complement what he wrote yet hardly explain it, but they make for a wrenching tale in their own right.

Kafka in Love

It is well known that Franz Kafka passed a harsh judgment on both his life and work. He instructed that his letters and unpublished manuscripts—including all three of his novels—be burned unread. Yet Kafka made the request to a friend, Max Brod, who had vowed he could never obey it. Walter Benjamin, Kafka's keenest interpreter, suggested that he was prepared to pass his work on but unwilling to be responsible to posterity for it.

But I doubt that Kafka, with Beckett the most pared down of modern writers, whose stories are sometimes no more than a paragraph, who dismissed his first book with the comment that "only its brevity is perfect," could have anticipated the publication of a thick volume of his letters to Felice Bauer, the bulkiest work ever to appear under his name: some 550 pages of the most heart-rending "love" letters ever written. Kafka had a macabre gift for coining aphorisms over the abyss; he was unable to write a bad sentence or be less than a fascinating person, even when, as in this astonishing collection, he reveals a side of his character that is almost unbearable, one that could even tempt us to dismiss him. The point about these letters is not to misuse them, not to treat them as gossip or mere neurosis, an occasion to cut a troubling figure down to size. We must be wary of reducing the writer to the rough contours of his personality.

Read with care this book not only unfolds a sad but remarkable story but furnishes new light on the most enigmatic writer of the twentieth century. This is an opportunity very much of the moment, for in these last years, just as we thought them tucked away in literary history, the great modern writers have returned to haunt us in a new guise, not the impersonal mask of their "works" but the messy informality of their sweating selves. Again and again—with the 1972 publication of the original manuscript of *The Waste Land*, full of revelations both technical and biographical; or Thomas Mann's diaries; or Forster's suppressed homosexual fiction; or the various Bloomsbury biographies, laying bare a whole cultural milieu—we have been asked to reconsider from a more personal angle writers whom we innocently imagined to have found their permanent niche. Kafka's *Letters to Felice* does not provide us with the most surprising of these revelations—we already knew too much about him—but surely the most painful, surpassing the uncut version of *The Waste Land* in the light it sheds on the private, neurotic mainsprings of great creative work.

Kafka met Felice Bauer in August 1912 and gingerly initiated a correspondence which lasted over five years, including two engagements, two estrangements, and many lesser ups and downs. It was the crucial period of his life, covering the years between his creative breakthrough and physical break-down; without doubt this stormy (though largely epistolary) relationship con-tributed much to both these turning points.

Two days after his first letter, in one long night's fever of composition, Kafka wrote his first great story, "The Judgment," about a man who becomes engaged and, as if in consequence, is sentenced by his father to "death by drowning," a de-cree which he hastens to execute on himself. The girl's initials are F.B. When the story was printed he dedicated it to Felice; in the letters he often refers to it as "her" story, and once even tells her to show it to her father! Five years later Kafka himself was sentenced to death by a pulmonary hemorrhage, the onset of tuber-culosis; he dolefully seized on the occasion to break with Felice, though he lived on until 1924. Felice married and had children soon after the split. She died in New York in 1960—one of the few people in Kafka's life to escape the Nazis, who killed all three of his sisters—and these letters first appeared in German in 1967.

Unfortunately, Felice's letters to Kafka have not survived, so half of their dialogue is missing and a residue of enigma remains. Kafka was twenty-nine when they met, she four years his junior. He lived in Prague, she in Berlin. He was taciturn, intense, moody, and unsocial; she was bright, outgoing, practical, a highly responsible working girl. Though Kafka's own office work remained the bane of his life (until he was rescued by illness), he later boasted that his fiancée had been "good at business"; he extravagantly admired every way in which she was his direct opposite.

Thus the seeds of their later discord were embedded in the relationship from the start, for Kafka's attraction to Felice was partly founded on fierce self-hatred and inner division. At several points in the letters he describes the feeling that two selves are at war within him. One is healthy and "normal"; its wish is to be with people, to get married and have children *comme les autres*. This is a deep and genuine strain in Kafka's sensibility. But the other, the stronger, is a cruel, monomaniacal demon whose whole life is bound up with writing ("the death of his dearest friend would seem no more than a hindrance—if only a temporary one—to his work").

In the first, unthreatening months with Felice these two personalities main-tain a tattered truce. Kafka's letters are exuberant—he is clearly happy—and his fiction, though somber (besides "The Judgment" he also writes his most ambitious and haunting story, "The Metamorphosis"), thrives as never before. But when the healthy self schemes to deepen his involvement, when Felice re-sponds, this prospect of intimacy poses an unbearable threat to his solitary habits and singleminded devotion to art. The second self takes revenge by going on strike. Kafka's writing goes to pieces; the demon takes over the affair, keeps it strictly epistolary, intrudes its obsessions into every letter. In terror at the "morasslike inner self" that seethes below, he groans that "the wrong sen-tences lie in wait about my pen, twine themselves around its point, and are dragged along into the letters."

Lying in wait—despite Felice's advice that he "live more in the real world" and "take things as you find them"—was an endless battery of complaints and charges, sometimes against Felice for not writing or not being responsive, more often and more violently against himself for making these demands of her, for presuming to fall in love with her, for existing. However much they may have poisoned the wellspring and brought unhappiness to both of them, these wrong and wronging words were a part of the emotional core of their relationship and provide us with most of the enlightenment to be found in these letters.

Kafka intermittently found the "right" sentences as well, and sipped hesitantly at a forbidden love and joy he strenuously excluded from his fiction. But this positive side of the correspondence is a trifle hollow. It's not until page 228, seven months after their first meeting, that Kafka and Felice dare to see each other again though they have been writing feverishly, often several times a day. (Kafka's last message the day before he came to Berlin was a two-word letter: "Still undecided.") Founded on so little actual acquaintance, the letters quickly become Kafkaesque in the way they pirouette around a missing center and create an exclusively mental universe. Like a patient projecting upon the invisible analyst he's only glimpsed for a moment, the letter writer spins out web upon web of fantasy. Kafka writes letters and letters about why he hasn't received more letters, and letters and letters about why he doesn't deserve to receive any letters. All this involves the most excruciating analysis of who he is and what he is. "You didn't know whom to write to," he says. "I am no target for letters." "Could it be that I still have some hope, or am toying with the hope, of being able to keep you? If this be so, as it sometimes seems to be, then it would be my duty to step out of myself and quite ruthlessly defend you against myself."

This wholly interior drama strikingly resembles psychoanalytic "transference," in which a neutral, vacant relationship becomes a blank slate on which the deepest unconscious conflicts can be inscribed. A "bony, empty face that wore its emptiness openly": this is how he described Felice in his diary. "I alienate myself from her a little by inspecting her so closely," he added. "What a state I'm in now, indeed, alienated in general from the whole of everything good." Kafka never allowed himself to respond to Felice as a full human being. Instead he put her on a pedestal and tried to worship her safely from a distance. He seized on her most ordinary traits and made them symbolize "the whole of everything good." He even grasped at her name, with its affected middle-class Gallicism, as the title to a simple felicity that had always eluded him. By turning her from a woman into a myth he guaranteed that it would elude him still, that he would sink even deeper into a sense of his own unworthiness. "I love her as far as I am capable of it," he writes in his diary, "but the love lies buried to the point of suffocation under fear and self-reproaches."

It is on this point that the letters to Felice intersect with what is after all the most important thing for us, which is his work. I remember how Kafka's books haunted my dreams even in high school, though I didn't "understand" them, and years later, when I looked curiously into some of the commentators, I could find nothing that answered to my experience of reading them. As with subsequent Kafkaesque works, such as Beckett's plays, there seemed to be a conspiracy to treat his fiction as some sort of allegory—about God, about totalitarianism, about bureaucracy, you name it; about everything but our feelings in reading them, the experiences *in* them, what actually happens. Critical ideas became a way of explaining things away or making them seem less disturbing.

As the letters show, Kafka often thought in images, and his stories, even those apparently so fantastic as "The Metamorphosis," tend to be expanded metaphors for real human situations. He develops them with perfect realism from their initial premises. Even when read literally the stories tell us more than all the fluff of interpretation: a doctor goes off on a house call and can never return; a traveling salesman who lives a buglike existence actually turns into a bug, and is finally swept out with the trash; a man without a full name is tried and executed for a crime that is never mentioned, by a court he never quite reaches or understands; a man with even less of a name, with only an initial, is summoned to a job that may or may not exist, by men who may or may not be men, who live in a castle that shimmers in the unapproachable distance. These stories are the work of a virtuoso of catastrophe, not at all depressing and "Kafkaesque" like their foolish imitators, but by turns wistful, grotesque, ironic, jokey, and horrific, a combination of Jewish gallows humor and precise Swiftian disgust. Kafka's problem was not with transcendence but with living in the world, in his own body, in some reciprocal relation with other people. When he asks in his diary, "What have I common with Jews?" he quickly adds, "I have almost nothing in common with myself and should stand very quietly in the corner, content that I can breathe." Ambivalent about sex, he sees "coitus as punishment for the happiness of being together."

Kafka had fantastic envy for the creature "who sits in himself as a first-class oarsman sits in his own boat," the man who "radiates mastery" and is "secure in his innermost being." His love for Felice, like the situations in his novels, was an attempt to open up an intercourse with the world, to communicate with something solid. Her letters become an addiction; he devours them and gets unnerved when a day passes without one. He wants to hear everything about her daily life, and more, about the past, "the thousands of days when there were no letters." But the script takes an unexpected turn, for despite his insatiable demands she begins to fall in love with him. The "world" actually beckons.

Alarmed, he turns from hectoring her to arraigning himself: she must know the "worst" about him. His health is bad; his prospects are uncertain; he's a misanthrope, who can't bear to be with people; literature is his whole life and leaves no room for other human beings. Gradually his letters escalate into the most sustained and furious self-loathing imaginable—though laced with intense expressions of love and accompanied by a rational clarity that sees exactly what his demon is trying to do. When her common sense proves unshakeable, he decides she merely loves him out of "compassion," or from a blind refusal to believe what he is saying. "I can never tear myself open wide enough to people to reveal everything and so frighten them away." Finally he writes in a shocking vein of self-denigration to her father, concluding: "I love her too much, and she cannot see me as I am. And perhaps she wants the impossible only out of compassion, no matter how much she may deny it. Well, now we are three. You be the judge!"

The father proved as impervious to this self-abasement as his sensible daughter, and Kafka blamed his own cunning for anticipating this—something else to feel guilty about! They were engaged twice: The first engagement took place in 1914, the second in 1917, both complete with stiff-collared middle-class formalities (which meant much to them, for different reasons), both to be dissolved within a few months. In the first case Felice seems to have decided—with his help no doubt—that he might really be impossible to live with. (She brought a sister and a friend to a summit meeting where, he felt, they "sat in judgment" on him.) In the second case he became convinced that his new illness was psychological in origin, a sign from mind and body alike that his five-year struggle to enter the world by way of conventional marriage went too deeply against the grain of his whole being. His head and lungs, he said, had conspired behind his back, and one of the combatants had landed a mortal blow.

It is deeply disquieting to read these letters, for they force us to reflect on this terrible story and confront the neurosis and unhappiness that were at the heart of his creative work. The letters show how much Kafka's genius was inseparable from his misery. The most self-condemning of the letters are also the most subtle, the most complex, the most fully imagined. Kafka's discovery of Felice led to a breakthrough in his writing, not because it held out the prospect of happiness but because it precipitated a crisis of "judgment": by her; by his father, whose position in life he would be encroaching upon, by her father; by the whole world into whose pale of formalities and arrangements, weddings and births, they would be intruding.

Similarly, the first break with Felice, when she had in fact "sat in judgment" on him, opened up another great creative surge in which he wrote, among other things, *The Trial,* "In the Penal Colony," and the stories later included in his book *The Country Doctor,* among them the great parable "Before the Law." With clarity and wit and a fanatical devotion to his writing, Kafka managed to turn his pain into art without losing touch with the pain. The naked suffering of the letters turns into something rich and strange, eternally open to new meaning, inexhaustible in the way only great myths and legends can be, even serene in the sense that Yeats said "Hamlet and Lear are gay; / Gaiety transfiguring all that dread."

To this day Kafka remains (even more than Joyce) the presiding genius of all experimental fiction in the West. When translated into narrative forms, Kafka's tenuous relations with the world became a self-created world, an alternate reality that overthrew the conventions of "reality" in fiction. From the second generation of modernists—Beckett, Agnon, Nabokov, Borges, Gombrowicz—to Alain Robbe-Grillet, the New Novelists, and American black humorists of the 1960s, including Philip Roth, Kafka's influence has been everywhere, the prism of a new reality, though sometimes abstractly, as a technique alone, an alienation "effect," without the solidity of detail that came from his own unappeasable hunger for the ordinary.

Down at the root of this body of work there remains the pain. A few hours of good writing could alleviate it, but nothing could provide any lasting relief. "You have no idea, Felice, what havoc literature creates inside certain heads. It is like monkeys leaping about in the treetops, instead of staying firmly on the ground. It is being lost and not being able to help it." "I have no literary interests, but am made of literature, am nothing else, and cannot be anything else."

Against this ferocity of commitment, this all-consuming totality, Felice can have little power: "The life that awaits you is not that of the happy couples you see strolling along before you in Westerland, no lighthearted chatter arm in arm, *but a monastic life at the side of a man who is peevish, miserable, silent, discontented, and sickly*; a man who, and this will seem to you akin to madness, is chained to invisible literature by invisible chains and screams when approached because, so he claims, someone is touching those chains."

From the epistolary beginnings to the final analysis of the effects of his illness, Kafka managed to sabotage the connection with Felice, much as he also needed and wanted it. Even after her marriage he continued to love and idealize her in his own way. "For F.—a happy mother of two children—I have the love an unfortunate commander has for a town he could never take, and which has nevertheless somehow become great." But Felice had won another sort of victory, for Kafka found he could never fully return to his solitary way of life, becoming instead involved with other women in the same destructive and tormented fashion. In all this there is nothing that any of us, healthy and well-adjusted as we surely are, can rightly feel superior to. As the letters to Felice (and also the later *Letters to Milena*) make clear, Kafka's neuroses are no different from ours, no more freakish, only more intense, more pure, more consistent, more brilliantly articulated, driven by genius to an integrity of unhappiness that most of us never approach.

The astonishing Milena Jesenská, a gifted literary figure in her own right, who fell in love with Kafka in the early 1920s, understood this; Felice apparently never did. She found him even more remarkable as a person than as a writer. "What his terror is," wrote Milena, "I know down to the last nerve. . . . I armored myself against it by understanding it." Yet neither of them was able to alter the pattern enough to break through. The surprise is that another woman about whom we know much less actually did. When Kafka met Dora Dymant in 1923 there was no thought of letters, no barrier in illness. He escaped from Prague and his family, went to live with her in Berlin. They dreamed of emigrating to Palestine. He even wrote to her father, a pious Jew, asking for permission to marry. In a truly Kafkaesque turn the father passed the letter on to his *rebbe*, who simply said, "No," without explanation. Not long afterward Kafka was dead, but not without a taste of the felicity and communion he had never found with Felice.

HOPE AGAINST HOPE: ORWELL AND THE FUTURE

VERY FEW BOOKS published in the twentieth century had the impact of *Nineteen Eighty-Four*. It crossed the line between a popular and a literary audience and intrigued students of politics as much as readers of futuristic fiction. It mirrored contemporary history but also influenced history by making the case against totalitarianism—especially Soviet-style Communism—so intelligible and unforgettable. It turned the longstanding themes of Orwell's journalism into a fable and the utopian claims for the workers' paradise into a nightmare. When I first read it in high school I was most taken with Orwell's ingenious phrasemaking: *Newspeak, Big Brother Is Watching You,* the *Anti-Sex League,* the *memory hole, unperson, doublethink.* I was no great fan of science fiction but I knew that the Cold War had found its authentic poet.

Rereading the book in 1984 itself, I marveled at how the ubiquitous surveillance in Orwell's future state anticipated later advances in the technology of snooping. I was struck too by Orwell's geopolitical vision, borrowed from the work of a well-known social critic, James Burnham, as he portrayed three large blocs in perpetual but limited war against each other—the Cold War and the "nonaligned group" in a nutshell. The early 1980s saw Orwell writ large in the last intense flare-up of the Cold War. In the aftermath of the Soviet takeover in Afghanistan, an American president revved up the arms race, campaigned against the "Evil Empire," and helped undo the conservative, geriatric leadership in the Kremlin. New long-range missiles were to be installed in Europe, provoking large-scale peace protests. There was still a dynamic, anti-American Third World bloc, spearheaded by the religious revolutionaries who had recently humiliated the United States in Iran. Since Orwell's future had formally arrived, discussions of the novel turned narrowly on his political forecasting, which was hardly the main purpose of *Nineteen Eighty-Four.*

Should we remember Orwell as a great writer, or simply a timely one? Was his work genuinely prophetic or merely an exaggeration of tendencies he decried in his own time? What kind of book was *Nineteen Eighty-Four* that readers could connect with it at so many different levels? If we raised these questions about his nonfiction work, it would be easy to demonstrate that he was one of the great essayists of the century. The social reportage of the first half of *The Road to Wigan Pier* and the lonely moral witness of *Homage to Catalonia* stamp them as extraordinary documents that at once illuminate and transcend their age. The first is a pioneering work on the culture of poverty, the second a testament to the duplicities of Stalinism. Early essays like "A Hanging" and "Shooting an Elephant" help us understand the workings of empire at ground level, while Orwell's essays on popular culture prefigure the whole field of cultural studies. Apart from Orwell's insight as an observer and critic, his essays can be singled out for their rhetorical effects alone: their deceptively straightforward yet memorable prose, their arresting openings and endings, their seductive way of anchoring the subject in Orwell's quirky personality and experiences—from Burma to Spain to the industrial north of England. A slight but perfect autobiographical essay like "Bookshop Memories," based on Orwell's months of working in a bookstore, stands out as a gallery of recognizable English types, a lethal Swiftian comedy of humors, deftly exposing some of the foibles of English eccentricity.

Despite his direct manner, Orwell was anything but a simple writer. In his signature piece, "Why I Write" (1946), which Sonia Orwell and Ian Angus placed at the head of his collected essays, the famous declaration that "good prose is like a window pane" is followed by a striking summary of his own work: "I see that it is invariably where I lacked a *political* purpose that I wrote lifeless books and was betrayed into purple passages, sentences without meaning, decorative adjectives and humbug generally." This is one of those memorable sentences easy to misread. Orwell's credo becomes clearer if we recall his definition of "political purpose" a few pages earlier: he was, as he said, "using the word 'political' in the widest possible sense. Desire to push the world in a certain direction, to alter other people's idea of the kind of society they should strive after." Described this way, political purpose can be seen as essential to all serious writing: Orwell soon declares that "no book is genuinely free from political bias." This follows hard upon his account of three other literary motives: the egoistic, the aesthetic, and the historical. He was determined, he tells us, "to make political writing into an art," crossing it with goals that had no clear connection to politics. "So long as I remain alive and well I shall continue to feel strongly about prose style, to love the surface of the earth, and to take pleasure in solid objects and scraps of useless information. It is no use trying to suppress that side of myself." Orwell's essays are the fruit of his mixed intentions, the sum of his contradictions. Orwell's description of himself as a political writer seems a good deal more nuanced when we read it in context.

When we turn to his last and most celebrated novel, the question of how good a writer Orwell is, and what kind of writer, becomes more challenging. In *Animal Farm* he had projected the details of Soviet history into a barnyard fable, beautifully simple and consistent, written in a bemused, childlike tone, and full of loving, concrete details of real farm life. *Nineteen Eighty-Four* would prove to be a more haphazard and ambitious work. Few serious Orwell readers think of it as their favorite among his books. He himself was aware of the novel's flaws, which were partly the result of his desperate effort to get it finished in the face of grave illness. ("I ballsed it up rather," he told Julian Symons, "partly owing to being so ill while I was writing it.") But *Nineteen Eighty-Four* also lies outside the mainstream of modern literature, which tends to be either realistic or formally inventive—focused either on creating a life-like, credible, self-contained world, like most classic novels, or on refining new techniques for exploring individual consciousness, as in Proust or Joyce. In different ways, both approaches aim for verisimilitude. The dystopian political novel, with its projection into the future, its anxious fascination with technology, and broad use of satire, allegory, and symbolism is at best an interesting minor current, though it included books Orwell admired and imitated, such as Jack London's *The Iron Heel* and Zamyatin's *We*. When, in another letter to Symons, Orwell acknowledged the "vulgarity of the 'Room 101' business," he was partly conceding the limits of the pulpy symbolism endemic to the genre. "I didn't know another way of getting somewhere near the effect I wanted."

If Winston Smith's horror of the rats in Room 101 is too crude and melodramatic, the torment he endures after his arrest is a weak echo of prison literature from Dostoevsky to Arthur Koestler's *Darkness at Noon*. While there is something impressive about Winston's mental disintegration, I doubt that I'm alone in finding his sadistic interrogator, O'Brien, a ludicrous and unconvincing figure. He is cast as a mouthpiece of the system, at once an intellectual and an executioner. Yet he merely repeats the specious logic of thought control that has already been explained by Winston and analyzed by the system's arch-enemy, Goldstein, in his subversive manuscript, which reads like an Orwell essay interpolated into the novel. Do we really need the diabolical O'Brien to tell us yet again about doublethink, about killing the sex instinct and abolishing the orgasm, about doctoring reality, abolishing memory, and consigning opponents to utter oblivion? It was one thing for Winston or the fictive "Goldstein" to dissect these features of the Nazi or Soviet system. It's quite another for an actual character to use Kafkaesque logic to boast about these ingenious forms of subjugation, which he is sure will last forever. O'Brien may embody the system but he cannot plausibly speak for it. O'Brien is no Grand Inquisitor, whose arguments he tries to match; he is not even in a class with the icy, relentless interrogator Gletkin in *Darkness at Noon*, a type Koestler knew at first hand.

We could salvage O'Brien, perhaps, by casting him not as an articulate sadist or spokesman but as a lunatic who manages to impose his sense of reality through mental and physical torture. But Orwell, whose fatalism was intensified by his own fatal illness, is determined to see these fiendish excesses not as an aberration, ghastly yet not necessarily permanent, but as the way history is actually heading. Though we hear of O'Brien's "exaltation," his "lunatic enthusiasm," and though Winston questions his own sanity for being out of step, the book offers little support for seeing this thuggish creature simply as a madman who plays mind-games with his victims while he happens to have his hand on the dial. When O'Brien tells Winston that the system's only goal is self-perpetuation—power for its own sake, torture for its own sake, dictatorship for its own sake—he becomes little more than an ideological construct. In the course of a suggestive analysis of O'Brien in his book *Contingency, Irony, and Solidarity*, the philosopher Richard Rorty argues that "he is as terrifying a character as we are likely to meet in a book," but to me he seems more a concept than a character. This is a major pitfall of this kind of allegory.

Nineteen Eighty-Four has several minor characters who also serve as emblems of Orwell's argument, including Syme the ideological zealot and Parsons, the slovenly, stupid true believer who is turned in by his own children, but they have a Dickensian vividness that makes them immediately credible. The most ingeniously conceived of these characters, Comrade Oglivy, that exemplary hero of the Revolution, never existed at all; he is simply the product of Winston Smith's talent for Orwellian fiction. His invented biography begins: "At the age of three Comrade Oglivy had refused all toys except a drum, a submachine gun, and a model helicopter. At six—a year early, by a special relaxation of the rules—he had joined the Spies; at nine he had been a troop leader. At eleven he had denounced his uncle to the Thought Police after overhearing a conversation which appeared to him to have criminal tendencies." Though Christopher Hitchens says that *Nineteen Eighty-Four* "contains absolutely no jokes," Orwell, for a change, is having some serious fun here. But as his own vitality waned, he allowed his bleak outlook to take over the novel, especially after Winston and Julia are apprehended.

Winston's fate is determined from the moment he buys a diary and begins writing, falls in love, and rents a room of his own, but Orwell allows him a small pinhole of hope that makes all the difference, for it energizes the first three-quarters of the novel. While a fear of the future, especially the inhuman effects of technology, links *Nineteen Eighty-Four* to the mainstream of science fiction, Orwell softens his own foreboding: he gives Winston not only moments of respite, pleasure, and rebellion but a curious faith in the future, not for himself but for what he personifies, a knotty residue of individuality, a stubborn resistance to regimentation. Orwell's appeal to posterity brings to mind poems like Whitman's "Crossing Brooklyn Ferry" or Brecht's "An die Nachgeborenen" ("To Posterity"), which begins, "Truly, I live in the dark ages," and ends with an appeal for understanding: "Think back on us / With kindness." Winston scribbles in his diary, as Orwell writes the novel, "for the future, for the unborn," though he wonders if communication is really possible under a system that claims it can wipe out any trace of him. In "Why I Write," Orwell describes the writer's historical purpose as a "desire to see things as they are, to find out true facts and store them up for the use of posterity." If Winston (like Orwell himself) already feels like a dead man, a corpse waiting to be interred, the book throws out a lifeline to some future time, a message in a bottle. Writing what he knows will be a posthumous novel, Orwell lends Winston his own sense of mission and purpose.

What is the basis for Winston's secret hope, the flicker of optimism that lights up *Nineteen Eighty-Four?* The Party tells him that "who controls the past controls the future: who controls the present controls the past." O'Brien makes him strip naked to see how puny and emaciated he has become. But Winston has put his trust in the proles, whose ordinary lives, still grounded in the past, lived outside of history, somehow preserve the continuity, the fellow feeling, that the Party has tried to stamp out. "They were not loyal to a party or a country or an idea, they were loyal to one another. . . . The proles had stayed human. They had not become hardened inside. They had held onto the primitive emotions which he himself had to relearn by conscious effort." Orwell always believed that ordinary people had more sense than most intellectuals, for at least they trusted the evidence of their senses. Yet he describes their popular culture as trashy and mechanical, and when Winston tries to learn about earlier times from one old man, he gets a mass of irrelevant details. Orwell idealizes the proles but denies them any capacity for reflection or agency, for connecting the dots.

Winston also puts his faith in the biology of sex and desire that brought him and Julia to this room, where day after day they can hear a woman below, as ample of girth as he feels wan and wasted, as fertile as he feels sterile, singing contentedly as she hangs out her wash. *Nineteen Eighty-Four* offers many such touches that reverberate against the book's ultimate gloom. The room itself is more than a love nest and refuge. Like the small crystal paperweight that Winston cherishes, it stands for the private life that resists being leveled and mobilized into any system. Though the room is finally a trap, set up and bugged by the Thought Police, and the paperweight is shattered when the police come to arrest them, they evoke traces of longing, tiny bits of individual happiness that no system can fully efface. "The room was a world, a pocket of the past where extinct animals could walk." Gazing at the paperweight, he feels that "it was as though the surface of the glass had been the arch of the sky, enclosing a tiny world with its atmosphere complete. He had the feeling that he could get inside it, and that in fact he was inside it. . . . The paperweight was the room he was in, and the coral was Julia's life and his own, fixed in a sort of eternity at the heart of the crystal."

All this comes to a head in a stirring passage in which Winston imagines what it might be like to be in the hands of the police, which he knows will happen soon enough:

> Facts, at any rate, could not be kept hidden. They could be tracked down by inquiry, they could be squeezed out of you by torture. But if the object was not to stay alive but to stay human, what difference did it ultimately make? They could not alter your feelings; for that matter you could not alter them yourself, even if you wanted to. They could lay bare in the utmost detail everything you had done or said or thought; but the inner heart, whose workings were mysterious even to yourself, remained impregnable.

Sartre, during his existentialist period, also argued that the willingness to die was the ultimate basis of freedom. But the last part of Orwell's book, the O'Brien part, is designed—unconvincingly, I think—to refute this faith, to show that the "inner heart," the feelings, were anything but impregnable. In passages like the ones I've quoted, however, Orwell gives us poignant images that counter the barbarous bureaucratic poetry of Newspeak and Ingsoc, images of a private world of desire and enclosure that survives from a dimly remembered past. They are linked to the book's positive values—truth, decency, loyalty, family feeling—but also to the memory of ordinary things that seem suddenly valuable when they can no longer be taken for granted, as one might feel in wartime or grave illness. Hearing a snatch of an old tune about church bells, Winston "had the illusion of actually hearing bells, the bells of a lost London that still existed somewhere or other, disguised and forgotten." In bed with Julia, listening to the woman singing in the courtyard and the distant shouts of children, "he wondered vaguely whether in the abolished past it had been a normal experience to lie in bed like this, in the cool of a summer evening, a man and a woman with no clothes on, making love when they chose, talking of what they chose, not feeling any compulsion to get up, simply lying there and listening to peaceful sounds outside. Surely there could never have been a time when that seemed ordinary."

This lyrical strain complicates *Nineteen Eighty-Four* and helps make it a great book, but it is rarely noticed by readers who focus on Orwell's grim picture of the future or his parable of totalitarianism. The very syntax of Orwell's sinuous sentence about lying in bed evokes the languid condition it describes. But moments like this also undercut the widely accepted view that Orwell was blind to the potential for resistance, the enduring force of human values even under the most crushing tyranny. Though he is strangely proud of his work for the system, simply because it is well done, Winston feels an irresistible pressure to shout out obscenities, to step across the line. But by describing totalitarianism as a self-perpetuating monolith, virtually impossible to overthrow from within, Orwell did not quite foresee how totalitarian systems could decay and evolve. Yet Orwell the essayist made exactly this point about the huge slave states described by James Burnham, even arguing that "the Russian regime will either democratize itself, or it will perish." The year after 1984, Mikhail Gorbachev came to power in the Soviet Union, and within six years the Soviet Union itself no longer existed. But in *Nineteen Eighty-Four* Orwell was not so much predicting what would happen in four decades as extrapolating from the world he actually saw around him.

Many futuristic novels are welded together from conceptual abstractions, often labored, occasionally ingenious; their setting is mechanical, their characters lack flesh and blood. Orwell's novel is a more hybrid work. It has often been noted that the world of *Nineteen Eighty-Four* resembles nothing so much as the England of the 1940s: the austerity of wartime and postwar rationing, the dreadful food and decaying, scruffy countryside, the shabby environs of the new welfare state. Orwell has a positive gift for Graham Greene–ish descriptions of gray, threadbare, rubble-strewn settings, reminiscent of London in the blitz, that induce a chronic feeling of sensory deprivation. Orwell infused this monochromatic late-Dickensian world with something that couldn't be more different: the new technology of mass destruction, surveillance, and indoctrination. His sources were as close as Chaplin's *Modern Times*, in which a barking forerunner of Big Brother uses a telescreen to oversee workers on an assembly line that has reduced them to cogs in the industrial machine. Orwell was also one of the first to describe a new kind of terror state that had evolved since 1930, in which older forms of resistance, including what we today call civil society, could no longer function. Active opposition was wiped out by the secret police, and mental opposition was leveled just as effectively by new tools for lying, spying, and propaganda.

The germ of Orwell's account of the new order can be found in *Homage to Catalonia* and in many essays and reviews, most explicitly in "Looking Back on the Spanish War" (1943), "Arthur Koestler" (1944), and "The Prevention of Literature" (1946). "Since about 1930 the world has given no reason for optimism whatever," he writes in the Koestler essay. "Nothing is in sight except a welter of lies, hatred, cruelty and ignorance, and beyond our present troubles loom vaster ones that are only now entering into the European consciousness." In the essay on the Spanish war he asks himself whether it is "perhaps childish or morbid to terrify oneself with visions of a totalitarian future." Yet he ends the essay with a poem about fortitude that evokes the inner heart as a "crystal spirit" that can never be smashed. "No bomb that ever burst / Shatters the crystal spirit," he writes, prefiguring the significance of the crystal paperweight in *Nineteen Eighty-Four*. Surely, this tension between Orwell's fear of the future and his obstinate faith in some innate power of resistance is the kernel from which the novel grew.

In the essay he notes, "before writing off the totalitarian world as a nightmare that can't come true, just remember that in 1925 the world of today [1943] would have seemed a nightmare that couldn't come true." Orwell observes that the literature of ideological disillusionment barely exists in English; it is a Central European phenomenon. He speaks to the civilized English distaste for extreme visions of any kind: "We in England underrate the danger of this kind of thing, because our traditions and our past security have given us a sentimental belief that it all comes right in the end and the thing you most fear never really happens. Nourished for hundreds of years on a literature in which Right invariably triumphs in the last chapter, we believe half-instinctively that evil always defeats itself in the long run." In *Nineteen Eighty-Four*, as in this essay, Orwell insists that it *could* happen here. He grafts features of the Soviet police state, the Nazi terror, the Holocaust, and the Cold War onto a contemporary English setting. Alarmed and disgusted by the sympathy of English intellectuals for both fascism and Communism, Orwell tries to show that even England, complacent in its poky traditions of liberal individualism, was not immune to the specious appeal of totalitarianism.

Those who argue that Orwell was a dying man who projected his own illness into a deeply pessimistic world picture are not completely off the mark. At thirty-nine, Winston Smith feels like a sick man, ashamed to reveal his gaunt body to a young woman but drawing vitality from her youth, health, and sensual abandon. Yet he also connects sex with death and, even as he grasps at life, has "the sensation of stepping into the dampness of a grave." Repeatedly he thinks of himself as an ambulatory corpse, like the three spectral Party leaders when they were temporarily reprieved before being arrested again and executed. But Orwell, perhaps feeling hopeless for himself, turns his hopes to posterity instead. Winston tries to convince Julia, who lives for the moment, "that there was no such thing as happiness, that the only victory lay far in the future, long after you were dead, that from the moment of declaring war on the Party it was better to think of yourself as a corpse." "We are the dead," he says in his frequent refrain, ironically echoing a tribute the gladiators paid to the Roman emperor before fighting in the arena.

Commentators go astray in assuming that Orwell's dark personal feelings somehow distort the picture he draws of the larger system. This may be true of the garish horrors of the last part of the book, fueled by a well-documented streak of sadomasochism in Orwell's own makeup, but not of *Nineteen Eighty-Four* as a whole. His personal stake in this story is mostly a source of strength. In his indispensable essay on the withering effects of totalitarianism on writing, "The Prevention of Literature," Orwell compares what censorship does to the journalist and its effects on the imaginative writer.

> The journalist is unfree, and is conscious of unfreedom, when he is forced to write lies or suppress what seems to him important news: the imaginative writer is unfree when he has to falsify his subjective feelings, which from his point of view are facts. He may distort and caricature reality to make his meaning clearer, but he cannot misrepresent the scenery of his own mind: he cannot say with any conviction that he likes what he dislikes, or believes what he disbelieves. If he is forced to do so, the only result is that his creative faculties dry up.

Orwell insisted that his best writing always had a political purpose, yet he also believed that creative writing is ineluctably personal, whatever its subject. As he says here, the novelist writes from his "subjective feelings, which from his point of view are facts." The "facts" of the case are to be found in the subjective landscape of his own mind. By investing his own feelings in Winston Smith's fate, and by making the setting an England he had experienced, one that his readers would recognize, Orwell rescues *Nineteen Eighty-Four* from the merely speculative horizon of most futuristic writing; he lends an emotional unity, an authentic immediacy, to an otherwise eclectic and occasionally contradictory work.

Pursuing his point in "The Prevention of Literature," Orwell adds that "even a single taboo can have an all-round crippling effect upon the mind, because there is always the danger that any thought which is freely followed up may lead to the forbidden thought. It follows that the atmosphere of totalitarianism is deadly to any kind of prose writer." As Orwell makes clear, any *political* taboo quickly becomes a mental one; political repression translates into repression as the psychoanalyst understands it. The kind of censorship that would guarantee the failure of an analysis also ensures a failure of imagination. Orwell's emphasis on the psychological effects of totalitarianism points to powerful elements in *Nineteen Eighty-Four* that go beyond the work of H. G. Wells and Jack London, Zamyatin, Huxley, and Orwell's other literary models. Orwell's treatment of language, truth, and history, a main concern of his essays over the previous decade, makes for the most original feature of the novel. Winston instinctively recoils from a regime that unhinges language from reality, history from memory, and he finally breaks down when his own sense of reality has been undermined.

In his essay on the Spanish war—the conflict that was the testing ground for both the weaponry and the propaganda of the great war that followed—Orwell looks back at how the war was reported and distorted. He voices the fear that its true history would never be written, that under the pressure of ideology "the very concept of objective truth is fading out of the world." All governments lie, he says, and "history is for the most part inaccurate and biased, but what is peculiar to our own age is the abandonment of the idea that history *could* be truthfully written." Anticipating a key theme of *Nineteen Eighty-Four*, he worries about the coming of "a nightmare world in which the Leader, or some ruling clique, controls not only the future but *the past*. If the Leader says of such and such an event, 'It never happened'—well, it never happened. If he says two and two are five— well, two and two are five. This prospect frightens me more than bombs."

Repeated in *Nineteen Eighty-Four*, this numerical example is perhaps not the best illustration of totalitarian control, and it is even less effective as an argument against the postmodern skepticism and relativism that Orwell so clearly anticipated. But like so much in *Nineteen Eighty-Four*, it is simple, stark and unforgettable; this helps explain why Orwell's fable has struck a chord in millions of readers, including many who grew up under the kind of system he describes but never actually saw. That so much of the novel has become a permanent part of our thinking and terminology testifies to its power as myth and to its cartoonish accuracy. We almost never think of insidious modern techniques of surveillance and persuasion—some of which invade our own lives, from the workplace to the bureaucracy—without using terms like *Big Brother* and *Newspeak* that Orwell invented. They are all summed up in that elastic and overused adjective "Orwellian," which we apply promiscuously not only to the worst dictatorships but to sundry forms of political lying, techno-jargon, public relations, electronic spying, and mass indoctrination—in short, everywhere language is used to obscure and falsify (or simply to "spin") what is actually happening. In that respect, Orwell's celebrated essay on "Politics and the English Language," which analyzes the political effects of this linguistic smokescreen, is the perfect discursive pendant to the novel.

Orwell's position on language and truth, history and fact, is a moral one, rooted in his faith in common sense, including the intuitive savvy of ordinary people. He prided himself on a notion of fact as straightforward as his firmest values, such as decency and candor. Orwell's no-nonsense views of objective truth can be traced to a bluff British empiricism, which puts all its stress on firsthand experience and direct perception. Yet this limitation also contributes to Orwell's strength as a reporter, an intellectual, and a political man. Whatever Orwell's efforts to declass himself, to expiate his sense of social guilt for growing up middle-class, going to St. Cyprian's and Eton, and serving the empire, the net result of his downward mobility was a determination to see things with his own eyes, whether in Wigan Pier or in Spain, and to describe precisely what he saw. His calling as a journalist, along with his fundamental honesty, entailed a descent into the particular. He was appalled by journalists and intellectuals who indulged their high-minded idealism; as he saw it, they put the idea, the theory, before the plain fact, the long-range political goal before the immediate human reality.

In Orwell's view, the responsible journalist, like the novelist, would surely emerge with a point of view, but it had to begin from what he actually saw— the facts on the ground, the words on the page. From early on Orwell knew that he "had a facility with words and a power of facing unpleasant facts." But Orwell did not carefully distinguish between fact and interpretation. Historians typically differ less on the facts than on what they mean. By drawing attention to the most extreme, even transient features of the totalitarian system—the wholesale rewriting of the past, the constantly shifting political line, the outright doctoring of texts and pictures, the deification, relentless demonization, or total elimination of historical figures, even the outright denial of simple fact (two plus two is four)—Orwell anticipates the postmodern debate about truth and language, yet falls short of contributing to it.

He had an exaggerated faith in objectivity, which his own polemical writing—confident, opinionated, sometimes blatantly unfair—did not always exemplify. Orwell is nothing if not definite, whatever the issue, even when he himself has changed his mind. But he gives an indelible picture of what happens when truth, memory, and history are made to serve political ends. His nightmare was the system that aims to control not only public but also private behavior, not only action but thinking and feeling, including memory, the sense of the past. He indicts the complicity of intellectuals whose *bien-pensant* ideals override common sense and allow them to excuse heinous deeds with a clear conscience.

Nineteen Eighty-Four is a flawed novel but seminal as an act of witness to the most odious features of twentieth-century history, especially the barbarism of the Nazi and Soviet dictatorships, with their cult of personality and their scorn for ordinary standards of truth and decency, to say nothing of their intrinsic violence and contempt for human life. Orwell's propaganda work for the BBC, his observations of England in the 1940s, the state of mind induced by his illness, his experience in Spain, the scars of his battles with the fellow-traveling left, his continuing faith in the working class and hopes for English socialism, his horror of the Cold War and fears of impending atomic war—all these give his monitory tale an emotional weight, a density of experience unusual in books of this kind. Orwell understood that genre writing, especially science fiction, for all its drawbacks, could be a more effective tool for portraying the daily grit of a totalitarian world than any straightforward realism. The unprecedented impact and enduring popularity of the novel have borne this out. His famous image of the future as "a boot stamping on a human face—forever" is less a forecast than a warning, by way of a grim, perhaps sadistic metaphor that no one would ever forget. On the other hand, his terminal illness lent a lyrical glow to the fugitive pleasures of ordinary life.

The bleak side of Orwell's novel, its punishing sense of entrapment, is closely linked to popular film genres of the same period, including film noir, horror, and science fiction, which responded to the same postwar traumas, including anxieties about nuclear war, permanent stalemate, and the loss of individuality. They too were grounded in the fear that the individual could somehow be "vaporised," effaced. Though reviewers stressed the anti-Communism of *Nineteen Eighty-Four*, the book found an unexpected echo in works that sounded the alarm against conformity and intimidation during the McCarthy era, which began not long after Orwell died in 1950. The new science fiction, spun off from Orwell, included Ray Bradbury's 1953 novel *Fahrenheit 451*, where the Thought Police become the firemen who burn objectionable books, and Don Siegel's 1956 movie *Invasion of the Body Snatchers*, in which ordinary citizens become happy zombies, mere physical replicas of themselves, bereft of individual thought and emotion, and only one couple, much like Winston and Julia, hold out desperately against the collective tide. Such works lack the political reach of Orwell's novel, whose original title was "The Last Man in Europe," but they demonstrate the power of his fable about those who hold out precariously in a world where the rudiments of human freedom and difference have been virtually wiped out.

MAGICAL REALISM

The Pornography of Power

EARLY IN 1961 Philip Roth complained in a much-discussed essay that reality in America had grown so bizarre, so grotesque, that it had outstripped the novelist's ability to handle it in a credible way. Roth was certainly right about the limits of the cautious domestic realism that surfaced in the 1950s. Focusing on "relationships" that seemed to unfold in a vacuum, some novelists had retreated to the pinched arena of the personal, giving up any effort to connect individual lives to the larger realities of the age. But in his attempt to explain this withdrawal into the self, Roth could not have been more wrong about the future direction of fiction, including his own.

Later that year a book of the most wildly inventive imagination was published. Many writers had already written about World War II with an awed solemnity that sought to match the ponderous gravity of the event itself. Joseph Heller's *Catch-22*, on the other hand, set out to compete with reality in outrageousness, using fantasy and comic exaggeration to mount a fictional assault on the historical world. Heller, and later Pynchon and Vonnegut, took the irreverence of black humor and applied it to history, politics, and war, where a more serious approach was expected from the novelist. They aimed to subvert the established order through mockery rather than muckraking; they found brilliant equivalents for the enormities of our time through fictive fabrication rather than documentary realism. They responded to Roth's challenge by taking a different tack, a seemingly irresponsible one, as Roth himself would later do.

At much the same time, impelled by enormities even more unspeakable than those in the North, a similar conversion from realism to a populist modernism was taking place in Latin America. Of all the fictional worlds created in the 1960s, the town of Macondo in García Márquez's *One Hundred Years of Solitude* (1967) is probably the most solidly imagined and widely beloved. Though a backwater and a magical place, it vibrates in its own way to all the shocks of Latin American history. The comic-opera wars between Liberals and Conservatives are faithful caricatures of the civil wars that ravaged the author's native Colombia through much of the nineteenth century.

Tremendously influenced by Faulkner's family sagas, with their recurring names and haunted lives, steeped in oral traditions rather than precise chronology, the book is a repository of lived history, remembered history, rather than the history of the textbooks. With its surfeit of pointless plot, its bizarre and stifling repetition of names and events, the hundred-year history of the Buendía family satisfies lovers of the generational chronicle while blowing up the genre from within. It told us that the names and dates in the textbooks were a fraud, that progress in Latin America had yet to take place, that what passed for history there was a delusion, a series of botched beginnings. This would have a wide impact not only south of the border but on North American fiction as well.

That a book with so mordant a message could be so lovable is one of the wonders of modern literature. One reason was García Márquez's thorough immersion in the folk consciousness—his love for magic, folklore, and superstition—which, assimilated to a post-Joycean literary consciousness, gave him a new technique to develop his antihistorical theme. García Márquez substituted memory for time, legend for chronology, a circle of associations for any linear cause and effect. The figure of the author in the book itself is the gypsy magus Melquiades, whose prophetic history of the family, written in Sanskrit, is only decoded on the last page, at the moment of its demise. In this book, "Melquiades had not put events in the order of man's conventional time, but had concentrated a century of daily episodes in such a way that they coexisted in one instant." Melquiades' method is a key to the author's own. By stretching out time to a hundred years, by giving us some members of the family for over five generations and others who barely last five pages, all with overlapping names and diminishing personalities, García Márquez envelops his wild anecdotes in an aura of timelessness, capturing the essence of Latin American "history" in a single embracing instant of awareness—while still ingratiating us with an endless supply of winsome detail.

In his next novel, *The Autumn of the Patriarch*, García Márquez deployed his technique of mythical realism to sum up the essence of Caribbean politics. Where the earlier book, full of lore he had imbibed at his grandmother's knee, apparently came to García Márquez in one great rush (with barely a word altered before publication), the later book, his most experimental, seemed willed into being by a ferocious mental effort. It deals with life from the point of view of the dictator's palace rather than the backwater village, but it weaves around the dictator such a web of myth, fantasy, and Rabelaisian exaggeration that the "real" man is finally lost in the legends; indeed, he can hardly be said to exist outside other people's awareness of him. He is no more than the fixed point in an absurd and chaotic world, "for the only thing that gave us security on earth was the certainty that he was there, invulnerable to plague and hurricane . . . invulnerable to time, dedicated to the messianic happiness of thinking for us, knowing that he would not take any decision for us that did not have our measure."

I suspect that the last thing García Márquez wanted to write was a novel about a Caribbean strongman. As an authentic modernist, what interested him most was the kind of public consciousness that creates such a phenomenon. The book is not only a meditation on power but also on the myths and illusions that sustain power even as they denature and devour its absolute possessors. In its mixed feeling of empathy and disgusted fascination with the dictator, in the peculiar pathos of its tone, the book initially brought to mind the baroque revelations about the last years of the reclusive and eccentric Howard Hughes in the 1970s, as well as complex dramatic treatments of the ambiguities of authority from *King Lear* to *Citizen Kane* and Chaplin's *The Great Dictator*.

The Autumn of the Patriarch is composed of six sections, each a single paragraph forty to fifty pages long, divided into rolling, run-on sentences that continue for several pages—hurtling inventories of fantastic and magical thinking in which the point of view changes from word to word, line to line. In the loss of syntactic and chronological structure, we somehow experience the sheer endlessness and proliferation of the dictator's rule. The result is sometimes unbearably tedious to read, at other times dazzling in its quicksilver flow of brilliantly inventive details. It creates a mesh of multiple awareness that consumes the comic-opera tyrant within the gargantuan dimensions of his image. The coarsest of peasants, he is wily only at surviving. His image is his substance; he *is* what others see in him.

In light of the book's political seriousness, combined with an unquenchable appetite for revolting details, its sludge of narrative accretion flows on with surprising comic gusto. The book begins and ends with the grotesque death of the tyrant, at an indeterminate age between 107 and 232; each chapter is a flashback from that "good news that the uncountable time of eternity had come to an end." Each movement combines the narrative subtlety of Kafka and Joyce with the comic-strip mentality of a Vonnegut or an R. Crumb. The chapters are each a theme and variations on a single piece of the tyrant's image, a chunk of his mythic baggage: his faithful double, his loyal general, his ancient, earthy mother, the mistress of his dreams who eludes him, the "official" wife who manipulates him, the chief inquisitor who outdoes him in torture and imprisons him in an airless space of perfect obedience. Through the interminable reign, the chronology remains vague; the same events are repeated again and again, as in *Catch-22*, until they emerge into a gemlike clarity, gradually, like a photographic image in the caustic bath of a printing solution. On the last pages we learn things that enable us to make more sense of the first pages. Ideally, we should begin again and read right through a second time, as I once did with Pynchon's *V.* and would do again with García Márquez's brilliant novella *Chronicle of a Death Foretold*, which also begins and ends with the death of the protagonist. As in Ambrose Bierce's celebrated story of an execution, "An Occurrence at Owl Creek Bridge," the time of this novella is a suspended moment, like the hub of a wheel surrounded by radiating spokes of plot, motive, and chance.

In *The Autumn of the Patriarch*, the timelessness and circularity of this method shows up the tyrant as a stay against history, a bulwark against the disorderly confusions of common life. The structure of the book reflects the dictator's suspension of the flow of time and change, his self-transformation into legend and hearsay. Finally, the mythic details of his existence dissolve into a figment of the people's imagination. García Márquez turns the tables on our morbid interest in this strange creature, our pornographic fascination with celebrity and power, for his subject is not the tyrant himself but the awe and fear he inspires, the fascinated subservience of his people. These "mind-forg'd manacles," as William Blake called them, are his surest instruments of control.

Finally the tyrant is his own victim, like Citizen Kane: loveless, solitary, decrepit, a figure of displaced sympathy. Animated by disgust, absurdity, and a sense of comic horror, *The Autumn of the Patriarch*, like its brutal hero, nurtures a soft core of sentimental lyricism, an incurable nostalgia for a simpler kind of life. That core may be hollow, but around it is the hard shell of an intricate and distinguished novel that amply rewards the close attention it relentlessly demands.

A Fishy Tale

A gargantuan fable that spans a period from the Stone Age to the 1970s, *The Flounder*, first published in English in 1978, was Günter Grass's first major novel in fifteen years and one of the most exuberantly inventive works in recent European fiction. The books which made Grass's literary reputation—the brilliant, quasi-autobiographical *The Tin Drum*, his novella *Cat and Mouse*, and the mammoth Joycean *Dog Years*—were all published between 1959 and 1963. By 1965 Grass had merrily plunged into West German electoral politics as a one-man Chatauqua on behalf of the Social Democrats and his good friend Willy Brandt.

After that sensational success, Grass, along with his fellow novelist Heinrich Böll, remained an irrepressible gadfly of German society, a liberal democrat opposed to both the doctrinaire left and the antiterrorist backlash of the 1970s that threatened to erode civil liberties in West Germany. He would become a strong opponent of the stationing of American missiles in Germany in the early 1980s and the premature reunification of the country after the fall of the Berlin wall. Admirable as all this activity was in a country whose writers and intellectuals traditionally (and catastrophically) kept away from politics, it proved of no benefit to his writing, though he produced a steady stream of poems, plays, essays, speeches, and minor fiction.

If Grass often found himself distracted from literature, sometimes serving as the national conscience, *The Flounder* marked a return to his roots, a summoning of his fictional powers; even if it had proved to be a literary disaster, it could never be seen as minor, for everything in it runs to excess. *The Flounder* is one of those monstrous miscellanies like Rabelais' *Gargantua and Pantagruel*, Burton's *Anatomy of Melancholy*, Sterne's *Tristram Shandy*, Melville's *Moby-Dick* (a Grass favorite), Flaubert's *Bouvard and Pécuchet*, and (in our century) Joyce's *Ulysses*, which take on the guise of narrative fictions but whose wilder energies lie elsewhere. They come across as inflatable vessels of bizarre information, vehicles for all kinds of encyclopedic, mythological, and historical lore. (Pynchon's *Gravity's Rainbow* and Barth's *Sot-Weed Factor* and *Giles Goat-Boy* were massive American contributions to this genre.)

Frequently these are scabrous and scandalous books, more blatantly obscene than other kinds of fiction—Grass is no exception here—yet they're also the work of intensely bookish men, anal types, collectors and compilers, shy but lecherous antiquarians. One of the things they collect is words, language; they have a passion for lists as well as facts, for epic catalogues and literary parodies. Where many novelists use language as a transparent medium for picturing the familiar world, these novels are entranced with language itself and are written in a spectrum of styles as wide-ranging as their subject matter. Their subjects run more to myths and fables than to social realism; theirs is the comedy of humors rather than manners.

The Flounder reads more like Boccaccio or Chaucer than like Flaubert; venturing less into parody than Grass's other novels, it is more engaged in storytelling than in language games. Within the framework of a modern fable, Grass tells and retells an endless assortment of historical anecdotes, ribald tales, and full-scale novellas—all variations on the battle of the sexes through the ages, but each neatly keyed to a particular food staple. The framing story is a free adaptation of the famous Grimm fairy tale "The Fisherman and His Wife," in which a greedy woman forces her husband to keep asking a talking flounder (really an enchanted prince) for more and still more, until she asks for the sky and they wind up in the same miserable pot where they began.

Grass expands this slanderous parable of nagging womanhood into a raucous treatment of women in history: from primitive matriarchy, in which "mother right" supposedly held sway, to the women's liberation movement, which puts the principle of male dominance on trial. That principle is embodied in the legendary Flounder himself, whom we see on the dust jacket (sketched by Grass himself), whispering mischievously in the masculine ear.

Attached to that ear is the nameless narrator of the book, whose present life bears some resemblance to that of Günter Grass. (Grass, like García Márquez, has often put himself into his books, blurring the separation between fact and fiction and anchoring them in his real activity as a writer.) Married to Ilsebill, the nagging wife of the fairy tale, who is now pregnant and asking for dishwashers and the like, the narrator keeps running off to do things a famous writer must (like visiting Calcutta as a cultural emissary and narrating a TV documentary about his native Danzig, now the Polish city of Gdansk). In previous incarnations, however, the narrator, always with the advice of the Flounder, has been involved with nine (or eleven) women, all of them cooks, each belonging to a different phase of history or prehistory. With the Flounder's aid the narrator—and society—have managed to overcome matriarchy and put women in their place, in the kitchen, in bed, while men learned to make history by advancing technology and pursuing war and conquest.

Eventually, as the modern world grows more insanely destructive, the Flounder becomes disenchanted with the male cause and finally, late in the twentieth century, offers his services to some feminists, who instead put him on trial for his past sins. Before a satiric Bertrand Russell–style tribunal, where splintering factions of militant feminists preside, we hear tales from the lives of all those cooks and the men they served (and sometimes dominated). These stories are served up to us with large helpings of popular anthropology and German history, along with staggering quantities of culinary information for each period. Grass evidently believes that society travels on its stomach; a rough but elaborate historical cookbook could be extracted from his mounds of out-of-the-way data. Finally, with much ideological phrasemaking, the Flounder is convicted, but a moderate faction prevails and the talking fish is thrown back into the Baltic rather than killed and eaten. Meanwhile the narrator's wife, who had conceived in the opening pages—the book is divided into the nine months of her pregnancy, which parallel the nine cooks of history—at last gives birth: to yet another girl-child, another omen of female continuity.

This sounds almost as confusing as a summary of Joyce or Rabelais would. It is filled out with as dazzling a variety of dishes as any literary menu since *Gravity's Rainbow*, but is the meal digestible? As in many such unusual concoctions, some of the ingredients come out half-cooked and a few of the courses seem to go on forever, such as the send-up of anthropological lore in the opening chapters and the increasingly tedious gibes at women's lib as the book goes on. But the risks of tedium and excess are built into this kind of encyclopedic satire. "At first I was only going to write about my nine or eleven cooks," says the narrator, "some kind of history of human foodstuffs—from manna grass to millet to the potato. But then the Flounder provided a counterweight. He and his trial." Only gradually, I take it, did the woman question impose itself as the framework of the satires, and then without the insistence, the inevitability, of the prewar and Third Reich material that made Grass's first three novels so impressive.

Grass was born and grew up in the Free City of Danzig, a Baltic seaport 96 percent German, surrounded by Poland, under the doubtful "protection" of the League of Nations. One of the world's most frequently besieged and contested cities (as Grass loves to emphasize), Danzig in the 1930s was a symbol of Germany's lost territories and a focus of Nazi agitation. By the end of the war it was buried in rubble, and its entire German population had been driven out. It's a truism to say that, except for Southerners like Faulkner, who inherited the consequences of the Civil War, American writers have a relatively undeveloped sense of history. But even among Europeans Grass was unusually well situated to learn how history buffets and batters local dreams and individual lives.

As a comic epic stuffed with maniacal research and ingenious analogies, *The Flounder* is by far the most audacious product of his rich historical imagination. Not in its feminist theme, however, which already seemed dated when the book first appeared. Grass's recoil from feminism looks instinctive, not thought through; by temperament Grass seems attached to his masculine prerogatives, though depressed at the havoc they have wrought in this world. But even the challenge of feminism does not possess his imagination the way the spectacle of the Nazis once did. The sardonic ferocity of *The Tin Drum* turns more pensive and playful here; the author's will does the work of the imagination. This lesser part of the book belongs on the shelf beside Mailer's *The Prisoner of Sex* and Thomas Berger's *Regiment of Women* as a beleaguered masculine response to the new feminism of the 1970s.

What stands up as vividly authentic in *The Flounder* is its original conception, the use of culinary history and sexual history as a vehicle for History. As with Joyce's Dublin, or García Márquez's Macondo, or even John Barth's tidewater country on the Maryland shore, Grass's sweeping panoramas of human life gain effectiveness by being concretely localized. But Grass is an exile, an orphan. Like the shtetl that haunts many Yiddish writers, German Danzig has come to exist almost exclusively in his work. "Men survive only in the written word," saith the Flounder. In this novel Grass undertakes to record and preserve not only the lost world of his childhood, as he did in *The Tin Drum*, but all of Danzig's history back to the Stone Age.

This is where the nine or eleven cooks prove so ingenious a device, like that other protagonist, the dwarfish Oskar banging his tin drum. Oskar adamantly refused to grow after his third birthday—and hence developed an unusual perspective on the adult world, which in its own way was more stunted and freakish than he is. Grass is an earthy and Rabelaisian writer with a coarse sense of humor, a bubbling sensual gusto, and an infectious appetite for life. Not a conventional realist, he diffracts history through symbols and parables, using distortion and exaggeration to limn the essentials of the real world all the more sharply. He revels in the traditional German affinity for the grotesque, but he has kept away from the stylized solemnity of Gothic painters and expressionist playwrights; instead, with a special mixture of comedy and horror—as when Oskar's father dies swallowing his Nazi Party pin—he became one of the tutelary spirits of the comic apocalyptic writers of the sixties.

But where American black humorists sometimes settled for a casual nihilism, a send-up of history as an absurdist joke, Grass, despite his comic extravagance, remained a committed socialist, obsessed with what history means and where it is going. This impelled him to his political work, though it damaged him as a writer. He has had Chile on his mind, Watergate, the Yom Kippur War, the slums of Calcutta, and this sometimes diluted his writing into topical discursiveness. His works depart as much from pure fiction as from art for art's sake. In *The Flounder* Grass's cooks save him, for they give body to his

politics and unite them with his gustatory temperament. Though comic creations, Grass's cooks, like Oskar, are all unyielding, obsessional types, hedonists,
ascetics, patriots, all mute but enduring witnesses to the horrors of their age.
Cooking tripe, boiling potatoes, hunting for mushrooms or ladling out soup at
every stage of Europe's history, the cooks bring Grass the novelist together with
Grass the socialist, for they make it possible for this burly Falstaffian imagination
to conceive "history from below." Under the sign of the animal appetites, which
no social coercion has ever managed to stifle, Grass recovers the point of view of
the anonymous masses and bares the deeply rooted impulses left out of official
history. In other words, despite the massive chunks of history sliced and grated
into it, *The Flounder* manages to meld these ingredients into a real novel.

TALKING DOGS AND PIONEERS

Despite the international acclaim enjoyed by contemporary Israeli writers, including Amos Oz, A. B. Yehoshua, Aharon Appelfeld, David Grossman, and
the poet Yehuda Amichai, the modern Hebrew literature that influenced
them remains an undiscovered continent. S. Y. Agnon, who died in 1970, is
always honored as the greatest Hebrew novelist of the century yet his work is
scarcely known in the English-speaking world. The 1966 Nobel Prize for literature stimulated a handful of translations of his fiction, which entranced reviewers without attracting many ordinary readers.

With its layers of biblical, rabbinic, and learned Hebrew, Agnon's writing
presents daunting problems for translator and reader alike. It is dense with allusions to Jewish texts, legends, and rituals that demand a glossary and can
make rough going even for the initiated. Like I. B. Singer, Agnon is less a novelist than a teller of tales, a master of short forms stripped of everything
inessential. He has rightly been acclaimed as a modernist, but there is a bewildering variety to his fiction, ranging from pious legends to Kafkaesque fables to
contemporary studies of unhappy relationships. In longer works Agnon's tone
can shift unpredictably from the folkloric to the witheringly ironic, from
Yiddish-style oral storytelling to keen psychological realism, all reflecting his
rich, unresolved ambivalence toward tradition and modernity. Classically
terse, tinged with archaic touches that subtly link past and present, Agnon's
supple Hebrew turns stiff and pedantic in most English translations.

All these problems come to a head in Barbara Harshav's lively translation of
his immense historical novel *Only Yesterday* (1945), the first English version of
a work widely considered Agnon's masterpiece. Agnon loves mimicking the
God-haunted speech of the orthodox, with its midrashic cadences, biblical
citations, pious homilies, and homely anecdotes. No translation can do full justice to ordinary sentences peppered with references to "the Holy-One-Blessed-
Be-He," in which God's will and purpose bob up at every turn. By trying to

capture every nuance of the Hebrew—its archaism, its piety, its textual echoes, even the exact word order—Barbara Harshav occasionally sacrifices readability for literal accuracy. For better or worse she follows Agnon closely when he slips into rhyme, parodies Sholem Aleichem, or imitates Talmudic syllogisms. The characters "ascend" to "the Land" or "descend" to something called "Outside the Land," all literal renditions of familiar Hebrew phrases that sound awkward in English.

Such minor blemishes do not really obscure Agnon's gigantic achievement. The novel is set in Ottoman Palestine between 1907 and 1911, the period of the so-called Second Aliyah, when hundreds of young Russian socialists, who would later become the elite of the new state, brought their Zionist labor ideology to Palestine with the hope of redeeming the land by working the soil. Determined to shed the ghetto personalities shaped by exile, persecution, poverty, petty trade, and a surfeit of otherworldly faith and learning, they had a double dream of creating a nation and recreating themselves.

Born in 1887 in Polish Galicia, now part of Ukraine, Agnon himself spent four or five years in Palestine between 1908 and 1912 before moving on to Germany, where his stories would bring him fame in Jewish literary circles. (He did not return to settle in Jerusalem until 1924, after a fire destroyed his Berlin apartment, incinerating many books and manuscripts.) His three novels of the 1930s, *The Bridal Canopy*, *A Simple Story*, and *A Guest for the Night*, were largely set in the shtetl world of Eastern Europe, evoking its heyday as well as its evident disintegration. But by the midthirties he realized that the rude Jewish settlements he had seen three decades earlier were fading into heroic legend, just as the rise of Nazism lent a terrible new urgency to the Zionist project. In *Only Yesterday* he set about to thicken the historical record, at once enshrining and debunking the fading memories of Jewish Palestine in its formative years. Like the later revisionist historians, he was reexamining some of Israel's cherished founding myths. Yet the book stretches the limits of realism when it modulates into the fantastic to work out the fate of its protagonist.

In his classic study of the historical novel, also written in the 1930s, Georg Lukács showed that such books at their most authentic were built not around the movers and shakers of history but around more commonplace characters—"middling heroes," he called them—who see history flash by in a blur without grasping its design, characters like young Fabrice at the battle of Waterloo in *The Charterhouse of Parma*. Lukács also insisted that the greatest historical novels are set not in the costumed world of the distant past (like Scott's *Ivanhoe*) but within living memory (like *Waverley*), the past as it incubates the present.

This is exactly what Agnon does in *Only Yesterday*. The novel centers not on the leading politicians of the Yishuv, or Jewish settlement, but on a generic Zionist youth named Isaac Kumer, who comes from Agnon's own town in Galicia, mocked and celebrated in his earlier fiction. Standing apart from the ideological passions of his fellow migrants, Isaac is less the pioneer than the dreamer, shy, unreflective, sexually passive, more acted upon than acting.

After failing to secure farm work because the landowners prefer cheap Arab labor to hotheaded Jewish socialists, Isaac drifts into the life of a house painter, becoming an artisan rather than an artist, a "smearer," not a builder, first in the freewheeling port city of Jaffa, just before the building of Tel Aviv, then in the perfervid atmosphere of Jerusalem. There he resumes some of the religious observance that he (like the author) had discarded in Jaffa. Kumer becomes our point of view, a malleable, colorless Everyman whose wanderings allow Agnon to explore every corner of the Yishuv. But his prolonged and gruesome death also opens up questions of ultimate meaning that transcend historical reportage. This transition is reflected in striking changes in style. *Only Yesterday* begins as a realistic novel about the small Jewish community in Palestine before World War I, then turns into a comically surreal fable (published, after all, in 1945) with despairing, nihilistic implications about God's wisdom and justice.

Though he was immersed in German literature from childhood, Agnon was always skittish about his European literary influences. But with its very ordinary hero caught in this swirl of the real and the phantasmagorical, *Only Yesterday* shows its kinship with other "common man" epics of the interwar years, beginning with Joyce's *Ulysses*, Jaroslav Hašek's *Good Soldier Svejk*, and Alfred Döblin's Joycean *Berlin Alexanderplatz*. (This tradition would resume after the war in seriocomic masterpieces like Ralph Ellison's *Invisible Man*, also indebted to Joyce, and Günter Grass's *The Tin Drum*, written largely under the spell of Döblin.) The collective title for such Chaplinesque works could be Hans Fallada's widely read *Little Man, What Now?* (1933), a phrase Agnon might have coveted. Typically, these are picaresque, episodic, wildly inventive novels, almost programmatic in their unevenness and excess. Propelled by dazzling verbal effects, they expose their lowly heroes to turbulent social scenes they have little power to master or comprehend. In place of Joyce's Dublin and Döblin's Berlin, Agnon gives us a tale of two cities, secular Jaffa, the commercial and literary center of the Yishuv, and sacred Jerusalem, parched by dust, poverty, and drought, home to every stripe of simple faith and burning fanaticism.

This doubling effect underscores the binary character of Agnon's book and makes it such an inclusive yet ambivalent vision of Jewish life. From the moment Isaac meets an elderly religious couple aboard ship to Palestine, the lines are drawn between Zionism and orthodoxy in a way that resonates through the novel and makes it surprisingly current. Looking back to 1910 from the 1940s, Agnon could already see an Israel divided between the secular social life of the coastal plain and the religious passions seething in Jerusalem. To the old people, who, in their mind's eye, see Israel as a land of "synagogues and prayer houses," Isaac belongs "to the cult of Zionists who want to strip the Land of its holiness and make it like all other lands." To him the old man is useless, since he is simply going home "to add another grave to the Land of Israel." In fact it is Isaac who will die, though both will be disabused of their rosy expectations of "the Land."

Only Yesterday undercuts both Zionism and religious faith as utopian dreams conceived in exile and oblivious to the harsh realities of Palestine, yet the skeptical author somehow remains committed to both of them. In the novel's opening paragraph, which lays out Isaac's fantasies in ripe biblical prose, he is described, for the first of many times, as "a man of imagination" (*ba'al dimyonot*), which is Agnon's sly way of telling us that he resists taking in what his own eyes see. In this respect he resembles Reb Yudel Hasid, the Quixotic hero of *The Bridal Canopy*, who is in fact his great-great-grandfather and a point of reference for his own more mundane adventures. Reb Yudel too had made his way to the Holy Land. His tale, complete with a happy ending, was full of trials and wonders, but since "miracles don't happen to every person, especially not to a fellow like Isaac," the younger man is doomed to be defeated.

This split between hard facts and wishful images, which nostalgically embellish the past as well as the future, is one of the crucial doubling effects in *Only Yesterday*. It shows Agnon's debt to Cervantes but also his fascination with the Jewish messianic tradition. The hard facts are as alien to the literati of Jaffa—including Hemdat, a version of the young Agnon, who dreamt of the Land from afar, but now finds he cannot write about it—as to the religious factions in Jerusalem, with their poisonous intolerance and excommunications. The naive Isaac wonders "how can Zionists who come there to work the Land make sects on top of sects that crush the Land into sections."

But as Amos Oz shows in his spiky, sardonic study of Agnon, *The Silence of Heaven*, the older writer felt no need to choose between the realists and the idealists, since every setback merely postpones but cannot undo the radiant future. "Ugly reality neither cancels nor refutes messianic visions but keeps them as a song for the future," says Oz in his impassioned and closely argued tribute to his literary forebear. Oz cherishes Agnon as a radical modernist and he teases out dark subtexts even from his most traditional-looking works. The messianic paradox is a key to Agnon's seemingly anomalous religious position. Oz concedes that, for all his mischievous irony and profound doubt, Agnon is ultimately elusive, a man who, in his own words, "stood at times among the worshippers, at times among those who question." The numinous Jerusalem inhabited by his pious dreamers, including the halt and the blind, is as real to him as the squalid conditions in which they actually live. As a novelist he is free not to choose.

Not so his characters. Isaac Kumer is caught not only between two cities, two ways of life, each perfectly satisfying to him, but between two women, the freethinking Russian girl, Sonya, who relieves him of his yeshiva-boy virginity but soon tires of him, and the cloistered Shifra, daughter of a religious zealot, who falls into turmoil as she finds herself attracted to him. Isaac's grim fate is determined, however, by yet another erotically charged encounter, when he gratuitously paints the words "Crazy Dog" on the back of a harmless stray animal who is whimpering for his attention. Shunned by the Jews who fear he is rabid, miserable among the gentiles whose food he dislikes, at home only under the billowing robe of a half-demented revivalist preacher, this talking dog (misnamed Balak after the Moabite king) becomes a central figure in the second half of the novel.

Roaming around Jerusalem, the dog becomes our guide to a city already attuned to signs and wonders. Striking terror in the Jews (who can read his scary inscription), he becomes the subject of a raging public debate that comically anticipates the varied interpretations developed by Agnon's later readers. Isaac's relation to him begins with a piece of writing, a marker that eventually turns into literal fact. As an outcast pining for acceptance, this creature seems to carry the burden of Jewish exile, the poignancy of exclusion, even the longing for Zion. Critics agree that he is Isaac's alter ego, the bearer of a timid man's suppressed aggression and eroticism. Yet most of the time, until he actually turns rabid, his behavior is neither aggressive nor sexual.

What most impresses me is this creature's desperate search for knowledge, his need to understand, within the doggy limits of his thinking, why he is so mistreated. The pathos of his position reminds me of Frankenstein's monster (not the movie version but Mary Shelley's more sympathetic original)—essentially an innocent and intelligent being, shunned for his botched appearance. Abandoned by his creator, marked as a threat when he is merely starved for human affection, the monster, like Balak, finally becomes the menace they see in him and takes revenge on the man who deformed and discarded him. In a novel completed in 1943, this inevitably suggests the degrading labels the Nazis attached to the Jews as they tried to extrude them from the human community.

Only Yesterday has its longueurs, especially in the Jaffa sections, but Balak's story, with its nihilistic conclusion, brings out not only Agnon's philosophical demon but his linguistic exuberance. As Balak modulates from Job-like complaints about his suffering to inchoate thoughts of revenge and finally to a rabid thirst for truth and meaning, Agnon's writing takes on a crisp intensity that is startling. Balak comes to stand for the questioning spirit itself, dogged by the confines of its own powers of comprehension:

> Balak shouts in torment, Oh, why am I hounded out of the whole world, everyone who sees me wants to kill me. Did I ever do anybody any harm, did I ever bite any of them. So why do they hound me and not leave my bones alone. Balak complains to Heaven and shouts, Arf, arf, give me a place to rest, give me righteousness and justice. And when Balak's shout is heard, they assault him with stones and sticks. Balak bites the stones and the dirt and screams. The stones and dirt say, Why are you shouting at us? Do we have a choice?

As in *The Tin Drum* or *Catch-22*, this is comedy on the far side of horror. From a burning sense of curiosity, estrangement, and protest, Balak finally turns toward the unfathomable depths of metaphysics:

> Because of Balak's yearnings for truth, his heart pounded like a pestle in a mortar. And in his innocence, he imagined he would grasp the truth, and wondered, Now I should rejoice but in the end, I don't. His insides shriveled and his kidneys grew cold and he couldn't bear the coldness of his spleen. Black bile overcame him and he saw himself leaving the world and not grasping the truth.

When he bites Isaac, the only one who is sure he is *not* crazy, he not only turns the man into a mad dog but foils his own quest to understand what happened to him: "After he dug himself a hole in the flesh of the painter and dripped the truth from it, the truth should have filled all his being, but in the end there is no truth and no nothing. And he is still at the beginning, as if he hadn't done a thing. Could it be that all his trouble was for nothing?" This last encounter between the painter and his shadow echoes the first, and seems equally pointless. The drip of the paint becomes the spilling of blood but with no infusion of meaning. In the most absurd manner possible, Isaac has inscribed his own destiny on the back of a dog, and it returns to destroy him. Essentially blameless but raving and violent, lashed to his bed in an obvious allusion to the binding of the biblical Isaac, he becomes a sacrifice to an absent God, to a truth he can embody but cannot know or impart.

POSTWAR FICTION IN CONTEXT

Genealogies

SEA CHANGE: CÉLINE IN AMERICA

MORE THAN FOUR decades after his death, almost six decades after his flight from France as a collaborator during the Nazi occupation, Louis-Ferdinand Céline's notoriety survives him. Even more remarkably, so does his vast literary influence, not only in France but in the United States. His impact on American writers has been enormous, though his eruptive, vernacular style should have made him the most untranslatable of authors. How do we place this still-controversial figure, who somehow transcended the times in which he nonetheless remains firmly anchored? Does he still belong primarily to France, where he remains at once a classic and an outlaw, or to the wider world that knows him only through his best writings? Is he a different writer at home and abroad? How did his work alter the direction of American fiction?

Born more than a century ago, in the same year the Dreyfus affair broke out, in some ways he belongs irretrievably to another era: before the Holocaust, even before 1914. Do we situate him, with all his local prejudices, in the parochial world of the lower middle class—with the small shopkeepers of the Passage Choiseul, where he grew up—or in the shadowy constellation of literary modernism in its 1930s phase? How well has he traveled, how much has he been transformed, if we examine him through an American lens? In the light of the notorious anti-Semitic diatribes he began publishing in 1937, which perhaps will never appear in English, should anyone at all be eager to claim him?

I ask these questions with considerable humility, more as a reader than as a literary scholar. More than with most writers, Céline's effect on us is a personal one. To read his greatest books, even without knowledge of his life or his politics, is to feel the impact of a blow: the shock of a dark, disillusioned, almost savage view of the human struggle. His first novel was written in the worst years of the Depression, between 1929 and 1932, when many writers lost their illusions, often in the process of acquiring other, perhaps revolutionary illusions or illusions about the uncomplicated virtue of society's victims.

These purely social writers, caught up in a worldwide economic crisis, with its attendant human misery, belong to their times. Some of them are of immense historical interest, often of direct personal interest too. But they do not reach across the decades to strike a blow at us, to puncture our hopes and wound our self-esteem. It was a time when morale was low, when survival itself seemed at stake. But thanks to the faith propagated by the Communists and the hopes fostered in America by the New Deal, the thirties were also in many ways an optimistic period. A sense of solidarity, the dream of a better future influenced many artists, though a few darker spirits were not to be placated. A mysterious, powerful writer named Tom Kromer dedicated *Waiting for Nothing*, his 1935 novel about the suicidally down and out, to "Jolene, who turned off the gas." He never completed another book. One of the most Célinean of all American writers, Nathanael West, who went to school with the French surrealists of the 1920s, made a specialty of deflating tawdry dreams and illusions in such tightly written novellas as *Miss Lonelyhearts*, *A Cool Million*, and *The Day of the Locust*, depressive, minimalist works in Céline's own comic apocalyptic mode.

There were other American writers of the thirties who said "No" to the optimism of both the official culture and its left opposition. Like West and Kromer, these writers typically were ignored or quickly forgotten in their time, then retrieved from neglect two or three decades later. Here I would include writers as different as William Faulkner, Tillie Olsen, and the Henry Roth of *Call It Sleep*, social writers who dwell not simply on class but on traumatic family conflict. I bring up these writers not because they closely resemble Céline or were influenced by him—few of them could have read him before they wrote their major books—but to draw attention to a time lag that was significant for Céline's reception in America. Like them, Céline, with his strenuous, disquieting challenge to his readers, had to wait three decades for the world to catch up with him.

As a visiting presence in American literature, Céline's volcanic bitterness, his bleakness and emotional intensity, belongs properly to the 1960s rather than the 1930s. His savage humor, his mockery of all forms of idealism as rhetorical delusions, could no more be appreciated by the thirties than Nathanael West's. Because his wretched characters are poor and desperate, Céline's first two books, with their low-life milieu, could be taken as a dire variant on the proletarian novel. Like the early Orwell, he could be seen as a picaresque writer venturing among the bottom dogs of society, an allegorist of the "little man": the aimless, innocent Everyman of Hans Fallada's widely read *Little Man, What Now?*, Hašek's Czech national mock-epic, *The Good Soldier Svejk*, Döblin's Weimar classic, *Berlin Alexanderplatz*, even Joyce's *Ulysses*. No wonder Trotsky tried to read Céline's *Voyage au bout de la nuit* (*Journey to the End of the Night*) as the inchoate work of a *lumpen* revolutionary, the instinctive exposure of a corrupt and rotten system.

This political reading of Céline had its limits, but it contributed to the celebrity and ambiguity of that first novel, especially in Paris, where his work was closely scanned for its ideological tendency. Though the Céline of *Voyage au bout de la nuit* had none of the identifiable loyalties of a left-wing writer, his broadly satiric treatment of the First World War could be read as pacifist, the surreal African expedition as anticolonialist, the episode in Detroit as anticapitalist, and his protagonist's life as a doctor back home among the poor as somehow proletarian. There is some truth to each of these readings. Yet the savagery of the African section, with its pervasive sense of rot and decay, human and material, takes us closer to the grotesque humor, the infinite sense of absurdity, of Conrad's *Heart of Darkness* than to any political writing. Céline at the time called himself "an anarchist to the core," but no two reviewers could agree on the political import of his novel.

At least French readers could *locate* Céline, linguistically and socially, as American readers never could. They knew the mentality and milieu he came from, perhaps even the argot he used to express its values. Céline would not fully come into his own style until *Mort à credit* (*Death on the Installment Plan*) in 1936, but his virtuoso use of slang, even in the earlier book, was a radical assault on the strict classical traditions of French literary prose. Similarly, even before the delirious account of his family in the second novel, the language of *Voyage* anchored the narrative in the cynical and suspicious outlook of the lower middle class. American readers would assimilate very little of this. The process by which a work is transmitted into another culture highlights not only the barriers of language but the differences between a writer's local and universal appeal. Céline's stylistic innovations, which were at the heart of his shock effect on French writers and readers, made very little impression abroad, especially in the toned-down, rather gentrified translations by John Marks in the 1930s. Céline would make his memorable mark among American readers as a voice, not a style.

In any case, English literature, looking back to Chaucer and Shakespeare as its great originals, shows far more variety and colloquial energy than we find in the more purified diction of classical French. As Dickens is rooted in the comic traditions of the eighteenth century, especially the work of Fielding, Smollett, and Sterne, Céline reaches back to the linguistic and narrative volatility of Rabelais and Cervantes. For many American readers, Céline became a kind of low-life Parisian Dickens, a comic voyager among social outcasts. At least until the new Ralph Manheim translations began appearing in 1966, Americans were largely deaf to his linguistic innovations, but they still could read Céline for his Dickensian vividness and comic hyperbole, his propulsive narrative energy. Starting with Henry Miller in the thirties, who read him in French even before Céline's first book appeared, and extending to the Beats of the fifties and the countercultural writers and black humorists of the sixties, the English-language Céline helped give new life to the loose-limbed, picaresque, autobiographical tradition in American fiction.

Why were American writers and American audiences so responsive to Céline? One obvious reason, of course, was that they knew so much less than the French about his political history. If Céline couldn't carry over the rhythm and virtuosity of his language into English, neither did he bear the heavy baggage of his social origins and political sins. Thus Céline's bottomless bitterness took on a more purely literary character in English: it became a fresh and liberating attitude toward life, not a tonality with a specific political past. Céline in English became less paranoid, less misanthropic, more ebullient, even curiously gay, buoyant, and life-affirming. Above all, his work played into a literature which, unlike French literature, had a long vernacular tradition behind it.

The greatest tribute to this American vernacular was Hemingway's famous remark that "all modern American literature comes from one book by Mark Twain
called *Huckleberry Finn*." Yet this same comment points to the relative rarity of
speech-oriented writing among classic American authors, especially in the New
England tradition. As Lionel Trilling remarked, "the young nation was inclined
to think that the mark of a truly literary product was a grandiosity and elegance
not to be found in the common speech." Despite Twain's bracing influence, this
conflict between the literary and the vernacular continued well into the twentieth century. For many years, our colloquial writing was largely confined to popular humor, pulp fiction, dialect stories, and regional writing, while serious
authors hewed to more refined and rarefied English models. There were exceptions like Stephen Crane and Gertrude Stein, who both influenced Hemingway;
Ezra Pound, who insisted that great poetry should be at least as well written as
prose, succinct, direct, clear, and concrete; perhaps Ring Lardner, a real writer's
writer, mislabeled a humorist; and Sinclair Lewis, who listened carefully, albeit
satirically, to the dizzying varieties of American speech. But when our first Célinean, Henry Miller, initially tried writing fiction in the 1920s, he was caught up in
a literary artificiality which gave him little access to his only subject: his own life.

Miller was a sponge who absorbed many different influences, but there can
be no question that reading *Voyage au bout de la nuit* shortly before it was published had a powerful effect on him. Céline helped Miller break away from the
kind of stiff and formal writing we find in earlier literary efforts like *Moloch* and
Crazy Cock, two posthumously published novels of no literary interest whatever. Céline enabled Miller to write in the first person, to write as he spoke,
and to tell the story first of his Paris life, then of his earlier New York life, with
a new directness and transparency. He helped turn Miller from a clumsy writer
into a pure storyteller, a supple voice that captures and holds us no matter
what the subject. Céline provided the model of a fictionalized autobiography—
exaggerated, outrageous, often fantastic. Miller's work is held together by sheer
verbal fluency, the spell of the barroom raconteur, not by a well-knit plot or developing characters. His voice gives his stories a mesmerizing immediacy that
compensates for his outrageous egotism. All of Miller's books can be strung
together, like Céline's, into a single autobiographical narrative whose hero
is not himself, his *real* self, but a wildly exaggerated projection of the author:
a deliberate confusion between art and life, fact and invention. Above all,
Céline helped him create a character he called Henry, or Val, an almost lovable
scoundrel who could use his own history to convey his mordant, ribald sense of
life. (Jack Kerouac, on the other hand, would later use Céline's work as a model
for his autobiographical chronicles without creating a strong central character,
instead projecting the colorful, Rabelaisian role on other figures—the Neal
Cassady character, for example.)

The only time I taught Miller's work was in the early 1970s, the heyday of
the first wave of postsixties feminism, when Kate Millett (in *Sexual Politics*) had

pinpointed Miller along with D. H. Lawrence and Norman Mailer as the villains of the new gender wars. Several students complained bitterly that Miller *used* women; true enough, but I argued that Miller used *everyone*, that his whole view of life was to get as much as he could, to give as little as he had to, to live on impulse and avoid being hemmed in by any sense of duty or responsibility. When George Orwell was on his way to fight in Spain in 1936, Miller called him a fool for risking his life for a political cause; he could imagine doing so out of personal curiosity or a sense of adventure, but not from a feeling of social or moral obligation. Any form of altruism made no sense to him.

Just as biographers have been telling us that Céline, unlike his fictional alter ego, was actually a good soldier, a conscientious and caring doctor, and a devoted son, Miller's recent chroniclers have shown us that he too was different from the happy-go-lucky cocksman of his books. Yet this was a character Miller needed to create, for Céline taught him to write picaresque fiction in modern terms by giving us a rogue we could identify with, a selfish heel who saw through everyone's motives, who undercut all idealistic pretensions and saw through to the seamy side of life.

We have always seen Miller as a distinctively American version of Céline, much more benign. Influenced by Whitman, Emerson, and Thoreau, he falls into moments of cosmic expansiveness or spiritual elation in which he "accepts" the universe, as no European would dream of doing. Orwell even described *Tropic of Cancer* as a rare example of a book by "a man who is happy," while calling *Journey to the End of the Night* "exactly the opposite": "a cry of unbearable disgust, a voice from the cesspool." Orwell is probably wrong about Céline—this is Céline as the thirties saw him—but there is no doubt about how much the "American" Miller is influenced by Céline's ranting, misanthropic flow of language.

Even more than Kafka, Céline had perhaps the greatest negative energy of any modern writer, the power of vituperation, the eloquent gift of pure hatred. Set down in New York, Céline's first protagonist, Ferdinand Bardamu, finds to his amazement that "there were no concierges in the whole city. A city without concierges has no history, no savor, it's as insipid as a soup without pepper and salt, nondescript slop."

> Year in and year out, as we may as well admit, our concierges in France provide anyone who knows how to take it and coddle it close to his heart with a free-gratis supply of all-purpose hatred, enough to blow up the world. In New York, they're cruelly lacking in this vital spice, so sordid and irrefutably alive, without which the spirit is stifled, condemned to vague slanders and pallid bumbled calumnies. Without a concierge you get nothing that stings, wounds, lacerates, torments, obsesses, and adds without fail to the world's stock of hatred, illumining it with thousands of undeniable details.

In this comic set piece, so typical of the fulminating little digressions in *Journey to the End of the Night*, hatred turns apocalyptic while remaining amusing.

Hatred is the spice of life, the ground of a sordid and irrefutable vitality. The hatred of the concierge kindles an inspired language, a malicious storytelling filled with "thousands of undeniable details." The concierge is a kind of novelist whose malicious words—words that sting, wound, lacerate, torment, and obsess—take us behind the bland facade of the world's respectability. The very subject inspires Céline into Rabelaisian word-riffs of his own—call it "concierge language"—a cascading verbal energy that will later fuel Miller's style.

For Céline's hatred, Miller's hero substitutes a roguish lout's all-purpose cynicism. Like Céline he loves puncturing hypocrisy, exposing the selfishness and stupidity of everyone's behavior, the baseness of motives, including his own. But he does this with perfect equanimity, even relish, because he holds himself apart from others, always looking out for himself with friend and foe, wife and lover alike. Whether he's been stealing a fuck or cadging a meal, Miller takes pleasure in showing people up, in boasting about what he got from them and how he got away with it. He is the genial con-man as talebearer and truth-teller.

Yet Céline is the more serious writer. We can laugh at the fantastic quality of Miller's sexual escapades, at his pitiless, unsentimental, even predatory treatment of his friends. But Bardamu's icy detachment at the death of his friend Robinson, like earlier scenes betraying his fatalism and passivity with patients who are dying, takes us to a realm of human inadequacy beyond laughter. "We've pushed pity to the bottom of our bowels, along with our shit," he says.

> I stayed with Leon to commiserate, I had never felt so embarrassed. I couldn't manage it . . . He couldn't find me . . . it was driving him wild . . . He must have been looking for another Ferdinand, somebody much bigger than me, to help him die more easily . . . But there was only me, just me, me all alone, beside him, the genuine Ferdinand, who was short of anything that would make a man bigger than his own bare life, short of love for other people's lives. Of that I had none, or so little that there was no use showing it. I wasn't as big as death. I was a lot smaller.

Instead of the mocking, boastful laughter of the antihero that we find in Miller, we find the genuine humility of the man who is not large enough for pity, who knows he is not as large as death, and of the novelist who will not lie about it, who will not let his character slip into another, more heroic, more literary pose. Like so many other Depression writers, Céline and Miller focus on the common man, but they also demystify this populist myth by refusing to sentimentalize him, refusing to substitute a larger figure for the ordinary man they know.

For both writers the common man, far from noble, is the *lumpen* figure tied to his appetites, bound to the body, immune to the rhetoric of ideals and duties the world uses to manipulate him. Nothing that isn't palpable makes any sense. These characters learn to resist or evade any demands that come from outside themselves. In *Journey to the End of the Night* Ferdinand learns this from the insanity of the war; in *Death on the Installment Plan* he picks it up even earlier, from his parents' frantic, pinched, fear-ridden lives. As Patrick McCarthy noted in his 1975 biography, "Céline's art aims at turning life into a series of random catastrophes. *Voyage* has no preamble to explain why Bardamu went to fight. . . . Instead Bardamu starts out with 'It all began just like that.' In the middle of a café conversation he rushes off to join the army."

Within a few pages, Bardamu's goal is to get away from the war, "because suddenly the whole business looked to me like a great big miserable mistake." The war has become to him no more than a "monstrous frenzy that was driving half of humanity . . . to send the other half to the slaughterhouse." He discovers that "you can be a virgin in horror as well as in sex": "How, when I left the Place Clichy, could I have imagined such horror? Who could have suspected, before getting really into the war, all the ingredients that go to make up the rotten, heroic, good-for-nothing soul of man? And there I was, caught up in a mass flight into collective murder, into the fiery furnace."

But in *Death on the Installment Plan* this hatred, fear, and suspicion develop in him at a much earlier age; they are the mental legacies of his family and class, with less of the comic valence they had in the first book. They are built into the wretched life of the shopkeepers of the Passage: the glee of his grandmother's tenants, who destroy their houses and watch avidly as she plunges into their blocked toilets with both arms to clean out their shit; the persecution mania of Ferdinand's father, who rails incessantly against Jews and Freemasons; the lousy jobs the boy is forced to take, which, like everything else in his life, always turn sour before too long. In this kind of life, hatred works its way into the very core of your being: "If you haven't been through that you'll never know what obsessive hatred really smells like . . . the hatred that goes through your guts, all the way to your heart." Ferdinand compares this to a more conventional kind of social griping, which is merely a mental reflex grounded in disappointment:

> Nowadays I'm always meeting characters who complain, who bristle with indignation . . . They're just poor bastards that aren't getting anywhere . . . jerks . . . dinner-table failures . . . that kind of rebellion is for weak sisters . . . they didn't pay for it, they got it for nothing . . . They're drips.

Such people, he implies, are the mere flotsam of the Depression years, the people who never knew the score, who really expected to do better. Or else they're the professional protesters, the middle-class crybabies who learned their social attitudes at school, or in some political movement ("they didn't pay for it, they got it for nothing").

> Where did they get it from? . . . no place . . . the *lycée* maybe . . . It's a lot of talk, hot air. Real hatred comes from deep down, from a defenseless childhood crushed with work. That's the hatred that kills you. There'll be more of it, so deep and thick there will always be some left, enough to go around . . . It will ooze out over the earth . . . and poison it so nothing will grow but viciousness, among the dead, among men.

None of the American writers influenced by Céline could match this level of negation, this apocalyptic nihilism so firmly planted in early misery and deprivation, real or imagined, in the unhappiness and paranoia of the mean, demeaning world of the Passage. Instead, Céline's admirers imitate the maledictions of his style, the leveling effect of his tirades, word-riffs, verbal inventories, and his way of levitating from an unsatisfying reality toward fantasy and comic delirium. For Allen Ginsberg—whose work evolved like Henry Miller's from the literary to the oral—Céline's breathless, eruptive rhythm, punctuated by the celebrated three dots, gives an incantatory effect to the long line Ginsberg borrows from Whitman, Blake, and Christopher Smart. In Célinean poems like "Ignu" and "Death to Van Gogh's Ear!" as in *Howl* itself, the trajectory of voice is not linear but aphoristic, staccato, repetitive, intensifying. The Céline who lies behind these poems is a master of anathema, the great vilifier; Ginsberg rains down curses on the Moloch of a society dominated by money, machinery, and the illusions created by advertising:

> Money-chant of soapers—toothpaste apes in television sets—deodorizers on
>   hypnotic chairs—
> petroleum mongers in Texas—jet plane streaks among the clouds—
> sky writers liars in the face of Divinity . . .
> Money! Money! Money! shrieking mad celestial money of illusion! Money
>   made of nothing, starvation, suicide! Money of failure! Money of death!
> Money against Eternity! and eternity's strong mills grind out vast paper of
>   illusion!

If Ginsberg, veering perilously close to doggerel, turns Céline's fury into Blakean prophecy, his friend William Burroughs—who actually introduced both Ginsberg and Kerouac to Céline—concentrates on the bleak nihilistic humor of Céline's death-soaked world. Much of Burroughs's *Naked Lunch* is a grotesque comedy of the body, a horrific twist on the sheer physicality of Céline's or Miller's universe. As Miller in his more ecstatic moods had transposed sexuality into something primeval, a "Land of Fuck" in which ancient, prehensile, scarcely human organs copulate amphibiously, Burroughs dissolves the body into something primitive and undifferentiated, the material for science fiction, sick humor, drug fantasy, and pornographic reverie. His mad scientist, Dr. Benway, has a dry, caustic humor quite different from the volcanic eruptions of Céline or Miller, yet he can also sound like a Céline character, right down to the three dots:

> Soon we'll be operating by remote control on patients we never see. . . . We'll
> be nothing but button pushers. All the skill is going out of surgery. . . . All the
> know-how and make-do . . . Did I ever tell you about the time I performed an
> appendectomy with a rusty sardine can? And once I was caught short without
> instrument one and removed a uterine tumor with my teeth.

Benway may even be Burroughs's version of Céline himself, collapsing the writer's vision into the practice of a mad doctor. This kind of sick humor reverberates throughout the book: "The finance company is repossessing your wife's artificial kidney. . . . They are evicting your grandmother from her iron lung." Burroughs's humanoid characters are cartoon figures going though comical-horrible catastrophes, endlessly being hanged, eaten, liquefied, dying and being reborn; they are the raw material of an anal fantasy of total control.

Céline can hardly be held responsible for the frequently disgusting, often incoherent excesses of this style, which combines many influences, including drugs and science fiction. But whether we consider this mutation of the novel a breakthrough or a breakdown, Céline is one of the writers who made it possible, who helped determine its tone and form. At a time when history itself was taking a nightmarish turn, Céline, like Kafka, found a way to chart its downward spiral, Yeats's sense that "things fall apart; the centre cannot hold." He broke down the form of the novel into the autobiographical harangue, the fantastic tirade, and this became part of the equipment of every alienated writer who followed him, even one as well-mannered as J. D. Salinger.

In the hands of Henry Miller, the Beats, and then the black humorists, Céline's anger and delirium, often his voice itself, were hijacked by rebellious figures whose work he would scarcely have recognized. Something like this can happen in any negotiation or transmission between cultures. A writer's work goes through a sea change as it is abstracted from its local roots, from the concrete conditions that shaped it, from the writer's own ideas and prejudices. If it survives the transition, and few works do, it takes on a new context, an unexpected relevance within another culture, another language, another era. (Think of Shakespeare in Germany, Dante in late Victorian England, Faulkner in Latin America.) As Céline himself became an anti-Semite, a collaborator, a figure of questionable sanity—a replica of the half-mad father he had mocked in Death on the Installment Plan—his earlier work became part of the permanent American counterculture, the enduring literary arsenal of the transgressive. It merged with influences as varied as the revival of Whitman, the improvisational flow of jazz, the renewal of the vernacular tradition (including black English), and the rippling effects of literary modernism and the banned and half-forgotten writers of the 1930s.

When Ralph Manheim published his translation of Death on the Installment Plan in 1966, the Célinean wave had been building for a decade—the decade of Howl, "The White Negro," An American Dream, Last Exit to Brooklyn, and The Crying of Lot 49. In an extremely unusual publishing move, the work appeared simultaneously in a limited hardcover edition from New Directions, a small literary publisher, and in a mass-market paperback from Signet-New American Library. Signet presented the novel in an iconoclastic 1960s manner as a banned book, a dirty and shocking work too strong for the taste of an earlier era: the cover described it as "the first COMPLETE and UNEXPURGATED

English version of the novel that shocked the literary underground in Europe and revolutionized contemporary fiction." The book was thus associated with published-in-Paris titles like *Tropic of Cancer*, *Naked Lunch*, *Lady Chatterly's Lover*, and *Lolita*, scandalous books which really had once been banned or expurgated, not to be published in America till the end of the fifties, when they helped foster a new wave of deliberately transgressive writing, eager to shock and offend. In this atmosphere, Céline's work was transformed: his style became a vehicle for exploring addiction, violence, and polymorphous sexuality. Thanks to the efforts of Grove Press and New Directions, the novel as nightmare, the novel as delirium, the novel as a shriek of pain or protest, was becoming a major outpost of American fiction. LeRoi Jones would even plagiarize Céline's best title by calling an early book of poems *Preface to a Twenty Volume Suicide Note* (1961).

Céline could hardly have anticipated the raucous 1960s, which gave his books their new and sensational currency in the United States—or the revival of interest in World War II, which created a receptive audience for his final trilogy—but he did understand his books' compatibility with American audiences and even with the Jewish critics and novelists who proved, paradoxically, to be among his most fervent admirers. Céline's work connects not only with the American vernacular tradition but with one of the oldest forms of American writing, the jeremiad, which Sacvan Bercovitch, in *The American Jeremiad*, traced from the Puritans and the Transcendentalists through the New Journalists of the 1960s. The latter group includes writers like Norman Mailer, Tom Wolfe, and Hunter Thompson, who were among those most strongly influenced by Céline's mode of prophetic or apocalyptic invective, and who helped make its fiercely hurried rhythm part of the lingua franca of the decade. Ignoring Céline's politics, these writers invariably saw Céline as a liberator in a decade when "liberation" was an ideological battle cry and paranoia passed for simple realism.

The strong affinity of Jews for Céline is even easier to understand. (Alfred Kazin and Clifton Fadiman were among the first reviewers to acclaim his work in the 1930s, and Milton Hindus, who would be disillusioned when he finally met him, was the first American academic to write a book about him.) Jews feel at home with Céline, as they do with Dostoevsky, because of his emotional intensity, his immense need for self-dramatization, his oral and verbal gift, his operatic fears and anxieties, his excesses and exaggerations, and his apocalyptic sense of defeat, rooted in his feelings as an outsider, a loser, a perpetual victim. While Céline's protagonists are hardly shlemiels, they see themselves as marginal men, history's victims, who occupy their lives not with heroic, foolhardy acts but with stratagems of survival, the shifty, cunning maneuvers of the powerless.

I'll conclude this account of Céline's impact on American writers by examining briefly two of the best books written under his influence, both by American

Jews, Joseph Heller's *Catch-22*, which came out in 1961, the year of Céline's death, and Philip Roth's breakthrough book, *Portnoy's Complaint* (1969), which showed the first effects of Manheim's new translation. Heller told an interviewer, Paul Krassner, in 1962 that "Céline's book *Journey to the End of Night* was one of those which gave me a direct inspiration for the form and tone of *Catch-22*." The influence comes largely from Céline's treatment of the war in the novel's first hundred pages, but extends beyond that. For Céline, as for Heller, war is a form of lunacy, of licensed mass murder, in which heroism and bravery are truly madness, while cowardice and escape are the only forms of sanity. Like Bardamu, Heller's Yossarian likes nothing more than to be in the hospital, where the novel begins and to which he repairs as often as possible. There death is at least an orderly, regulated process.

> There was a much lower death rate inside the hospital than outside the hospital, and a much healthier death rate. Few people died unnecessarily. People knew a lot more about dying inside the hospital and made a much neater, more orderly job of it. They couldn't dominate Death inside the hospital, but they certainly made her behave.

Characters who die in battle lack the imagination to see that the world is set on killing them. Heller's open-hearted Clevinger, the Harvard-educated intellectual, may descend from Céline's brave colonel, who is comically oblivious of all danger, ignoring the whizzing bullets that will turn him into a piece of bleeding meat. "Clevinger was dead," one chapter of *Catch-22* begins. "That was the basic flaw in his philosophy." Céline's version was this:

> The colonel never had any imagination. That was the source of all his trouble, and of ours even more so. Was I the only man in that regiment that had any imagination about death? I preferred my own kind of death, the kind that comes late. . . . A man's entitled to an opinion about his own death.

Heller took over the rueful, jokey side of Céline's tone but also the raw sense of horror. Like Céline, he conveys the sheer physicality of human life in the heightened, surreal conditions of war: a sense of the putrid, fragile vulnerability of the flesh. The deaths of the brutal sergeant and the quixotically brave colonel in Céline set the stage for the deaths of Kid Sampson and Snowden in *Catch-22*, with their message that flesh is matter, bleeding garbage. Céline's version is harsh and graphic:

> The colonel's belly was wide open, and he was making a nasty face about it. It must have hurt when it happened. Tough shit for him! If he'd beat it when the shooting started, it wouldn't have happened.
> All that tangled meat was bleeding profusely.

The tangled meat of the colonel becomes the liver and lungs of Kid Sampson, raining all over the beach, or the kidneys, ribs, and stomach of poor Snowden, endlessly dying throughout the novel as Yossarian tries to repair the gaping hole in his side. Staring at these organs as they spill out, Yossarian feels he has discovered the meaning of life, the spur to his determination to protect his own skin.

"I wasn't very bright myself," says Bardamu, "but at least I had the sense to opt for cowardice once and for all." Or as he says much later, "One can never be too anxious. Thanks to a certain ingenuity, I lost nothing but what self-respect I had left." Falstaff himself, that great apologist for cowardly cunning under fire, could scarcely have put it better. What Céline lent Heller and other writers was not simply an antiheroic attitude, a manual for ignoble survival in a world become a madhouse and slaughterhouse. He gave them a mode of black comedy on the far side of horror, a slashing, jeering tone of rueful bitterness, a needling sarcasm that became a dominant note in American writing in the 1960s as another war began to drive a nation crazy.

Céline's cynicism was the authentic voice of the persecuted, misunderstood, rather despicable little guy—Everyman as perpetual victim—with no ideals, but with a chip on his shoulder, a sense of always being dumped on, oppressed. This character's hard-edged raillery burlesques everything, mocks all social and impersonal claims, keeping his real feelings out of sight. Céline lived this psychological outlook with an intensity later antiwar writers like Heller and Vonnegut could not really muster. Though grounded in the authors' own wartime experiences, their shlemiel-like characters were much more stylized, more literary conceptions. Céline's boiling resentment, his verbal savagery, lay outside their ken.

Heller's chief innovation, inspiring Roth and other black humorists of the sixties, was to turn all this negation and humiliation into stand-up comedy, into vaudeville routines with roots in Jewish humor. Jewish comedians often transposed the ironies of fate, or the social contempt of others, into a particular kind of joking, a defensive self-mockery that was actually a survival strategy. Jewish writers (like Jewish comedians) turned pathos into punch lines without losing the undercurrent of pathos. What Heller did for war, Roth did for the nuclear family, turning it into the epic battleground that few could survive without serious wounds.

Roth's specialty was the Oedipal novel of Jewish family life, the kind of book no serious writer could attempt again after its definitive send-up in *Portnoy*. Roth's novel is indebted less to Bellow and Malamud than to *Death on the Installment Plan*, a work that, with only minimal adjustment, could sit on the shelf of Jewish American classics. In the three books he published before *Portnoy*, Roth had developed a reputation for Jamesian craft and subtle, fluent technique, not for any kind of Célinean excess. Although one of the books was called *Letting Go*, it was really about the inhibited lives of 1950s graduate students, prematurely aged, prematurely married and responsible, unable to let go in any way. Like Céline, Roth was known among his friends as a brilliant mimic, a man of many voices, almost a borscht-circuit comedian, but his early books aimed at moral subtlety and psychological refinement in the prescribed 1950s manner.

Portnoy, on the other hand, cast in the first person as a psychoanalytic monologue, was an outrageous cartoon rather than a Jamesian *nouvelle*. It centers on a constipated father, always at the end of his rope, an emotionally overbearing mother to end all Jewish mothers, and an endlessly masturbating son trying to free himself from the emotional and moral suffocation of his upbringing. If the book was new territory for Roth, there were undoubtedly many influences that contributed to it, above all, as he himself later acknowledged, the influence of the sixties itself, a rebellious, iconoclastic atmosphere that relished excess and encouraged writers to let it all hang out. In a sense, *Portnoy* was the product of *all* those banned books and the climate that allowed them finally to be published. In interviews at the time of *Portnoy*'s publication, Roth gave credit to the scabrous comedy of Lenny Bruce, and even to the political climate, but didn't mention Céline. Yet consider the striking similarities between *Portnoy* and *Death on the Installment Plan*: the masturbation, the shrill, hysterical mother, the father's miserable job with an insurance company—above all the heightened, farcical tone of the monologue, the sense of pain at the heart of laughter, which had little precedent in Roth's work.

There's one substantial difference: Céline's Ferdinand is always being told how bad he is, how much his behavior is bankrupting and disgracing his family, while Portnoy is the good boy desperately trying to be bad. Yet both have been raised in a moral and emotional maelstrom, both have been schooled in the parsimonious constraints of the lower middle class, both have been swimming all their lives in a sea of anxiety, the children of fearful, manipulative, operatically intense parents. "Look, am I exaggerating to think it's practically mysterious that I'm ambulatory," says Portnoy. "The hysteria and the superstition! The watch-its and the be-carefuls! You mustn't do this, you can't do that . . ."

> Do you get what I'm *saying*? I was raised by Hottentots and Zulus! I couldn't even contemplate drinking a glass of milk with my salami sandwich without giving serious offense to God Almighty. Imagine what my conscience gave me for all that jerking off! The guilt, the fears—the terror bred into my bones! What in their world was not charged with danger, dripping with germs, fraught with peril? Oh, where was the gusto, where was the boldness and courage? Who filled these parents of mine with such fearful sense of life?

For Ferdinand, the watchword of his parents' lives is also fear—fear and an awesome sense of responsibility, heightened by the emotional blackmail they practice on him. When he loses his first job, he is treated like an utter monster, a mutant who is sure to shame the family and bring it down. "I was incorrigible . . . I myself was crushed, I searched the depths of my soul, trying to figure out what enormous vices, what unprecedented depravities I could be guilty of." As Bardamu says in *Journey*, "[L]ike my mother, I could never feel entirely innocent of any horrible thing that happened." Guilt-ridden Portnoy staggered under the same moral baggage.

When, through the intercession of his uncle, Ferdinand is sent off to boarding school in England, in a final effort to salvage the reprobate, his parents enact a hysterical scene at the Gare du Nord—hysterical at least in Céline's wild retelling of it:

> I looked at my parents, they were trembling all over . . . They couldn't hold back the tears . . . I began to bawl too. I was terribly ashamed, I was breaking down like a girl, I didn't think much of myself. My mother clutched me in her arms. [. . .]
>
> I begged her to control herself, I implored her amid the kisses, the blowing whistles, the racket . . . But it was too much for her . . . I extricated myself from her embrace, I jumped on the step, I didn't want her to start in again . . . I didn't dare admit it, but in a way I was curious . . . I would have liked to know how far she could go in her effusions . . . From what nauseating depths was she digging up all this slop?

This is Sophie Portnoy *avant la lettre*, but in the final lines Céline goes over the top, melding fascination and disgust, family feeling and sheer nausea in a way that was beyond his American admirers. For all their debt to his gift of vituperation, his autobiographical excess, his emotional exaggeration, his freedom from fictional conventions, his endlessly resourceful paranoia, his verbal energy and virtuosity, and his bottomless skepticism about the rhetoric of culture and its noble ideals, Céline's American followers, perhaps to their credit, lacked his power of negation, along with his curious Nietzschean gaiety. Miller, Heller, and Roth, though they preach the limits of conventional morality, are finally moralists. *Portnoy's Complaint* in the end is a series of brilliantly effective stand-up routines (I know many of them almost by heart), while *Death on the Installment Plan* is a great novel, ruthless and unsettling.

Looking back I see I've emphasized the comic side of Céline's American impact, his liberating effect rather than his darker legacy, which can be seen in punk and postmodernist writers of the past two decades. Along with a dozen other influences from Whitman to Lenny Bruce, Céline helped reorient the American novel—indeed, he himself, through Manheim's translations, became an ingrained part of the American tradition. In Philip Roth's case alone, Céline's dark power continued to deepen, from *My Life as a Man* (1974) and *The Anatomy Lesson* (1983) to the misanthropic, *Lear*-like tirades of *Sabbath's Theater* (1995). One writer almost immune to his influence, John Updike, suggested that its effect left something to be desired. It led, he argued, to a form of "*nouveau picaresque*, with its comfortable paranoia, its pleasant assumption that the world is uniformly zany and corrupt and therefore cannot be analyzed, only experienced at random. . . . Without any consequential development linking events, the reader is led along by the writer's voice alone, and its promise of ever-new prodigies of horror or style." Ever the realist, last of the traditional craftsmen, Updike complained that "the constant company of his first-person voice shelters us from the kind of confrontation with massive, inexorable reality that the great third-person novels provide."

Updike wrote this in 1975, after a decade in which minor, often trite Célinean novels, formless and egomaniacal, had become routine in American fiction, virtually identified with the style of the 1960s. But like the two world wars and the Vietnam War, the world of the 1960s, which often defied credibility, was not amenable to massive, objective documentation. For many American novelists after the war, the old methods of realism and even the formal experiments of modernism no longer served. They saw around them an unstable society that had veered out of control, patterns of behavior so perverse that the psychic depths beneath them felt bottomless. They could trust only their own frayed nerves. They would portray the world by refracting it through their own egos, and Céline's wild, subjective novels helped show them the way.

In the 1960s even the journalists followed suit. Céline's style inspired sixties journalists like Tom Wolfe and Hunter Thompson. The Célinean novel, like the Kafkaesque short story, was created less by the willful aberrations of a single talent than by conditions which made its eruptive manner and grim outlook inescapable. Céline's delayed transatlantic voyage came only when America was ready for him, when it became more like the phantasmagoria that he, like Dickens, had once keenly observed here. His grasp on reality was not always very firm, but there were times when paranoia, exaggeration, disgust, and emotional excess were the only way of telling the truth.

THE COMPLEX FATE OF
THE JEWISH AMERICAN WRITER

As EARLY AS the 1960s, influential critics argued that American Jewish writing no longer counted as a distinct or innovative literary project, for younger Jews had grown so assimilated, so remote from traditional Jewish life, that only nostalgia kept it going. Ted Solotaroff wrote some exasperated pieces about young writers whose work already seemed to him derivative—thin, tiresome, voguish, strained, or sentimental. Irving Howe and Robert Alter launched similar complaints. I once heard the Israeli writer Aharon Appelfeld tell a New York audience that Jewish writing was grounded in the Yiddish culture and way of life that had flourished in Eastern Europe, something that died with I. B. Singer in New York and S. Y. Agnon in Israel. Gazing down benignly at an audience that included his good friend Philip Roth and the novelist E. L. Doctorow, he said that while there were certainly writers who happened to be Jews, there really were no more Jewish writers.

Other observers have been equally firm in anchoring American Jewish writing to the immigrant experience, a point brought home by Irving Howe in a famous attack on Philip Roth in *Commentary* in 1972. Howe saw Roth, whose first book he had warmly acclaimed, as a writer with "a thin personal culture," the kind of writer who "comes at the end of a tradition which can no longer nourish his imagination" or simply has "chosen to tear himself away from that tradition." Certainly there was very little sense of history, Jewish or otherwise, in Roth's finely crafted early fiction. Yet in the light of his humor, his characters, his subjects, and above all his later development, Roth hardly stood outside the Jewish tradition; instead he had a family quarrel with the Jewish world that profoundly affected everything he wrote. Yet Howe's charge struck home. A good deal of Roth's subsequent writing can be seen as a rejoinder to Howe's wrongheaded attack, which so rankled him that a decade later he wrote a furious novel, *The Anatomy Lesson*, lampooning Howe as a hypocrite, a pompous moralist, and even, in a remarkable twist, a motor-mouthed pornographer.

What was the heart of the Jewish literary tradition that Howe and Roth, two of its most gifted figures, could come to such angry blows over it? My subject here is how Jewish writing has changed and even grown, how it survived even the best-informed predictions of its demise. The conflict between Roth and Howe was partly temperamental, but some of it was generational. Howe was the product of the Yiddish-speaking ghetto, of socialism and the Depression; Roth came of age in postwar America, a world he would alternately satirize and recall with nostalgia. There is a streak of the moralist, the puritan, in

Howe's criticism, while Roth took pride, especially when he wrote *Portnoy's Complaint*, in playing the immoralist, or at least in treating Jewish moral inhibitions as an ordeal, a source of conflict. For Howe, as for writers of his generation like Bernard Malamud, this moral burden was the essence of our humanity; for Roth it led to neurosis, anger, and dark, painful comedy.

It comes as a surprise to realize that the major current of Jewish writing in America dates only from the Second World War. Irving Howe once compared the Jewish and the Southern literary schools with a provocative comment: "In both instances," he said, "a subculture finds its voice and its passion at exactly the moment it approaches disintegration." But in what sense was Jewish life in America approaching disintegration in the first two decades after the war, when the best Jewish writers emerged? What was dying, quite simply, was the vibrant immigrant culture evoked by Howe in *World of Our Fathers*. After the war Jews became freer, richer, more influential. As they moved up the economic ladder, professions like academic life opened up to them that had previously been off-limits. Thanks largely to the vague sense of shame induced by the Holocaust, social anti-Semitism in America became virtually a thing of the past. Surely the great literary flowering owed much to the way Jews in America had finally arrived, although the writers were often critical of what their middle-class brethren did with their freedom.

In any ethnic subculture, it's almost never the immigrant generation that writes the books. The immigrants don't have the language; their lives are focused on survival, on gaining a foothold in the new world and ensuring an education for their children. That education not only makes literature possible; it ignites a conflict of values that makes it urgent and inevitable. The handful of excellent novels by individual writers before the war belongs less to a major literary movement than to the process by which the children of immigrants claimed their own identity. In powerful works of the twenties and thirties like Anzia Yezierska's *Bread Givers*, Mike Gold's *Jews Without Money*, and Henry Roth's *Call It Sleep*, the writers pay tribute to the struggles of their parents yet declare their independence from what they see as their narrow and limited world. These works could be classed with Sherwood Anderson's *Winesburg, Ohio* and Sinclair Lewis's *Main Street* as part of what Carl Van Doren called the "revolt from the village," the rebellion against local mores and patriarchal authority in the name of a freer, more universal humanity.

Ironically, the parochial world these writers rejected was the only authentic material they had. Their painful memories of small-mindedness and poverty, parental intolerance and religious coercion, fueled their imagination as nothing else could. In these works the driving impulse of the sensitive, autobiographical protagonist—Sara Smolinsky in *Bread Givers*, little Mike Gold in *Jews Without Money*, the impetuous Ralph Berger, hungry for life, in Clifford Odets's play *Awake and Sing!*, even young David Schearl in *Call It Sleep*—is to get away from the ghetto, with its physical deprivation, its materialism and lack of privacy, its desperately limited horizons, but also to get away from the suffocating embrace of the Jewish family—the loving but overly emotional mother, the domineering but ineffectual father, and the inescapable crowd of siblings, aunts, uncles, cousins, and neighbors, all completely entwined in each other's lives. These works were a blow for freedom, a highly ambivalent chronicle of emancipation, and often, sadly, they were the only books these writers could write. Their autonomy was hard-won but incomplete; this new identity liberated them personally but did little to fire their imagination.

Henry Roth once told me that only when he began to depart from the facts of his life did his novel begin to take on a life of its own; it then proceeded almost to write itself. In *Beyond Despair*, Aharon Appelfeld made the same point to explain his preference for fiction over autobiography. It gave him the freedom he needed to reshape his own recollections, especially the wartime experiences that bordered on the incredible. "To write things as they happened means to enslave oneself to memory, which is only a minor element in the creative process." The early Jewish American novelists were not so lucky. They were stuck not only with what they remembered but with a naturalistic technique that could not do full justice to their experience. Their escape from their origins, never fully achieved, became a mixed blessing; they found themselves caught between memory and imagination, ghetto sociology and personal need. Mere rebellion and recollection, it seemed, could not nurture a full career. Their literary development was stymied. Only the postwar writers managed to break through this sterile pattern.

Saul Bellow, Bernard Malamud, Delmore Schwartz, Paul Goodman, and their Yiddish cousin, I. B. Singer, were the first Jewish writers in America to sustain major careers, not as immigrant writers but in the mainstream of American letters. As modernism replaced naturalism as the dominant literary mode, as fresh influences like psychoanalysis and existentialism exploded the sociological approach of many prewar writers, a new generation found powerful new vehicles for dealing with their experience. Straightforward realism was never an option for Jewish writers in America; it belonged to those who knew their society from within, who had a bird's-eye view, an easy grasp of its manners and values. As newcomers dealing with complex questions of identity, Jews instead became specialists in alienation who gravitated toward outrageous or poetic forms of humor, metaphor, and parable—styles they helped establish in American writing after the war.

The key to the new writers was partly their exposure to the great modernists—Kafka, Mann, Henry James—but also their purchase on Jews not simply as autobiographical figures in a social drama of rebellion and acculturation but as parables of the human condition. Though Saul Bellow admired the power of an authentic naturalist like Theodore Dreiser, though Flaubert helped forge his aesthetic conscience, his first two novels, *Dangling Man* and *The Victim*, were more influenced by Dostoevsky and Kafka than by any writers in the realist tradition. Bellow and his friends were the children of the Holocaust rather than the ghetto. They did not write about the recent events in Europe—they hadn't directly experienced them—but those horrors cast their shadow on every page of their work, including the many pages of desperate comedy.

The atrocities of the Holocaust, the psychology of Freud, and the dark vision of certain modern masters encouraged Jewish writers to find some universal significance in their own experience. Kafka was the prophet, not of totalitarianism—that was too facile—but of a world cut loose from will and meaning, the world as they experienced it in the 1940s. Saul Bellow's engagement with the themes of modernist culture can be traced from novel to novel, but even a writer as private as Malamud was able to combine the stylized speech rhythms of the ghetto with a form adapted from Hawthorne and Kafka to turn parochial Jewish tales into chilling fables of modern life. This was the brief period when the Jew became the modern Everyman, everyone's favorite victim, shlemiel, and secular saint. Yet there was also an innovation in language, a nervous mixture of the literary and the colloquial, of art talk and street talk, that was almost poetic in its effects. Bellow himself brought the buoyant, syncopated rhythms of the vernacular into his prose. As he put it in his eulogy of Malamud after his death in 1986:

> Well, we were here, first-generation Americans, our language was English and a language is a spiritual mansion from which no one can evict us. Malamud in his novels and stories discovered a sort of communicative genius in the impoverished, harsh jargon of immigrant New York. He was a myth maker, a fabulist, a writer of exquisite parables.

We can find these effects almost anywhere we turn in Malamud's stories, from such animal fables as "The Jewbird" and "Talking Horse" to wrenching tales like "Take Pity," which he put at the head of his last collection of stories. It includes the following bit of dialogue, supposedly between a census taker, Davidov, and a recalcitrant citizen named Rosen:

> "How did he die?"
> "On this I am not an expert," Rosen replied. "You know better than me."
> "How did he die?" Davidov spoke impatiently. "Say in one word."
> "From what he died?—he died, that's all."
> "Answer, please, this question."
> "Broke in him something. That's how."
> "Broke what?"
> "Broke what breaks."

Eventually we discover that the man answering the questions in this Kafkaesque exchange is himself dead, and his reckoning with the "census taker" takes place in some bare, shabby room of heaven or hell, though it feels like a forlorn pocket of the ghetto. (Malamud himself later described it as "an institutional place in limbo.") Rosen, an ex-coffee salesman, has killed himself in a last-ditch effort to impose his charity, pity, or love on the fiercely independent widow of the man who died. Rosen takes pity on her, but she will not *take* his pity. Even after he turns on the gas and leaves her everything, she appears at the window, adrift in space, alive or dead, imploring or berating him in a final gesture of defiance.

Like all of Malamud's best work, this is a story of few words but resonant meanings. Anticipating Beckett, Malamud strips down the sociology of the ghetto into a spare, postapocalyptic landscape of essential, even primitive emotions, finding uncanny comedy on the far side of horror. After her husband's death, as the business disintegrated, the woman and her children came close to starving, but the story is less about poverty than about the perverseness of the human will. Again and again Rosen tries to help the widow, but she adamantly refuses to be helped. Both are stubborn unto death, and the story explores the fine line between goodness and aggression, generosity and control, independence and self-sacrifice. Rosen will get the proud woman to take his help, whether she wants to or not, but neither can truly pity the other; their unshakable self-will isolates and destroys them. And the interrogator, standing in for both author and reader, makes no effort to judge between them. The story leaves us with a sense of the sheer human mystery.

The raw power of Malamud's stories is based on a simple principle: that every moral impulse has its Nietzschean dark side, its streak of lust or the will to power, just as every self has its antiself, a double or shadow that exposes its vulnerabilities and limitations. This dialectic of self and other is at the heart of Malamud's stories and novels. The "self" in his stories is often a stand-in for the writer, the artist as assimilated Jew—someone fairly young but never youthful, well educated but not especially successful, Jewish but nervously assimilated, full of choked-up feeling. Repeatedly, this figure is brought up short by his encounter with some ghetto trickster, a wonder-working rabbi, an ethnic con man who represents the suppressed, tribal part of his own tightly controlled personality.

Malamud's work is full of examples of such symbolic figures, half real, half legendary, including the ghetto rat, Susskind, a stateless refugee in Rome in "The Last Mohican," who steals the hero's manuscript on Giotto, and Salzman, the marriage broker in "The Magic Barrel," whose ultimate gift to a young rabbinical student is his own fallen daughter. These old-world characters point to the ambiguous, even disreputable qualities that the young hero has bleached out of his own identity. They are slightly magical figures who come and go with almost supernatural ease. At different times they stand for ethnic Jewishness, carnality, wild emotion, even a sense of magic and the irrational. Or else they are figures from another culture—the Italian helper in *The*

Assistant, the black writer in *The Tenants*—who test the limits of the protagonist's humanity and sometimes put him on a tentative path toward redemption
and self-recognition.

There's a later treatment of this theme in a story called "The Silver Crown."
The main character is a high school teacher called Gans (or "goose"), and the
figure who puts him to the test is a rather dubious wonder rabbi named Lifschitz. For an odd sum of money, this Lifschitz promises to cure Gans's ailing
father by fashioning a silver crown. We never discover whether Rabbi Lifschitz is a holy man, a con man, or both. But when the skeptical Gans eventually loses faith, curses his father and demands his money back, the old man
quickly expires. This could be a coincidence—Malamud loves ambiguity—but
he leads us to suspect that the son, who seemed so desperate to save his father,
actually does him in. His suspicions about the rabbi and the money signified
an unconscious ambivalence, even a hostility toward the father that he couldn't
directly express. Seemingly sensible and cautious, he's only the stunted husk of
a man, going from filial piety to symbolic parricide in just a few lines. Malamud
took this story from one of the newspapers, but he shaped it into something
entirely his own, a test of the moral limitations of our assimilated selves, our
rational and secular humanity, which has killed off some essential part of who
we are.

Malamud's own piety toward the past is not much in evidence in the next generation. Coming of age in the late 1950s and early 1960s, writers like Philip
Roth belonged to a new group of rebellious sons and daughters, some of them
even parricidal, like Malamud's Albert Gans. This was the black-humor generation, rebelling not against the constraints of the ghetto—they were too
young to have known any real ghetto—but against the mental ghetto of Jewish morality and the Jewish family. If Anzia Yezierska or Clifford Odets in-
veighed against the actual power of the Jewish father or mother, Roth and his
contemporaries, who grew up with every apparent freedom, were doing battle
with the internal censor, the mother or father in the head. (Much later Roth
would build *The Human Stain* around a character who jettisons his whole family, including his doting mother, to seek a clean slate and grasp a new identity
for himself.)

The work of these writers proved deliberately provocative and hugely entertaining; always flirting with bad taste, it was often very funny, but with an
edge of pain and giddiness that borders on hysteria. As Portnoy gradually discovers that he's living inside a Jewish joke, the novel's comic spirits turn self-
lacerating. Like Roth, writers such as Stanley Elkin, Bruce Jay Friedman,
Joseph Heller, Jerome Charyn, and Mark Mirsky practice an art of incongruity,
deploying a wild mockery in place of the old moral gravity. Howe's charge
against Roth—that he writes out of a "thin personal culture"—could be leveled against them as well, but it would be more accurate to say they looked to

a different culture, satirical, performative, intensely oral. They identified less with modernists like Kafka and Dostoevsky than with provocateurs like Céline, Nathanael West, and Lenny Bruce. They looked less to literature than to stand-up comedy, the oral tradition of the Jewish jokes that Freud collected, the tirade of insults that ventilated aggression, the vaudeville *shtick* that brought Jews to the forefront of American entertainment.

The usual targets of their derision, besides Jewish mothers and Jewish husbands, were the new suburban Jews who had made it after the war, the vulgar, wealthy Patimkins in *Goodbye, Columbus*, who live in a posh Newark suburb, play tennis and send their daughter to Radcliffe, and—this got me when I first read it—have a separate refrigerator for fruit in their finished basement. (Actually, it was their *old* fridge, which they were thrifty enough to save, the way they've held onto remnants of their old Newark personality.) As a foil to the Patimkins of Short Hills, Roth gives us the inner-city blacks of Newark, where the Jews used to live. We get glimpses of black workmen ordered around by the Patimkins' callow son, and especially of a young boy who runs into trouble simply because he wants to read a book on Gauguin in the local public library. At the heart of the book, then, for all its irreverence, is a sentimental idea of the virtue of poverty and the simple life, something the upwardly mobile Jews have left behind but the black boy still seeks in Gauguin's noble vision of Tahiti.

Goodbye, Columbus was published in 1960, at the outset of a decade in which outrage and irreverence would become the accepted cultural norms. Even Saul Bellow would take a spin with black humor in *Herzog* (1964), as Bernard Malamud would do, unconvincingly, in *Pictures of Fidelman* in 1969. Here these stern moralists dipped into sexual comedy as never before, the comedy of adultery in Bellow, of sexual hunger and humiliation in Malamud. But they were soon outflanked by their literary son, Philip Roth, who in *Portnoy's Complaint* would make epic comedy out of Jewish dietary laws, rabbinical pomposity, furtive masturbation, plaintive longing for *shikses*, and above all the family romance. With its deliberately coarse comic stereotypes, especially of the histrionic Jewish mother, the longsuffering father, and their son, the young Jewish prince, this was the work that elicited Irving Howe's attack, the book that turned the vulgar spritz of stand-up comedy into literature.

The Oedipal pattern in *Portnoy* belongs to a larger history: Roth and other black humorists were rebelling not only against their biological parents but against their literary ones, the moralists of the previous generation, who were still around and did not take kindly to it. Bellow responded to the carnival aspect of the 1960s by taking on the voice of the censorious Jewish sage in *Mr. Sammler's Planet*, arraigning middle-aged adulterers along with women, blacks, and young people in one sweeping image of moral decay—of "sexual niggerhood," as he put it in one indelible phrase. The date was 1970, the bitter end of that tumultuous decade; Bellow's and Howe's responses were extreme but typical of the overheated rhetoric of the generation gap and the culture wars.

Bellow's outrage perhaps was tinged with the envy that so many middle-aged Americans, not simply Jews, felt toward the new sexual freedoms of the young.

Bernard Malamud responded just as pointedly in a 1968 story called "An Exorcism," but it is scarcely known because he never reprinted it in his own lifetime. More than any other text, this story brings to a head the Oedipal tensions among Jewish writers, shedding light on some key differences. It is closely related to another story of generational conflict Malamud wrote the same year, "My Son the Murderer," about a bitter stand-off between an anxious, intrusive father and his twenty-two-year-old son, who is angry at everyone, unhinged by images from Vietnam, and grimly awaiting his own draft notice. (Malamud had a son just the same age.) The central figure in "An Exorcism" is an austere older writer—like Malamud himself, but far less successful—a lonely man rigorously devoted to his craft, a kind of saint and hero of art. An aspiring writer, a young sixties type, attaches himself to the older man at writers' conferences—virtually the only places he ventures out. The older man, Fogel, is grudging and taciturn, but gradually his defenses drop, for he feels "grateful to the youth for lifting him, almost against his will, out of his solitude." Having won his confidence, the boy betrays him; he publishes a story based on an embarrassing sexual episode in the life of the older man. Fogel first confronts, then forgives him. But when the student, as a provocative stunt, seduces three women in a single night, the writer feels a wave of nausea and violently exorcizes him from his life.

Not given to wielding fiction as cultural polemic, Malamud clearly felt uneasy with the naked anger of this story, which indicts not simply one unscrupulous young man but a whole generation for its freewheeling life and confessional style. In the eyes of an exacting craftsman who fears that *his* kind of art is no longer valued, these facile new writers simply don't invent enough. (Fogel accuses the young man of doing outrageous things simply to write about them, of being little more than "a walking tape recorder" of his "personal experiences.") When Fogel tells his surrogate son that "Imagination is not necessarily Id," Malamud could even be referring to Portnoy's recent line about "putting the Id back in Yid." Roth would give his own version of his spiritual apprenticeship to Malamud and Bellow ten years later in *The Ghost Writer*. In any case, "An Exorcism" remained unknown, while *Portnoy's Complaint* became the ultimate piece of second-generation black humor, a hilarious whine against the neurotic effects of a prolonged exposure to Jewish morality and the Jewish family.

Portnoy's complaint was an Oedipal complaint, but even at the time, long before he published *Patrimony*, his affecting 1991 memoir of the death of his father, it was clear how deeply attached Roth was to the parents he mocked and mythologized—the eternally constipated father, the effusively overbearing mother who loved and forgave him as no other woman could, loved him even for his transgressions. All through the 1970s Roth kept rewriting the novel in increasingly strident works like *The Breast*, a misconceived fantasy; *My Life as a Man*, a vengeful account of his first marriage; and *The Professor of Desire*. Roth seemed unable to escape the facts of his life but also seemed desperate to offend. He attacked critics for taking his work as autobiographical yet repeatedly fell back on exaggerated versions of the known facts. In *My Life as a Man* (and later in a directly autobiographical narrative called *The Facts*), he even played on the relationship between fact and invention by giving us what he claimed to be the "real" story behind some fictional versions. But of course he felt free to make up this version as well.

None of these almost military maneuvers against critics and readers, which Roth also carried on in essays and interviews, quite prepared us for his next book, *The Ghost Writer*, which launched the next stage of Jewish American writing, the one we are still in today. Let's call it the return, or the homecoming. If the second stage was debunking and satiric, even parricidal, the third stage began with Roth's filial homage to the two writers with whom his name had always been linked. Malamud appears in the book as E. I. Lonoff, very much the ascetic devotee of craft we meet in Malamud's own late work. Bellow (with a touch of Mailer) figures as the prolific, much-married, world-shaking Felix Abravanel, a man who, as it turns out, "was clearly not in the market for a twenty-three-year-old son." Roth himself appears as the young Nathan Zuckerman, a dead ringer for the author at that age. Zuckerman has just published his first, controversial stories, as Roth himself had done, and his own father is angry at him for washing the family linen in public. ("Well, Nathan, you certainly didn't leave anything out, did you?") His father has gotten the elders of the Jewish community on his case, in the person of one Judge Leopold Wapter, who sends him a questionnaire (!) that concludes: "Can you honestly say there is anything in your short story that would not warm the heart of a Julius Streicher or a Joseph Goebbels?"

Judge Wapter stands for all the professional Jews and rabbinical critics who had been upset by Roth's early stories—which, after all, had surely been written to ruffle people's feathers, even to offend. With very broad satirical strokes, the older Roth is now caricaturing his enemies, nursing old grievances, parading his victimization as wounded virtue. Roth demands from his readers what only his parents had given him: unconditional love. He wants to transgress and wants to be forgiven, wants to be outrageous yet also to be accepted, to be wickedly clever and be adored for it. When his lovers or his critics fail to give this to him, he lashes out at them. This rehearsal of old grievances is the tired and familiar part of *The Ghost Writer*, but the book included much that, in retrospect, was daringly fresh.

First, there is a surprising and resonant literariness that matches the book's evocative tone and warm filial theme. Roth's angry iconoclasm, his need to offend and outrage, has for now been set aside. *The Ghost Writer* deals with Nathan Zuckerman's literary beginnings, and Roth's virtuoso portraits of the older writers are perfectly in tune with the literary allusions that form the backdrop of the story—references to Isaac Babel, the great Soviet-Jewish writer murdered by Stalin; to Henry James's story "The Middle Years," which also deals with a young acolyte's relation to an older writer; and most importantly, to the diary of Anne Frank. She is the figure behind Amy Bellette, the young woman in Roth's story who may actually *be* Anne Frank, and who may be having an affair with Lonoff.

Second, for all the *shtick* and satire in Roth's previous fiction, this is in some ways his most Jewish book so far, not only in his tribute to earlier Jewish writers but in his tender retelling of Anne Frank's story. Both the literariness and the Jewishness had always been latent in Roth's work, just barely masked by its satiric edge, its willed vulgarity. Roth's literary bent had been evident in his essays on contemporary fiction, his brilliant story about Kafka, the interviews he had published about each of his novels, and especially the invaluable series he was editing for Penguin, "Writers from the Other Europe," which launched the Western careers of little-known Polish and Czech writers such as Milan Kundera. No critic, to my knowledge, has yet tried to gauge the effect of this large editorial enterprise on Roth's later fiction. As his own work bogged down in *Portnoy* imitations and paranoia, this project took Roth frequently to Eastern Europe, where he made a wealth of literary contacts. Thus Roth found himself editing morally serious and formally innovative work that, despite its congenial absurdism, cut sharply against the grain of what he himself was writing. This material exposed Roth to both the Holocaust and Soviet totalitarianism, and ultimately gave his work a historical dimension, and especially a Jewish dimension, it had previously lacked. These books brought him back to his distant European roots. The angry young man, the prodigal son, was gradually coming home.

In *The Ghost Writer* Roth still nurses his old quarrel with the Jewish community, just as he would pursue his vendetta against Irving Howe in *The Anatomy Lesson*. He eulogizes Lonoff as "the Jew who got away," the Jew of the heart, or art—the noninstitutional Jew—and portrays Anne Frank as a secular, detached Jew like himself. In a bizarre moment, Zuckerman even imagines himself *marrying* Anne Frank, perhaps the ultimate rejoinder to his Jewish critics, to all the Judge Wapters of the world. But apart from this defensiveness, there's a strain of reverence toward art in the book, toward the Jewish historical experience, even toward the Jewish family, which creates something really new in Roth. Instead of rebelling against the father, he wants to be anointed by him: he's come "to submit myself for candidacy as nothing less than E. I. Lonoff's spiritual son." Adopted by Lonoff, married to Anne Frank, he will no longer be vulnerable to the Howes and Wapters who criticize his writing for not being Jewish or tasteful enough.

In retrospect we can see how so much of value in Roth's later work—the wider political horizons in *The Counterlife* and *Operation Shylock*, the unexpected play with metafiction and magic realism in both those books, with their ingenious variations on what is made up and what is "real," and finally, his loving tribute to his late father in *Patrimony* and to the figure of the Good Father in *American Pastoral*—can be shown to have originated in *The Ghost Writer*. Moreover, they are strikingly typical of what I call the third phase of American Jewish writing, when the Jewishness that once seemed to be disappearing returned with a vengeance. In this phase the inevitability of assimilation gives way to the work of memory.

There's nothing so surprising about this pattern. The great historian of immigration, Marcus Lee Hansen, long ago enunciated the influential three-generation thesis that came to be known as Hansen's Law: "What the son wishes to forget the grandson wishes to remember." Sociologists have shown that this return actually begins in the twilight years of the second generation as it seeks to recover its own buried past. In *Patrimony* Roth presents his aged father as in some ways a pain in the neck but also as the keeper of the past, the storyteller, the Great Rememberer. Driving around Newark with his son, the former insurance agent, like a real census taker, recalls every occupant of every building. "You mustn't forget anything—that's the inscription on his coat of arms," his son writes. "To be alive, to him, is to be made of memory."

The father's motto is also part of the artistic credo of the son. Roth's protagonists are always astonished to meet old friends who fail to recall every single minute of their mutual childhood. This is why the narcissistic side of Roth, obsessed with self-scrutiny, cannot let go of any of his old grievances. Every object in his life—the old typewriter he got for his bar mitzvah, for example, which his first wife pawned—carries some heavy baggage of personal history. It leads him to idealize his youth in *Portnoy*, to see the postwar years as a golden age in *American Pastoral*. It enables him to remember his past with a hallucinatory intensity. Yet by the mideighties Roth also developed a wider historical purview, a sense of all that life that was lived before him, or far away from him—in Eastern Europe, where he sets "The Prague Orgy"; in England or Israel, where some of the best parts of *The Counterlife*, *Deception*, and *Operation Shylock* take place. This is a more cosmopolitan Roth, reaching outside himself for almost the first time, in dialogue with Zionism, acutely sensitive to anti-Semitism, finding new life in the Jewish identity he had once mocked and scorned.

Much of *The Counterlife* still belongs to the old self-involved Roth of the Zuckerman saga—the fears of impotence, the scabrous comedy, the Wagnerian family uproar—but the sections set in England and Israel are something else. Until the early 1980s, there was as little trace of the Jewish state in American fiction as there was of the old European diaspora in Israeli writing. American writers by and large were not Zionists, and Israeli writers were not nostalgic for the shtetl or the Pale. With its insistence on nationhood as the solution to the Jewish problem, Israel was perhaps too tribal, too insular to capture the attention of assimilated writers, however much it preoccupied ordinary American

Jews. Israel was the place where Portnoy couldn't get an erection—surely the least memorable part of that larger-than-life novel.

But more than a decade later, when Zuckerman's brother Henry becomes a *baal t'shuva*, a penitent, and Zuckerman looks him up among the zealots of the West Bank, Roth's work crosses that of Amos Oz and David Grossman, novelists who had written so well about the tensions dividing Israeli society. Like them, Roth gives ample hearing to great talkers who can articulate sharp ideological differences, which also reflect his own inner conflicts. He begins to relish the sheer play of ideas, the emotional bite of Jewish argument. This will be central to all his subsequent work. *The Counterlife* inaugurates a dialogic phase of Roth's writing that gets played out in *Deception*, an experimental novel which is all dialogue; *The Facts*, where Nathan Zuckerman appears at the end to offer a rebuttal to Roth's memoir; and *Operation Shylock*, which returns to the Israeli setting of *The Counterlife*. In this new fiction of ideas, Roth's work acquires a real historical dimension, which would also, beginning with *American Pastoral*, lead to an acclaimed but uneven trilogy about postwar America.

Zuckerman in Israel, like Zuckerman recounting other people's stories in the American books, is also Roth escaping from the self-absorption of his earlier work. In England, cast among the not-so-genteel anti-Semites, Zuckerman develops an extraordinary pride, aggressiveness, and sensitivity about being Jewish. With their layers within layers, both *The Counterlife* and *Operation Shylock* are among Roth's most Jewish books, even as Zuckerman defends himself (and Jewish life in the diaspora) against the imperious claims of orthodoxy and Zionism. They mark his return to the fold, as well as his most formally complex fiction, pointing not only to the confusions between art and life but to the multiple layers of Roth's identity.

By giving so much attention to Roth, I run the risk of making it seem as though it's only *his* development that is at stake, not larger changes in American Jewish writing. But every facet of Roth's later work has its parallel in other writers who have emerged in the last twenty years: the more explicit and informed Jewishness, the wider historical framework, the play with metafiction or magical realism, and the more intense literariness. In line with the wave of identity politics in America, there has been a persistent search for roots among younger Jewish writers, as well as older writers from assimilated backgrounds, such as Leslie Epstein (who grew up in Hollywood, the son of a famous screenwriter), Anne Roiphe (who grew up rich on New York's Park Avenue), and Alan Isler (who grew up in England). If we add to the themes listed above a concern with gender and sexual preference and a fascination with strict religious traditions, we would have a complete inventory of issues that have attracted the younger generation, including such varied writers as Steve Stern, Allegra Goodman, Lev Raphael, Thane Rosenbaum, Melvin Jules Bukiet, Pearl Abraham, Rebecca Goldstein, Michael Chabon, Ethan Canin, Aryeh

Lev Stollman, Ehud Havazelet, Nathan Englander, Myla Goldberg, Tova Mirvis, Jon Papernick, Jonathan Safran Foer, Dara Horn, Gary Shteyngart, and Gabriel Brownstein. They have dealt with subjects as remote from the work of their predecessors as the old and new Jews of Memphis, the lives of young Jews in Oxford and Hawaii, the orthodox communities of New York and Israel, the attractions of Jewish folklore and mysticism, the lives of Russian Jews in America, the problems of gay Jewish identity, the surreal experiences of the walking wounded—Holocaust survivors and their children—and the distantly remembered world of the shtetl and of Europe after the war. Some of their writing, arduously researched, smells of the library, while other parts of it are autobiographical or fantastic—or a mixture of both. These writers are drawn more to magical realism than to kitchen-sink realism. Michael Chabon's *Amazing Adventures of Kavalier and Clay* reinvents the young Jewish men who conceived the great comic-book characters of the late thirties and early forties. The novel offered an ingenious angle on a whole historical period, projecting these superheroes as boyish fantasies that compensated for the sense of Jewish powerlessness. Usually these new writers work best in short novels like Stollman's hypnotic *The Far Euphrates*, which explored Jewish mysticism, or in collections of overlapping stories like Goodman's *The Family Markowitz*, composed of scenes and vignettes that allude nostalgically to the old-style family chronicle. They write knowingly about life in Israel, as in the stories included in Englander's *For the Relief of Unbearable Urges* or Papernick's *The Ascent of Eli Israel*, and make resonant use of the kind of intricate moral fable perfected by Singer and Malamud, half ironic, half traditional. The larger synthesis so far eludes them.

The marked Jewish accent and interests of these emerging writers were foreshadowed not only by shifting stance of Philip Roth but by themes explored by another older writer, Cynthia Ozick. Like Roth she spent many years indentured to the 1950s gospel of art according to Henry James, and only later discovered her own vein of Jewish storytelling, typical of what I've called the third stage. To put it bluntly, Ozick's work is far more Jewish than that of her main predecessors, richer with cultural information, proudly nationalistic, even sentimentally orthodox. Some of her stories and essays, such as her angry piece in *The New Yorker* on Anne Frank's diary (reprinted in *Quarrel & Quandary*), launched stinging attacks on secular Jews. Yet she began as a feminist and became the most articulate woman in a largely patriarchal line that rarely produced strong writing by women, apart from such isolated figures as Emma Lazarus, Mary Antin, Anzia Yezierska, Grace Paley, or Tillie Olsen. This is something else that has changed dramatically since 1970.

Bellow and Malamud had Jewishness in their bones, but what they actually knew about Judaism could have been written down on a single page. They knew the ghetto neighborhoods, the character types, the speech patterns, and whatever else they took in at the kitchen table. They were born into Yiddish-speaking homes. Their Judaism was instinctive, domestic, introspective. But their determination to navigate the literary mainstream deterred them from getting too caught up with specifically Jewish subjects. They refused to be consigned to any literary ghetto. "I conceived of myself as a cosmopolitan man enjoying his freedom," said Malamud. Ozick, on the other hand, like I. B. Singer or Steve Stern, was fascinated by the whole magical side of Judaism—the popular lore and legend, the dybbuks and golems of Jewish mystical tradition. For Singer this was part of his experience of growing up in Poland, the curious son of a learned rabbi, entranced by hidden and forbidden byways of the Jewish tradition. What we find in Ozick and Stern is sometimes a bookish, vicarious Judaism based on reading and research. But this very bookishness—a certain remoteness from life—becomes a key theme in their work.

Until recently a fear haunted Jewish American writing: that the subject was exhausted, that we live in inferior times, that giants once walked the earth and said everything that had to be said; the rest is commentary. From her first important story, "Envy, or, Yiddish in America," in 1969 to her keynote story, "Usurpation: Other People's Stories," in the mid 1970s to *The Messiah of Stockholm* and *The Puttermesser Papers*, Ozick repeatedly writes stories about writers, or stories about other people's stories. This is a latecomer's literature, almost a textbook example of the postmodern profusion of texts upon texts or of Harold Bloom's famous theory of the anxiety of influence, which emphasizes the Oedipal relations between writers and their precursors. We risk becoming footnotes to our forebears.

Like *The Ghost Writer*, Ozick's "Envy"—the very title is revealing—is most memorable for its portraits of two older writers, one a lethal caricature of I. B. Singer—widely translated, fabulously successful, yet cruel, egotistical, and rejected by most other Yiddish writers—the other loosely based on the great poet Jacob Glatstein, celebrated among fellow Yiddishists yet never properly translated into English. (Ozick herself later did some translations of his work.) But the key figure is a young woman, perhaps based on Ozick herself, whom the embittered poet seizes upon as his life-line into English, the potential savior of all of Yiddish culture.

This poet is envious of the Singer character but even more contemptuous of American Jewish writers for their ignorance: "*Jewish* novelists! Savages!" he says bitterly. "Their Yiddish! One word here, one word there. *Shikseh* on one page, *putz* on the other, and that's the whole vocabulary." Like Roth's novella, this is a kind of ghost story; the characters embody a dead culture trying to come alive. But it's also a vampire tale, since the young woman eventually rejects them as blood-suckers trying to live at her expense. Fascinated by the high drama of an expiring Yiddish culture, she decides she cannot allow it to take over her own life. Cynthia Ozick is thought of as some kind of pious traditionalist, but this, her best story, written with ferocious energy and style, is a work that radiates hostility from first to last, reminding the reader of the polemical turn she often takes in her essays.

In Ozick's story "Usurpation," the spirit of envy takes over the protagonist herself. It begins with a young author at the 92nd Street Y listening to a reading by a famous older writer. After two or three sentences, her ears begin to burn, for she feels he's telling a story that truly belongs to her, that she was born to write. As it happens, the writer and the story can easily be identified, since Ozick retells it. It is "The Silver Crown," Malamud's tale of the wonder rabbi, which is precisely about the conflict of generations that is virtually the signature of this third or latecomer's generation. It's also a story of the kind of Jewish mystery and magic so dear to Ozick that she feels sharp regret at not having written it herself. Malamud had been there first, but Ozick, like Steve Stern, makes her literary belatedness the theme of her story.

It's no accident that Ozick's stories overlap with her eloquent literary essays, or that metafiction and postmodernism here make a surprising entry into Jewish writing. Postmodernism, as I understand it, conveys the sense that all texts are provisional, that we live in a world already crowded with familiar texts and images, that originality is a Romantic illusion and techniques like collage, pastiche, and pseudocommentary are better than realism for conveying our sense of belatedness and repletion. At the heart of Ozick's fine story "Puttemesser Paired" (in *The Puttermesser Papers*) are some brilliantly told episodes from the life of George Eliot, which the heroine partly reenacts, just as Ozick weaves a lost novel by the murdered Polish writer Bruno Schulz into *The Messiah of Stockholm*. As in the work of Jorge Luis Borges, this is writing about writing, situated vicariously on the fine line between commentary and invention.

It's not often that literary history so closely mirrors social history, but the conflict of literary generations I've described here is part of a larger pattern. It's no news that America has experienced a revival of ethnicity, or that the world has been rocked by waves of resurgent nationalism. With their longstanding commitment to the universalism of the Enlightenment, to which they owed their emancipation, Jews have been ambivalent about participating in this process. Thanks to the near-disappearance of anti-Semitism, Jewish life in America has become far more assimilated, but younger Jewish writers have both taken advantage of this and sharply criticized it. They have turned to Israel, to feminism, to the Holocaust, to earlier Jewish history, and to their own varied spiritual itineraries, ranging from neo-Orthodoxy and mysticism to Eastern religion, as a way of redefining their relation to both Jewish tradition and contemporary culture. If they have lost the old connection to Europe, to Yiddish, or to immigrant life, they have begun to substitute their own distinctive Jewish and American experiences. They are not simply living on the inherited capital of past literary generations. The new writing so far may lack the power of a Malamud, a Bellow, or a Grace Paley, but it is certainly not enervated by the bland, assimilated aspects of Jewish life. As Jews have gained acceptance as full-fledged Americans, the writers have taken the measure of what might be lost, and looked to deepen a culture of their own. Jewish writers have quarreled with each other and with themselves, but these have been family quarrels, not holy wars. Whatever tension this creates, it certainly gives no sign that Jewish American writing is about to give up the ghost, especially now that the ghost, the past, has taken on new flesh and blood.

THE FACE IN THE MIRROR: THE ECLIPSE
OF DISTANCE IN CONTEMPORARY FICTION

WE LIVE IN a confessional age; we are forever trying to unburden ourselves of the intimate baggage of our own experiences. As Michel Foucault writes in *The History of Sexuality*, "One confesses in public and in private, to one's parents, one's educators, one's doctor, to those one loves: one admits to oneself, in pleasure and in pain, things it would be impossible to tell anyone else, the things people write books about." The disquieting thing about this confessional wave is that it often involves little introspection and less self-knowledge. Rousseau scoffed at his predecessor, Montaigne, for having owned up to only petty vices, but some writers go much further and confess mainly to the sins of others. Contemporary writing is full of examples of the confessional *victim*, blameless, self-absorbed, more sinned against than sinning. In them the failure of introspection is usually matched by the paucity of insight into the mind and feelings of those around them.

This kind of narcissism would seem to be poor ground for the creation of fiction, whose sine qua non is certainly the imagining of other people, the conception of a plausible human context for the self. But literary developments after the 1960s blurred the rigid demarcations between fiction, autobiography, history, and journalism. The need to "create" characters gradually yielded to a tendency to anchor them in an autobiographical protagonist. Certainly there was no less experience in fiction in the forties and fifties, but Henry James's notions of craft and T. S. Eliot's theories of impersonality then prescribed a considerable degree of authorial distance, even objectification. In a famous passage of "Tradition and the Individual Talent" that seems remarkably quaint today (and not simply due to its gender reference), Eliot wrote: "The more perfect the artist, the more completely separate in him will be the man who suffers and the mind which creates; the more perfectly will the mind digest and transmute the passions which are its material."

Eliot, as we have come to see, was a closet romantic all along; he makes this clear in his use of "the man who suffers" as an emblem of experience, the passion he sees at the root of all art and poetry. But this is not how he was read in the 1950s, when the emphasis was on the transmutation: experience in art was so thoroughly chewed and digested that it sometimes turned into an exercise in style. The lines between life and art remained sharply drawn. The mystique of "creative writing" hung like a soft, low fog over literature courses and short-story workshops. Poems and novels were intimidating—as fragile as porcelain, as magical as incantations—and only the precious few who had received the call to Art could conjure them up.

This mystique of art could never fully explain a form as impure as the novel. Even under the influence of Flaubert and James, fiction couldn't fully shake off the traces of travel literature, memoirs, history writing, journalism, fairy tales, romances, popular melodrama, and other prose forms out of which that bastard genre was born. Besides, for all the importance of craft and invention, no art but figurative painting put so much stress on verisimilitude. Where painters might get by on a keen eye, an exacting sense of line, and a fine palette, the verbal medium demanded a range of feeling, a psychological insight, that writers could elicit only from their own experience. A novel had to be credible about setting, character, motivation. There might be child prodigies in math, chess, science, or music but never in fiction. Many novels are disguised autobiography, first novels painfully so; in the fifties, the fictive disguises for the author's own experience could be tedious and transparent; the cosmetic changes were often unconvincing and sometimes read like a defense against painful feelings and burning memories. In this literary climate, which demanded that fiction seem truly fictional, despite the actualities that lay behind it, what was gained in art could be lost in immediacy; what was gained in form was often lost in feeling.

The confessional thrust in the writing of the sixties, which began in poetry with Lowell and Ginsberg, and was advanced in prose by Mailer, Bellow, Kerouac, and Roth, aimed to liberate art from a stagnant formalism and bring it closer to experience. American poetry and prose became more directly autobiographical. Already in the late 1950s, literary form became more open and flexible and literary language more colloquial. As the 1960s unfolded, the lines between different kinds of writing—and between art and life—blurred. With *In Cold Blood* Truman Capote claimed to have invented the "nonfiction novel"; in *The Armies of the Night* Mailer breached the barrier between the novel and history; Tom Wolfe imported colorful fictional techniques into his journalism; for their first books, Frank Conroy and Frederick Exley set a pattern for many later writers by publishing novelistic autobiographies instead of autobiographical novels; Philip Roth in *Portnoy's Complaint* developed a cross between a novel and a vaudeville *shtick*; and Borges, by example, taught a generation to write stories that looked more like essays and sketches than fictional narratives. Everyone had a tale to tell. The priestly hush that attended the worship of art in the fifties was dispelled.

It was easy to mock the populist manifestations of this new mood, but for restless, unpredictable talents this blurring of boundaries could lead to thrilling innovations. Film, painting, poetry, and drama were shaken up by this creative ferment, and so was the art of the novel. Instead of disappearing behind the objective facade of the finished work, as they generally had in the fifties, novelists, like the new confessional poets, learned to place themselves in the foreground of what looked more and more like their own story. Suddenly it seemed that every writer, as if exhausted by the strenuous effort of imagining other people, simply made a version of himself—and, increasingly, *herself*—into his or her protagonist. Perhaps it was the immediacy of the movies that helped bring this about; and as films like $8\frac{1}{2}$ turned toward the personal and the subjective, the spirit of the later Fellini descended on American fiction. Heightened, stylized autobiography became a prevailing fictional mode; the speaking voice of a very personal narrator, full of charm and insinuation, replaced the more remote sounds of the omniscient storyteller.

Modernists like John Barth, who maintained that their stories were just artifacts, structures of words rather than windows on life, insisted on exposing the gears of their fiction-making machinery. At the other end of the spectrum, more subjective writers like Roth and a legion of feminist successors found it difficult to imagine a world that was not a function of their own bruised egos. Writers who felt blocked by the demands of art began spilling out their own histories, including tales of writer's block. Soon, what began as a breakthrough threatened to dissolve into an adventure in solipsism.

By the late 1970s this raw quality had become a lazy convention, producing innumerable poems that were not poems, stories that were not stories, shapeless novels that read like straight autobiography, higher gossip, or dispatches from the gender wars. Lacking a boldly elaborated plot or fully imagined characters, these novels seemed trapped in the minds of their protagonists. The formalist critic John Crowe Ransom had said of Flannery O'Connor's first stories that they were really *written*. Despite her reliance on a handful of situations from her own life, particularly in her later work when she was confined by illness, her stories were intricately plotted and richly textured. But during the 1970s the liberating thrust of direct personal expression gave way to an unimaginative dependence on the writer's own story. According to an imaginary writer named T. S. Garp, "The *worst* reason for anything being part of a novel was that it really happened." ("Garp would say that the autobiographical bug—if there even was one—was the least interesting level on which to read a novel. He would always say that the art of fiction was the act of *imagining* truly—was, like any art, a process of selection.") Yet Garp was the hero of a hugely successful novel, *The World According to Garp*, in which he happened to be a writer and a wrestler, an unusual combination he shared with his creator, John Irving. *Garp* was a portrait of the artist as the alter ego of his creator. Garp even writes a lurid book, *The World According to Bensenhaver*, which is marketed on this basis, and becomes his first great commercial success, just as *The World According to Garp* would be a popular breakthrough for Irving. The book thus anticipated its own publishing history. According to an imaginary critic quoted in the book, "Garp's work was progressively weakened by its closer and closer parallels to personal history." The same can be said of a number of other novels of the same period by prominent writers, all built around characters who are the very self and voice of the author, with barely a fig leaf of fictionalization.

In short order, William Styron in *Sophie's Choice* described an episode from the early life of a writer who, in the mid-1940s, had not yet written books that sound strikingly like his own *Lie Down in Darkness*, *The Long March*, and *The Confessions of Nat Turner*. Philip Roth in *The Ghost Writer* sketched a tale from the life of a promising young writer who, in the mid-1950s, has published some stories that, though praised by discerning critics, have brought down on him the wrath of his family and the official guardians of the Jewish community. In *Dubin's Lives*, Bernard Malamud told the gray and depressing story of a middle-aged writer—in this case a biographer, a student of other people's "lives"—who wrestles with his writing block and his fears of decline in a small New England town, where he nurtures the remains of a long, quiescent marriage and carries on an affair with a girl the age of his own daughter. Though each of these novels had moments that were touching and true, they were marred by self-absorption. This was fiction constrained by tunnel vision—narrow, intense, isolated from any context—fiction in which the whine of personal feeling drowns out the muffled hum of the great world.

Books like *Sophie's Choice*, *The Ghost Writer*, *Dubin's Lives*, and *The World According to Garp* leaned so heavily on recognizable details of their authors' lives that they amounted to self-plagiarism. And because they turned so narrowly on parochial problems of authorship, these books also seemed very much like each other. They were confessional yet owned up to very little. They rarely showed their authors in a bad light. They tried to be personal yet avoided the mysteries of personality for the more mundane dilemmas of writer's block, relations with older writers and publishers, middle-aged affairs, and literary reputations. Only Malamud even bothered to change the kind of writing the character did, making the protagonist of *Dubin's Lives* a biographer rather than a novelist, but the book remained as self-absorbed, as focused on the writer's mind and craft as the others.

It's important to distinguish books like these from modernist works that make authors and their techniques a part of the subject, and comment in a self-conscious way about the nature of art and the creative process. Among the great modern writers, Joyce, Mann, and James all painted complex, ambiguous portraits of the artist—potentially a fascinating subject for fiction, capable of carrying an enormous freight of myth and meaning beyond straight autobiography. But many postsixties writers simply anchored their undercooked tales in the facts of their own experiences, sometimes counting on the reader to recognize the parallels with their lives, which became common knowledge as authors increasingly were marketed as personalities. "Whenever Garp would try to write, he would see only the dull, undeveloped facts of his personal life." Writers grew unwilling to risk the terrors of invention and the strain of imagining other selves. As opposed to personal history, genuine storytelling has a logic of its own. A character's life can elude the author's best-laid plans. Writers need a plot not simply to keep the reader engaged but to understand their characters by seeing them through the eyes of others.

The impression we get from the opening monologue of Dostoevsky's *Notes from Underground* is altered and complicated by the brilliant novella that follows: observing the protagonist in action, we fathom him in a way we couldn't from his own self-conscious and manipulative harangue. Another distancing device is irony, which can be seen at its most subtle and sinuous in *Death in Venice*, Thomas Mann's novella about a distinguished writer who develops a corrosive passion for a beautiful young boy he sees on the beach. The book includes a slightly parodistic survey of the great man's "works," works that Mann himself had once contemplated writing. No one could fully count the ways in which Gustave von Aschenbach was or was not Mann himself, or some future fate he fears or foresees. The posthumous publication of Mann's letters and diaries, along with revealing biographies, showed that the character was much closer to the author than anyone could then have imagined. The same ambiguity hangs over the complex twists and turns of Henry James's portraits of writers and artists in stories like "The Middle Years" and "The Lesson of the Master." Willfully or ineptly, our contemporary authors of tales about writers deny themselves—and us—such a prismatic view of their central characters. When a novel or story is fully imagined, it takes on a subtle autonomy. If it genuinely grips us, we scarcely bother to think about its autobiographical basis, if there is one. The James stories, like Mann's novella, may be rooted in his own dreams and disappointments, but they are finally about art and life, not about Mann or James. *The Ghost Writer* echoes "The Middle Years," but we never doubt that *its* subject lives closer to home. Roth would make this conundrum the basis of his later work.

Merely autobiographical novels are neither modernist experiments nor parables of the artistic life, though they appeal to the precedent of such earlier works. Far from extending the form in any way, Roth, Styron, Malamud, and Irving were conservative novelists writing less about art than about themselves, though Roth, smarting under the charge of being strictly a confessional writer, would later defect to his own corner of the postmodern camp. Beginning with works like *The Anatomy Lesson* and *The Counterlife*, he would offer alternate versions of the same stories, repeatedly blurring the line or showing where life and art, fact and invention, diverged. Even in *The Ghost Writer*, Roth was exceptional in providing real centers of interest besides the authorial self, perhaps because it is modeled directly on the artist fables of James, particularly "The Middle Years," which gets retold in the course of the novel. *The Ghost Writer* is built on the classic Jamesian situation of the worshipful acolyte, the newcomer to art, confronting the old lion, who is by now almost too world-weary to dispense the wisdom of a lifetime. The eager, ambitious young man is obviously Roth himself at twenty-three—the book is set in the mid-1950s—the author of those famous or infamous early stories.

Roth's treatment of not one but two older writers proved to be a real tour de force. With his gift for mimicry and pastiche, Roth did a virtual survey of modern Jewish letters. E. I. Lonoff, whom our hero visits, is based on Malamud ("with his 'translated' English to lend a mildly ironic flavor to even the most commonplace expression"), while Lonoff's more worldly rival, Felix Abravanel, crosses Bellow with a bit of Mailer. When Lonoff tells our young hero, Nathan Zuckerman, "And what about you? . . . Aren't you a New World cousin in this Babel clan, too? What is Zuckerman in all this?" the young Roth was claiming his own place in the Jewish pantheon of Bellow-Malamud-Roth, a gilded ghetto to which these writers generally disliked being confined.

It was not in the portrayal of Lonoff and Abravanel that the book went wrong; Roth has the perfect ear of a born satirist, and his malicious eye for the damning detail never fails him. As the ascetic Lonoff says of Abravanel:

> I admire what he puts his nervous system through. I admire his passion for the front-row seat. Beautiful wives, beautiful mistresses, alimony the size of the national debt, polar expeditions, war-front reportage, famous friends, famous enemies, breakdowns, public lectures, five-hundred-page novels every third year, and still, as you said before, time and energy left over for all that self-absorption. The gigantic types in his books have to be that big to give him something to think about to rival himself. . . . It's no picnic up there in the egosphere.

One could hardly imagine a better description of the titanic, self-involved writer. Self-absorption on a colossal scale, as we find it in Mailer and Bellow (and echoed in Abravanel), can be a kind of self-transcendence, a wrestling with history and destiny, not vulgar self-promotion. This is the vein of self-absorption that lights up the American classics, going back to Emerson, Whitman, Melville, and Emily Dickinson; the writer's inner life becomes a lens that filters and interprets the world. It's in the depiction of Zuckerman that the book runs into trouble. When Lonoff says lamely that "Zuckerman has the most compelling voice I've encountered in years, certainly for somebody starting out," Roth's language gives way to his ego. This is the self-regarding chatter we hear about the writings of T. S. Garp or about Dubin's sacramental devotion to the art of biography, for which, like Lonoff, he neglects wife, children, people in general—in short, neglects to live. In their inflationary self-portraits as writers, Roth, Irving, and Malamud turned self-concerned on a pettier scale than Mailer or Bellow—concerned with getting words down, with reputation, etcetera. The picture we get of their alter egos' lives seems inert and literal, not grandiose and suggestive.

This may be unfair to *The Ghost Writer* and even to *Garp*. Roth, after all, provides us with three different writers, an unhappy wife for Lonoff who isn't simply a figment of the male imagination, and a convincing though familiar family background for Zuckerman. He also dreams up Zuckerman's fantasy that Lonoff's young protégée, Amy Bellette, is really Anne Frank, who survived the war incognito. Roth's sober literary side, his Dr. Jekyll persona with its civilized morality, has always competed for our attention with his satiric, borscht belt side. In Roth's erotic and historical reverie about Anne Frank, his id and superego come together—though, as a mere daydream, it strains the unity of *The Ghost Writer* as a novel. A friend of mine, a novelist, remarked that the book would have been better if Amy really *were* Anne Frank, that is, if Roth had had the courage of his fictional invention. Yet this speculative possibility foreshadows the alternate plots, the unstable dialectic of the real and the imagined, that brilliantly complicates Roth's later books.

We can see what Roth was trying to do: like Styron in *Sophie's Choice* but with more control and economy, he was using autobiography to launch himself into territory far outside himself, to the history of the Holocaust, which hardly any writer had yet been able to encompass in fiction. Where Styron turned his vast research into melodrama, trying in a futile way to paint the whole picture of the Holocaust, Roth used Anne Frank's diary with great restraint as the part that stands for the whole—one individual fate that makes six million more meaningful. And where Stingo, Styron's alter ego, remained too remote and detached—not nearly as obsessed with the poor Polish refugee Sophie and her doomed Jewish lover Nathan as he often claims to be—Roth tried to harness Anne Frank's story to his personal history. Just as Zuckerman admires Lonoff as a man free of tribal attachments, a kind of non-Jewish Jew, Roth portrays Otto Frank's family as assimilated Jews like himself, who were nevertheless persecuted as Jews. Roth tries to appropriate their story, now sanctified into Jewish legend, as his response to his own persecutors, the censorious Judge Wapters and Irving Howes of this world. "Oh, marry me, Anne Frank," thinks Zuckerman, "exonerate me before my outraged elders of this idiotic indictment! Heedless of Jewish feeling? Indifferent to Jewish survival? Brutish about their well-being? Who dares accuse of such unthinking crimes the husband of Anne Frank!"

A moment later, in an ingenious twist, Zuckerman/Roth recognizes the futility of using Anne Frank's story—that is, his own fictional invention—to purify himself, to be a child again. His "marriage" to Anne, "far from acquitting me of their charges and restoring me to cherished blamelessness," would prove, like *The Ghost Writer* itself, "a fiction that would seem to them a desecration even more vile than the one they had read." You can't go home again, Roth finally admits, and you can't use fiction to establish your claims to personal virtue. But like Anne herself, he can't put aside "this seeming passion to 'come back' as the avenging ghost." Roth's revenge-inspired books (like *I Married a Communist*), directed at specific people in his life—ex-wives, critics, former friends—would always show him at his least attractive.

Styron's novel, like Roth's, is driven by a desire to take possession of history and put it on display as evidence of a deep and resonant humanity. But where Roth tries hard to tie the pieces together, Styron's book breaks apart into two separate and unequal halves: Stingo's autobiography and the drama of Sophie at Auschwitz and her later affair with Nathan in New York. Though Stingo at twenty-two is an unpublished Southern writer and an intensely frustrated virgin, his dreams of literary and erotic glory intersect at several points with those of his slightly more advanced counterpart, Zuckerman. Stingo does not make it with Sophie until page 496—this is a languorous novel by any standard—but Styron's graphic though baroque treatment of his sexual fantasies, masturbatory habits, and comic near-misses would have not been possible without the liberties Roth took in *Portnoy*. Styron can also be warmly evocative, as Roth is in *The Ghost Writer*, about the ecstasies, ambitions, and disappointments of a young writer just starting out, "those faraway afternoons of First Novelhood (so long before middle age and the drowsy slack tides in inanition, gloomy boredom with fiction, and the pooping out of ego and ambition) when immortal longings impelled your every hyphen and semicolon and you had the faith of a child in the beauty you were destined to bring forth."

Unfortunately, Styron cannot write even about writing without falling into overwriting; his mock-epic enthusiasm—what the critic Robert Towers described as his "prolixity and facetiousness"—smacks of insincerity. Working with a sliver of experience from his early days as a writer and a mountain of indigestible research on the Holocaust, Styron had no choice but to embellish, and this betrayed the book's lack of conviction and formal organization. Styron has a habit of substituting lush prose, full of overelaborated metaphors and irrelevant sensory details, for an inward grasp of character, and his control of plot seems improvisational in its slackness. This kind of writing showed its limitations in his earlier treatment of Nat Turner, whose character and point of view were smothered in overripe eloquence. Stingo is a far more convincing figure, a comical redneck in search of love and fame in the big city; but even here Styron can't decide whether he's a bumbling innocent or a budding genius. He is so close to the character that he hasn't thought him through.

Worst of all, anchoring a novel in an autobiographical figure puts him on a different plane from those conceived fictionally, like Sophie and Nathan. Stingo's humiliations as a purveyor of the slush pile at McGraw-Hill in the first chapter are much more believable than Sophie's gruesome trials as a typist for Rudolf Höss, the commandant of Auschwitz (who after all, like Nat Turner, really existed, and can't simply be appropriated fictionally). Sophie's position in the camp is far too atypical to carry the burden of the Auschwitz experience. As Georg Lukács demonstrated in *The Historical Novel*, when such books rely too heavily on key historical figures and the characters' unlikely proximity to them, we end up with costume drama in a confected historical setting rather than an authentic sense of the past.

Sophie's attempts to seduce and manipulate Höss are the stuff out of which "serious" movies are made, movies like Lina Wertmüller's *Seven Beauties*, with its bogus, aestheticized version of a concentration camp. Besides, as the book

moves back from postwar New York to prewar and wartime Poland, it founders technically: Stingo keeps falling into the role of the omniscient narrator,
telling us stories, with ever-diminishing credibility, which he could not have
known at first hand. Styron's own detailed research on the Holocaust keeps
poking its ribs through the bare flesh of the fictional narrative. Despite its basis
in fact, or because of it, this kind of novel has a way of becoming factitious,
underimagined.

When *Sophie's Choice* first appeared, it seemed worthwhile to wonder why
Styron, in a book so subjective that parts of it scarcely read like fiction at all,
should have intruded another book set so far from his usual imaginative terrain. Overlaid and entangled, Stingo's story and Sophie's story never merged.
No doubt the Holocaust had an intrinsic moral interest for a writer concerned
with sin, passion, and the darker recesses of the human heart. But the book itself hinted at a reason closer to home. As early as 1947 (which is when the
framing story takes place), Styron claims to have been aware of the waning
star of Southern writing and the rising literary star of the Jews. Most improba-
bly, Styron has Nathan, a biologist, tell Stingo that "Southern writing as a
force is going to be over within a few years. Another genre is going to have to
take its place." Nathan even asks him whether he's heard of *Dangling Man* by
Saul Bellow (his first and only published book at the time, and hardly noticed
outside a small literary circle).

As usual Styron, who recalls minute inflections of thought and feeling going back thirty-two years—the way Stingo unfolds a panoramic knowledge
of Sophie's life before he met her—is projecting his later concerns onto an in-
appropriate character. Styron was going one up on the Jewish novel, as Updike
tried to do in his stories about Henry Bech. If black novelists were hesitant to
tackle the subject of slavery, Styron appropriated it from them in *Nat Turner*;
if Jewish writers shrank back from the enormity of the Holocaust, Styron
stepped in to show them how it could be done—and with a Polish heroine to
boot, as if to remind us that others besides the Jews suffered. He even built up
an analogy between those gallant romantic Poles, beautiful losers, and the
dashing spirit of the American South. And what were the Jews, he says ab-
surdly, but the blacks of Poland? It was not that Styron approached the Holocaust with anything less than a serious, conscientious spirit. But his failure to
encompass it, his melodramatic reduction of it, like his overripe impersonation of Nat Turner, helps us understand why so many other writers, whose anguish seems more authentic, held these pressing subjects at bay, or honored
them with their silence.

Like all autobiographical writers when they step outside their own experience, Styron and Roth risked betraying large subjects by assimilating them to
themselves. In the infinite night of the Absolute, said Hegel mockingly, all cows
are black; here, in the dark night of the soul, all other figures grow dim. *The
Ghost Writer* and *Sophie's Choice*, anchored in their young literary protagonists,

are in some ways the lean and fat versions of the same story. Equally bizarre were the intersections between Roth's novel, with its Malamud-like figure, Lonoff, and Malamud's own *Dubin's Lives*. Dubin was an author about Malamud's age, and he too lived in a small New England town, as Lonoff does. In both books this character—austere, moral, ascetic—resists being seduced by a young woman, though Dubin eventually goes off with her to Italy, as Roth's Lonoff only dreams of doing. In the end, both characters cling to a basically loveless life with their long-suffering wives, though it's much less clear why the wives also stick with them.

In Lonoff's case the presumed genius of the man, his single-minded fidelity to his art, excuses many sins and makes the vagaries of personal life seem secondary. But Dubin is no more than a self-absorbed biographer whose moral and emotional gyrations are harder to justify. What seems authentic about Dubin is the fear of getting old, the sense of one's powers slipping away, the ferocious wish to hang on to life and be reborn with a younger woman. (There's one short section on the "age of aging"—on pages 308 to 323 of the hardcover edition—that is as good as anything on the subject in contemporary fiction.)

But as with other novels centering on writers, Malamud's failure to achieve distance from Dubin prevented him from making sensible judgments about his behavior and kept readers from seeing other characters except through Dubin's unreliable eyes. In many ways a generous man, an altruist nailed to the cross of duty and humanity, Dubin priggishly treats his women and his children as functions of his need and uses his work to blot out any awareness of *their* needs. But the novel, which describes him in hushed tones as "the biographer," and collaborates egregiously with his self-importance, remains only haphazardly aware of this.

Genuflecting before the sanctities of art, Malamud loses the rich and poignant humor of his early books: the novel grows as stolid and solemn as its protagonist. The riveting poetic quality of Malamud's language in his wonderful short stories disappears; straining for eloquence, eschewing fluent colloquialism, the book falls into a stylized shorthand that inadvertently parodies the great prose of *The Assistant* and *A New Life*. The book moves so slowly, so little happens for such long stretches, that it almost seems to move backward; as Dr. Johnson said tactfully of *Paradise Lost*, no one would wish it longer than it is. For a book that dwells minutely on nature, rich with echoes of Thoreau, the style feels remarkable unnatural.

Like so many of these novels about authors, *Dubin's Lives* seems haunted by echoes of other writers. Obsessed with literature, such books invariably become too literary, inviting comparisons that make them look bad. *The Ghost Writer* is a kind of homage to James, a "blest *nouvelle*" in his airy and sparkling manner, on one of his favorite themes. But the complex relation between the old writer and his young admirer in James's "The Middle Years" simply beggars imitation; their intricate interaction reverses itself several times in the last three pages alone. One of James's relatively minor works, it makes Roth's story seem minor as well.

The same result ensued from the competition Malamud set up with Thoreau and D. H. Lawrence. Both are said to be subjects of Dubin biographies, yet they're also meant to comment on his relation to nature and his sexual traumas and adventures. Malamud deserves full credit for working up this Lawrence material well—this was no superficial dip into *Lady Chatterley*-land. (He later wrote some interesting biographical stories about Virginia Woolf and Alma Mahler.) Dubin may not be a credible biographer yet his Lawrence was a precisely articulated subject. But by no stretch of the imagination does Lawrence's sexual philosophy or his tempestuous married life with Frieda shed much light on Dubin's more banal predicament, the belated midlife crisis of a proper married man having an affair with a girl half his age. This is a faintly ridiculous situation, more suitable for farce than for the Wagnerian intensities of *Women in Love*. Molière could have handled it well; the Malamud who wrote the early Fidelman stories, with their wild and touching humor, could have handled it well. But here, fatally wrapped up in Dubin's viewpoint, he lost perspective. Half the book was taken up with Dubin's depressions, and Malamud became as portentously solemn about Dubin's love life as he was about his work. The book's blinkered vision is symptomatic of the problems that can afflict writers writing about writers as surrogates for themselves.

Every writer works out of a limited stock of feelings and experiences. But if the writing is not to remain private, the novelist must also depend on keen observation, along with unusual powers of empathy and intuition, must (in James's phrase) be one on whom nothing is lost, very much like good actors with their fund of personalities and gestures, their readiness to get inside someone else's skin. Yet the *process* of writing, though it involves a kind of performance, *is* intensely private—the least worldly, the least social of all callings. Writers are creatures who can live in their heads and tolerate long stretches of solitude.

This came to mind when I read in John Irving's book that "Garp spent a lot of time trying to imagine what it would be like to have a job." Soon he decides that he actually wants one. "It was for his writing that he was thinking he needed a job. I am running out of people I can imagine, he thought." With typical comic bravado he thinks of setting up as a marriage counselor, since he must be as expert in human relations as the licensed professionals. But it remains startlingly true that few modern novels tell what it feels like to hold down a job, least of all *The World According to Garp*. In contemporary fiction we usually get more of a sense of society from popular novelists than from serious ones: the debased progeny of Balzac are on the best-seller list, not in the literature courses. Popular novelists like James Michener became famous for the diligence of their research, though their characters were wooden, their material journalistic, their plots melodramatic.

Garp never follows through on marriage counseling—he soon has enough trouble with his own marriage—but when he finds it hard to go on writing, he does become a wrestling coach. (Irving himself, as everyone soon learned, had also been a wrestler.) "There were only two things in the world that T. S. Garp ever learned to do: he could write and he could wrestle." Of course the novel was about more than writing and wrestling, but it was weakened by the eclipse of distance between author and protagonist. As a fictive novelist and literary celebrity, Garp, like his progenitor, frequently expresses his dislike of autobiographical fiction and claims to love nothing more than storytelling, imagination, making things up. "The only reason for something to happen in a novel," says Garp, "is that it's the perfect thing to have happen at that time." "Tell me *anything* that's ever happened to you," he tells an interviewer, "and I can improve upon the story; I can make the details better than they were." This makes good sense, and implies a devastating judgment on the kind of autobiographical novel I have been considering here. But these very words convict themselves: they are a writer's way of jerking off in print, sounding off about writing rather than telling a story.

To his credit Irving did what few writers in this genre dare to do: he gave us big chunks of Garp's fiction. I found these extracts less enthralling than Irving did, but they showed more invention than Irving's own book (of which they were, of course, an invented part—wheels within wheels!). *Garp* was at times a delightful and ingratiating book. It mixed the playful with the solemn, the arbitrary with the inevitable. It initiated an important literary career. But like the later Salinger, like Vonnegut at his weaker moments, it fell too frequently into cuteness and even bathos—which may account for its popularity. For all his intelligence, Irving is an incurably sentimental writer as well as a didactic one. As the book goes on, he allows Garp a vein of simplistic moralizing about art and life that takes us behind the character and back to the author. "He knew he oversimplified the things that made him angry." But he also oversimplifies the things he loves, the ideas he preaches and parodies. For this reason the first hundred or so pages of the book were easily the best: the story of Garp's mother, Jenny Fields; his almost immaculate conception, which is a wonderful comic take-off on all those myths of the birth of the hero; her career as a famous feminist and their years together at Steering School and then in Vienna, where both begin trying to write.

When Garp finally becomes a published author, this kind of inspired fantasy material diminishes in the book. (It returns later in the gratuitous form of sudden, grotesquely comical violence, which became a trademark of Irving's). The distance between Irving and Garp nearly disappears, the mythic humor and resonance of the book die down, and more solemn matters of craft and literary apprenticeship take their place. There's no pain (but not much gain) in reading about the older Garp as a housekeeper, husband, and affectionate but anxious parent. But by this point the book's comic spirit has ebbed and a good deal of discursive babble begins to clutter up the narrative. The disintegration and death of Garp read like the author's self-pitying daydream. The long epilogue, "Life After Garp," sketching in the lives of all the surviving characters, is so bad that it raises troubling questions about the whole novel. What makes these figures so flimsy and puppetlike, unable to resist such heavy-handed manipulation? It turns out that except for his mother, Jenny, who is already dead, these characters have no life apart from Garp; his presence has energized them, kept them in orbit around his needs, his being. Once the author's surrogate drops out, the book lapses into a sentimental reverie about early death and posthumous fame, and the other characters fall like matchsticks. Apparently, they were never that real to begin with.

I hope I haven't implied that the only way out of this quandary for American fiction is simply a return to a more impersonal mode of plot, setting, and characterization. These books leaned on autobiography like a crutch, but what hobbled them was not subjectivity but the failure of subjectivity to be forcefully realized. Eventually, because of these limitations, they gave way to a vogue for memoirs that dispensed entirely with these fictional trappings. But even straight autobiographies succeed not by retelling the past but by imagining a world, establishing a voice, propounding a myth, or finding the pattern that lends meaning to a life history. There are no easy answers to the vexing question of how experience gets into fiction. Writers may rely lamely on what "really happened," whether they portray their protagonists as authors or not. By the same token, a novel about a writer, and even about oneself, can be full of style, wit, subtlety, color, and an intuitive feeling for other people. As fictional creations authors need not simply be people who write, any more than painters are only people who paint. They can have twenty selves and play as many roles from week to week, hundreds more if we include their fantasy lives. Each of us has dimensions of personality, powers of empathy, observation, and imagination, that are almost infinite if we could tap into them creatively. Hawthorne, whose temperament was reclusive, could recreate the world while poring over old books and papers in the attic, or "in the deserted parlor, lighted only by the glimmering coal-fire and the moon" (as he tells us in the introduction to *The Scarlet Letter*). But these writer-centered novels by Malamud, Roth, Styron, Irving, and others take little cognizance of the many selves of the person who writes, the artist who creates. Roth made this discovery in the early 1980s, no doubt irritated by the kind of criticism developed here, and it led him to write postmodern novels like *The Counterlife* and *Operation Shylock*, in which the autobiographical writer seems to shuffle the deck of alternative selves.

One of the strategies of modernism in all the arts was to bring the creator into the work, to dispel illusion and the hackneyed imitation of life, and to make the audience more conscious of form, more cognizant of the creative process. Books about authors, if they are daring enough—think of Vladimir Nabokov's *Pale Fire*—can become verbal equivalents of action painting or *pointillisme*: they seem to compose and decompose before our very eyes (a clever illusion if there ever was one). But when a rare novel of Nabokovian ingenuity came along, like Jonathan Baumbach's *Chez Charlotte and Emily*, reviewers were frightened off by its complexity, just as they were terrified or offended by the early works of modernism. Baumbach's multilayered book was about an "author" who is making up a good deal of the book himself, like a Saul Steinberg figure in the act of drawing or erasing the very cartoon in which he appears. The book explored not the humdrum existence of the writer but the fiction-making powers we all have, the relation between what we imagine and who we are—a theme as old as Cervantes yet as new as our best experimental writers.

The narrowly autobiographical books I've examined in this essay were not experimental works; they took advantage of territory gained by others long ago. They were conservative books that fell back on the convention of realism without paying their dues, without the hard work of plotting, characterization, milieu, and historical insight that gave the realistic novel its glory. Writers appeared in these books simply as themselves, not as reflexive devices raising serious questions about reality and representation. They didn't enable us to look behind the scenery to the artistic process, to watch the work watching itself as it was being articulated. But neither were they fully fictionalized characters, limitless in their potential for mystery and surprise. Instead they were just people who wrote: getting their stuff written was their main problem, though they also made love and war with characters who lived in the reflected glow of their overbearing presence.

Flatly autobiographical novels may arise from laziness, or self-absorption, or a failure of imagination, or even from a cultural atmosphere that devalues craft and invention and puts a premium on self-expression—a sort of Me Generation attitude that worked its way into the arts yet lost its creative thrust. When I put the question informally to Norman Mailer, he inclined toward another explanation: creative panic, the writer's fear that the last book was his last book, that it has sucked him dry, emptied him out. This panic may lead writers to solicit their own experience too directly: not sure they can still create, still dream, they fall back on remembering.

For all I know, a gripping novel like Scott Spencer's much-admired *Endless Love*, published around the same time as the novels discussed here, may have been just as autobiographical; in its relentless focus on a single adolescent love affair, it was certainly as narrow and obsessive. But obsession and the fatality of love were precisely the book's subjects; its white-hot emotion swept us past all questions of personal history. As a piece of confessional writing, the hero's erotomania, including one of the longest sex scenes in contemporary literature, could be seen as boastful and embarrassing. Knowing no limits, it propelled him toward madness, yet also into an erotic utopia dreamed of by mystics, from which he seemed unlikely ever to recover. But because this confession takes place in a genuine novel, not on a talk show or in a tell-all memoir, the book knows all this and puts it into perspective. This is what pornography is like when it happens to real people: gloomy, ecstatic, suffocating, and pure. It shows that authentic fiction can still be written, even as an exorcism of personal demons.

ORDINARY PEOPLE: CARVER, FORD, AND BLUE-COLLAR REALISM

THE DEATH OF John Cheever, Bernard Malamud, Donald Barthelme, and Raymond Carver during the 1980s seemed to mark the symbolic passing of three separate generations in American fiction. There were many other important writers, but somehow these four seemed especially emblematic of the postwar decades when their best work emerged. Along with Flannery O'Connor, who died prematurely in 1965, and a few younger writers like Alice Munro and John Updike who have since become our older masters, they were among the greatest contemporary practitioners of the short story.

At a time when the Wasp novel of manners had already expired in America, Cheever, in a series of brilliant stories for *The New Yorker*, chronicled the hidden anxieties of a postwar generation of young urban professionals who were now raising children in the fashionable suburbs. Despite his lighthearted tone and a taste for whimsy and fantasy, Cheever was a scrupulous realist and a keen social observer. Yet his stories were also rooted in his own obsessions and concealments, which have become clearer since his death: his ambivalence toward his family, his half-suppressed homosexuality, his self-destructive alcoholism—all couched behind the facade of the country gentleman. But as time passes, his work has emerged as a painstaking record of American morals and manners in the years immediately following the war.

Bernard Malamud's poor, luckless ghetto Jews seem a world away from Cheever's tennis-playing, hard-drinking Wasps. Though Saul Bellow, with his more varied body of work, was able to maintain his creative edge for a longer period, Malamud, who died in 1986, was (at his best) the purest, most deeply moving of the Jewish-American writers who emerged in the forties and fifties. Like Cheever, he showed little interest in the larger world of politics and society. His wraithlike characters, who barely live in the world yet suffer grievously from it, are caught up in their own private troubles, which are relieved only by Malamud's comic (and cosmic) sense of the irony, his bittersweet Jewish imagination of disaster. Much more than Cheever, Malamud was a fabulist, a descendant of Hawthorne and Kafka, who turned each story into moral allegory, a parable of his own characters' distance from life and their desperate hunger for it.

By the late 1960s, Malamud's style of wrenching moral anguish had worn as thin as Cheever's vein of sparkling social observation. If Malamud seemed too grimly involved, too earnest, Cheever appeared altogether too smoothly detached and well defended. Both were consummate craftsmen, yet their stories, like Flannery O'Connor's, seemed too *written*, too finished, for a world that appeared to be coming apart. The explosive contradictions of the age, with its noisy public confrontations and wild loss of inhibitions, demanded a fiction that was more fragmentary and surreal, more sophisticated yet also more carnivalesque. The age demanded Donald Barthelme, whose inspired *bricolage* swept up everything from Snow White to Tolstoy, from Robert Kennedy to Kierkegaard.

Barthelme's early stories, with their haunting illustrations and obscure titles, were a Sargasso Sea of the history of culture. The taste of the sixties, grounded in Pop Art, had undone the old cultural hierarchies, especially those that divided trash from art. It fostered a metafiction that would look more assembled than written, a two-dimensional, open-ended fiction toying with its own devices, acutely conscious of its fictionality. But Barthelme went beyond this clever reflexiveness; his work was elegant and dry, witty and detached, facetiously mock-serious. Yet, for a few years in the late 1960s, it was also full of powerful intimations of mystery and pathos. For all his debts to playful, non-linear writers of the past, from Laurence Sterne to Borges, Barthelme was an original, a writer with a different tone, a new way of processing cultural waste.

Barthelme, like Thomas Pynchon, situated himself neatly "on the leading edge of this trash phenomenon," but with the passage of time his work became flatter and less magical; his prose remained elegant, his wit undimmed, but the deeper current of feeling ran dry, the ironies grew predictable. He had gone to the well once too often. The 1970s, with its fuel crises and chronic recessions and political disasters, from the loss of Vietnam to the fiasco of Watergate, were in every way a more pinched and depressed period than the sixties. As the economy soured and America's role in the world seemed to contract, the culture needed a writer who reflected the downbeat mood, the sense of frustration and failure that worked its way into the fiber of individual lives. The age demanded a writer like Raymond Carver.

No writer was less suited to play the role of social prophet than Carver. Despite his meticulous craftsmanship, a thick fog of depression hangs over his early collections of stories. Yet they tell us a great deal about forgotten American lives. Most of Carver's stories are set in the Pacific Northwest; his blue-collar characters live far from the mainstream of upper-middle-class life, with its chic urban sophistication. These stories deal not with cosmic dilemmas but with the routine unhappiness of marriage and family life, with trite subjects like alcoholism, casual infidelity, dull jobs, and unemployment. Carver's characters are not especially sensitive or introspective, but he never condescends to them or directly judges them; instead he works their constricted awareness into his technique. In Carver's mature work, less is more: less psychology, less literary language, less continuous narration, only spare, disjunctive details which we ourselves as readers must assemble. A Carver story is like a do-it-yourself fiction kit.

After the exhaustion of metafiction, Carver's work, along with that of Ann Beattie, Bobbie Ann Mason, Richard Ford, and Tobias Wolff, represented a return to realism and regionalism in American fiction, a rediscovery of "ordinary" life and ordinary people—that is, of life as it is lived among the shopping malls and K-Marts, in suburban ranch houses and in factory jobs, lives pitted by divorce, family violence, and a general sense of defeat. Carver's characters are losers, people who mess up, who invariably make the wrong choices, and his "realism" is as narrow in its horizons as these people's hopes. Many of his stories are barely anecdotes, with little apparent shape or resolution. They record the *disjecta membra* of experience without the emotion or understanding that would give them meaning. Yet this uneventfulness, at once casual and arbitrary, is as deceptive as the realistic surface.

Carver's famous minimalism was a post-Beckett realism that had been through the forge of modernist skepticism and despair. Carver avoided physical description, narrative texture, atmospheric detail, and authorial commentary, even began to remove them from stories he'd already published. In addition to his regular collections, Carver put out several small-press chapbooks of his poetry and prose, such as a 1977 book of stories called *Furious Seasons*. Some of the pieces in *Furious Seasons* were short prose experiments that Carver never reprinted; they show his restless attempts to develop some fictional form that would perfectly match his dark vision. But three longer stories, "Dummy," "Distance," and "So Much Water So Close to Home," reappeared in his next regular collection, *What We Talk About When We Talk About Love*, but so drastically rewritten that they are almost unrecognizable. These changes showed how deliberately Carver worked at the style that would prove irresistible to other American writers.

Few other writers have given us stories in such strikingly different versions. In these revisions we see Carver ruthlessly paring these tales down, roughing up the narrative, removing descriptive details, metaphors, and all traces of wistful, coming-of-age lyricism; abetted or incited by his editor, Gordon Lish, he turned long rolling paragraphs into choppy, staccato bulletins, often just fragments of dialogue separated by silence and vacancy. Everything "literary" became colloquial and demotic: instead of a generalized narration, a "normal" language of storytelling, we heard in these new versions the talky cadence of someone's off-beat voice, the same voice that sounded in the tinny, repetitious titles that became a Carver trademark ("Will You Please Be Quiet, Please?" "What We Talk About When We Talk About Love").

The revised stories even get different titles; thus "Dummy" becomes "The Third Thing That Killed My Father Off," and "Distance" turns into "Everything Stuck to Him." The third story, "So Much Water So Close to Home," keeps its title but loses three-quarters of its text, as if a Giacometti sculpting with words had hacked away at it in a wild frenzy. It becomes skeletal, fragmentary, discontinuous, detached from all explanation: the enigmatic, boiled-down essence of the story it had been. The characters are the same, even the "story" is the same, but now the meaning, the pattern, must take shape in the mind of the reader; it's nowhere explicit in the words on the page.

In Carver's work, the surreal, associative logic of a Barthelme collage infil-
trated the terrain of a minute domestic realism, making it wild and jazzy and
grimly comical. Just as there is an infinite sadness buried in Barthelme's worldliness and cultivation, there's a zany nihilistic humor at the heart of Carver's
low-rent tragedies. Malamud and Cheever, like their great contemporary Flannery O'Connor, were masters of the kind of story that could say so much so
quickly, stories that were perfectly condensed, lapidary, wise. Barthelme and
Carver, in their different ways, took the story into a period when writers understood less and less of what was happening, when all meanings were a jumble
and short takes became attractive because they were modest and fragmentary
and took so little purchase on reality. Carver's so-called minimalism—its implications were anything but minimal—was perfectly suited to a period when
Americans were lowering their expectations, learning to live with limitation,
to make fewer demands in their own lives.

In the last phase of his career, before he died in 1988, Carver himself
changed. While some of his reductions reflected the turns of his own sensibility, others had come about under pressure from his editor, Lish, which Carver
eventually began to resist. As his own life grew happier, as the nation itself, led
by a relentless cheerleader, began recovering some of its morale, his stories became longer, less cacophonous, more fluent and optimistic. In his final revisions, Carver, even before he found a new publisher and editor, now began to
add, not substract. "Distance" recovered its title and some of its lost text. Only
two years after it appeared, one of his saddest stories, "The Bath," became "A
Small, Good Thing," which was one of his most quietly affirmative. Here, the
accidental death of a young boy, so harsh and meaningless in the earlier text,
sets the stage for a moment of quiet human contact as Carver shows us how
life goes on, even for the bereaved parents.

Carver's last story, "Errand," is about the death of Chekhov, but even more
about the glass of champagne he drinks before his death, and about the doctor
and the woman at his bedside, and especially about the room-service boy who
brings the bottle. Soon to be facing death himself, Carver focused on survival—
yet also, true to himself, emphasized the banal details that make death and survival more bearable, more ordinary. At the end Carver sacrificed the spareness
of Hemingway (the first minimalist) and the bleakness of Kafka for the elemental human warmth he found in Chekhov. His work lost some of its creepy
edge, its dead-end aura of desperation and defeat, but gained something as
well, a renewed sense of human possibility.

It would be hard to overestimate the effect of Carver's work on American
writers of the 1980s. When Cheever, Malamud, and Barthelme died, their best
work was long behind them; they were the venerable markers of certain key
moments in American letters. Carver, for all his genuine modesty, passed from
the scene at the height of his influence, with the evidence of his handiwork all
around him. "Encountering Carver's fiction early in the 1970s was a transforming

experience for many writers of my generation," wrote Jay McInerney, the ultra-hip author of *Bright Lights, Big City.* "No other writer was as much discussed and mimicked by the writers one met at readings and writers' conferences." His influence was everywhere, from brat-pack novelists like McInerney, Bret Easton Ellis (*Less Than Zero*), and Tama Janowitz (*Slaves of New York*) to fastidious minimalists like Amy Hempel (*Reasons to Live*), Frederick Barthelme (*Second Marriage*), and Mary Robison (*Oh!, Days*).

What these trendy writers learned from Carver—or rather, misunderstood in him—proved disastrous for them. He taught them to focus on observed details, to listen for snatches of revealing talk, as all writers must. But somehow (like the early imitators of Hemingway) they came to believe that the essence of fiction was leaving things out, not only literary texture but the shaping of a plot, not only psychology and description but all emotional involvement. No matter what happened, they seemed too cool to care, or too damaged to react. They avoided the easy pattern of anecdotal complication and epiphany of the traditional story but had little but sheer sensation to substitute; their random slices of life were too thin to be nourishing. At the height of its newfound prestige, the short story was going nowhere.

What these writers largely missed in Carver was the social and emotional anchor of his work. Carver himself was something of a dead-end character. Many of the blue-collar jobs he described he himself had held. He could be as self-destructive, could feel as defeated, as anyone in his work. He knew the lives of auto mechanics and grocery clerks and recovering alcoholics from the inside. The laconic flatness, the dogged ordinariness of his prose belonged to the way of life of a definite region, a class, even a certain landscape. The modest humanism of his last phase was a hard-won achievement. His style could not easily be transposed to the fashionable disco world of New York or the moneyed teen-age drug scene in L.A.—let alone the brand-name world of a yuppie serial killer. It could not be reduced to a distancing device or an experiment in literary language. Ellis's flat, horrific *American Psycho* was the ultimate mismatch of style and subject.

The writers who best reflected Carver's vision were those who shared his regional and class background, his feeling for the unhappy lives of ordinary Americans. Two of the most promising to emerge in the 1980s were Richard Ford, who came from Mississippi, and Russell Banks, who grew up in New Hampshire. Before American literature was urbanized, writers who escaped from the small towns and provincial Midwestern cities had always written with a mixture of sympathy and horror about the worlds that produced them, the Winesburg, Ohios, and Gopher Prairies. More recently, John Updike in his Rabbit novels, Bobbie Ann Mason in *Shiloh and Other Stories*, and Joyce Carol Oates in *Marya* and other works set in western New York showed how powerfully they could identify with the joyless lives that might easily have entrapped them back home. But Richard Ford in *Rock Springs*, a brilliant collection of related stories mostly set in his adopted Northwest, came closest to matching Carver on his own ground.

Though Ford gives it his own coloring, this is straight Carver country: as men go off hunting and fishing, and come back drunken and violent, we watch marriages disintegrating, people drifting apart, children losing all contact with parents. A mood of ineffable sadness infuses these stories, as it does in Ford's best-known novel, *The Sportswriter* (1986), which has a more middle-class setting. The novel is a long, slow work in which very little happens, a book whose hero suffers from depressive fits of "dreaminess" dispelled only toward the end, when he begins to give up his secret mourning for his lost child, his dead marriage, his aborted career as a writer. Until then, Ford's alter ego clings to the surface of the familiar as a refuge from depression. When a friend kills himself, he is puzzled. "He could've hunted up a reason to keep breathing," he thinks. "What else is the ordinary world good for except to supply reasons not to check out early."

The relentless yet lyrical banality of *The Sportswriter*—which reminded me of the quietly desperate musings of Walker Percy's 1961 novel *The Moviegoer*—is the very definition of the contemporary fiction of the ordinary. Yet Ford shrewdly makes this cheery suburban emptiness part of his hero's problem, his defensive mask, something he must finally learn to put behind him. Ford's narrator, Frank Bascombe, like Percy's, takes remarkable satisfaction in the small rituals of daily life. Ford learned from Carver and Percy how to find meaning, even deep feeling, in banal situations and seemingly uneventful lives.

In *Rock Springs* (and its companion piece, the short novel *Wildlife*) Ford evokes the ordinariness of his characters' lives in a different way, as if he were shaping a myth around it. Unlike Carver, who avoided all "literary" flourishes, Ford treats these people as if they were the material of legend. At his worst Ford strains too hard for a resonant simplicity; he can sound like the Old Man of the Mountain, imparting timeless wisdom around a cracker-barrel. But Ford, like Updike, also restores the lyricism Carver mercilessly pruned from his early stories. The speaker in Ford's fiction is often the same character, a man about forty, depressed, emotionally disabled, gazing back with fatal clarity at the early twists and turns which made his life whatever it became: a father's sudden act of violence, a mother's abandonment of the family, a husband's chronic infidelity, a teenage boy's numb acquiescence to disaster.

The mood of *Rock Springs* is best expressed by the opening of "Great Falls": "This is not a happy story. I warn you." Most of the stories are told in the first person, in a tone of portentous simplicity—mournful, resigned—at times touching, even heartbreaking, but also occasionally mannered and unconvincing. Ford learned from Carver how to pull the reader right into the story, to pare it down to elemental details and put an unexpected spin on every sentence. But Ford's stories are longer and more complex than Carver's; their narration reaches, not always successfully, for an emotional pitch that Carver implies but rarely underlines. His stories often end in large unanswerable questions that point to some hollowness, some huge inevitability that underlies human relationships. "Great Falls" concludes with just such a large gesture, an appeal to "some coldness in us all, some helplessness that causes us to misunderstand life when it is pure and plain, makes our existence seem like a border between two nothings, and makes us no more or less than animals who meet on the road, desperate and without patience and without hope."

"Great Falls" is little more than an anecdote, though it involves the end of a marriage. The boy's father comes home to find his wife with a gentleman caller; he holds a gun to the man's neck as he threatens and rags him but then simply sends him away. The son's recollections, many years later, are strung together with short, declarative sentences: "The house itself is gone now—I have been to the spot." "It is a true thing that my father did not know limits." They are so uninflected they sound like pieces of folk wisdom: the narrator reaches for insight he did not have when these events took place. His memories reflect not only what happened then, which marked him forever, but other nameless blows life had in store for him. This brooding sense of the unspoken prepares us for the story's final lines and gives them surprising resonance.

Like Hemingway in his Nick Adams stories, Ford used such silences to lend weight to the young man's initiation into unhappy manhood. This rite of passage, which sometimes involves hunting and fishing, or drinking and women, but also a tremulous fear and sensitivity, takes place in the heart of Hemingway territory, in a Montana that seems more like a great emptiness than a natural paradise. Nature offers moments of almost sublime beauty, like the flight of the wild geese in the last story, "Communist," but the towns and cities, with their transient inhabitants, become in memory "a place that seemed not even to exist, an empty place you could stay in for a long time and never find a thing you admired or loved or hoped to keep." Here, aimless people make the wrong choices, or no choices, on the way to their own special form of unhappiness.

Though Ford's stories focus on ordinary lives in commonplace settings, what happens in them, however trivial or arbitrary it may at first seem, becomes a turning point, the moment when hope began to fail, when a marriage fell apart, when a boy was suddenly thrust out on his own, glimpsing life in all its darker shadings. At such times, always matter-of-factly described, the fault lines of character, the stresses of a relationship, suddenly come to the surface, and the narrator discovers that "the most important things of your life can change so suddenly, so unrecoverably." As he later wrote in "Good Raymond," a brief memoir, Ford shared with Carver a fatalistic sense "that life goes this way or life goes that way; that chance is always involved, and that living is usually just dealing with consequences." This is the fatalism of the powerless, inured to the inevitable.

In another story, "Optimists," the father comes home to find his wife not with a lover but simply playing canasta with friends. But he himself is terribly upset: the labor situation on the railroad is bad, hard times are coming, and he has just seen a man die under the wheels of a boxcar. When one of the guests goads him provocatively, he kills the man with a single punch, setting in motion a train of consequences that transform all their lives. Though the father had not meant to do what he does, it lands him in prison, destroys his marriage, and changes his son's outlook: "I saw him as a man who made mistakes, as a man who could hurt people, ruin lives, risk their happiness. A man who did not understand enough." The same could be said about all the men in Ford's stories. They educate the young protagonist to a world of violent impulses, thoughtless behavior, and irretrievable effects. And people simply drift apart, as if something in the Western air kept them from staying together. By the end of the story, when the narrator runs into his mother at a convenience store, he has seen neither of his parents for many years.

The one undoubted masterpiece in *Rock Springs* is "Communist," an initiation story that strikes a fine balance between unspoiled natural beauty and the wayward human presence. Here the father is already dead; the main character is the mother's boyfriend, Glen Baxter, who takes the young man hunting for wild geese—creatures that, unlike people, are said to mate forever. The mother is not happy: "Hunt, kill, maim. Your father did that too." But the boy is enthralled. His father has already taught him to box; Glen will teach him to kill. He is enraptured by the sight and sound of the geese, "a sound that made your chest rise and your shoulders tighten with expectancy." Ford gives the young man's voice an accent all its own: "It was a thing to see, I will tell you now. Five thousand white geese all in the air around you, making a noise like you have never heard before. And I thought to myself then: this is something I will never see again. I will never forget this. And I was right."

"I don't know why I shoot 'em," says Glen. "They're so beautiful." But in a moment of truth, Glen refuses to finish off a goose he has wounded, then kills it in a burst of fury, and this undoes him in the eyes of both mother and son. "You don't have a heart, Glen," she says. "There's nothing to love in you." And the boy, now grown older, sees Glen not as "a bad man, only a man scared of something he'd never seen before—something soft in himself—his life going a way he didn't like. A woman with a son. Who could blame him there?" Like many of Ford's stories, "Communist" turns on almost nothing but makes it everything, a defining moment that shifts the course of people's lives. The boy's eagerness to become a man leads him to the manly perception that life is more complicated than he knew; an initiation into the hunt becomes an initiation into the mysteries of life, as the boy discovers how "a light can go out in the heart."

Ford's portentous endings test the limits of introspection for characters who are not obviously so insightful. The narrator of "Rock Springs," a petty car thief with a daughter and girlfriend in tow, inspects his life from every angle, but when he appeals for the reader's empathy in the final line ("Would you think he was anybody like you?"), he speaks for the author more than for himself. Despite its unity of tone and setting, its strong characters and memorable atmosphere, *Rock Springs* is an uneven collection. There is something factitious, an aura of unearned wisdom, about the poker-faced simplicity of weaker stories such as "Winterkill." Ford's rhetorical gestures are just what any sensible editor would urge the writer to eliminate, but their effect can be exhilarating, heartbreaking. At their best, they echo with a bottomless sadness, yet give an almost cosmic dignity to the disappointments of routinely stunted, marginal lives.

Russell Banks's major novels, with their melodramatic intensity and strong narrative drive, show nothing of Carver's tight-lipped, slangy style. But Carver's example may have liberated Banks to deal directly with his own blue-collar background. Banks began as a metafictional writer who published his first stories with the experimental Fiction Collective. But in large books like *Continental Drift* (1985) and *Affliction* (1989) and more intimate works like *The Sweet Hereafter* (1991), he shifted to a powerful realism that centered, as Carver's work did, on the self-destructiveness of the blue-collar male—"lonely, poor, depressed, alcoholic and violent"—the dreamy man-child who never thinks things through, the perfect loser with a genius for the wrong choice, who's sure that "you can't escape certain awful things in life," whose every attempt to escape is bound to make things worse—to leave his children scarred, his wife bitter, and his own life in shambles. These are people "whose lives . . . were ordinary and, despite the ordinariness, gave them constant trouble."

Yet Banks was also a writer in reaction against the narrow-gauge minimalism that Carver's style unwittingly encouraged but scarcely exemplified. It was no surprise when he turned to large-scale historical fiction in *Cloudsplitter* (1998), his exhaustively researched novel about John Brown. Like such wide-ranging maximalists as Robert Stone, Norman Mailer, or Don DeLillo—the latter's fix on the violent blue-collar male was part of his portrait of Lee Harvey Oswald in *Libra*—Banks was willing to harness his acute perceptions about people to a thriller plot, with elements of murder, suicide, and suspense. In doing so he gave his fatal vision a headlong momentum and connected individual lives to a larger social world, especially in *Continental Drift*. (This book, with its vast metaphorical title and topical Haitian counterplot, reminded readers not of the minimal side of Hemingway but of the Caribbean adventurers of *To Have and Have Not*.)

In the end Banks, like the Hemingway of the 1930s, risked sentimentalizing his loser into the "common man," a figure of some special decency. But by showing us how distant lives and different worlds converge, Banks's work, like Carver's last stories, suggested that minimalism had run its brief course in America. Once again, in the hands of hugely ambitious writers like Stone,

Banks, DeLillo, Toni Morrison, and Jonathan Franzen, the future lay in some transformed and heightened version of the social novel. The exhaustion of minimalism encouraged a return to a more expansive, more full-bodied fiction, a fiction embracing the larger world that surrounds our individual lives, a fiction at once more intricately written, more richly emotional, and more densely political.

TEXTURES OF MEMORY

Late Bellow: Thinking about the Dead

THERE'S SOMETHING gratifying about being outflanked by an author, about finding something radically unfamiliar in a long-familiar body of work. As a reader I was late in appreciating Saul Bellow. His work meant little to me before *Herzog* appeared in 1964; much of it I had not yet read. This was years after I had come upon unexpected fragments of my own life in the stories of Bernard Malamud, Grace Paley, and the young Philip Roth. I was gripped by their stories: I felt an immediate sense of recognition I didn't as yet experience with Bellow. But *Herzog* was different in a way I found entrancing. Unlike many works of Jewish American fiction, it didn't dwell on the Lower East Side, on Jewish families and immigrant lives. Instead it reveled in the twists and turns of the modern mind as refracted through the breakdown of one zanily intense Jewish intellectual. To be an existential thinker like Moses Herzog, a self-absorbed genius (or crackpot) with world-historical ambitions but little talent for daily life—this was something I could imagine for myself, something at moments I thought I *was*. Like many of my friends from Columbia, I took special pleasure in the Big Idea, the epic drama of modern culture. For years afterward I was fond of quoting Herzog's imagined letters, delicious in their intellectual comedy: *"Dear Doktor Professor Heidegger, I should like to know what you mean by the expression 'the fall into the quotidian.' When did this fall occur? Where were we standing when it happened?"* I was a lowly graduate student in 1964, but like Herzog I was especially taken with the drama of Romanticism and its Nietzschean aftermath. (Herzog had made his reputation with a book on "Romanticism and Christianity.") During the night there were times when Herzog's letters and ideas seemed to help me over the bumps in my thesis, though by morning such shafts of insight invariably slipped away. Beleaguered Herzog was the modern mind in extremis, and I was its faithful student.

I wasn't much interested in *Herzog* as a novel; its apparent shapelessness exhilarated me, for it seemed inexorably tied to the dissolution of the main character, above all his manic bursts of letter writing. His turmoil served as prologue to a turbulent decade in American life that would later come to appall Bellow. But Bellow has had a long career, with a good deal of time for both the writer and his readers to entertain second thoughts. His later stories, including his last novel, *Ravelstein* (2000), and even the curious arrangement of his *Collected Stories* (2002), have provided unexpected instruction in how to reread him. Above all they remind us that Bellow, for all his admiration for the great realists like Dreiser, is a poet of memory whose deepest feelings are rooted in his earliest experiences.

No one reading *Herzog* could miss Bellow's affecting memories of growing up on Napoleon Street in Montreal; they appeared separately in *Commentary* before the book came out. Herzog's anguished clinging to a distant past comes through as both a badge of honor and a symptom of his mental distress. At one point he thinks he's been shunned by a childhood friend, a man in flight from all Herzog remembers, for "all the dead and the mad are in my custody, and I am the nemesis of the would-be forgotten." His words highlight the disturbing impact of the novelist on his readers. "I bind others to my feelings, and oppress them," he says. But Herzog's inability to let go also expresses his illness. "To haunt the past like this—to love the dead! Moses warned himself not to yield so greatly to this temptation, this peculiar weakness of his character. He was a depressive. Depressives cannot surrender childhood—not even the pains of childhood."

But almost four decades later, Bellow bookended his *Collected Stories* with its two most recently written pieces, the uncollected "By the St. Lawrence" (1995), which grew out of a visit to his Canadian birthplace after a near-fatal illness, and "Something to Remember Me By" (1990), which looks back at his guilt and confusion over the death of his mother when he was seventeen— he simply could not deal with the fact that she was dying—yet is cast as a gift of remembrance to the main character's only child and grandchildren, his posterity. Both stories unfold the nagging recollections of an old man facing mortality. They show us how much Bellow himself indulged "this peculiar weakness of his character" and put it at the center of his late work. Unlike so many writers whose well ran dry, Bellow turned old age itself into a gift.

These and other stories since *Herzog* draw attention to things I first neglected in that novel: family feeling, first of all, and piety toward the past, which I must have found less glittering than the intellectual fireworks or the comedy of adultery. But because I was so taken with the subject, and with the links between his intellectual brio and his breakdown, I paid little attention to the technical side of the novel, to how the story is told. To put it very simply, most of the action takes place in Herzog's mind. As he knocks about the house, buys some new clothes, sits in a cab, or heads up to Martha's Vineyard on a train, Herzog broods about his troubles and remembers, remembers. To an astonishing degree in the works of fiction that followed, the present "action" would be that of a man thinking.

Herzog was a great literary and commercial success. It catapulted Bellow into a different order of fame. This must have heightened the contrast with his modest beginnings: between where he came from and what he had become. What Bellow dramatized in *Herzog* as the self-absorption of a troubled soul was transformed, in the works that followed, into the calm ruminations of a man, invariably the writer's alter ego, reflecting on his long life. This self-absorption (or self-indulgence) could make longer works like *The Dean's December* (1982) and *More Die of Heartbreak* (1987) seem thin and distracted, like interminable self-interviews or aimless inventories of the author's mind. Bellow became much freer in venting his own ideas, almost as if they were major characters in these novels. This kind of inward gaze would add a streak of rancor and Olympian disdain to the eloquence of *Mr. Sammler's Planet* (1970). But under the more rigorous discipline of short fiction, especially in the family stories that began with "The Old System" (1967), this meditative reflection, seemingly almost formless, could develop into a strikingly powerful literary device.

What happens in these late stories? A man of some fame and distinction—perhaps a scientist, perhaps a scholar, but clearly a stand-in for the celebrated author—pauses to take stock of people who've mattered to him in his long life. In the prototype for these stories, "The Old System," Dr. Braun has "given up his afternoon to the hopeless pleasure of thinking affectionately about his dead." They may be long-dead parents, "stifled in clay. Two crates, side by side." They may be more recent deaths triggering unusually strong emotions that renew his first attachments. These deeply felt reflections show how far he has come yet paradoxically how close he remains to where he set out. They remind him that for all his standing in the world, for all the inner tumult of ideas and feelings, he too will one day be extinguished. "Now a content, now a vacancy," he muses. "Now an important individual, a force, a necessary existence; suddenly nothing." This bleak recognition could be banal, a mere insult to his self-importance. Instead Bellow turns these monologues into aching meditations on what makes us human. Long-lived writers rarely do their best work toward the end. But late Bellow is often great Bellow, in part because of this current of rumination on ultimate things, on the stark contrast between the little disturbances of man and the cosmic chill of constellations "cast outward by a great begetting spasm billions of years ago" (as Bellow concludes "The Old System").

Invariably, the protagonist's fixation on early memories makes no sense to those around him, especially his worldly, practical siblings. "During this last visit with Brother Philip, I tried to get him to speak about Mother," says the musicologist narrator of "Him with His Foot in His Mouth." He has no luck. "You've got such a memory hang-up—what use is it?" Philip tells him. Not by chance, his brother is also swindling him, perhaps as the consequence of a defective sense of kinship. Bellow's own surrogate characters have no choice. "The cousins are the elect of my memory," says the eminent protagonist of "Cousins," whose aging relations are ill or in trouble and need something from him. He has long been apart from their world but his feeling for them, laid in early, forms the ground of his emotional life. As a young man he marveled at their busy energy, their quarrels and maneuvers; they anchored him in real life. In times past they offered a field for his exuberance, basic training for his affections. "Once under way, these relationships have to be played to the end."

These family ties bind him to an "old system" of moral obligations and tribal loyalty that the modern world has conspired to dissipate. "By such actions, I had rejected certain revolutionary developments of the past centuries, the advanced views of the enlightened, the contempt for parents." In "The Old System" a dying woman demands twenty thousand dollars from her estranged brother in exchange for permitting him to visit her in the hospital. The money means little to either of them, but morally, Dr. Braun thinks, her behavior is revolutionary. "Cousin Tina discovered that one need not be bound by the old rules. . . . From her bed she seemed to be directing this research." Adamant in her grievances, a virtuoso of will and feeling, she "had seized upon the force of death to create a situation of opera, which at the same time was a situation of parody."

Side by side with this recoil from the moral tenor of modern life, which gets full play in *Mr. Sammler's Planet* but comes through more subtly in the family stories, there is a metaphysical argument. For Bellow's protagonists, such precious memories and family feelings are portals to understanding, signposts of the soul. Bellow has been disturbing readers with such "higher" thinking ever since he flirted with Rudolf Steiner and "anthroposophy" in *Humboldt's Gift* (1975), but never so effectively as in these stories. Family ties shape the research he himself has been directing. The Bellow man is often on the defensive about such attachments and spiritual intimations, but they never blur the concrete forms of his world or still its boisterous humanity. For the central character in "Cousins," this spiritual quest "was not an abstract project. I did not learn it over the seminar table. It was a constitutional necessity, physiological, temperamental, based on sympathies which could not be acquired. Human absorption in faces, deeds, bodies, drew me towards metaphysics. I had these peculiar metaphysics as flying creatures have their radar." Here the character's involuntary absorption in his extended family anticipates the writer's keen absorption in people, especially their faces and bodies. Memory is bound up with the writer's own faculty of attention and capacity for feeling.

Bellow is guided by his belief in the intimate link between soul and body; he thinks our appearance changes at the behest of the inner being. This helps explain the concentration on physiognomy and human form that yields some of his most remarkable metaphors and sentences. Of one cousin's shady operations, the narrator writes: "Much knowledge of such happenings was in Tanky's looks, in the puffiness of his face—an edema of deadly secrets." Waiting to be sentenced for a crime, this once-robust man "didn't look good. He didn't have fast colors after all. His big face was swelled out by years of brutal business. . . . His inner man was toying with a stroke as the alternative to jail." Another cousin shows her age: "I remembered Riva as a full-figured, dark-haired, plump, straight-legged woman. Now all the geometry of her figure had changed. She had come down in the knees like the jack of a car, to a diamond posture. She still made an effort to move with speed, as if she were dancing after the Riva she had once been."

To me this sounds less like love of kin than an unsparing focus on human frailty as a clue to the unknown. In "By the St. Lawrence," the latest-written story, Bellow disputes this distinction. "These observations, Rexler was to learn, were his whole life—his being—and love was what produced them. For each physical trait there was a corresponding feeling. Paired, pair by pair, they walked back and forth, in and out of his soul." Whatever its source, the yield is abundant: Bellow's descriptive powers, like his comic gift for names, rival those of Dickens. For all his loving portraits of intellectuals, always more erratic and colorful than himself, for all his exuberant play with ideas, the Bellow man (like Chick in *Ravelstein*) is most drawn to the surface of things, their revealing outline and texture. Real intellectuals like Zetland (based on his friend and rival Isaac Rosenfeld), "though fond of the world . . . were not long detained by surface phenomena." Their Platonic abstractions, their dreams of perfection, differ from the novelist's love of appearances, which for him are windows to the soul.

One key to Bellow's late work is that he cannot tell this story, any story, except by placing himself in it, creating a surrogate observer, musing, interacting, recollecting. In this respect Bellow is postmodern, factoring the observer into the thing observed, which his mind endlessly alters and reshapes. Not for him the omniscient narrator freely inhabiting each character's thinking, or the memoir tied strictly to the facts, or the wholly invented tale with no grounding in his personal history. This framing device—along with the metaphorical prose—puts people at one remove, always filtered through a scrim of memories and impressions, for the stories are less about the characters themselves, let alone their real-life originals, than about his feeling for them and the news about life and death he draws from them, or projects onto them. This is why Bellow's portrait of Humboldt (based on Delmore Schwartz) needs the bland, time-serving Citrine as a foil, why Ravelstein (a dead-on version of Allan Bloom) has Chick as his on-camera biographer, why the story of Zetland is laid out for us, as the subtitle indicates, "By a Character Witness," who is not so much telling a story as testifying to a personality. Self-protective instinct enabled them to prosper, to endure, but recollection redeems them. Much of late Bellow has this Ishmael-like quality of witness. Bellow's favorite intellectuals were uproarious, gaudily self-destructive; they lived incautiously, with panache, not forethought. He fulfils the more mundane obligations of the survivor. They live on in his self-examination, the tonal registries of his retrospection. Their stories pass through him and accrue to his inner strength.

This power of witness, with its obscure metaphysics, cuts even deeper in the family memories than in his finely etched recollections of Allan Bloom, Isaac Rosenfeld, Harold Rosenberg, or Delmore Schwartz. The last pages of "The Old System," like so many other Bellow endings (*Seize the Day*, even *The Dean's December*), give us something few modern writers attempt, a really long view, an almost unbearably eloquent reach toward the infinite. Recalling how a brother and sister could create such commotion in each other's breast, and now in his own, Dr. Braun wonders bitterly "what emotions were. What good were they! What were they for!" He thinks of Yeats, another survivor. "Perhaps the cold eye was better. On life, on death. But, again, the cold of the eye would be proportional to the degree of heat within." As a scientist examining specimens of humanity, he feels defensive about his own temperamental detachment. He considers whether the passions that make us human have not also been exploited "for the sake of exciting disturbance, to make an uproar, a crude circus of feelings." And this leads him to think of the Jews from whom he sprang, with "their feelings, their hearts! Dr. Braun often wanted nothing more than to stop all this. For what came of it? One after another you gave over your dying. One by one they went. You went. Childhood, family, friendship, love were stifled in the grave. And these tears! . . . But what did you understand? Again, *nothing!* It was only an intimation of understanding." He cannot answer his own questions, "why life, why death?" or even "why these particular forms—these Isaacs and these Tinas?," these unquiet souls.

Bellow's late work appears to have been written in search of such fugitive intimations of understanding. Haunted by memories that will die with them, plagued by dim hints and unanswerable questions, Bellow's fictional surrogates reach back to the past to project themselves into an unfathomable future. Like all writers, they envision a form of survival. "The rule of the dead is that they should be forgotten," says Chick in *Ravelstein*. "After burial there is a universal gradual progress toward oblivion. But with Ravelstein this didn't altogether work." Out of indelible recollections of their dead and piercing interrogations of themselves, his characters make a mark or shape a legacy that gives us something to remember them by.

SAINTS AND SINNERS: WILLIAM KENNEDY'S ALBANY CYCLE

William Kennedy's best novel, *Ironweed* (1983), begins with a remarkable scene of an itinerant tramp, Francis Phelan, sober for the moment, making his way through a cemetery, where he has picked up a day's work digging graves. But from the opening sentence Kennedy passes swiftly beyond this "factual" situation:

> Riding up the winding road of Saint Agnes Cemetery in the back of a rattling old truck, Francis Phelan became aware that the dead, even more than the living, settled down in neighborhoods.

The dead include his own parents, whose graves he has not seen in many years, and his infant son, whose accidental death twenty-two years earlier still haunts him, especially since it caused him to abandon his wife and family. But this is no ordinary graveyard visit, for we soon learn that "Francis's mother twitched nervously in her grave as the truck carried him nearer to her; and Francis's father lit his pipe, smiled at his wife's discomfort, and looked out from his own bit of sod to catch a glimpse of how much his son had changed since the train accident."

When I first read these lines two decades ago I was gripped but mildly annoyed. What were we to make of these frisky dead, still very much themselves, who keep reappearing not only in the minds of the living but as real presences before their eyes, almost as full-fledged characters? And what of grim Francis, down but not entirely out, whose dead uncles recognize in his face "the familiar scars of alcoholic desolation" which they knew all too well? The place is Albany, New York, the backwater town from which Francis fled many years earlier, the corruption-ridden state capital 150 miles north of New York City. The time is 1938, which led critics to see Francis as a hobo and drifter out of Depression fiction, a down-at-heels man but one driven by remorse for his sins rather than poverty. To other critics the voluble dead brought to mind not proletarian writing but a magical realism mixing social history and fantasy. A decade later Francis reappeared in *Very Old Bones* (1992), a novel about his younger brother Peter, an artist, who envies Francis as "a man who pursued his own direction freely, even if it led to the gutter and the grave. Francis was a wreck of a man, a lost soul on a dead-end street, yet in him was no deference to the awful finality of his condition. He did not seem to notice it."

This suggests that Francis was less a figure out of García Márquez than a specimen of urban lowlife who also, with echoes of Beckett and Joyce, gave us a window on the state of a man's soul. Kennedy himself had left his native city in the 1950s and worked for five years as a journalist in Puerto Rico, where he met his wife and, just as fortuitously, studied writing with a visiting young novelist, Saul Bellow, who became his most important mentor. When his father's illness drew him back to Albany in 1960, Kennedy came home to a mother lode of Bellovian material: a legendary Democratic political machine that had controlled the city for four decades, a rich history of crime, bootlegging, gambling, and prostitution, tolerated by the law and tied in with the machine, and through it all a complex network of families descended from nineteenth-century Irish Catholic immigrants. "It was in these years," he later wrote, "that my mind changed on Albany, that I came to see it as an inexhaustible context for the stories I planned to write." Though the circumstances are different, Francis's flight and his return to Albany stand in for the author's own homecoming, both physical and imaginative. Francis's vivid encounters with the dead conjure up Kennedy's enormous appetite for local lore, his Faulknerian sense that the past is not dead, it is not even past. Like an intuitive social novelist, Francis discerns "neighborhoods" and overhears family conversations even in the cemetery. His mind, like Bellow's, is infused with the flavor of remembrance; opening a trunk in the attic of his old home, he feels "drugged by the scent of the reconstituted past."

Kennedy's near-flawless 1975 novel *Legs*, the first book of the Albany cycle, emerged from this intoxicating sense of the past. In his ebullient history *O Albany!* (1983), Kennedy comes across as an endlessly curious journalist and storyteller who has spent countless hours debriefing townsmen about the city's history and their own. One of his favorite subjects is the sensational murder of gangster Jack "Legs" Diamond in an Albany rooming house, a building in which Kennedy himself—this may be hard to believe—has since set up his own office. Set at the beginning of the thirties, at the height of America's love affair with the gangster, *Legs* is both the story of one notorious criminal specimen and a study of the collective imagination that turned these men into icons. Kennedy's portrait is curiously sympathetic yet also shows us how these brutal thugs, who went to the movies like everyone else, became legends even to themselves. We see Diamond through the eyes of a *Gatsby*-like narrator, a brilliant but un-scrupulous lawyer named Marcus Gorman, who is seduced by his client's amoral energy and style. "I make no case for Jack as a moderate," he says, "only as a man in touch with primal needs." The same could be said of Kennedy's whole body of work. Writing more than forty years after Diamond's death, Marcus compares him favorably to Richard Nixon, "who left significant history in his wake, but no legend; whose corruption . . . lacked the admirably white core fantasy that can give evil a mythical dimension." What distinguishes Jack from the politicians who emulate him is their hypocrisy, for he is at least straightforward in his cor-ruption, a "predator wolf" but also "a venal man of integrity," who remains vul-nerable to "punishment, death, and damnation."

With this turn Kennedy reshapes the gangster myth and gives it a strong Catholic coloring. Where Bellow's protagonists (like Herzog and Mr. Sammler) are essentially upright men fascinated by the moral underworld—their vice is self-righteousness, not sin itself—Kennedy's heroes are fallible creatures, case studies in moral ambiguity, whose lives are said nevertheless to have a "luminous quality." By avoiding self-deception, staying in touch with their own propensity for evildoing, which the author sees as universal, they achieve a kind of bleak sainthood in the face of human limitation, as we might note in Peter Phelan's awestruck view of his derelict brother. Their ruling vices—lust, violence, or greed—not only make them more exciting to us but more fully human. They be-come the "underside," the mirror image, of our own respectable lives.

This is why *Ironweed* remains the definitive Kennedy novel. Once a gifted baseball player, Francis is surprised to realize that he was destined to become the "family killer," the violent man who has also broken up his own family. The ghosts who haunt him are not simply those he neglected and left behind but people he actually killed, usually without intending to do so: a scab in a trolley strike, his own infant child, another tramp who threatened him, the "demon" who was part of a vigilante mob wantonly destroying the makeshift shanties of the homeless. Looking down at his own hands he sees the scars of past violence written on his body. Kennedy portrays him as a man "going nowhere," caught in a time warp, yet so exquisitely attuned to the past, living so intimately with his guilt, that he becomes a kind of saint. The dead in the cemetery witness his "regeneration," which continues through the whole novel.

This temptation to sainthood is the besetting vice of Kennedy's fiction. His novels have the tough, sardonic surface of hardboiled fiction. He writes like a man without illusions, someone who expects the worst and is therefore amused, not outraged by it. His feeling for urban corruption, for the society of gamblers, crooked cops, bootleggers, politicians, and big-hearted whores, links him with Bellow and makes him a good match for Hammett and Chandler. But like Chandler he tends to romanticize his heroes into knightly figures, men who do nasty jobs and clean up the messes others have left behind. With small adjustments, Chandler's famous tribute—"Down these mean streets a man must go who is not himself mean, who is neither tarnished nor afraid"— could be applied to Roscoe Conway, the hero of Kennedy's much-acclaimed novel *Roscoe* (2002), the seventh in the Albany cycle. He is a figure of Falstaffian girth and appetite, a lawyer and fixer whose whole life for twenty-six years has been the fabled Albany political machine. Now he wants to quit but it's 1945, a war is ending and a mayoral election is coming up, and everyone depends on him. Disappointed in love—the woman he loved married his closest friend, scion of a rich family—Roscoe goes through the novel dealing with other people's problems: the mysterious suicide of his friend, which is a blow to the machine; an ugly custody battle that soon follows; the politically ambitious governor's efforts to crack down on corruption; assorted quarrels and killings that also threaten the party's lock on power. Roscoe's instincts are always to cover things up, to put pressure on newspapers not to run stories, to lie in court, yet also to comfort those in trouble, to give them a shoulder to lean on, even though he himself feels ill and increasingly exhausted. But Roscoe, as much as Francis Phelan, is also a fulcrum of memory, and what he mainly remembers are episodes from the history of Albany politics from 1919 to 1945.

This is a book Kennedy was born to write, but he may have waited too long to write it. It's the moment of history that is most alive to him, the wild spree of Prohibition with the bleak aftermath of the Depression, a strange time when

> the illusion of beer would replace beer, the illusion of gin would replace gin, and the illusion of jurisprudence and justice would transform the populace into hoodlums, chronic lawbreakers, professional hypocrites, defiant drunks, and political wizards.

As Kennedy writes in *O Albany!*: "Prohibition in Albany was a contradiction in terms. Very little was ever prohibited in this city." Instead, "drinking exploded ridiculously in the 1920s when people were told they couldn't drink." This sounds cynical, worldly, but the mood of the novel is mellow and valedictory; Kennedy's protagonist is physically damaged and turning philosophical.

His memories of politics, sin, and skullduggery can be evocative but lack the zest of similar stories in *O Albany!*, especially the great journalistic sketches of Albany's longtime Democratic boss Dan O'Connell (d. 1977) and his main man, the city's almost permanent mayor, Erastus Corning (d. 1983). Both play minor roles in the novel, but the character of Roscoe is an invention, Kennedy's way of processing this history through the eyes of an insider, who is also, like Homer's Achilles, tired of the fray, the warrior who wants to withdraw from the battle. Roscoe has heart problems, the metaphoric kind but also the kind that require surgery, and he even compares himself at one point to Philoctetes ("that fellow with the wound that never heals").

The first hundred pages of *Roscoe* are magical. The book begins on V-J day, and Kennedy, with his whimsical humor, gets that heady moment of triumph exactly right. No one can rival Kennedy in recreating the atmosphere of a small American city and showing us how politics operate at the local level. For three decades, while American fiction grew ever more autobiographical and self-absorbed, Kennedy, with his rich Irish sense of family and clan, carved out a piece of social terrain that could be compared to the densely imagined local worlds of Faulkner and Joyce. As in Faulkner's Yoknapatawpha or John O'Hara's Gibbsville, it was exhilarating to see a minor character or subplot in one novel exfoliate into a novel of its own, as if the living tissue of a whole society were being filled in.

But Kennedy's books invariably pivot on their protagonists, and this novel is as much about Roscoe himself as the world his memories recapture. If *Legs* sometimes reminds us of *The Great Gatsby*, one model for *Roscoe* was surely Nathanael West's *Miss Lonelyhearts*, a stations-of-the cross novel that unfolds in panels reminiscent of comic strips around its depressed central figure. Kennedy takes just such a prismatic approach to Roscoe. Each chapter is headed with a title like "Roscoe and the Pope," "Roscoe and the Silent Music," or "Roscoe among the Saints" and begins with a brief, dreamlike, often wacky prologue that pinpoints a moment in Roscoe's spiritual journey. Here we find the kind of fantasy material we recall warmly from *Ironweed*, including conversations with the dead, but gradually the raffish character we first knew dissolves into a candidate for sainthood. As Roscoe is idealized into a Tiresias-like figure who has seen it all yet stays the course, his character grows dimmer, not sharper; he becomes a meditative authorial consciousness, like the protagonists in late Bellow. A novel of ideas, an abstract moral fable, begins eating its way inexorably into Kennedy's graphic character study and social history.

Nothing that happens in the book's nebulous plot quite justifies the high tenor of Roscoe's reflections on "the human proclivity for deceit," or on the paradox of "an entire society structured on extortion and subordination: what a way to live." (For the earlier Roscoe, who was so much more down-to-earth, things were far simpler: "Can one sensibly retreat to the moral high ground when major money is on the table?") In one of Roscoe's fantasies, when his late friend's credentials for sainthood are challenged by a devil's advocate, he counters that "not morality but fraudulence is the necessary modality for human existence. Nothing is, or ever was, what it seems." He recalls his friend "saying in a black moment that everything eventually comes to nothing. 'That's the secret you don't tell the children,' he said, 'and even if you did, they wouldn't accept it.'" Just as Addie in Faulkner's *As I Lay Dying* reviews her life from inside her coffin, on her bumpy way to her own burial, Roscoe muses on why men seek power over each other on the operating table, where the surgeon has laid open his heart.

It's not clear why Roscoe needed to become such a wisdom figure. We miss the charming scoundrel he left behind. Perhaps, at seventy-four, Kennedy himself had earned his autumnal tone, but his protagonist carries too much freight of meaning. In the novel's denouement, Kennedy's crisp writing turns slack as Roscoe tries to resume the love affair with his old flame, his friend's widow. Their long separation, her marriage to his friend, obsess him. ("I regret that with every breath we both take, every breath of yours that might have been mine," he tells her.) Her final rejection plays into his black mood, his dark Catholic sense of some ultimate futility.

For all his lifetime of chicanery, Roscoe is portrayed as an honorable man, a prince among thieves. Kennedy describes him as an honest man except in politics, but his memories lack the obsessive drive of the guilt feelings that so powerfully haunt Francis Phelan and fuel his spiritual regeneration. His remembered dead seem less essential, more accidental. Francis is an individual, but also *merely* an individual, one wayward man who achieves a modest salvation and self-forgiveness as he rejoins the human community. Roscoe's recollections are less convincing but have a wider scope: they embrace key pieces of America's public history, such as the effects of Prohibition, the pivotal 1932 election, and the impact of both world wars, things that hold no interest for a tramp like Phelan, who has fallen off the social map.

Kennedy's best work shows that a sense of universal corruption need not flatten but can actually enrich a writer's pleasure in his people's motives and contradictions. Kennedy's characters enjoy the game even when they see through it. Their lives have a rich immediacy that their creator relishes. Their nagging conscience heightens their worldliness and lust for life; their misdeeds and misgivings go hand in hand; they live more fully for wagering their souls. This does not quite work in *Roscoe*, for all its incidental pleasures. Unlike *Ironweed*, it succeeds better as a still-vivid Irish political novel than as a parable of spiritual redemption.

READING AND HISTORY

DAMAGED LITERACY: THE DECAY OF READING

IT'S A PARADOX that we use of the same word, reading, for the most elementary forms of literacy and also for professional forms in literary commentary, some of them quite technical, as when we talk of new "readings" of poems and stories. The gap between ordinary reading and critical reading was not always so great. When a far smaller proportion of our population was literate, the critic felt obliged to speak for the common reader, to make judgments that expressed not simply a personal view but an ideal social consensus—and to do so in language that might actually reach a majority of readers. This cannot simply be because the audience was socially homogeneous, since readership was expanding to include the new middle class. An old-style critic and man of letters like Joseph Addison would express the values of this audience yet also work to improve its taste and standards. As Terry Eagleton pointed out in *The Function of Criticism*, criticism developed in the eighteenth century as part of what Jürgen Habermas has called "the public sphere," the new arena of public opinion, civic debate, social improvement, and cultural self-invention that became a counterweight to the absolute state, paving the way for the middle-class revolutions of 1789 and afterward. The educational mission of critics like Addison and *philosophes* like Diderot took on political weight.

As literacy spread beyond the middle class and a genuinely popular reading public developed, the cultural function of criticism changed. Without losing their sense of having an important social role to play, critics began to define themselves not as part of a community of readers but as defenders of Culture against the philistines, as stalwart opponents or improvers of mass taste. Finally even this public mission began to wane. Modern artists set themselves firmly against culture as a consumable, marketable commodity: as an escape or a status symbol, an adornment or refinement of middle-class life. They rejected the appeal to a mass audience. In the same spirit, critics schooled on modernism turned their backs on consumable criticism, writing for little magazines or academic journals, devoting themselves to technical commentary on distant or difficult works. Abandoning some time-honored functions of criticism, they left the instruction of popular taste to the middlebrow bookmen, consumer guidance to the book reviewers and literary journalists.

Eventually critics made their way into the universities, where their work became even more specialized and recondite. They continued, of course, to carry on regular lives apart from the arcane craft of literary analysis. They learned to read with two quite different selves, as ordinary readers consuming information—taking in newspapers, reading for pleasure, gobbling up junk fiction at bedtime—and as subtle readers bringing other kinds of news from a cordoned-off realm of culture and art. Because university departments were organized into "fields," many critics became specialized scholars, working in areas that were remote from what modern readers knew and read.

In those days, in the forties and fifties, for example, when the university was rapidly expanding, English departments gave no encouragement to critics with strongly contemporary interests. It took a long time for academic criticism to catch up with modern writing, which was too fresh, anarchic, and seemingly outside the tradition. Academic critics often lacked literary taste; they were antiquarians rather than intellectuals, researchers and textual editors rather than critics. The business then of the liberal arts was culture and scholarship of a more traditional kind, confined safely to canonical works from earlier periods.

Meanwhile, the popular audience went on reading in its own way—reading for the plot, the characters, the archetypal situations, reading for sex, for thrills, for escape, for sheer human interest. Margaret Mitchell's *Gone with the Wind*, first published in 1936, once sold fifty thousand copies in a single day (just as bookstores fifty-four years later found it impossible to meet the insatiable demand for the manufactured sequel, *Scarlett*, despite its atrocious reviews). By 1939, the invention of the cheap paperback would enormously enlarge the reading audience, especially for genre fiction. In the same year, the runaway success of the film version of Mitchell's novel would demonstrate how the movies could staggeringly multiply the audience for a popular novel.

The surprising thing about the factitious *Scarlett* was not that it was written, quite badly, by a hired author but that this calculated piece of exploitation was so long in coming. Popular reading, like popular moviegoing, is an adjunct of the culture industry, not because this audience has no taste of its own but because it loves sequels and remakes, loves to find out what happened next and, usually, to see it all happen again. Popular reading is essentially rereading—the pursuit of a known quantity, a familiar experience: this is where culture and commerce meet. The dream of pop culture is an endlessly reproducible commodity, a story that never ends, no matter how many times it's been told and retold.

With genre films, as with genre fiction, the audience knows what to expect: a mixture of the fresh and the familiar, the original and the archetypal. This is what makes the marketing of popular culture so different from the creation of an audience for literary fiction or modernist art. The avant garde, even when it slips into known formulas, always aims for experiences that are one of a kind, unsettling, disquieting, dislocating. Shock and surprise are not endlessly repeatable, even in horror films. Experimental freshness is always a rare commodity.

As popular literature evolved into media culture, traditional critics and alarmed educators sounded the death knell of reading. Guardians of public morality regularly condemn the level of sex and violence in film and video, as they deplored the bad taste of Gothic fiction in the eighteenth century. I myself grew up on the cusp between a reading culture and a film and television culture. As a precociously highbrow kid, I played hooky from school to attend cheap matinées of Broadway plays, and even to sit reading for endless hours in the local public library. The Seward Park branch, around the corner from my school on the Lower East Side, had already served generations of immigrants and their children, giving them access to American experiences and an American language they could not find at home. When my family moved to suburban Queens, I ate my way through the library there, gorging myself indiscriminately on anything between covers. I had the pleasant illusion of mastering whole fields in a single weekend. I learned about sex from Margaret Mead's brisk studies of adolescents in Samoa and New Guinea, and even gained access to the Locked Shelf that held forbidden works like Norman Mailer's *Barbary Shore*, which didn't do much for a fourteen-year old.

A few years ago a bright undergraduate, struggling out of class origins far humbler than my own, fighting an angry father who resisted his desperate longing for more education, blurted out how much he envied me because I "grew up before television." "You've already read a lot," I said to him. "But I have so much more I want to read," he said plaintively. "I feel I'll never catch up. All that lost time." Yet I remembered how much I resented not having a television at home when so many other families already did. My student was projecting on me his ideal reading fantasies: an infinite amount of free time, a clear channel to the culture of the past, a precious treasure locked up in the pages of books.

What he was saying with his jealous tribute was that I belonged to the last of the reading generation, which is partly the case for writers and intellectuals my age. But the fact that he said it showed it couldn't be entirely true. I still encounter students who have the same euphoria about reading that I had at their age, but more often than not their real passion is for music, just as in the sixties and early seventies it was for film, for politics, or for drugs. For them the barrier to reading is not lack of time, as my student imagined, but something more perceptual, something in their rhythm of apprehending experience. Since they grew up with television, with the music videos of MTV, with the VCR and the Internet, reading and writing seemed clumsy and primitive compared to electronic communication. I see their thrill of surprise, their disbelief, when they get excited by a literary text. It's an unfamiliar sensation, almost as good as music, as good as sex.

These kids are literate; they have all the basic skills. But the obstacles that keep them from reading aren't so different from some of the social barriers to literacy itself. It's hard for a critic to assess the widespread anxiety about literacy among educators today, but the statistics are real enough, including falling scores on college aptitude tests through the seventies and much of the eighties, especially in the upper reaches of those tested. According to a useful symposium,

Literacy: An Overview by Fourteen Experts (1991), there remain persistent pockets of adult illiteracy in America. The late Timothy Healy, director of the New York Public Library, said that "New York City has an estimated 1.5 million people over the age of sixteen who cannot read a newspaper or the instructions on a bottle of medicine," while Joseph Murphy, the former chancellor of the City University, added that "there are as many as 60 million illiterate and semiliterate adults in America today." But an even graver concern is the more limited literacy of many who have the basic skills. Thus, in the same volume, Daniel P. Resnick and Laren B. Resnick stress the difference between minimal literacy as a passive skill and the kind of reading that gives power and pleasure, encouraging conceptualization and independent judgment.

For all these critics the problem is not just educational but political and economic. Murphy says that "because poverty and illiteracy go hand in hand, the poor are disenfranchised, cut off from the democratic process." For Leon Botstein, the president of Bard College, the problem is not so much illiteracy as "damaged literacy," and it is not confined to the poor:

> Before the age of mass literacy in the nineteenth century, illiteracy meant simply the almost total inability to read or write. Today, illiteracy has become a species of the ability to read and write, a severely crippled and limited form of literacy. . . . The modern form of illiteracy—inadequate literacies—is perhaps most devastating and widespread among those who otherwise would qualify, demographically, as part of a social and economic elite capable of serious literacy.

Most observers agree that literacy is a key to both economic advancement and political participation, not just for individuals but for whole societies that need technical and linguistic skills to remain competitive. Many workers who lost their jobs in America's shrinking industrial base tried to retrain themselves for more sophisticated work, much of it brain work; others slipped down into the service economy, working for minimum wages without union protection or fringe benefits; still others, like so many of the workers in England's northern industrial towns, have remained permanently unemployed (or "redundant," as the British put it more vividly).

These severe economic dislocations can hardly be blamed on reading problems, and certainly not on watching too much television or listening to rock music, the convenient reasons for decline that are advanced in best-selling conservative tracts on "the closing of the American mind." But damaged literacy made it difficult for Americans in the 1970s and 1980s to adjust to economic competition from Europe and Asia, just as it had long made them vulnerable to the demagogic campaigns that manipulated media images and popular symbols. Political participation depends on literacy, on access to complex information. Total dependence on electronic media distorts the public sphere, turning citizens into objects of spin control, image management, and negative campaigning. Media campaigns too often simply pull the wool over voters' eyes, distracting them from real issues and separating them from their own interests. The political consequences have been enormous.

At this point I must shift gears and turn again to those other readers, the professionals, who are exceptionally sensitive about being manipulated by what they see and read. Many critics today, as if in violent reaction to the reading habits of the ordinary citizen, are haunted by the fear of becoming passive consumers of ideological subtexts or messages. They feel surrounded by schemes to manipulate their perceptions. As the country grew more conservative in the 1980s, many academic critics turned more radical, and this led to an onslaught by national magazines and media pundits on "political correctness," the supposed left-wing and multicultural orthodoxy in American universities.

Here we encounter a number of puzzling paradoxes about "reading" in America today. As reading diminishes—not in absolute terms but relative to other ways of receiving information—as reading loses its hold on people, the metaphor of reading constantly expands. Molecular biologists like Robert Pollack talk about "reading DNA," the structure of genetic transmission in each living cell. Students of urban life discuss "the city as text" and how to read it, as they did at a conference I attended in 1989. Film scholars publish books about "how to read a film," reflecting our constantly expanding (and increasingly undifferentiated) notion of what constitutes a text. And literary critics over the past seventy years have developed ever more subtle and complex ways of reading those texts, often using obscure, specialized language that itself resists being read, besides reducing too much of the real world to its textual traces.

As educators worry about the role of video and electronic media in displacing the written word, as the skills of ordinary readers seem to languish, the sophistication and territorial ambitions of academic readers continue to grow, widening a split that has been one of the hallmarks of the modern period. This doesn't mean that the common reader no longer exists. But many professional readers dissociate themselves on principle from the habits of the tribe: they deliberately read against the grain of the text, against common sense, against most people's way of reading—indeed, against their own way of reading in their ordinary lives. If the reader of *Scarlett* or *Gone with the Wind* reads passively, wanting to be possessed and carried away by a book, as by an old-fashioned movie or an impassioned piece of music, the critical reader, influenced by theory and by the New Historicism, has developed an active, aggressive, even adversarial approach to writing. What Paul Ricoeur, in his book on Freud, called the "hermeneutics of suspicion" has become a primary feature of academic criticism, which aims above all to disclose the institutional pressures and ideological formations that speak through texts and influence us as we read.

This adversarial way of reading is scarcely new. Freud was determined to penetrate the screen-memories, evasions, and self-deceptions that kept his patients from self-knowledge. The New Critics spoke of the "intentional fallacy"—the error of trying to interpret works according to the author's own expressed views—and liked to quote D. H. Lawrence's dictum: Trust the tale, not the teller. For all their differences, Freud and the New Critics were agreed that language itself revealed what people concealed—what they hid even from themselves. Both looked for the subtext in every text: for Freud, the slip of the tongue, the latent rather than manifest content of the dream; for the New Critic, the revelations of the image, the symbol, or the elements of irony, paradox, and ambiguity that could be found even in poems that seemed simple and direct.

In the sixties and seventies, deconstructionists like Paul de Man and Jacques Derrida took this one step further. Stressing the ambiguity of language even more than the New Critics, they went from manifest and latent meaning to no-meaning. Infinitely subtle and paradoxical readers, they turned reading against itself. They were far more interested in the tricky process of *how* things meant, or seemed to mean, than in *what* they meant. Where others saw meaning, they saw blockage, misperception, and internal contradiction. Nothing meant what it seemed to mean because language itself stood in the way.

Turning to linguistic theories that stressed the arbitrary relation between the sign and its referent, they insisted on what de Man, in a 1972 essay on Roland Barthes, called "the autotelic, nonreferential aspect of literature," its obedience to its own linguistic rules, independent of the world it appears to portray. This, he says, "cannot seriously be contested, but the question remains why it is always again and systematically being overlooked, as if it were a threat that had to be repressed. . . . All theoretical findings about literature confirm that it can never be reduced to a specific meaning or set of meanings, yet it is always being interpreted reductively as if it were a statement or message." Literary study, he adds, has had the "unsettling experience of being unable to cleanse its own discourse of aberrantly referential implications."

Here de Man neatly combined a hint from linguistics with the psychoanalytic vocabulary of resistance and repression (as he would do again in his most cited essay, "The Resistance to Theory"). But this kind of "repression" may primarily be in the eye of the observer. Once I heard the sociologist Philip Rieff describe the key to Freud's work as "the repression of the sacred"—religion was what then interested him, Rieff, but Freud, alas, wasn't buying it; ergo, he must have been avoiding or suppressing it. Most people have always read literature referentially, that is, in relation to the larger world of social meaning and an inner world of personal feeling. That literature cannot be "reduced to a specific meaning or set of meanings" scarcely proves that it is entirely self-referential, or that any effort to grapple with meaning boils down to an extractable "statement or message." This view is itself reductive, designed to render all interpretation invalid—little more than a misguided nostalgia for easy-to-read messages. No theory of reading had ever departed so far from what we ordinarily expect out of reading: some kind of meaningful insight, however fragile and partial, into ourselves and our world.

But if de Man pitted reading against itself, the New Historicists of the 1980s pitted writers against themselves. Like de Man, they looked for the little gaps and contradictions that would reveal what the writer had repressed, but they saw these subtexts as ideological formations, the unconscious assumptions by which a society propagates its values. It is true that the further we get from a writer's era, the more such basic assumptions stand out; they appear as dated as the clothes, the decor, and the conversation. No criticism can avoid dealing with the role of received ideas, prejudices, and social constructions in any literary work. Outsider groups—women, blacks, Jews, Asians—have every right to resist being caricatured by what they see and read and to examine the social and ideological nature of such projections. Our culture is full of unexamined myths that cry out to be deconstructed, as Roland Barthes showed long ago in his scintillating *Mythologies*.

What has marked so much of our most advanced criticism is the suspicion and hostility with which it performs these operations: its failure to distinguish art from propaganda, literature from advertising, its fierce resistance to the mental framework of the works it examines. "All right, what's wrong with this book?" said one militant instructor to the students in her humanities class, to make sure they didn't get taken in by those "great" books: how is the author trying to seduce and deceive us, even indoctrinate us? Some of our recent ideological criticism turns the social understanding of literature, which can be intrinsically valuable, into an all-too-predictable exercise in debunking and demystification.

One controversial example is a widely discussed essay on Wordsworth's "Tintern Abbey" by Marjorie Levinson, which can be found in her book *Wordsworth's Great Period Poems*. Everyone will recall that the poem is a long, brooding, troubled meditation in which the poet returns to the Wye valley, near the border of England and Wales, and realizes how much he has changed in the five years since he last saw it. The ruin of Tintern Abbey actually has nothing to do with the poem, except—in the topographical manner of the eighteenth century—to help us locate the neighboring landscape. But Levinson, picking up a lead from Mary Moorman's 1957 biography of Wordsworth, learned from a guidebook of the period that Tintern Abbey, far from being simply a picturesque ruin, was also a place where beggars and homeless people congregated, and the Wye River, besides being a sylvan stream, also contained a good deal of commercial and industrial traffic, perhaps even pollution.

From these observations, Levinson essentially argues that the poem is a lie and a fraud, or at best some kind of half-truth. Wordsworth, she says, who had once had strong political feelings—inspired, as we all know, by his sympathy

for the French Revolution and by the pinched and impoverished lives he witnessed as a boy in the Lake District—is now taking refuge from history in a
self-involved world of inner meditation. "Given the sort of issues raised by
'Tintern Abbey''s occasion," says Levinson, "it follows that the primary poetic
action is the suppression of the social." Wordsworth's failure to mention the
beggars, or indeed the abbey itself (outside his title), here becomes a deliberate act of mystification. This supposed turn from politics and society toward
subjectivity—a poetry of the individual mind—becomes the archetype not
only of Wordsworth's career but of Romantic poetry in general. " 'Tintern
Abbey''s suppression of historical consciousness," she says, "is exactly what
makes it so Romantic a poem."

I cannot do full justice to Levinson's detailed argument in this summary, but
it's fair to say that she uses "Tintern Abbey" first as the smoking gun of Romantic self-betrayal—in exactly the same way that the Lake poets were denounced as political turncoats by young radicals of their own day—and then
as her demonstration model for a new way of doing criticism. Like other recent
ideological critics and New Historicists, Levinson insists that critical interpreters, like cultural anthropologists, must avoid being taken in by the outlook
of the works they're reading. They cannot be limited, for example, to what a
poem is about, but must concern themselves with all it's *not* about, what it sup-
presses and leaves out, including the supposed historical truth about the old
abbey and the busy river. "Wordsworth's pastoral prospect is a fragile affair,"
Levinson says, "artfully assembled by acts of exclusion."

Art thus becomes a way of cunningly hoodwinking the reader, reducing him
or her to (pleasurable) passivity as a naive victim of indoctrination. The role
of the enlightened reader, the professional reader, is to ask rude questions, to
point a finger at what has been left out. We should withhold our reverence
even from great writers, restrain our pleasure and admiration, and take full advantage of our historical distance from what we read. The worst thing we can
do, she says, is "to forget ourselves through a facile sympathy, and lose our
enabling, alienated purchase on the poems we study." This evidently is Levinson's view of how we ordinarily read: whether we are serious critics or romance
readers, we "forget ourselves through a facile sympathy" with writers and their
works; we lose our critical alienation and, in act of self-surrender, identify with
the author, the story, the characters and their fates.

Levinson tries to counter this by introducing a suppressed social context.
But it's hard to see the relevance of the river traffic or the beggars at the abbey
to what Wordsworth is writing: a meditative or pastoral poem, which inevitably involves a projection onto the landscape. Levinson essentially attacks
him for not writing a different poem. Can Wordsworth really be said to have
neglected the poor? Other poems he wrote at the same time, such as "The Ruined Cottage," "Old Man Travelling," "The Old Cumberland Beggar," and the
early books of *The Prelude*, contain the most indelible, heartrending portraits

of the blind, the poor, the homeless, and the destitute to be found anywhere in English poetry. Wordsworth's humanity can scarcely be the issue; neither can his social conscience.

Levinson is right to say that a merely worshipful attitude toward literary genius and Great Books can lead to myopia or blindness; critics and serious readers shouldn't have to be like rock fans, prostrating themselves at the altar of their idols. She properly insists on looking outside the work itself, seeing it through modern eyes yet searching for the apt historical detail.

But she herself has fallen into another form of myopia: the blind confidence of the intrusive, adversarial critic who knows exactly what's being suppressed and why—the critic caught in present-day concerns, quick to denounce literature and expose its "ideology" for failing to accord with her own views. Where the deconstructionist critic searched out subtexts and linguistic lacunae from a deep-seated skepticism, trying to show how language itself was slippery and duplicitous, the ideological critic writes out of a misplaced certainty, comparing the poor writer's partial, deceptive outlook to her own more complete and truthful picture. This is not only politically correct criticism; it's epistemologically correct criticism, ratifying the wisdom and superiority of the critic over the writer.

De Man's skepticism about interpretation has been turned here into political hostility, founded on some remarkable presumptions about the history the poet is supposedly leaving out. Where de Man imagined critics experiencing vertigo in trying to cleanse their discourse of "aberrantly referential implications," the ideological critic, also looking for gaps and suppressions, has brought back reference to the "real" world with a vengeance, in the most literal fashion imaginable.

Both approaches give us samples of reading against the text by professionals who have lost touch with how ordinary readers read, including the ordinary readers in themselves. More than that, they've set out to undermine the kind of naively respectful reading that (to my mind) is largely a thing of the past. A "facile sympathy" for great writers is hardly one of the current dilemmas of higher education or even of literary criticism. Levinson's more skeptical approach might have been a bracing challenge during the last stages of the New Criticism, when professional reading grew slack and idolatrous, and pedantic interpreters went to ridiculous extremes to sanctify Art and harmonize every detail of what they read. They saw the text as a fine organic unity and invariably uncovered evidence to prove it.

This is hardly the case today. The subtle, infinitely complicated, and highly adversarial analysis of literature comes at a time when fewer people are reading, when print culture has lost much of its former prestige, when any goal beyond minimum literacy seems as elusive as ever. The populist suspicion of literature at the bottom end of the reading curve is paralleled by the "hermeneutics of suspicion" at the high end. The indiscriminate sense among postmodern critics that everything is a text matches the leveling attitude of the TV generation, which makes everything accessible by changing channels or surfing websites, and diminishes literature to a media buzz.

The worst part of the alienation of criticism from literature is the loss of the public sphere. Not so long ago this was reflected most in the jargon and abstruseness of academic writing; indeed, in the heated debate over political correctness in the early 1990s, when literature professors were chastised, sometimes unfairly, for their political orthodoxy and intolerance, they had no effective public vocabulary for their reply. Their very language seemed to convict them. Habituated to talking only to each other, contemptuous of the wider audience and more accessible style that critics had once cultivated, academics were unprepared for attacks in *Newsweek* or *New York* magazine or for televised debates and interviews. In the face of such challenges they turned defensive or sarcastic; in the public eye, their cause folded like an undefended city.

Just as people who are illiterate have, quite involuntarily, lost access to the public sphere, critics and literary intellectuals who were fundamentally hostile to literature, who treated it only as linguistic or social evidence, suffered in their own way a kind of "damaged literacy." They opted out of the community of readers, in which critical discourse contributes to public debate. (On the other hand, following the debacle over political correctness, there was a significant reversal of direction, as some gifted literary scholars turned toward essayistic criticism, literary journalism, autobiography, and op-ed writing.) Why a critic like de Man should have abandoned the public sphere, becoming skeptical about history itself, could be more readily understood when we learned of his former public role as a featured writer for Belgian newspapers under the Nazi occupation. But a historical critic like Levinson came explicitly to assert the claims of public truth against private meditation; she castigated Romantic poets for failing in their social responsibility. But she turned her back on the common reader and common sense as dramatically as de Man.

Paul de Man of course believed that all literacy was damaged literacy, that all reading inevitably resulted in misreading, just as Levinson seems to believe that an undue respect for writers is a risk to our moral health. In the prefaces to his novels, Henry James urged that we grant writers their *donnée*, their creative premise, so that criticism could show where the execution succeeded or fell short. Instead, advanced critics disregard the intent and attack the writer for writing the wrong work. The book reviewer has been described as someone who arrives on the field after the battle is over, to finish off the survivors. In this spirit, academic critics have come along to deconstruct the reading process after it has already self-destructed.

The role of the critic is not to read notionally and cleverly, and certainly not to arraign writers for their politics, but to raise ordinary reading to a higher power—to make it more insightful, more acute, without losing the vital authenticity of a deeply personal reaction. Criticism can remain intuitive even as it turns analytical; its communal speech has private sources. It is surely ironic to speak for the social responsibility of the writer while betraying the public sphere of reading. Criticism, even academic criticism, is neither a sect nor a priesthood but ultimately a public trust, mediating between artists or writers and their often puzzled audience.

Nietzsche warned of the interpreter's will to power over the text, the desire, born of envy, to possess and appropriate it. Geoffrey Hartman, in his essay "The Fate of Reading," countered with the example of Dr. Johnson, who preserved a boyish sense of wonder within the moral will of the mature critic. This is the excited feeling that Keats conveyed in his sonnet on sitting down to read Chapman's Homer and Stephen Greenblatt highlights in his book about voyages of discovery, *Marvelous Possessions*. While it is surely impossible, even undesirable, for scholars to revert to an unself-conscious form of reading, especially when reading and literacy have remained under siege, this sense of wonder may yet provide some basis to reconcile the common reader and the critical reader, and help restore criticism to its place in the public sphere, where cultural commentary meets political and civic discourse.

A naive reading, anchored in wonder, must remain an indispensable moment of a more self-conscious reading, not just a piece of scaffolding to be kicked away as our suspicion and professionalism take over. We need a better balance between the naive and suspicious readers in ourselves: between the willing suspension of disbelief and our ability to withhold ourselves and read skeptically; between our appreciation of art and the knowledge of its persuasive power; between a sympathy for the author as an individual like ourselves—working out creative problems, making contingent choices—and our critical sense of a literary work as the discursive formation of a cultural moment, which (as Michel Foucault once said) "speaks" the author rather than is spoken *by* him. We need such a balance to remain strong readers, avoiding the cheerfully nihilistic skepticism of a deconstructive critic like Paul de Man as well as the reductive, politically motivated criticism of would-be historical critics like Marjorie Levinson—approaches that, far from advancing the cause of literacy, only confirm its beleaguered position.

FINDING THE RIGHT WORDS

IN ANY DISCUSSION of the reader, the political critic, or the public intellectual in the second half of the twentieth century, it would be hard to find a figure more exemplary or more controversial than Irving Howe. Since Howe's death in 1993, at the age of seventy-two, his work and even his personal aura have had a strong afterlife. Literary criticism, like most political writing, usually fades with time. Once off the scene, the writer can no longer bring old ideas up to date or lend them coherence by sheer force of personality. Irving Howe, on the other hand, remains a vivid presence, and not simply among his acolytes. His death was followed by many memorial tributes, along with attacks by prominent neoconservatives who saw him still as a thorn in their side—too smart a writer, too biting a critic to be easily set aside. More comment followed when his son, Nicholas Howe, brought out his last and most literary work, *A Critic's Notebook*. With his sharp-tongued humor and debater's edge, Howe played a central role in an excellent documentary about four New York intellectuals, Joseph Dorman's *Arguing the World*. A leading professional journal, *American Jewish History*, devoted a whole issue to a not altogether friendly reconsideration of Howe's masterpiece, *World of Our Fathers*, which lies like a lion across the path of historians of Jewish immigrant life. There have already been two well-researched intellectual biographies, one by a militant conservative, Edward Alexander (1998), who is critical of Howe's politics, early and late, the other by a sympathetic liberal, Gerald Sorin (2002). John Rodden, who has written about Orwell and Trilling, recently edited two collections of essays about Howe and his work.

More than a decade after his death Howe continues to attract fierce censure and grateful praise. I'm not the only writer who still hears his voice echoing in my head, wondering at times what he might have thought of this or that book, this or that twist or turn in politics. *Dissent*, the social democratic journal he founded with Lewis Coser in 1954, remains intellectually robust—an ecumenical magazine of the beleaguered left, as flexible in its social criticism as he became in his lifelong commitment to socialism. As in the 1950s, it finds itself trying to carve out a "decent" left in a period when conservatives are dominant, liberals often feel demoralized, and radicals blame the United States for all the world's ills. Moreover, *Dissent* now embraces many cultural issues Howe tended to exclude from what he conceived as a forum for discussing politics and social policy. In his last decade, he made his peace with the aging radicals of the sixties generation, though he didn't always approve of where they stood, and thus insured that the magazine would not only survive but flourish, even as the world's political agenda dramatically changed.

Howe saw himself as a perpetual dissenter, but there were always others ready to follow where he led. His socialism seemed an anomaly in the 1950s, as American power grew and intellectuals grew more complacent and self-satisfied. Yet he also felt shunted aside by the young leftists of the 1960s and responded with a steady barrage of criticism so intemperate that it might have permanently alienated him from those who shared his deepest aims. (He certainly earned the enduring enmity of Tom Hayden.) But three decades later there is no writer more revered by intellectuals who combine hopes for greater economic equality with a stubborn faith in democracy, who criticize their country for falling short of its ideals but refuse to see it as the root of evil in the world. For political writers like Richard Rorty, Michael Walzer, Todd Gittlin, and Paul Berman, he remains a model of the activist thinker who somehow escaped the clutches of what Orwell called the "smelly little orthodoxies" of the twentieth century, very much as his old antagonist, the protean Ralph Ellison, became the unlikely model for a generation of black intellectuals who had outgrown the ideologies on which they cut their teeth, including black nationalism and Marxism.

The changing fortunes of Howe as a literary critic tell a similar story. The rise of theory, including deconstruction, academic feminism, ideological critique, and postmodernism, isolated him even more dramatically than the waves of conservatism and radical leftism. His style as a critic was marked by the vehement clarity of someone schooled in political argument, who had also learned his craft in the late 1940s as a rebellious protégé of Dwight Macdonald and an anonymous book reviewer for *Time* magazine. Even in his longest literary essays Howe remained a working journalist who made sure to deliver a clear, vigorous account of a writer's career, a character's human density, a book's texture and style, and its compelling claim on the reader—an approach that went out of fashion in academic criticism after 1970.

Howe saw this happening even earlier. In a stinging attack on Leslie Fiedler's *Love and Death in the American Novel*, he anticipated what would later be called "the hermeneutics of suspicion," the critic's search for a buried subtext that could reveal the writer's unconscious motives or be used to indict the work itself. "Like a mass-culture imitation of a psychoanalyst, Fiedler refuses on principle to honor the 'surface' events, characters, statements and meanings of a novel. . . . He engages not in formal description or historical placement or critical evaluation, but in a relentless and joyless exposure. The work of literature comes before him as if it were a defendant without defense, or an enemy intent on deceiving him so that he will not see through its moral claims and coverings." Writing in 1960, Howe had little inkling of how fashionable this adversarial posture would become for later academic critics.

Beginning with his first major work, *Politics and the Novel* (1957), Howe made his reputation as a social and political critic of literature, not a strictly aesthetic one. But in trying to connect intimately with the literary text and make sense of it to a broader public, he cast his lot, surprisingly, with the formal critics, both New and old, whose approach was already going out of style. After a period of "painful soul-searching" around 1948, he reacted sharply against his own sectarian background and the Marxist criticism it had fostered. He felt a growing delight in literature itself, apart from its ideological tendency. Fiedler's imperious psychoanalytic method, he says, "disregards the work of literature as something 'made,' a construct of mind and imagination through the medium of language, requiring attention on its own terms and according to its own structure." We rightly think of Howe as a historical critic, yet he always grounds his commentary in a writer's language and style, the emotional patterns revealed in the work, and the unique or familiar ways the writer remakes the world.

For many years the clarity of Howe's prose, along with this focus on the individual author, the individual work, made him seem like an old-fashioned figure on the critical scene, more the journalist and omnivorous reviewer than the full-fledged critic. Yet on writers as different as T. E. Lawrence, Sholem Aleichem, Louis-Ferdinand Céline, Ignazio Silone, George Orwell, I. B. Singer, Edith Wharton, Isaac Babel, and Theodore Dreiser, his essays were often the first place the general reader might turn for critical illumination. As a sometime radical with a deep, abiding sense of privacy, Howe did not reveal much of himself in these essays. Yet his grasp of these writers was so immediate, so personal, so determined to find the living pulse of their work—and to articulate something almost unsayable in his own intuitive response—that we come to feel we know him intimately. His sharp, relentless, often scathingly funny voice is no doubt indebted to his political writing but also reenacts his probing, jabbing way of reading. Even his longtime antagonist Philip Roth acknowledged that Howe was a real *reader*, one of the chosen, whose criticism could cut to the quick.

Like Lionel Trilling, Howe took every literary work, as he took many political issues, as a moral challenge, a set of embodied convictions on how to live. This led him into sweeping polemics in which he would play the provocateur, evoke passionate controversy, but at times go badly astray. It was the outraged moralist in him that led him to attack James Baldwin and Ralph Ellison for betraying the legacy of rage in the work of their mentor, Richard Wright, and to revile Roth in *Portnoy's Complaint* for putting his talent "to the service of a creative vision deeply marred by vulgarity." The same puritanical streak led him to travesty the "new sensibility" of the 1960s as a toxic dose of primitive innocence, a form of moral anarchy, and to wonder "whether this outlook is compatible with a high order of culture or a complex civilization." Despite a lifetime's work fighting for social justice, Howe, like other Jewish writers (including Freud and Trilling), found himself caught up in a tragic vision that stressed an almost insoluble moral tension, an irreconcilable conflict. In a brief essay on Isaac Babel, he picks up Trilling's cue that Babel, riding with the Red Cossacks through territory dotted with his fellow Jews, "was captivated by the vision of two ways of being, the way of violence and the way of peace, and he was torn between them." But typically, Howe, speaking out of his own sense of the conflicts between politics and art, gives a historical coloring to Trillling's timeless observation, seeing the soldiers' brutality in political terms: "Babel understood with absolute sureness the problem that has obsessed all modern novelists who deal with politics: the problem of action in both its heroic necessity and its ugly self-contamination." In other words, though radical goals may be admirable, the means at hand to realize them could easily prove offensive, unpalatable. In one story Babel's protagonist, part journalist, part combatant, is bitterly berated by a Russian soldier for riding through battle without cartridges in his revolver. "Crouching beneath the crown of death," the writer ends up "begging fate for the simplest ability—the ability to kill a man." In another story he meets an old Jew who feels as abused by the Revolution as by the feudal Polish landowners who are fighting against it, and longs for something "unattainable," a "sweet Revolution," the "International of good people." Characteristically, Howe shows how this tension is enacted in Babel's famously laconic style, where it becomes a tremendous source of energy. Taking up John Berryman's comparison of Babel with Stephen Crane, he writes that "in both writers there is an obsessive concern with compression and explosion, a kinesthetic ferocity of control, a readiness to wrench language in order to gain nervous immediacy. Both use language to inflict a wound."

This is no casual insight, no imposed melodrama, but a remark dredged up from deep inside the critic's own psyche. Trilling and Howe, both conflicted Jews, respond strongly to the ambivalence about Jews, about violence, about revolution that makes Babel's *Red Cavalry* so starkly effective yet would one day make the author one of Stalin's victims. This personal identification gives power to Howe's essays, which are often obliquely autobiographical. In a memoir of one of his mentors, *Partisan Review* editor Philip Rahv, with whom he later quarreled, Howe describes how Rahv turned cautious in the conservative climate of the 1950s, provoking others (including Howe) to write the provocative critical essays Rahv himself might have written. By holding back, Rahv lost his "élan, his nervousness": "He could still turn out a lively piece full of the old fire and scorn, but he had made an estimate—politically mistaken, morally unheroic—that this wasn't the time to take chances. And by not taking chances (they didn't turn out to be such big chances either), he allowed his energy to dribble away, his voice to lose its forcefulness." Howe himself, at Rahv's urging, wrote the famous 1954 polemic "This Age of Conformity," one of the key dissenting texts of the decade, which Rahv then published in his magazine. In Howe's account, Rahv's cunning and timidity did him in; as Howe sees it, personal authenticity, keeping faith with one's convictions, is inseparable from political and moral daring. Rahv's flaw, his failure of nerve, gives Howe's portrait of him its tragic cast at the same time it justifies Howe's own zeal for controversy, his take-no-prisoners approach to public argument, his lifelong persistence as a political campaigner, and the peculiar nervous intensity of his own style.

Howe's personal voice, his refusal to rest or desist, brought him back into fashion as a critic in the same way that he became the political conscience for many in the younger generation. Just as he lived to see the end of the Reagan revolution and the fall of the Soviet Union, he saw the beginning of a tectonic shift in the world of literature and criticism. Thanks mainly to the humiliation of the left in the culture wars of the late eighties and early nineties, a new fascination with the public intellectual challenged the long dominance of theory, with its arcane professional languages. In an obituary tribute to Trilling written many years earlier, Howe recalled asking Trilling whether he wasn't terrified of the new methodologists who were taking over the field. (Trilling responded puckishly that he was terrified of everything.) By the time Howe died the theorists had more or less had their day, and Howe himself became an important model for young literary scholars like David Bromwich and Ilan Stavans, who were as interested in politics as in culture and were eager to write for larger audiences without intellectual compromise. For me he had always been such a model, ever since I began reading him as an undergraduate around 1960. When I published my first piece in *Partisan Review* in 1962, I got a complimentary note from Howe, always on the lookout for young talent. He invited me to write for *Dissent*, something I didn't actually get to do until twenty-five years later. I didn't meet him until the early seventies, and disliked much of what he wrote in the interim about politics and the arts in the 1960s. It amazed me that he could write a sympathetic essay on Berkeley's Free Speech movement one year, then publish a furious onslaught against the New Left barely a year later. When Philip Rahv criticized him for setting up "anti-Communism as the supreme test of political rectitude on the Left," when Raymond Williams attacked the "rancor" of his tone, its sense of "unjustified superiority," I completely agreed, though Rahv had scarcely earned the right to attack him from the left and Williams's position boiled down to the hoary dictum "No enemies on the Left."

Howe escaped from politics, as he had done since the fifties, through his invaluable work on Yiddish literature, editing a series of anthologies, with superb introductions, that brought this largely invisible body of work into the mainstream. Toward the end of the decade he also wrote two landmark essays summing up the culture of modernism and the world and style of the New York intellectuals, essays that showed not only his wide purview and bold synthesizing powers but his rueful sense, perhaps premature, that these chapters of cultural history were more or less behind us. Just as Howe saw himself as a latecomer to Yiddish literature, which paradoxically made him a pioneer in its dissemination to an English-speaking audience, he felt a sense of belatedness in both modernist culture and the fractious circle of the New York writers. Caught between vigorous participation and an elegiac sense of farewell, he became the boldly assertive chronicler who brought the whole subject into focus, as he had done with the work of many individual writers. Yet he also believed that cultures could flourish brilliantly in their moment of decline, as I. B. Singer, Chaim Grade, and Jacob Glatstein had shown in the waning days of Yiddish literature, as Southern writers and Jewish American writers had done when their cultural roots were (in his view) already disintegrating.

Not long after I met Howe, I joined his department, the doctoral program in English at the City University of New York, and very soon the wariness between us dissolved. In the face of rising neoconservative influence, he had turned left again in the early 1970s, bringing his *Dissent* colleagues along with him. But I was twenty years younger, with a certain awe of him, and he tended to be abrupt and impatient with everyone, which often made me feel I was keeping him from more important business, indeed, from getting his work done. The publication of *World of Our Fathers* in 1976 made him a household name in a way he never expected to become, and it also increased demands on his time. He had little small talk, and our conversations were swift, amusing, and often practical—a student to be examined, a wrinkle in a writer's work to be ironed out. (I remember one phone call in which he questioned me about the shifting names of the protagonists in Delmore Schwartz's elusive, mesmerizing stories.) I admired him for his political probity, literary intelligence, and scorching wit, and felt he was someone I would never really know well but was glad to have on my side. I came to know him better through his writing, which never failed to engage me, and through his public appearances, where he was always a master of argument, than through our snatches of conversation, which often seemed truncated. I find today that I annotated almost every page of his 1982 memoir, *A Margin of Hope*, agreeing and disagreeing more vigorously than I ever did when he was in the room. Yet when he died I felt a gap in my life that has never really been filled.

On an impulse, Howe retired from active teaching in 1986 but continued writing, editing, and lecturing until his death. In his reviews he often praised his subjects for staying the course, getting the work done, even in the face of defeat, discouragement, aging, and illness. He says of Edmund Wilson that "his career took on a heroic shape, the curve of the writer who attains magisterial lucidity in middle age and then, in the years of decline, struggles ferociously to keep his powers." In describing his flawed heroes, Howe often enriched the portrait by projecting his own fears. The illnesses of his last years often left him depressed, and more than once I heard him wonder whether the world really needed another book from him. But he enormously admired Norman Thomas, the perennial Socialist candidate, for sticking to his political mission and even for his eloquent style in debate ("he knew more, he talked faster, and—miracle of American miracles!—he came out with comely sentences and coherent paragraphs"). He described Thomas as "the only truly great man I have ever met." Howe reserved his contempt for the former radicals from his City College days who had grown up poor but turned comfortable and conservative, losing their feeling for the world they left behind and enjoying their new access to wealth and power. Another hero of his, a figure of genuine moral authority, was the Italian novelist Ignazio Silone, "the least bitter of ex-Communists, the most reflective of radical democrats," whose later books were nonetheless weakened by "his exhausting struggle with his own beliefs, the struggle of a socialist who has abandoned his dogmas yet wishes to preserve his animating values," something Howe himself understood very well.

It's hard not to see the touches of self-reflection in Howe's portraits of Wilson and Silone. Howe had begun redefining his socialism as early as the 1950s, transforming it from historical dogma to moral critique—"the name of our desire," as he called it, using Tolstoy's phrase. Eventually it became a more forceful extension of liberalism, an unwavering commitment to the labor movement and the welfare state, and a branch of the left wing of the Democratic Party. The very word, socialism, became a mantra for persistence and determination; it was his link to the radical past even as he was adapting it to the needs of the present. In the introduction to his 1966 collection of political essays, *Steady Work*, he described himself as "a man of the left, in dialogue with himself, asking which of his earlier ideas should be preserved, which modified, which discarded." This tentativeness was borne out not by the essays themselves, which are never less than emphatic, but by the unresolved conflicts between them. This was especially true of his essays on the New Left, which were marred by his impatience with a generation he clearly hoped would follow his political lead. Howe could be polemical, at times even infuriating, without losing his grasp of the complexity of the subject. Echoing Trilling's well-known critique of liberalism in *The Liberal Imagination*, he described a commitment to socialism in the mid–twentieth century as "a capacity for living with doubt, revaluation and crisis," yet also called it "an abiding ideal." Socialism for him became a politics of conscience rather than a specific program or a set of goals; he came to admire figures who put their conscience, as well as their powers of observation, before their theories and ideas.

Howe saw Orwell, like Silone, as a writer trying to live by a consistent set of values after they had lost their ideological underpinnings. Aside from *A Margin of Hope*, Howe's 1968 essay on Orwell is perhaps the closest thing he ever wrote to a self-portrait. He describes Orwell as someone who kept his head, "wrote with his bones," through the worst political episodes of the twentieth century: "the Depression, Hitlerism, Franco's victory in Spain, Stalinism, the collapse of bourgeois England in the thirties." Howe writes that "for a whole generation—mine—Orwell was an intellectual hero." He saw in Orwell many of the qualities he aspired to or regretted in himself. Like his other heroes, including Wilson, Orwell was an irascible, even "pugnacious" man, whose essays are rightly admired for their "blunt clarity of speech and ruthless determination to see what looms in front of one's nose." He notes, without really complaining, that Orwell "is reckless, he is ferociously polemical," even when arguing for a moderate position. In the face of those who see him as some kind of secular saint, he doubts that Orwell "was particularly virtuous or good."

Although Orwell "could be mean in polemics," he sometimes befriended those he had criticized, for he was driven not by personal animus but "by a passion to clarify ideas, correct errors, persuade readers, straighten things out in the world and in his mind." He admires Orwell's "peculiar sandpapery humor" and the "charged lucidity" of his prose, which nicely describes his own. Like Howe, Orwell "rejected the rituals of Good Form" and "turned away from the pretentiousness of the 'literary.'" He notes that Orwell "had a horror of exposing his private life," a theme that surfaces repeatedly in Howe's pieces (on Joyce, for example, and on Salinger) but also sets parameters for his own memoir. Finally, Howe examines the formal features of Orwell's essays, especially their superb endings. Beginning with Orwell as a moral exemplar who is himself a less than perfect man, who is in fact a difficult man, he ends by scanning Orwell's great essays for lessons on how to write. In Howe's final work, A Critic's Notebook, he is still searching and still learning.

The best responses to Howe's work were as attentive to his style as he was to the language of those he reviewed. A few reviewers took due note of his remarkable growth as a writer. Early on, in 1964, Ted Solotaroff observed how the critic and the socialist intellectual converged in him, not only in his sense of cultural crisis but in "his crisp, meticulous prose, his skill at literary description, his grasp of the relevant issue quite equal to any serious book or audience. He is almost always telling you something sound and worthwhile and he is almost always as clear as glass." In Howe's earlier work this could be a defect. His literary essays sometimes read like position papers, and one could almost discern a shadowy list of points, the skeleton of the argument, behind the merely efficient surface of the writing. But as Howe's politics and even his temperament lost their sharp edges, his feeling for the aesthetic, his exhilaration with the language, blossomed. Rereading the large body of Orwell's essays, he is surprised to find that "the sheer *pleasure* of it cannot be overstated . . . Orwell was an even better writer than I had supposed." In his review of Howe's 1973 collection The Critical Point, Roger Sale made a similar discovery about Howe himself: that "he seems to have grown over the years, and his prose is sharper, the insights more precise and flexible." He concluded that Howe "seems to be trusting his human and literary instincts more than he once did."

By attending to the touch and feel of a text, Howe became more of a genuine essayist. As he mellowed, the nuances, reservations, and exceptions that complicated his case became as important as the argument. He came to love the New York City Ballet, where he learned to appreciate Balanchine's dancers for their eloquence of the body, an eloquence beyond language. The felicity of his own prose, once merely workmanlike, burgeoned along with its complex powers of description. Struck by Howe's description of the "high radiance" of Frost's greatest poetry, Roger Sale remarked that "only the best critics are generous enough to find the right words for their authors." This laconic verbal precision, itself very literary, contrasts with the tedious elaboration that often mars academic writing, in which every point must be spelled out, every remark illustrated by five examples. Howe later paid tribute to the deeply troubled Delmore Schwartz as "a wondrous talker, a first-rate literary intelligence—the sort who can light up the work of a poet or novelist with a single quick phrase." For a true critic this is a talent as basic as breathing.

Howe never became as fluent a writer as Trilling or Alfred Kazin, or as direct and uncluttered as Orwell and Wilson, those masters of the plain style. Working rapidly, he developed a better ear for his subjects' prose than for his own. But he had gifts absolutely essential to a critic: the power of discrimination, the gift for striking the right note, and for getting under the writer's (and the reader's) skin. His literary judgment, his intuition, could create a benchmark, a point of reference, for serious readers, even those who disagreed with him. It could reach the writers themselves, as his well-known attacks touched a nerve in Ellison and Roth, galvanizing Ellison to an eloquent defense and perhaps moving Roth in a subtly new direction, toward work of greater historical scope and moral urgency.

As a writer himself, Howe acknowledged that his talent for metaphor was limited. I've always been struck by a certain clumsiness in his account of his "reconquest of Jewishness" in A Margin of Hope. But "Jewish Quandaries," the chapter in which this odd, soldierly phrase appears, is a penetrating essay (with illustrations from his own life) on the struggle of Jewish intellectuals with their ethnic background; it is also a frank analysis of how his own feelings had changed over the years. Speaking for many cosmopolitan radicals who once disdained merely tribal loyalties, he writes ruefully that "we had tried to 'make' our lives through acts of decision, 'programs' that thwarted the deeper, more intuitive parts of our own being." Embarrassed by the immigrant poverty and parochialism of his early years, indoctrinated by the universalism of his later Marxist faith, with its trust in collective movements and contempt for bourgeois individualism, Howe never found it easy to talk about himself. It went against the grain. Yet his memoir, if rarely intimate, showed how well he could *think* about himself, trusting his human and literary instincts as he had increasingly done in his criticism.

As with all the best critics, his work has a strong personal stamp, and he himself comes through on every page—awkward, funny, impatient, at moments ruthless, yet with an uncanny ability to get to the heart of the matter, to highlight what really counts. More than a decade younger than Trilling, Rahv, and their generation, he always felt like a latecomer, a brash young man among the grownups; but as a critic and cultural historian he was distinctly an original, a writer with sweeping powers of synthesis whose political savvy, humane moral outlook, and keen feeling for art ultimately enabled him to find his own voice and deploy it with unusual power.

THE SOCIAL USES OF FICTION

Is READING FICTION good for us? Does it enlarge our social sympathies or offer us little more than moments of escape from our humdrum lives? The novel came in with the modern world, the cocky young upstart among literary forms, and there have always been detractors skeptical of its social value. In the eighteenth century, novels were often disguised as plain fact yet sharply attacked for making things up. Puritans castigated novels as lurid and immoral, while sober realists scorned them for encouraging flights of fantasy. Marxists resisted their penchant for bourgeois individualism, their focus on the private lives of privileged people, yet sometimes appreciated the power of their social criticism. There were always intellectuals who loathed novels for being too popular, and solemn men of affairs who considered them irrelevant to the serious (male) business of running society.

To Martha Nussbaum, the novel is "a living form," still central to our culture, "morally serious yet popularly engaging." From early in the twentieth century, when the mass media began taking the place of popular fiction, the novel was refined by modernism into a more self-conscious art, just as films would be elevated into art by the challenge of television. But novel-reading, for all its refinements, has usually been seen as an intimate experience grounded in personal feeling, the domain of a largely female audience. Few critics, not even the great theorists of realism, such as Georg Lukács and Erich Auerbach, have mounted a case for its social benefits, as Martha C. Nussbaum did in her 1996 book *Poetic Justice: The Literary Imagination and Public Life*.

Nussbaum is a distinguished philosopher and classicist whose previous work centered on Greek tragedy, classical Greek philosophy, and Hellenistic ethics. But she also published a highly readable collection of essays on philosophy and literature, *Love's Knowledge* (1990), concentrating on novels by Dickens, Henry James, Proust, and Beckett. Where *Love's Knowledge* mapped the close connections between modern novels and ethical concerns, *Poetic Justice* set out bravely to apply the lessons of fiction to economics, social thought, and jurisprudence.

Since John Rawls published *A Theory of Justice* in 1971, an increasing number of philosophers, including Robert Nozick, Richard Rorty, Bernard Williams, Charles Taylor, Hilary Putnam, and Thomas Nagel, have entered into a broad conversation with economists, sociologists, legal thinkers, and political theorists about how our society should be organized. This discussion has not usually touched the general reader, since it dealt with fundamental principles rather than policy issues, but in *Poetic Justice* Nussbaum made a determined effort to reach a wider audience. Her previous work was by turns eloquent and verbose, brightly personal yet clogged with references to her own writings. *Poetic Justice*, based on a series of lectures, proved to be a more concise, accessible work; it was densely argued—it felt quite long for a rather short book—but also timely and urgent.

The unspoken context of *Poetic Justice* was the wave of budget cutting, cost/benefit analysis, and hardhearted social theory driving the new leadership in Congress after the Gingrich revolution in 1994, but also at the state and local level, which licensed a diminished sympathy for society's losers: the poor, the ill, and the elderly. This assault against the welfare state and the legacy of New Deal liberalism had begun during the Reagan years, when hardheartedness came into vogue and the well-to-do were told that it was fine to flaunt their wealth and privilege. But this became a legislative agenda only after the electoral success of Gingrich's so-called Contract with America, which swept conservative Republicans into power in both houses of Congress. Though the Speaker and his Contract soon fell from grace, the conservative dominance continued, especially in the House of Representatives.

Some of this backlash against welfare liberalism could be traced to class anger, race prejudice, and economic self-interest, but some of it arose from a willed ignorance of what the progressive reformer Jacob Riis called "how the other half lives." When housing and schooling are segregated by class and race, when members of the white middle class rarely meet someone whose life is radically different, the poor take on no individual reality; they remain part of an "underclass" known only through media images of violent crime or urban encounters marred by fear or disgust: panhandling, chronic homelessness, petty crime, the visible remnants of the drug culture. This ignorance of the actual lives of the poor reduces our empathy and makes possible what Martha Nussbaum calls "the economist's habit of reducing everything to calculation."

Like many previous critics of utilitarianism, she objects to seeing individuals as figures in a numbers game rather than creatures beset by conflict and moral choice. Utilitarian economists, she says, "perceive only those abstract features of people and situations that can easily be translated into economic calculations." Compared to novelists, they are "blind to the qualitative richness of the perceptible world; to the separateness of its people, to their inner depths, their hopes and loves and fears; blind to what it is like to live a human life and to try to endow it with a human meaning."

This attack on purely economic models was made brilliantly in the nineteenth century by John Stuart Mill, whose father, a radical reformer, worked closely with the founder of utilitarianism, Jeremy Bentham. The younger Mill saw Bentham as a great man whose reasoned critique swept away "the accumulated cobwebs of centuries," but who was limited by his "want of imagination" and his "small experience of human feelings." When Mill himself, brought up by his father to become a thinking machine, suffered a nervous breakdown at twenty, he turned for relief to the poetry of Wordsworth, which rescued him from depression and tapped a vein of deep feeling that had been scanted by his education.

Like Richard Rorty, who made an equally strong case for fiction in *Contingency, Irony, and Solidarity* (1989), Martha Nussbaum looks to novels (and to poets like Whitman) for exactly what Mill brought away from Wordsworth's poetry, a sense of the richness, mystery, and complication of individual lives. Where Bentham had developed a crude calculus of pleasure and pain as a way of insuring "the greatest happiness of the greatest number," Mill, like his contemporaries Carlyle and Ruskin, insisted on ethical distinctions that took account of the *quality* of life. Nussbaum picks up directly from this critique as it was slashingly fictionalized in Dickens's *Hard Times* (1854), an angry novel about workingmen, industrialism, and an inhuman system of education, a book admired by Ruskin and Shaw but largely forgotten until the English critic F. R. Leavis rediscovered it in 1948.

Just as Newt Gingrich, appealing to studies by historian Gertrude Himmelfarb, invoked "Victorian virtues" to bolster his crusade against the welfare state, Nussbaum turns back to Dickens to assail the economic-utilitarian rationale behind the right-wing legislative agenda. One focus of her criticism is the "law and economics" movement represented by Richard Posner, a federal judge and prolific legal scholar to whom the book is warmly dedicated. *Poetic Justice* is a Dickensian rejoinder to his readable and influential book *The Economics of Justice* (1981), which centers on "wealth maximization" as a principle of common law. Early in Nussbaum's book, he appears as the arch-calculator, the modern equivalent of Mr. Gradgrind, Dickens's "man of facts," who is "ready to weigh and measure any parcel of human nature, and tell you exactly what it comes to." But by the end Posner emerges as the model jurist, whose subtly written opinion in a sexual harassment case beautifully defines the novelistic insight of the "literary judge." (This tribute did not prevent him from sharply criticizing her book in his later work, *Public Intellectuals: A Study in Decline*, published in 2001.)

Poetic Justice was a tract for the times in the guise of a defense of the literary imagination. Nussbaum's tour de force is her inspired translation of *Hard Times* into the language of social theory, backed by briefer discussions of Richard Wright's *Native Son* and E. M. Forster's posthumously published *Maurice*, which explores homosexuality. Nussbaum shows how these novels, in their metaphoric language and their focus on individual feelings, give us rare knowledge of people in remote corners of society, the kinds of people many of us might never otherwise meet. She puts special emphasis on "the novel's interest in the ordinary," the way it enables readers, despite their distance and detachment, to get "close to the people and their actual experience." This is just the kind of personal identification she urges on legislators, ethical thinkers, and judges alike. Her notion of the "literary judge" who sees people as individuals, not simply as cases, is closely modeled on her conception of novel-reading, with "the literary imaginer as judicious spectator."

But she muddies her case for fiction as a genre by focusing on three social-problem novels dealing with hot-button issues of class, race, and sexual preference. Nussbaum does not distinguish between the fierce social polemic of *Hard Times*, which she gamely paraphrases and updates, and the formal properties it shares with other novels, which she too readily attributes to fiction at large. Is she making a case for "the novel" as a literary form or for this kind of polemical novel, written in direct response to social crisis? The pamphleteering immediacy of *Hard Times*—one of the only novels Dickens published in weekly rather than monthly installments—is scarcely typical of Dickens himself, let alone novels in general. Nussbaum says she is confining herself to realistic fiction, but *Hard Times* is perhaps the least realistic novel Dickens ever wrote. Written in white-hot anger and a spirit of bitter derision, with characters verging on broad caricatures, the book proves little about the value of fiction or its commitment to social justice.

This highlights the major misstep in *Poetic Justice*, which is Nussbaum's suggestion that because we identify with fictional characters, "a concern for the disadvantaged is built into the structure of the literary experience," a sweeping generalization that takes us far beyond realistic fiction. Are novels really this virtuous and humane? Reading can give us pleasure in illicit and unexpected ways. There are novels in which we identify with the rich and successful, not the "disadvantaged"; novels that turn people into butts of satire, even hatred; novels manipulating our fantasies rather than enlarging our sympathies; and finally, post-Brechtian or radically modernist novels that, compared to the classic works of realism, involve us much less with the fate of individual characters. Nussbaum's argument depends too much on novels in tune with today's liberal politics but strictly nineteenth-century in their Aristotelian storytelling conventions. "Indeed," she claims, "we can say of the mainstream realist novel what Aristotle said of tragic drama, that the very form constructs compassion in readers." Yet this compassion can be cruelly circumscribed, as we know from the oft-repeated example of the woman in the theater who weeps copiously at the play while her footman freezes out in the snow.

Far from finding literature intrinsically liberal, critics from Hazlitt to Trilling argued that its sympathies were often antidemocratic. "The language of poetry naturally falls in with the language of power," Hazlitt wrote of Shakespeare's *Coriolanus*. Novels, with their concern for the mundane and the ordinary, may well raise different issues, but recent academic critics have taken Hazlitt much further, regularly debunking art as a vehicle of ideology and social power. Nussbaum's love of literature is refreshingly old-fashioned; it no doubt stems from her training in philosophy and the classics rather than literary studies. When *Poetic Justice* first appeared, it was strikingly out of tune with the current wisdom in academic criticism, in Washington, and in the social-policy think tanks. It still is.

Her defense of fiction as an open form teeming with unruly humanity recalls how writers as different as Henry James and D. H. Lawrence once idealized the novel as "the one bright book of life." At a time when the legacy of the Gingrich revolution still dominates public policy, when conservative ideologues have deliberately used tax cuts for the well-to-do as a way of making social services unaffordable, and, at the other end of the cultural spectrum, when even the official guardians of literature seem to regard it with suspicion, Nussbaum's appeal to the outlook of fiction as a model for judicial and social policy seems bracingly utopian—no doubt unduly abstract but also immensely heartening. *Poetic Justice* is less a study of literature than a lay sermon for downhearted liberals, in which the novel serves as a potent metaphor for a deeper understanding of ordinary people's lives.

THE LIMITS OF HISTORICISM: LITERARY THEORY AND HISTORICAL UNDERSTANDING

WHEN I BEGAN teaching literature in the mid-1960s, the campus atmosphere was alive with conflict but the internal revolution that would transform scholarship in the humanities still lay ahead. National politics and the role of the university were the issues, not the methods used in any discipline. Every month brought demonstrations and teach-ins against the Vietnam War, the draft, the ROTC, and defense research, but the coming battle in literary and cultural studies was barely on the horizon. College and graduate courses were still parceled out in terms of conventional periods, genres, and major authors, with little attention paid to the premises of criticism itself or to literature published since 1945. But by 1980, many younger scholars had been trained in theory, and this curriculum was changing. The theory years had begun, accompanied by a wave of identity politics, though the deepest inroads were at first limited to a few elite universities. But soon even departments far from the mainstream made room for black studies and women's studies. Some had already slotted in at least a single theorist, usually a deconstructionist, whose role was to shake up the department and give it a fresher look, an orientation toward the future. Gradually, however, as the next generation gained a tenuous, then a tenured foothold, theory became less a specialty of its own, more a radical critique of how the whole field of literary studies operated. Yet despite its sweeping, sometimes apocalyptic language, its radicalism never took a genuinely political form. As theory gained acceptance in the university and prestige in the profession, it never challenged institutional patterns of control and advancement already in place. Where the sixties generation had thrown itself into radical lifestyles, communal living, and alternate forms of education, the young theorists, facing tougher economic times, merely sought a place at the table, sometimes playing on liberal guilt as a way of capturing a piece of academic turf.

A new generation was asserting its identity, but in an ambiguous way. Earlier generations of literature professors had seen themselves as guardians of the language against the professional deformations of social scientists and academic Marxists. Now, proponents of theory took a different turn. They tried to refashion the university into a radical enclave within an increasingly indifferent, self-centered society. They transformed the academic study of literature at the expense of its connections to the wider world. Theory turned its back on the kind of criticism that advances literacy, cherishes style, and honors clarity as it mediates between literature and its audience. The success of the political right in culture wars of the late 1980s and early 1990s, especially the battle over political correctness, was partly the result of theory's vulnerable position in the public sphere, its failure to develop a language in which it might defend itself in open debate. The new dispensation was mocked by traditionalists for its pseudosystematic ambitions, its paralyzing skepticism, its often impenetrable jargon, its focus on method at the expense of other important issues (or at the expense of literature itself), and the cults that surrounded its academic stars. This led eventually to a retreat from theory, a search for new ways of making literature meaningful, and a nostalgia for the kind of public intellectual, the accessible generalist, that theory had mocked and effectively undermined.

One result of the ferment over theory in the last two decades has been the revival of the historical method in the study of literature, the arts, and the world of ideas. Scholars who might once have focused on the linguistic patterns of Shakespeare's plays or Wordsworth's poetry have tried instead to explore their roots in the social history of their times. Art critics who, in the very recent past, would have analyzed impressionist or cubist canvases as configurations of light, color, line, and texture have looked more closely at their content and its links to the artists' lives. Critics once obsessed by theoretical problems of methodology and representation are now engaged with minute details of history and biography. A revolution has brought criticism back to the historical interests that were dominant in the late nineteenth century, the golden age of literary history and biography, before the rise of modernism and the New Criticism. The exclusive attention to the text has given way to a new concern for context as a key to critical interpretation. Now some scholars are applying this historical approach to criticism, especially the waves of literary theory that completely altered the academic study of literature between the late 1960s and early 1990s, including the reemergence of historicism itself.

As we look back at the theory years today, now that the fierce polemical passions have waned, the transformation of literary studies in a single generation seems astonishing. Where did it come from? What kind of residue has it left? In a relatively short time, conventional scholarship and criticism focused on individual writers and their works were displaced by a skeptical approach to all interpretation and an emphasis on elements of ideology that presumably lay embedded in all literary projects. Criticism shifted from a focus on literature to an examination of the instruments of criticism itself, or the social or linguistic conditions that bring literature into being. The emphasis on aesthetics, on the meaning and structure of the work itself, gave way to the social history characteristic of the New Historicism, the political commitments of radical feminism and queer theory, and the ideological scrutiny that became the hallmark of cultural studies. Literature and history were denied their power to convey the truth or depict the world, to achieve what Matthew Arnold quaintly called a "criticism of life." Instead they were seen as ideological formations and social or linguistic constructions.

In Paul de Man's later work, wars and revolutions were reduced to rhetorical terms, that is, to the terms in which they had been interpreted, or represented in language; the periods and movements of standard literary histories became "rather crude metaphors for figural patterns rather than historical events or acts." An iconoclastic exuberance lurks behind such dour, poker-faced pronouncements, a barely concealed delight in upsetting every applecart in sight. But the effect on the disciplines was not so amusing. The new history turned away from sequential narratives that told stories and made causal connections; it shifted instead toward excavations of deep-seated assumptions, projects designed to strike through the mask and expose rhetorical devices of control and representation. As one who remains at heart an old historicist, seeking a balance between the social context of literature and the power it achieves through language, voice, and formal expression, I am not the ideal person to explain this sharp turn. But I'm interested in the answers proposed by the young contributors to *Historicizing Theory*, a volume edited by Peter C. Herman that came out early in 2004. In an unexpected twist, they search out the historical basis of theory itself by examining the biographical circumstances that may have contributed to the work of Foucault, de Man, Baudrillard, Derrida, and even the New Historicists, such as Stephen Greenblatt. Herman begins by echoing the Marxist critic Fredric Jameson's first commandment, "Always historicize." To which I'm tempted to respond, "Why historicize?"—especially when these theorists have stubbornly resisted acknowledging the extraliterary influences that may have shaped them. And why "always" (and *how*) when the evidence can be quite slim, when some historical explanations are more revealing than others, and when competing models of historical understanding can differ dramatically in their approach and their results?

Nowadays, politically minded scholars tend too readily to think of the shift from the old historical approach to a new formal approach after 1945 as a function of the Cold War, a recoil from politics that can be observed not only in literary studies but in sociology, art criticism, analytic philosophy, and law. Yet no one has shown convincingly how the Cold War *caused* any of these changes, though it may have coincided with them. Still, there was a remarkable consistency. Historians turned their backs on the progressive traditions of Turner, Parrington, and Beard, which put history at the service of populist or democratic values. The New Criticism in literature, functionalism in sociology, analytic and positivist philosophy, and the formalist art criticism of Clement Greenberg were alike in turning their subjects into closed systems that left many important issues off-limits, especially social questions about class and power that had dominated discussion before the war.

But even as we look to find some historical basis for this turn against history, it is worth recalling the serious weaknesses of historical criticism that led to its decline. Modern poetry and painting could be exceptionally difficult. They broke sharply with nineteenth-century traditions of narration and visual representation. They took on forms of distortion or abstraction that seemed bent on effacing their origins. Historical criticism, on the other hand, except in the hands of an astute critic like Meyer Schapiro or Edmund Wilson, seemed badly suited to the formal complexity and sheer bravado of modern art. Some leading historical critics, like Georg Lukács and Van Wyck Brooks, rejected modernism outright as a form of reactionary obscurantism. But even critics who were more sympathetic could be reductive or obtuse about art, just as some New Historicists would later turn away from aesthetics as a formation of middle-class ideology.

Other historically oriented critics simply failed to get deeply *into* the work or rise to its personal challenge. Marxist critics could betray their subject into predictable formulas. Some historical critics dissolved the work of art into its background, with its undigested facts and broad generalities, in much the same way that unimaginative New Critics sometimes reduced it to mechanical patterns of imagery, or the way psychoanalytic critics could reduce it to the neurotic conflicts of its author. As formal methods could be subtle but narrow, as if the critic were wearing blinders, the historical approach could be expansive but superficial, eschewing the close-up for the wide-angle view. Historical criticism supplied the big picture but often routinely, in terms of movements and periods that hardly accounted for what truly mattered in the work of individual artists. With some exceptions, like the work of the Frankfurt school or of a few key art historians, historicism stood bewildered before the artistic revolutions of the twentieth century, with their premium on novelty, their demand for a radical transformation of consciousness. In the face of this challenge, many historical critics could offer little more than fierce resistance or soothing clichés about art movements, period styles, and social background.

Though it avoided many of the mistakes of its predecessors, the revived historical criticism after 1980 would not entirely escape such simplifications. Often it relied on interesting but remote social anecdotes that could point up an ingenious parallel to a literary work without convincing the reader that it was truly relevant or illuminating. Sometimes it proposed what simply looked like an analogy between the text and its imagined context, little more than a structural resemblance, a pattern of inference rather than a genuine source or point of origin. By avoiding the chronological approach of earlier historicists, which sought out the genesis of historical events and movements, it ran the risk of looking arbitrary or merely clever. It sought out the ideological key to literary works, the text or anecdote that would expose the networks of social power, but the keys did not always fit the designated locks. In an essay he contributed to *Historicizing Theory*, Ivo Kamps contrasts the new and old historicism very effectively. He shows how a narrative focused on small "particulars" served as a counterweight to the sequential narratives favored by social historians, which claimed access to history *wie es eigentlich gewesen*, as it actually happened, or unfolded in time. These traditional accounts have been seen as "pre-encoded" by the historian's own assumptions and categories, as in part they no doubt were. Yet this really is a caricature of the older history, which was just as likely to be tentative, empirical, and open to contingency. Narrative history is not simply a claim about how things happened but a method of interpretation, a way of shaping data and engaging the reader through story, of identifying causes and effects and weaving disparate strands together. At its best, it remains open to correction and transformation, to yet another account that will refine or supersede it.

In recent years, Renaissance and American Studies scholars have done valuable work in recovering what had been ignored or suppressed by earlier critics, including the viewpoints of outsiders—women, people of color, colonial subjects—but they could not always convince readers of its critical importance to the literary work. Apart from their political motivation, the hint of special pleading, their approach relied too much on what was absent or unexpressed in the work itself. This kind of argument by inference or analogy can be found in some very good essays in Herman's book. Derrida's emphasis on the break or rupture is traced to his own expulsion from school (and eventual departure from the country) as a young French Jew in Algeria; de Man's pessimism and sense of futility is linked to the sudden and catastrophic fall of Belgium to the Nazis; and Foucault's stress on totalitarian control within social institutions like the asylum and the prison is attributed to his own boyhood in occupied France during World War II. Yet these men adamantly resisted making such connections and denied that their work was grounded in their personal histories. Since they often argued that the self was a social construction or a linguistic formation, they balked at seeing their ideas peeled back to their biographical roots, especially when, in de Man's case, they had much to conceal about their earlier lives.

As Peter Herman points out, theorists may resist historical explanation because it can be used to debunk their work, as neoconservatives and hard leftists have sometimes done. A genetic approach may serve as a handy way to mock ideas without actually grappling with them. These theorists may also resist because, despite their relativism or skepticism, they think their beliefs are true, or at least convincing, and deserve to have a life of their own. We must also concede (as Herman notes) that all of us are badly positioned to lay bare the cultural roots of our own work, something only succeeding generations can do. These respectful probes by younger scholars confirm the waning of theory since the eighties and midnineties. Belonging to what Jeffrey Williams calls "the posttheory generation," they take a detached view of the landscape from which theory emerged, yet remain committed to the historical approach that succeeded theory in the 1980s. For European thinkers, they argue, the background is dominated by World War II, a period of defeat, occupation, ruthless brutality, moral compromise, and near-total control. For American critics, the story goes, the sixties, the Vietnam War, and the New Left provided the political crucible from which theory sprang forth. Certainly the left politics of most theorists seems to reflect the radicalism that marked that turbulent decade. More broadly, the attacks on traditional forms of historiography and literary scholarship might well owe something to the debunking spirit of the 1960s, its mockery of authority and disdain for tradition, including the liberal tradition. An astute critic of literary theory, Eugene Goodheart, gives us an incisive summary of this viewpoint in his recent memoir, *Confessions of a Secular Jew*:

> The radical students who made careers in the academy sublimated their radicalism in the various disciplines they occupied, particularly in the humanities. Radicalism became theories of interpretation, its targets literary and philosophical texts and social and political institutions. Having failed to transform society, it also became disillusioned, and already, beginning in the seventies, the most radically skeptical of theories, deconstructionism, became the rage. Its aim was to unsettle our convictions about the possibility of objective truth, spiritual transcendence, authoritative discourse. It asserted a doctrine of uncertainty in the most certain of tones. Is it fortuitous that its originator was a French Jew, Jacques Derrida?

In this partly ironic account, theory was both a product of radicalism and a marker of its defeat, which resembles the crushing sense of failure experienced by Europeans during World War II. Theory set out to revolutionize the academy where young insurgents and their followers took refuge from an unsympathetic society. It aimed at a radical transformation of the interpretive disciplines only to burden them with a sense of skepticism, disillusionment, and broken connections. During the backlash years of Nixonian demagoguery and Reaganite restoration, theory became catastrophe theory, a way of compensating for the sense of impotence, or of recouping failure by showing that it was inevitable, even as critics asserted their power over the text, their refusal to be dominated by its structures, themes, or rhetorical patterns. Emphasizing ideology over interpretation, literary scholarship became a way of seeing through literature, of not being taken in by it.

This linkage between literary theory and the 1960s is far more subtle than one would suppose from Allan Bloom's attacks on relativism in *The Closing of the American Mind*, which could be applied to virtually all modern thought since the Enlightenment, or the neoconservative argument that postmodern theory is simply revolutionary nihilism run amok. Neoconservatives always exaggerate the influence of the sixties as the source of all social and moral evil, including evils rooted in capitalism itself. But even Goodheart's version, which is reminiscent of Hazlitt's witty argument that Wordsworth and Coleridge applied the leveling principles of the French Revolution to poetic diction and rustic characters, raises some elusive historical issues. We can leave aside the objection that, to my knowledge, no major student radicals became literary theorists, and that those who did give theory its big push were generally older, had few political involvements, and (both in Europe and America) began publishing their work well before the sixties revolution hit its stride in 1968. Foucault's *Les Mots et les choses* appeared in France in 1966; Jacques Derrida published three major books in 1967, including *De la grammatologie*. Unlike their more committed predecessor, Sartre, they did not get engaged in the uprising of students and workers the following year. Back in the United States, most of those who became theory stars in the 1970s, including Paul de Man, Geoffrey Hartman, Harold Bloom, J. Hillis Miller, Edward Said, and Stanley Fish, had done their graduate work in the 1950s at Harvard or Yale. Their ambitions were academic and relatively traditional, and they were already becoming known for innovative work in their fields. None of them was especially political in the sixties. But we might say that it was not their own politics that linked theory to the sixties but the enthusiastic reception of their work among the foot soldiers of the younger generation.

Even so, serious problems remain in tracing the historical roots of theory to the 1960s. First of all, the politics of the sixties varied enormously through the course of the decade. The movement in the early sixties, grounded in the civil rights marches and the campaign against nuclear weapons, was humanistic, utopian, and democratic. The Port Huron Statement, with its emphasis on participatory democracy, was most influenced by the work of C. Wright Mills, John Dewey, and the American pragmatists. Poststructuralist theory, on the other hand, was nothing if not a critique of Western humanism, including the existential humanism of the sixties, across which it cast a large epistemological shadow. The radical students I taught in the late sixties were scarcely bent on deconstructing the residues of metaphysics in Western humanist texts. On the contrary, they responded with passion to the classics as subversive works whose humane promise remained unfulfilled. They connected almost viscerally with art and philosophy, not because it was canonical but because it felt so fresh and immediate—and visionary. Blake, Dickens, Ruskin, and Lawrence felt like their contemporaries, not like musty classics. Never had the Great Books felt more relevant than when the whole direction of society seemed in play. The lineage of deconstruction takes us back not to the politics of the sixties but to its ultimate betrayal and blockage.

A better case for the sources of theory can be made from the sour political mood of the late sixties, when the smashed hopes of earlier years turned to anger, skepticism, and suspicion. As Ivo Kamps puts it in his essay in *Historicizing Theory*, Vietnam was "a war in search of a narrative," at least until the surprise Tet offensive early in 1968, when media accounts of American embarrassment and failure overwhelmed the mundane facts of the defeat of the Viet Cong on the ground. By then the triumphal claims of America's military and political leaders had been so discredited that no one believed them, even when they happened to be true. In the Tet offensive, the Viet Cong had thrown everything they had into simultaneous strikes all around the country;

their cadres were decimated, not to be rebuilt for many months, though few people knew this at the time. Yet in the other war, the battle for public opinion that was waged on television, America suffered a humiliating and finally decisive setback. Soon President Johnson and his advisors decided that the war could not be won. The antiwar movement gained its greatest victories in the media, not in the halls of Congress, the White House, or the voting booth. As the administration repeatedly lied to the people with optimistic predictions, phony successes, and exaggerated body counts, a vast reservoir of disbelief built up in American life, a deep distrust of official information, which could have contributed to the later appeal of the "hermeneutics of suspicion" in literary theory. At the same time, as government pronouncements lost credibility, the virtual reality shaped by the media began to dominate public perception. In this sense, the rise of cultural studies might be linked to the darkening political climate of the late sixties.

Cultural studies in America is descended in part from the American Studies movement, which embraced popular culture along with the high arts, and it took off from the ever-expanding media scene. The overweening new interest in popular culture was licensed by the subtle and powerful pop culture of the sixties, especially the music, which made the hierarchical distinctions of earlier mass culture critics untenable. Cultural studies was also indebted to the rise of identity politics in the late sixties, beginning with black nationalism, feminism, and the gay pride movement. Rejecting the notion of a unified culture for an emphasis on diversity and difference, cultural studies was caught between an ethnically derived notion of group affirmation and a postmodern sense of fluid or constructed identity. For scholars who came of age in the sixties and seventies, issues of race and gender, like pop culture, were part of the air they breathed. Since this was also true for young writers, painters, and filmmakers, cultural studies developed in concert with an eclectic postmodernism in the arts, just as the earlier formalist criticism had responded to the strenuous innovations of modernism.

The pitfalls of using history as a key to explaining culture are clear enough. Even when it has freed itself of Hegelian notions of the Zeitgeist or Marxist certainties about historical inevitability, historical criticism is rarely as rigorous as formal analysis. In the words of John Kerrigan, writing in the London Review of Books, "as the heat goes out of the Theory wars, the literary critical mainstream has settled into a historicism that has never properly established which principles of relevance should apply." Historicist readings too often seem idiosyncratic, empirically tenuous, or merely suggestive. As David Shumway argued in a recent issue of the Minnesota Review, an eclectic journal sympathetic to theory, "performance has replaced persuasion as the standard by which scholarly practice is judged." Major academic careers have been made in recent decades with far-fetched readings that are more striking than convincing, interpretations that are widely discussed yet finally accepted by no one. Often they are deliberately counterintuitive, as if designed simply to attract attention, even outrage. Once they are out there, students feel obliged to build on them or grapple with them; they become part of the conversation, which they help distract or derail. This fault is not limited to historical readings; it is a professional deformation that marks all fashionable trends in scholarship. But historical interpretations are especially predictable in their political sympathies. Eager to weigh in on the side of the insulted and the injured, they appear predetermined by their well-meaning political agendas. Yet compared to other ways of reading, they call upon a larger knowledge of the world and often do more to link literature or theory to the actual flow of human life. They draw literary interpretation closer to the real world, a term they would never use.

The historical approach can be used polemically to belittle writers and movements by reducing them to the circumstances of their origin. But it can also serve to enhance them by anchoring them in actuality. To be reminded of how the "shaping nightmare" of World War II might have affected the young Foucault, how the sudden "decapitation" of Belgium by the Germans might have influenced Paul de Man, or how the trauma of the Algerian war might play itself out in the work of Derrida, who spent his early years there, can be a way of validating their abstractions, rightly or wrongly, by associating them with great social movements and deeply felt personal experiences. Yet this leaves open the question of why such formative, perhaps traumatic, events would take them in one direction rather than another. If Foucault was so deeply affected by the totalitarian climate of the Nazi occupation, why did he later apply this template almost exclusively to progressive institutions and liberal societies? There are diametrically opposed ways of reading the relationship between de Man's late work and his early collaborationist articles; partisan scholars bring their own agendas to these issues. But no serious thinker can be reduced to his or her biography, no matter how much the life illuminates the work.

In the end, the great justification for a historical approach to literature and criticism is that we must know everything, the life, the times, the intricate internal argument, the shape of the language. When a subject truly engages us, every detail is precious, every shred of evidence is worth considering. We want to know how life feeds into art, not simply how art feeds on itself. It's important that we bring to bear as much information and insight as possible, not just the curious sidelight or the odd, quirky, arresting analogy that takes an unexpected turn. Professional historians, who often find the work of New Historicists unconvincing, mostly remain committed to empirical canons of evidence, to narratives that emphasize beginnings and endings, cause and effect. They feel obliged to weigh competing explanations, as the best interpretive work has always done. This does not mean that criticism must be confined to a dispassionate, elusive objectivity. No great critic ever imagined this possible.

By the end of the 1950s, American academic criticism had fallen into a deadly and narrow common-sense approach that was constrained not by a rigorous formalism but by a deep failure of imagination. Themes were summarized, characters were characterized, images were scrutinized, but the questions being asked had grown less interesting. New Critical methods of close reading had contributed as much as they could, but now had thinned out to a point of diminishing returns. They were being applied to the wrong texts or to works that had already been exhaustively read. They were ferreting out subtexts where none needed to be found. They had grown mechanical and pedantic. Or else, like some later schools of theory, they developed ingenious readings remote from any immediate experience of the work in hand.

This is what made the essayistic approach of Blanchot, Barthes, and Benjamin seem so exciting at the time. Like the best critics of the past, they made arresting connections through paradoxical leaps of intuition and insight. They were essentially writers, not critics—writers whose aphoristic prose enforced its own suspension of disbelief. They were as imaginative, as gifted, as much fun to read, as most of the writers they wrote about. But they were also genuine readers who rose to the challenge of their subjects. This was what bold, unclassifiable American critics like Kenneth Burke and Alfred Kazin had been doing all along, but it hardly satisfied the demands of academic work as then construed. What these critics did could be emulated but not imitated: it offered no "method," and its effects could be disastrous in the hands of less agile practitioners. With such idiosyncratic critics, the reality check, the empirical constraints, came in the shock of recognition on the part of the reader, the shaft of illumination their essays provided.

Less gifted critics—we ourselves—can only operate through argument and evidence, the drama of persuasion and assent. Like other forms of criticism, historical interpretation can be well done or badly done, loopy or acute, ingenious or ingenuous. Yet setting things in context is always worth doing, and frequently revealing. It helps us enlarge the picture and justifies the calling of the critic as a Virgilian guide to the exacting mysteries of art. It peers behind the masks that writers or theorists take up to convince us they have given birth to themselves. There are always risks involved in searching out the figure in a carpet or shaping the multitude of possibilities into a single coherent narrative, but the return of historical criticism was an invigorating breath of fresh air. It released a burst of interpretive energy beyond the limited horizon of formalism and deconstruction. At a moment of intellectual exhaustion, it offered provocative new readings for old. Drawn to political advocacy, to sitting in judgment on the perceived power relationships of the past, it sometimes served as a well-meaning vehicle for its own preconceptions. Yet finally, historical interpretation is an indispensable way of comprehending culture and exploring the theories and practices through which it has always tried to make sense of itself. It paid its own way, and we are the richer for it.

SOURCES

Introduction: A Mirror in the Roadway

The introductory essay was written especially for this volume and is published here for the first time. Its sources, besides the contents of this book itself, are numerous. To clarify the passage from Stendhal's *The Red and the Black* from which I borrow the book's title, I used a French edition by Henri Martineau (Paris: Classiques Garnier, 1961) and translations by Lowell Bair (New York: Bantam, 1958) and Robert M. Adams (New York: W. W. Norton, 1969). The classic critics of European realism are still Georg Lukács, Erich Auerbach, and Ian Watt (in *The Rise of the Novel*). I relied upon Lukács's *Studies in European Realism*, trans. Edith Bone (London: Hillway, 1950) and Auerbach's *Mimesis: The Representation of Reality in Western Literature*, trans. Willard Trask (Princeton: Princeton University Press, 1953). Raymond Williams's "Realism and the Contemporary Novel" can be found in *The Long Revolution* (New York: Columbia University Press, 1961). Richard Wright's early and programmatic essay "Blueprint for Negro Writing" is reprinted in *The Portable Harlem Renaissance Reader*, ed. David Levering Lewis (New York: Viking, 1994). James Wood writes suggestively of realism and the real in *The Broken Estate: Essays on Literature and Belief* (New York: Modern Library, 2000). Among many important books on American realism are Amy Kaplan, *The Social Construction of American Realism* (Chicago: University of Chicago Press, 1988); Michael Davitt Bell, *The Problem of American Realism* (Chicago: University of Chicago Press, 1993); Miles Orvell, *The Real Thing* (Chapel Hill: University of North Carolina Press, 1989); David E. Shi, *Facing Facts: Realism in American Thought and Culture, 1850–1920* (New York: Oxford, 1995); Phillip Barrish, *American Literary Realism: Critical Theory and Intellectual Prestige, 1820–1995* (New York: Cambridge University Press, 2001); and Daniel Borus, *Writing Realism: Howells, James, and Norris in the Mass Market* (Chapel Hill: University of North Carolina Press, 1989). René Wellek's essay "The Concept of Realism in Literary Scholarship" can be found in *Concepts of Criticism*, ed. Stephen G. Nichols, Jr. (New Haven: Yale University Press, 1963). For Willa Cather's essays, see "The Magic of Contradictions," below. Edith Wharton's letter to F. Scott Fitzgerald can be found in Fitzgerald's *The Crack-Up*, ed. Edmund Wilson (New York: New Directions, 1945). Lionel Trilling's influential attack on Dreiser and American realism, "Reality in America," serves as the opening essay of *The Liberal Imagination* (New York: Viking, 1950). H. G. Wells reviews his differences with Henry James on the nature of fiction in his *Experiment in Autobiography* (1934; London: Faber & Faber, 1984). Wells made some of the same points about his own fiction in the opening pages of his novel *Tono-Bungay* (1909). I quote from Flaubert's 1852 letter to Louise Colet from *The Selected Letters of Gustave Flaubert*, ed. and trans. Francis Steegmuller (1953; New York: Vintage, 1957). See also James Wood on Flaubert in *The Broken Estate*.

Richard Rorty's critique of the mirror image of representation can be found in *Philosophy and the Mirror of Nature* (Princeton: Princeton University Press, 1979). Bernard

Williams takes a different view in *Truth and Truthfulness: An Essay in Genealogy* (Princeton: Princeton University Press, 2002). I quote Nietzsche from his posthumously assembled work *The Will to Power*, ed. Walter Kaufmann, trans. Walter Kaufmann and R. J. Hollingdale (New York: Vintage, 1968). The William James quotations are from *Pragmatism* (1907; New York: Meridian, 1957). Peter Gay questions the fidelity of fiction to history and society in *Savage Reprisals* (New York: W. W. Norton, 2002).

The City as Text: New York and the American Writer

This essay served as a keynote for the biennial convention of the Italian Association for North-American Studies in Porto Conte, Sardinia, in October 1989. It was first published in *RSA: Rivista di Studi Anglo-Americani* 8 (Chiarella-Sassari, 1990) and in a revised version in *TriQuarterly* 83 (Winter 1991–92). The following were some of the secondary works about New York and the modern city that proved helpful to me:

Bender, Thomas. *New York Intellect*. New York: Knopf, 1987.

Berman, Marshall. *All That Is Solid Melts into Air: The Experience of Modernity*. New York: Simon & Schuster, 1982.

Conrad, Peter. *The Art of the City: Views and Versions of New York*. New York: Oxford University Press, 1984.

Gelfant, Blanche Housman. *The American City Novel*. 2d ed. Norman: University of Oklahoma Press, 1970.

Jaye, Michael C., and Ann Chalmers Watts, eds. *Literature and the Urban Experience*. New Brunswick, NJ: Rutgers University Press, 1981.

James, Henry. *The American Scene*. 1907. Ed. Leon Edel. Bloomington: Indiana University Press, 1968.

Kazin, Alfred. *A Writer's America*. New York: Knopf, 1988.

Kazin, Alfred, and David Finn. *Our New York*. New York: Harper & Row, 1989.

Lankevich, George J., and Howard B. Furer. *A Brief History of New York City*. Port Washington, NY: Associated Faculty Press, 1984.

Morand, Paul. *New York*. Trans. Hamish Miles. Illus. Joaquin Vaquero. New York: Henry Holt, 1930.

Mumford, Lewis. *The Brown Decades*. 2d ed. New York: Dover, 1955.

———. *The City in History*. New York: Harcourt Brace Jovanovich, 1968.

———. *The Culture of Cities*. New York: Harcourt Brace Jovanovich, 1970.

Pickering, James H., ed. *The City in American Literature*. New York: Harper & Row, 1977.

Pike, Burton. *The Image of the City in Modern Literature*. Princeton, NJ: Princeton University Press, 1981.

Sennett, Richard, ed. *Classic Essays on the Culture of Cities*. New York: Appleton-Century-Crofts, 1969. Includes Georg Simmel's essay.

Sharpe, William, and Leonard Wallock, eds. *Visions of the Modern City*. Baltimore: Johns Hopkins University Press, 1987.

Sutcliffe, Anthony, ed. *Metropolis 1890–1940*. Chicago: University of Chicago Press, 1984. Includes Kenneth Jackson's essay.

Trachtenberg, Alan. *Brooklyn Bridge: Fact and Symbol*. 2d ed. Chicago: University of Chicago Press, 1979.

Wallock, Leonard, ed. *New York: Culture Capital of the World, 1940–1965*. New York: Rizzoli, 1988.

Weimer, David R. *The City as Metaphor*. New York: Random House, 1966.

Two especially good anthologies of New York writing are *New York: Poems*, ed. Howard Moss (New York: Avon, 1980), and *Writing New York: A Literary Anthology*, ed. Phillip Lopate (New York: Library of America, 1998).

The Second City

This brief essay about Chicago first appeared in the Outlook Section of the *Washington Post* (August 18, 1996). Theodore Dreiser's best writing about Chicago can be found in *Sister Carrie* (1900), which conveys his first impressions of the city, and in his financial novel, *The Titan* (1914). But see also his autobiographical works, *A Book about Myself* (1922) and *Dawn* (1931). Upton Sinclair's *The Jungle* (1906) is still the great exposé of the living and working conditions in early industrial Chicago (see below). Overshadowed by Dreiser were two of Chicago's leading social realists, Henry Blake Fuller (*The Cliff-Dwellers* [1893] and *With the Procession* [1895]) and Robert Herrick (*The Web of Life* [1900] and *The Memoirs of an American Citizen* [1905]). An indelible image of the city was created by Carl Sandburg's first book, *Chicago Poems* (1916).

Jane Addams's classic *Twenty Years at Hull-House* (1910) remains the best memoir about Chicago, but different facets of the city's life can be explored in the great architect Louis Sullivan's *The Autobiography of an Idea* (1924), Ben Hecht's vivid *A Child of the Century* (1954), and Richard Wright's *American Hunger* (1977), the suppressed second half of his great autobiography. Henry Adams described his 1893 visit to Chicago in *The Education of Henry Adams* (1918).

James T. Farrell's *Studs Lonigan* (1932–35) and Richard Wright's *Native Son* (1940) give amazingly detailed accounts of the city's Irish and black communities, focusing on the fate of wayward young men. The poetry of Chicago's low life and mean streets is on display in the stories collected in Nelson Algren's *The Neon Wilderness* (1947) and in his early novels, *Never Come Morning* (1942) and *The Man with the Golden Arm* (1949), as well as *Chicago: City on the Make* (1961), offbeat poetic essays. Much of Saul Bellow's finest writing about Chicago went into his spare wartime novella *Dangling Man* (1944), his sprawling picaresque novel *The Adventures of Augie March* (1953), and his disillusioned late work *The Dean's December* (1982). His 1951 story "Looking for Mr. Green" can be found in *Mosby's Memoirs and Other Stories* (1968) and in his *Collected Stories* (2001).

St. Clair Drake and Horace R. Cayton wrote a classic account of the black community of Chicago's South Side, with an introduction by Richard Wright, in *Black Metropolis* (1945; Chicago: University of Chicago Press, 1993). Norman Mailer's personal history of the 1968 Democratic Convention can be found in *Miami and the Siege of Chicago* (New York: Signet, 1968). The most thoughtful study of the classic Chicago writers is Carl Smith's *Chicago and the American Literary Imagination, 1880–1920* (Chicago: University of Chicago Press, 1984). A sweeping and beautifully written account of the city's early development and rapid growth is Donald L. Miller's *City of the Century: The Epic of Chicago and the Making of America* (New York: Simon & Schuster, 1996).

Upton Sinclair and the Urban Jungle

The essay on Upton Sinclair first appeared as an introduction to *The Jungle* (New York: Bantam Books, 1981) and was reprinted in *Upton Sinclair's* The Jungle: *Modern Critical Interpretations*, ed. Harold Bloom (Philadelphia: Chelsea House, 2002). Despite his huge influence, wide readership, and immense body of work, Sinclair has attracted few serious critics or biographers, though there are valuable essays by Michael Brewster Folsom, Emory Elliott, and others in the Bloom anthology. Most helpful to me were historical works such as James Weinstein, *The Decline of Socialism in America, 1912–1925* (New York: Monthly Review Press, 1967), and David Shannon, *The Socialist Party of America: A History* (New York: Macmillan, 1955). For Sinclair's place in the left-wing literary tradition, see Walter B. Rideout, *The Radical Novel in the United States, 1900–1954* (1956; New York: Columbia University Press, 1992). See also Sinclair, *My Lifetime in Letters* (1960) and *The Autobiography of Upton Sinclair* (1962).

A Radical Comedian

This essay on Sinclair Lewis first appeared as an introduction to *Main Street* (New York: Bantam Books, 1996). The standard biographies of Lewis are by Mark Schorer, *Sinclair Lewis: An American Life* (New York: McGraw-Hill, 1961), and Richard R. Lingeman, *Sinclair Lewis: Rebel from Main Street* (New York: Random House, 2002). Edith Wharton's letter to Lewis can be found in Schorer's capacious biography. Schorer also edited *Sinclair Lewis: A Collection of Critical Essays* (Englewood Cliffs, NJ: Prentice-Hall, 1962), Martin Bucco brought out *Critical Essays on Sinclair Lewis* (Boston: G. K. Hall, 1986), and Harold Bloom edited *Sinclair Lewis: Modern Critical Views* (New York: Chelsea House, 1987): See also the memoir of Grace Hegger Lewis, *With Love from Gracie* (New York: Harcourt Brace, 1955). Alfred Kazin juxtaposes Lewis with Sherwood Anderson as the "village atheist" and the "village mystic" in *On Native Grounds* (1942; New York: Harcourt, Brace, 1995). The liveliest social history of the 1920s remains Frederick Lewis Allen, *Only Yesterday* (1931; New York: Harper & Row, 1964). Few contemporary novelists owe much debt to Lewis, but there are fine essays by John Updike in *The New Yorker* (May 17, 1993) and Gore Vidal in the *New York Review of Books* (October 8, 1992). James M. Hutchisson clarifies the origins of the major novels in *The Rise of Sinclair Lewis, 1920–1930* (University Park: Pennsylvania State University Press, 1996).

The Magic of Contradictions: Willa Cather's Lost Lady

This essay on Willa Cather was first published in *The New Criterion* (February 1999). The most useful biographies of Cather are James Woodress's solid factual study, *Willa Cather: A Literary Life* (Lincoln: University of Nebraska Press, 1987), and Sharon O'Brien's strong feminist study of her early work, *Willa Cather: The Emerging Voice* (New York: Oxford University Press, 1987), but the first biography, by E. K. Brown, as completed by Leon Edel, *Willa Cather: A Critical Biography* (New York: Knopf, 1953), and the memoir by Cather's companion, Edith Lewis, *Willa Cather Living* (New York: Knopf, 1953), remain of interest. The freshest critical study is Hermione Lee, *Willa Cather: Double Lives* (New York: Pantheon, 1989), but an earlier brief account by David Daiches, *Willa Cather: A Critical Introduction* (Ithaca, NY: Cornell University Press, 1951), is still worth reading. Joan Acocella has written a bracing overview of Cather and her recent critics in *Willa Cather and the Politics of Criticism* (2000; New York, Vintage, 2002), an expanded version of an article that appeared in *The New Yorker* (November 27, 1995).

Three useful anthologies of essays on Cather are *Willa Cather and Her Critics*, ed. James Schroeter (Ithaca, NY: Cornell University Press, 1967), which documents the critical reception of Cather's work, including key essays and reviews; *Critical Essays on Willa Cather*, ed. John J. Murphy (Boston: G. K. Hall, 1984), with reviews and essays on each of her novels; and *Willa Cather: Modern Critical Views*, ed. Harold Bloom (New York: Chelsea House, 1985). Blanche Gelfant's influential 1971 essay on *My Ántonia* can be found in both the Murphy and Bloom collections. Gelfant also wrote a fine introduction to *O Pioneers!* (New York: Penguin, 1989). Cather's own essays from *Not Under Forty* are quoted from Willa Cather, *Stories, Poems, and Other Writings*, ed. Sharon O'Brien (New York: Library of America, 1992), part of an excellent three-volume edition of her most important work.

The Authority of Failure

This essay originated as a centennial lecture on Fitzgerald in 1996 at Princeton and elsewhere and first appeared in *The American Scholar* (Spring 2000), and then, with references, in *F. Scott Fitzgerald in the Twenty-first Century*, ed. Jackson R. Bryer, Ruth Prigozy, and Milton R. Stern (Tuscaloosa: University of Alabama Press, 2003). For me, the most important works for an understanding of Fitzgerald in the 1930s were the stories "The Rough Crossing" (1929), "One Trip Abroad" (1930), "Babylon Revisited" (1931), "Crazy Sunday" (1931); and *The Pat Hobby Stories* (New York: Scribner's, 1962); the essay "Echoes of the Jazz Age" (1931), in *The Fitzgerald Reader*, ed. Arthur Mizener (New York: Scribner's, 1963); the essays and journals collected in *The Crack-Up*, ed. Edmund Wilson (New York: New Directions, 1945), including "My Lost City" (1932), "The Crack-Up" (1936), and "Early Success" (1937); and the novels *Tender Is the Night* (1934) and *The Last Tycoon* (1941).

Among the many biographies of Fitzgerald, the most useful to me were Andrew Turnbull, *Scott Fitzgerald* (New York: Scribner's, 1962); Matthew J. Bruccoli, *Some Sort of Epic Grandeur: The Life of F. Scott Fitzgerald* (San Diego: Harcourt Brace Jovanovich, 1981); Scott Donaldson, *Fool For Love: F. Scott Fitzgerald* (New York: Congdon & Weed, 1983), James R. Mellow, *Invented Lives: F. Scott and Zelda Fitzgerald* (Boston: Houghton Mifflin, 1984); and Jeffrey Meyers, *Scott Fitzgerald: A Biography* (New York: HarperCollins, 1994). The critical literature on Fitzgerald is enormous and will go unrecorded here. Philip Rahv's *Daily Worker* review of *Tender Is the Night* can be found in his *Essays on Literature and Politics, 1932–1972*, ed. Arabel J. Porter and Andrew J. Dvosin (Boston: Houghton Mifflin, 1978). The review of Henry Roth's *Call It Sleep* is quoted in Walter B. Rideout, *The Radical Novel in the United States, 1900–1954* (1956; New York: Columbia University Press, 1992).

Edmund Wilson: Three Phases

The essay on Wilson originated in a series of panel discussions at the Mercantile Library in New York organized by Lewis M. Dabney, celebrating the centennial of Wilson's birth in 1895. It first appeared in *Partisan Review* (no. 4, 1997), then in *Edmund Wilson: Centennial Reflections*, ed. Lewis M. Dabney (Princeton: Princeton University Press, 1997). For the first phase of Wilson's career, the 1920s, the key works are *The Shores of Light* and *Axel's Castle*; for the Depression years, *The American Earthquake* and *To the Finland Station*; for the postwar years, *Patriotic Gore* and *A Piece of My Mind*, with its centerpiece, "The Author at Sixty." Elena Wilson edited Wilson's splendid *Letters on Literature and Politics, 1912–1972* (New York: Farrar, Straus & Giroux, 1977). The best critical study of Wilson is by George H. Douglas, *Edmund Wilson's America* (Lexington: University of Kentucky Press, 1983). There is a readable biography by Jeffrey Meyers, *Edmund Wilson: A Biography* (Boston: Houghton Mifflin, 1995). Besides the centennial volume, Lewis M. Dabney edited *The Portable Edmund Wilson* (New York: Viking, 1983). Meyer Schapiro's review of *To the Finland Station* appeared in *Partisan Review* in 1940. V. S. Pritchett's essay on Wilson came out in *The New Yorker* (December 23, 1972) and was reprinted in *The Tale Bearers* (New York: Random House, 1980). Kenneth Burke's 1939 essay on *Mein Kampf* ("The Rhetoric of Hitler's 'Battle'") can be found in *The Philosophy of Literary Form* (Berkeley: University of California Press, 1974).

A Glint of Malice

The essay on Mary McCarthy was written for a conference on her work at Bard College in October 1993. It was published in *Annandale*, the magazine of Bard College (May 1994), in *The Threepenny Review* (Fall 1994) and, with references, in *Twenty-Four Ways of Looking at Mary McCarthy*, ed. Eve Stwertka and Margo Viscusi (Westport, CT: Greenwood Press, 1996). Later I wrote "Mary McCarthy at 90," *The Nation* (September 2–9, 2002). I profited from two excellent biographies: Carol Gelderman, *Mary McCarthy: A Life* (New York: St. Martin's, 1988), which includes the quotation from Dwight Macdonald's letter; and Carol Brightman, *Writing Dangerously: Mary McCarthy and Her World* (New York: Clarkson N. Potter, 1992). Nearly all of McCarthy's books are published by Harcourt, but there is also a good selection of her essays edited by A. O. Scott, *A Bolt from the Blue and Other Essays* (New York: New York Review, 2002). For a discriminating early essay on her work by her friend Elizabeth Hardwick, see *A View of My Own* (New York: Farrar, Straus & Cudahy, 1962). Alfred Kazin's acid portrait of McCarthy can be found in *Starting Out in the Thirties* (Boston: Atlantic-Little, Brown, 1965); William Barrett's more star-struck view appeared in *The Truants: Adventures among the Intellectuals* (New York: Anchor Books, 1982).

Silence, Exile, Cunning

The essay on "The Modern Writer as Exile" was written as the keynote for a symposium at Nassau Community College in October 1997. It is published here for the first time.

The biblical quotations are from *Tanakh: A New Translation of the Holy Scriptures* (Philadelphia: Jewish Publication Society, 1985). Delmore Schwartz's 1945 essay on T. S. Eliot's internationalism can be found in *Selected Essays of Delmore Schwartz*, ed. Donald A. Dike and David H. Zucker (Chicago: University of Chicago Press, 1970). The Kafka quotations are from *The Diaries of Franz Kafka, 1910–23*, ed. Max Brod (Harmondsworth, U.K.: Penguin, 1964); *Letters to Felice*, ed. Erich Heller and Jürgen Born, trans. James Stern and Elisabeth Duckworth (New York: Schocken, 1973); Max Brod, *Franz Kafka: A Biography* (New York: Schocken, 1960); and *The Complete Stories*, ed. Nahum N. Glatzer (New York: Schocken, 1971). The letter to Milena Jesenská is quoted from Ernst Pawel, *The Nightmare of Reason: A Life of Franz Kafka* (New York: Farrar, Straus & Giroux, 1984), a superb biography. Other indispensable biographies included Richard Ellmann, *James Joyce* (New York: Oxford, 1959); Lyndall Gordon, *Eliot's Early Years* (New York: Oxford, 1977); and biographies of Beckett by James Knowlson and Anthony Cronin (see below).

Since this essay was written, there has been much valuable writing by and about exiled or expatriate writers. I would single out Alex Zwerdling, *Improvised Europeans: American Literary Expatriates and the Siege of London* (New York: Basic Books, 1998); André Aciman, ed., *Letters of Transit: Reflections on Exile and Memory* (New York: New Press, 1999); Edward Said, *Reflections on Exile and Other Essays* (Cambridge: Harvard University Press, 2001); and, for a more skeptical view as well as a sweeping overview, Ian Buruma, "The Romance of Exile," *The New Republic.* (February 12, 2001). There is an excellent anthology of exiled writers, *Altogether Elsewhere: Writers on Exile*, ed. Marc Robinson (San Diego and New York: Harcourt, Brace, 1994). For a striking recent novel about exile, including the relationship between Kafka and Milena, see Antonio Muñoz Molina, *Sepharad*, trans. Margaret Sayers Peden (New York: Harcourt, 2003).

The Beckett essay first appeared in the *New York Times Book Review* (August 3, 1997). Besides Beckett's own writings, mainly published by Grove Press, the two main sources are the now-standard (and excellent) biographies: James Knowlson, *Damned to Fame: The Life of Samuel Beckett* (New York: Simon & Schuster, 1996); and Anthony Cronin, *Samuel Beckett: The Last Modernist* (New York: HarperCollins, 1997). Beckett's somewhat reclusive and mysterious life, including his time in the French Resistance, was first explored by Deirdre Bair in *Samuel Beckett: A Biography* (New York: Random House, 1978). Kenneth Tynan's review of *Waiting for Godot* can be found in *Curtains* (New York: Atheneum, 1961). I also quote from A. Alvarez, *Samuel Beckett* (New York: Viking Press, 1973) and Hugh Kenner, *Samuel Beckett: A Critical Study* (New York: Grove Press, 1961).

This portrait of Kafka first appeared as a review of Kafka's *Letters to Felice* (see above) in the *New York Times Book Review* (September 30, 1973). Other sources include Kafka's *Diaries* and Max Brod's biography (see above). I learned much from Gustav Janouch, *Conversations with Kafka*, trans. Goronwy Rees, 2d ed. (New York: New Directions, 1971). Kafka's riveting *Letters to Milena* first appeared in English in a badly truncated edition by Willy Haas, trans. Tania and James Stern (New York: Schocken, 1953), but this was superseded by a much superior edition, trans. Philip Boehm (New York: Schocken, 1990), which includes four essays by Milena as well as her obituary of Kafka. Milena was the subject of a moving biography by Margarete Buber-Neumann, who knew her in the Ravensbrück concentration camp, where she died on May 17, 1944; see *Milena: The Story of a Remarkable Friendship*, trans. Ralph Manheim (New York: Schocken, 1988). There is now also a biography of the "woman about whom we know much less": Kathi Diamant, *Kafka's Last Love: The Mystery of Dora Diamant* (New York: Basic Books, 2003). Elias Canetti's 1968 meditation on the letters to Felice, "Kafka's Other Trial," can be found in *The Conscience of Words*, trans. Joachim Neugroschel (New York: Seabury Press, 1979).

Hope against Hope: Orwell and the Future

The essay on *Nineteen Eighty-Four* was written for a centennial conference on Orwell at Wellesley College in May 2003. It was first published in *The American Scholar* (Spring 2004) and in *George Orwell: Into the Twenty-First Century*, ed. Thomas Cushman and John Rodden (Boulder, CO: Paradigm Publishers, 2004). Orwell's essays and letters are quoted from *The Collected Essays, Journalism and Letters of George Orwell*, ed. Sonia Orwell and Ian Angus (Harmondsworth, U.K.: Penguin, 1970); and *Nineteen Eighty-Four* from the original American edition (New York: Harcourt, Brace, 1949). Richard Rorty's essay on Orwell and O'Brien can be found in *Contingency, Irony, and Solidarity* (New York: Cambridge University Press, 1989). Christopher Hitchens's *Why Orwell Matters*, (New York: Basic Books, 2002), is an incisive contribution, but the outstanding book on Orwell remains John Rodden's study of the reception of his work and the myths that accumulated around him, *The Politics of Literary Reputation: The Making and Claiming of "St. George" Orwell* (New York: Oxford, 1989). The standard biography is still Bernard Crick's *George Orwell: A Life* (1980; Harmondsworth, U.K.: Penguin, 1982), but I learned a good deal from Jeffrey Meyers's revisionist portrait, *Orwell: Wintry Conscience of a Generation* (New York: W. W. Norton, 2000). Of the many extraordinary essays on Orwell, I would single out Lionel Trilling's influential discussion in *The Opposing Self* (New York: Viking, 1955) and Irving Howe's essays in *Politics and the Novel* (New York: Meridian, 1957) and *Decline of the New* (New York: Horizon Press, 1970); but see also Trilling's review of *Nineteen Eighty-Four* in *Speaking of Literature and Society*, ed. Diana Trilling (New York: Harcourt Brace Jovanovich, 1980), and an article by Orwell's *Partisan Review* editor Philip Rahv in his *Literature and the Sixth Sense* (Boston: Houghton Mifflin, 1970), which expresses oblique reservations, which I share, about the role of the inquisitor O'Brien.

Magical Realism

The essays on García Márquez, Grass, and Agnon first appeared as reviews, respectively, in *Seven Days* (March 14, 1977), the *New York Times Book Review* (November 7, 1978), and the *Times Literary Supplement* (September 1, 2000). See Gabriel García Márquez, *The Autumn of the Patriarch*, trans. Gregory Rabassa (New York: Harper & Row, 1976); Günter Grass, *The Flounder*, trans. Ralph Manheim (New York: Harcourt Brace Jovanovich, 1978); and S. Y. Agnon, *Only Yesterday*, trans. Barbara Harshav (Princeton: Princeton University Press, 2000). All three writers were awarded the Nobel Prize for Literature. The first two have been widely read in acclaimed English translations; their work needs no further documentation here, though I can warmly recommend García Márquez's recent memoir, *Living to Tell the Tale*, trans. Edith Grossman (New York: Knopf, 2003). Though revered as one of the founders of modern Hebrew literature, Agnon has never enjoyed this kind of general readership here. To accompany their translation of *Only Yesterday*, Princeton published a book-length study by novelist Amos Oz, *The Silence of Heaven: Agnon's Fear of God*, also translated by Barbara Harshav. The most wide-ranging collection of Agnon's stories in English is *A Book That Was Lost and Other Stories*, ed. Alan Mintz and Anne Golomb Hoffman (New York: Schocken, 1995). One of the best English translations of an Agnon novel, because it is forceful and direct, is by Hillel Halkin, *A Simple Story* (New York: Schocken, 1985). Agnon's most illuminating critic in English is Robert Alter; see, for example, *Hebrew and Modernity* (Bloomington: Indiana University Press, 1985). There are also book-length critical studies by Baruch Hochman and Arnold Band. Benjamin Harshav contributes a valuable critical introduction to *Only Yesterday*.

Sea Change: Céline in America

This essay on Céline in America first appeared in a special issue of the *South Atlantic Quarterly* on "Céline, USA," edited by Alice Y. Kaplan and Philippe Roussin (Spring 1994). This issue includes a range of other essays by leading scholars (including Céline's French editor, Henri Godard) and by contemporary American writers. Of special interest is the editors' own essay, "Céline and Modernity." There are major biographies of Céline by Patrick McCarthy, *Céline* (New York: Richard Seaver/Viking, 1976), and Frédéric Vitoux, *Céline: A Biography*, trans. Jesse Browner (New York: Paragon House, 1992), as well as a more recent biography in English by Nicholas Hewitt, *The Life of Céline: A Critical Biography* (Malden, MA: Blackwell, 1999). Ralph Manheim's classic translations of *Journey to the End of the Night*, *Death on the Installment Plan*, and Céline's postwar trilogy, *Castle to Castle*, *North*, and the posthumous *Rigadoon*, were published between 1966 and 1983, the first two by New Directions, the last three by Delacorte and Penguin. Lionel Trilling is quoted from *The Liberal Imagination* (New York: Viking, 1950); George Orwell from his essay "Inside the Whale," in vol. 1 of *The Collected Essays, Journalism and Letters of George Orwell*, ed. Sonia Orwell and Ian Angus (Harmondsworth, U.K.: Penguin, 1970); and John Updike from *Hugging the Shore: Essays and Criticism* (New York: Knopf, 1983).

The Complex Fate of the Jewish American Writer

This essay began as a lecture at Williams College and many other venues, including the Jewish Book Council in London, the Hebrew University of Jerusalem, and the New York Public Library. It first appeared in *The Nation* (October 22, 2001) and, in a longer version with full references, in *Ideology and Jewish Identity in American and Israeli Literature*, ed. Emily Miller Budick (Albany: SUNY Press, 2001). The sources are almost too numerous to include here. Irving Howe's 1972 essay "Philip Roth Reconsidered" was reprinted in *The Critical Point* (New York: Horizon Press, 1973). See also his essay "Strangers" (1977) in *Celebrations and Attacks* (New York: Horizon Press, 1979) and his introduction to *Jewish-American Stories* (New York: New American Library, 1977). Aharon Appelfeld's views of Jewish writing and of his own work can be found in "The Rise and Fall of the Jewish Author," trans. Jeffrey Green, in *The Pakn-Treger* 25

(Summer 1997), and in *Beyond Despair*, trans. Jeffrey M. Green (New York: Fromm International, 1994). Saul Bellow's eulogy of Malamud is quoted by Robert Giroux in his introduction to Malamud, *The People and Uncollected Stories*, ed. Robert Giroux (New York: Farrar, Straus & Giroux, 1989), which also includes Malamud's story "An Exorcism." Malamud's "Take Pity," can be found in *The Stories of Bernard Malamud* (New York: Farrar, Straus & Giroux, 1983). Both stories, along with "The Silver Crown," have also been reprinted in Malamud, *The Complete Stories*, ed. Robert Giroux (New York: Farrar, Straus & Giroux, 1997). Cynthia Ozick's story "Envy; or, Yiddish in America," was collected in *The Pagan Rabbi and Other Stories* (1971; New York, Schocken Books, 1976). The best anthologies of new Jewish American writers give special emphasis to the emergence of women. See especially *Writing Our Way Home: Contemporary Stories by American Jewish Writers*, ed. Ted Solotaroff and Nessa Rapoport (New York: Schocken Books, 1992); and *Lost Tribes: Jewish Fiction from the Edge*, ed. Paul Zakrzewski (New York: HarperCollins Perennial, 2003).

The Face in the Mirror: The Eclipse of Distance in Contemporary Fiction

This essay on autobiographical fiction is a revised and much enlarged version of "The World in a Mirror: Problems of Distance in Contemporary Fiction," *Sewanee Review* (Summer 1981), but it also includes substantial portions of "The Autobiography Bug," *Harper's* (June 1980). Both pieces were inspired by a group of novels published toward the end of the 1970s, including John Irving, *The World According to Garp* (New York: E. P. Dutton, 1978); Bernard Malamud, *Dubin's Lives* (New York: Farrar, Straus & Giroux, 1979); Philip Roth, *The Ghost Writer* (New York: Farrar, Straus & Giroux, 1979); and William Styron, *Sophie's Choice* (New York: Random House, 1979); along with contemporaneous fiction of a different stripe, such as Jonathan Baumbach, *Chez Charlotte and Emily* (New York: Fiction Collective, 1979); and Scott Spencer, *Endless Love* (New York: Knopf, 1979).

Ordinary People: Carver, Ford, and Blue-Collar Realism

The essay on Raymond Carver and his influence first appeared in French as "Fiction: La quête de la vie ordinaire," in *Le Magazine Littéraire* (October 1990), a special issue on American writing, 1960–90, edited by Marc Chénetier, who also did the French translation. It was published in English in *Partisan Review* (Summer 1991). The present version is revised and expanded, incorporating passages from my essay on Richard Ford for *The Columbia Companion to the Twentieth-Century American Short Story*, ed. Blanche H. Gelfant (New York: Columbia University Press, 2001). Ford's memoir "Good Raymond" appeared in the *New Yorker* (October 5, 1998).

Textures of Memory

The essay on Bellow was written for a symposium on him in *Literary Imagination* (Winter 2002), a welcome occasion for me since I had often found myself critical of his work, going back to "For Art's Sake," *Partisan Review* (Fall 1966), a rejoinder I wrote as a graduate student to a cranky PEN speech by Bellow. Other contributors to the 2002 tribute included Stanley Crouch, Eugene Goodheart, and Christopher Ricks. Bellow had somehow turned old age into a gift, and this essay was largely inspired by his most recent books, *Ravelstein* (New York: Viking, 2000) and *Collected Stories* (New York: Viking, 2001). See also my review of *Collected Stories* in the *Times Literary Supplement* (January 18, 2002).

The piece on William Kennedy and his Albany cycle first appeared in the *Times Literary Supplement* (November 1, 2002). The novels mentioned include *Legs* (1975; New York: Penguin, 1983); *Ironweed* (New York: Viking, 1983); *Very Old Bones* (New York: Viking, 1992); and *Roscoe* (New York: Viking, 2002). Because of the abundance of local lore in his fiction, his novels are illuminated by his lively panorama of Albany history, *O Albany!* (New York: Viking, 1983) and his nonfiction collection, *Riding the Yellow Trolley Car* (New York: Viking, 1993). They include profiles of the colorful political bosses and gangland chieftains whose careers figure in *Legs*, *Roscoe*, and other novels of the Albany cycle.

Damaged Literacy: The Decay of Reading

This essay on reading and literacy was written for "Reading in America," a conference at the University of Paris VII in December 1991. It was first published in French as "Lire et écrire: Le savoir détérioré," trans. Dominique Rinaudo, in *Cahiers Charles V 14* (1992). It appeared in English in *Profession 93* (New York: Modern Language Association, 1994). Terry Eagleton's *The Function of Criticism* (London: Verso, 1984) usefully invokes Jürgen Habermas's notion of the public sphere. All the essays cited on literacy, including the piece by Leon Botstein from which I took my title, can be found in *Literacy: An Overview by Fourteen Experts*, ed. Stephen R. Graubard (New York: Hill & Wang, 1991). Paul de Man's essay "Roland Barthes and the Limits of Structuralism," though written in 1972 for the *New York Review of Books*, was first published posthumously in *Yale French Studies* 77 (1990). Marjorie Levinson's controversial reading of Wordsworth's "Lines Composed a Few Miles Above Tintern Abbey" can be found in *Wordsworth's Great Period Poems* (New York: Cambridge University Press, 1986). The sense of wonder is wonderfully explored in Stephen Greenblatt, *Marvelous Possessions*. (Chicago: University of Chicago Press, 1991); and Geoffrey Hartman, "The Fate of Reading," in *The Fate of Reading and Other Essays* (Chicago: University of Chicago Press, 1975).

Finding the Right Words

This essay on Irving Howe was written as an afterword to *Irving Howe and the Critics: Celebrations and Attacks*, ed. John Rodden (Lincoln: University of Nebraska Press, 2005). The discussions of Howe's criticism by Roger Sale and Ted Solotaroff can be conveniently found in their own collections: Roger Sale, *On Not Being Good Enough* (New York: Oxford, 1979) and Theodore Solotaroff, *The Red Hot Vacuum and Other Pieces on the Writing of the Sixties* (New York: Atheneum, 1970). See also Rodden's *The*

Worlds of Irving Howe: A Critical Legacy (Boulder, CO: Paradigm Publishers, 2005). The quotations from his critical journalism come primarily from Howe's own *Celebrations and Attacks* (New York: Horizon Press, 1979). His portrait of Orwell can be found in *Decline of the New* (New York: Horizon, 1970). His critique of Philip Roth appears in *The Critical Point* (New York: Horizon, 1973). Other critical essays were collected in *Politics and the Novel* (New York: Meridian, 1957) and *A World More Attractive* (New York: Horizon, 1963). His political essays were collected in *Steady Work* (New York: Harcourt, Brace, 1966). Howe's memoir of Philip Rahv came out in *The American Scholar* (Autumn 1979). See also his 1982 memoir, *A Margin of Hope: An Intellectual Autobiography* (New York: Harcourt, 1982) and his final work, *A Critic's Notebook*, ed. Nicholas Howe (New York: Harcourt, 1994).

The Social Uses of Fiction

This discussion of Martha Nussbaum and fiction is expanded from a review in the *New York Times Book Review* (April 7, 1996). The books discussed or mentioned include Nussbaum, *Poetic Justice: The Literary Imagination and Public Life* (Boston: Beacon Press, 1996) and *Love's Knowledge: Essays on Philosophy and Literature* (New York: Oxford, 1990); Richard Posner, *The Economics of Justice* (Cambridge: Harvard University Press, 1981) and *Public Intellectuals: A Study in Decline* (Cambridge: Harvard University Press, 2001); and Richard Rorty, *Contingency, Irony, and Solidarity* (New York: Cambridge, 1989).

The Limits of Historicism: Literary Theory and Historical Understanding

This essay on historicism was written as the afterword to *Historicizing Theory*, ed. Peter C. Herman (Albany: SUNY Press, 2004). The present edited version was published in the *Chronicle of Higher Education* (May 23, 2003). The essays cited by Ivo Kamps and David Shumway can be found in *Historicizing Theory*, but I also quote from Shumway, "The Star System Revisited," *Minnesota Review*, nos. 52–54 (Fall 2001); Eugene Goodheart, *Confessions of a Secular Jew: A Memoir* (Woodstock and New York: Overlook Press, 2001); and John Kerrigan, "Touching and Being Touched," a review of Valentine Cunningham, *Reading after Theory*, in the *London Review of Books* (September 19, 2002). Jeffrey Williams's essay on the "posttheory generation" can be found in *Day Late, Dollar Short: The Next Generation and the New Academy*, ed. Peter C. Herman (Albany: SUNY Press, 2000). See also Herman's introduction to that volume. On various trends in criticism that have encroached on theory and to some degree supplanted it, including autobiographical criticism, public intellectual writing, and literary journalism, see Williams's essay "The New Belletrism," *Style* 33.3 (Fall 1999).

INDEX